FOCUS
ON
GRAMMAR
AN INTEGRATED SKILLS APPROACH

THIRD EDITION

SILVIA CAROLINA TIBERIO

PEARSON
Longman

FOCUS ON GRAMMAR 3: An Integrated Skills Approach
Teacher's Manual

Pearson Education, 10 Bank Street, White Plains, NY 10606

Staff credits: The people who made up the *Focus on Grammar 3 Teacher's Manual* team,
    representing editorial, production, design, and manufacturing, are: Rhea Banker, Nancy
    Blodgett, Christine Edmonds, Nancy Flaggman, Ann France, Margot Gramer, Laura
    Le Dréan, and Laurie Neaman.
Cover images: (background) Comstock Images RF, (background center) Nick Koudis RF;
    (center) Harold Sund RM
Text composition: ElectraGraphics, Inc.
Text font: 11/13 Sabon, 10/13 Myriad Roman
Illustrator: PC & F p. 199

ISBN: 0-13-189987-2

LONGMAN ON THE **WEB**

Longman.com offers online resources for
teachers and students. Access our Companion
Websites, our online catalog, and our local
offices around the world.

Visit us at **longman.com.**

Printed in the United States of America
    5 6 7 8 9 10—BAH—12 11 10 09 08

Contents

An Introduction to the Series   iv

About the Teacher's Manual   viii

General Teaching Tips   1
Strategies   11
Frequently Asked Questions (FAQ)   12

Unit-by-Unit Teaching Tips   15

Supplementary Activities   143

Scoring Rubrics   158

Audioscript   160

Student Book Answer Key   175

Introduction

The *Focus on Grammar* series

Written by ESL/EFL professionals, *Focus on Grammar: An Integrated Skills Approach* helps students to understand and practice English grammar. The primary aim of the course is for students to gain confidence in their ability to speak and write English accurately and fluently.

The **third edition** retains this popular series' focus on English grammar through lively listening, speaking, reading, and writing activities. The new *Focus on Grammar* also maintains the same five-level progression as the second edition:

- Level 1 (Beginning, formerly Introductory)
- Level 2 (High-Beginning, formerly Basic)
- Level 3 (Intermediate)
- Level 4 (High-Intermediate)
- Level 5 (Advanced)

What is the *Focus on Grammar* methodology?

Both controlled and communicative practice

While students expect and need to learn the formal rules of a language, it is crucial that they also practice new structures in a variety of contexts in order to internalize and master them. To this end, *Focus on Grammar* provides an abundance of both controlled and communicative exercises so that students can bridge the gap between knowing grammatical structures and using them. The many communicative activities in each Student Book unit provide opportunities for critical thinking while enabling students to personalize what they have learned.

A unique four-step approach

The series follows a four-step approach:

Step 1: Grammar in Context shows the new structures in natural contexts, such as articles and conversations.

Step 2: Grammar Presentation presents the structures in clear and accessible grammar charts, notes, and examples.

Step 3: Focused Practice of both form and meaning of the new structures is provided in numerous and varied controlled exercises.

Step 4: Communication Practice allows students to use the new structures freely and creatively in motivating, open-ended activities.

Thorough recycling

Underpinning the scope and sequence of the *Focus on Grammar* series is the belief that students need to use target structures many times, in different contexts, and at increasing levels of difficulty. For this reason, new grammar is constantly recycled throughout the book so that students have maximum exposure to the target forms and become comfortable using them in speech and in writing.

A complete classroom text and reference guide

A major goal in the development of *Focus on Grammar* has been to provide students with books that serve not only as vehicles for classroom instruction but also as resources for reference and self-study. In each Student Book, the combination of grammar charts, grammar notes, a glossary of grammar terms, and extensive appendices provides a complete and invaluable reference guide for students.

Ongoing assessment

Review Tests at the end of each part of the Student Book allow for self-assessment. In addition, the tests in the new *Focus on Grammar* Assessment Package provide teachers with a valid, reliable, and practical means of determining students' appropriate levels of placement in the course and of assessing students' achievement throughout the course. At Levels 4 (High-Intermediate) and 5 (Advanced), Proficiency Tests give teachers an overview of their students' general grammar knowledge.

What are the components of each level of *Focus on Grammar*?

Student Book

The Student Book is divided into eight or more parts, depending on the level. Each part contains grammatically related units, with each unit focusing on specific grammatical structures; where appropriate, units present contrasting forms. The exercises in each unit are thematically related to one another, and all units have the same clear, easy-to-follow format.

Teacher's Manual

The Teacher's Manual contains a variety of suggestions and information to enrich the material in the Student Book. It includes general teaching suggestions for each section of a typical unit, answers to frequently asked questions, unit-by-unit teaching tips with ideas for further communicative practice, and a supplementary activity section. Answers to the Student Book exercises and audioscripts of the listening activities are found at the back of the Teacher's Manual. Also included in the Teacher's Manual is a CD-ROM that includes PowerPoint® presentations that offer alternative ways of presenting selected grammar structures.

Workbook

The Workbook accompanying each level of *Focus on Grammar* provides additional exercises for self-study of the target grammar for each unit. Tests included in each Workbook provide students with additional opportunities for self-assessment.

Audio Programs

The Student Book Class Audio Program includes the listening activities, the Grammar in Context passages, and various other exercises. The symbol ⌒ identifies audio for the listening exercises. The symbol ⌒ next to the Grammar in Context passages and other exercises indicates that the listening is optional. Audioscripts for the listening exercises are located in the back of the Teacher's Manual.

Some Student Books are packaged with a Student Audio CD. This CD includes the listening exercise from each unit.

CD-ROM

The *Focus on Grammar* CD-ROM provides students with individualized practice and immediate feedback. Fully contextualized and interactive, the activities extend practice of the grammatical structures in the reading, writing, speaking, and listening skills areas. The CD-ROM includes grammar review, review tests, score-based remedial practice, games, and all relevant reference material from the Student Book. It can also be used in conjunction with the *Longman Interactive American Dictionary* CD-ROM.

Assessment Package (NEW)

A comprehensive Assessment Package has been developed for each level of the third edition of *Focus on Grammar*. The components of the Assessment Package are:

1. Placement, Diagnostic, and Achievement Tests

- a Placement Test to screen students and place them into the correct level
- Diagnostic Tests for each part of the Student Book
- Unit Achievement Tests for each unit of the Student Book
- Part Achievement Tests for each part of the Student Book

2. General Proficiency Tests

- two Proficiency Tests at Level 4 (High-Intermediate)
- two Proficiency Tests at Level 5 (Advanced)

These tests can be administered at any point in the course.

3. Audio CD

- Audio CDs include the listening portions of the Placement, Diagnostic, and Achievement Tests.
- The audioscripts for the tests are located in the Assessment Package.

4. Test-Generating Software

The test-bank software provides thousands of questions from which teachers can create class-appropriate tests. All items are labeled according to the grammar structure they are testing, so teachers can easily select relevant items; they can also design their own items to add to their tests.

Transparencies (NEW)

Transparencies of all the grammar charts in the Student Book are also available. These transparencies are classroom visual aids that help instructors point out and explain important patterns and structures of grammar.

Companion Website

The *Focus on Grammar* companion website (www. longman.com/focusongrammar) contains a wealth of information and activities for both teachers and students. In addition to general information about the course pedagogy, the website provides extensive practice exercises for the classroom, a language lab, or at home.

 ## What's new in the third edition of the Student Book?

In response to users' requests, this edition has:

- a new four-color design
- easy-to-read color coding for the four steps
- new and updated reading texts for Grammar in Context
- post-reading activities (in addition to the pre-reading questions)
- more exercise items
- an editing (error analysis) exercise in each unit
- an Internet activity in each unit
- a Glossary of Grammar Terms
- expanded Appendices

 ## References

Alexander, L. G. (1988). *Longman English Grammar.* White Plains: Longman.

Biber, D., S. Conrad, E. Finegan, S. Johansson, and G. Leech (1999). *Longman Grammar of Spoken and Written English.* White Plains: Longman.

Celce-Murcia, M., and D. Freeman (1999). *The Grammar Book.* Boston: Heinle and Heinle.

Celce-Murcia, M., and S. Hilles (1988). *Techniques and Resources in Teaching Grammar.* New York: Oxford University Press.

Firsten, R. (2002). *The ELT Grammar Book.* Burlingame, CA: Alta Book Center Publishers.

Garner, B. (2003). *Garner's Modern American Usage.* New York: Oxford University Press.

Greenbaum, S. (1996). *The Oxford English Grammar.* New York: Oxford University Press.

Leech, G. (2004). *Meaning and the English Verb.* Harlow, UK: Pearson.

Lewis, M. (1997). *Implementing the Lexical Approach.* Hove, East Sussex, UK: Language Teaching Publications.

Longman (2002). *Longman Dictionary of English Language and Culture.* Harlow, UK: Longman.

Willis, D. (2003). *Rules, Patterns and Words.* New York: Cambridge University Press.

About the *Focus on Grammar* Teacher's Manual

This Teacher's Manual offers a multitude of ideas for working with the material in *Focus on Grammar 3: An Integrated Skills Approach,* third edition. In this manual, you will find the following information:

- **General Teaching Tips** (pages 1–14) describe the principles underlying the course and give suggestions for teaching the activities in the Student Book. A Strategies for Teaching Grammar page offers a quick reference for some of the most common and useful grammar teaching techniques. A Frequently Asked Questions section answers some of the most common issues encountered by teachers.
- **Unit-by-Unit Teaching Tips** (pages 15–141) give you additional ideas for completing the activities unique to each unit.
- **Supplementary Activities** (pages 143–157) provide extra practice exercises for use during your presentation of a grammar point.
- **Scoring Rubrics for Speaking and Writing** are provided on pages 158 and 159 of the Teacher's Manual. You can use the rubrics to assess various speaking and writing tasks throughout the Student Book.
- **Audioscripts** and the **Student Book Answer Key** are included at the back of the Teacher's Manual for easy reference.

The **PowerPoint® presentations CD-ROM** bound into this Teacher's Manual includes additional teaching tools and resources:

- **PowerPoint® presentations** for selected units in the Student Book offer an innovative method for the contextualized instruction of grammar. These theme-based, user-friendly presentations contain a variety of colorful graphics and animations to engage a wide range of learning styles. In addition to providing a stimulating visual reinforcement of the Grammar Notes, these presentations also include interactive practice activities.
- A **PowerPoint® presentation Guide,** included on the CD-ROM in PDF format, offers guidelines for using the **PowerPoint® presentations.** It contains a variety of suggestions for getting the most out of the presentations in terms of both instructional benefit and learner participation.
- **Transparencies** of all Grammar Charts in the Student Book offer an additional teaching tool for presenting the target grammar points in the classroom.
- **Graphic Organizers** can be printed out and used in the classroom or assigned as homework. The graphic organizers provide support through the steps of pre-writing and writing a first draft.
- **Rubrics for assessing speaking and writing tasks** help teachers provide helpful feedback to students. Teachers are encouraged to use the scoring system provided, as well as write specific notes based on each student's performance.

General Teaching Tips

These tips are designed to guide you in teaching the recurring sections of the Teacher's Manual and Student Book. Experimenting with the various options will enliven your classroom and appeal to students' different learning styles.

In the following section and in the Unit-by-Unit Teaching Tips, the icon ⏰ indicates an optional step you may wish to include if time permits.

Unit Overview

The Unit Overview (offered in the Teacher's Manual) highlights the most important grammar points of each unit. It also points out common grammar trouble spots for students. You may also find it helpful to review the Grammar Charts and Grammar Notes in the Student Book before teaching each unit.

Grammar in Context

Each unit of the Student Book begins with a reading selection designed to raise students' interest and expose them to the target grammar in a realistic, natural context. The selections include newspaper and magazine excerpts, websites, newsletters, advertisements, conversations, and other formats that students may encounter in their day-to-day lives. All of the texts are also available on the Audio Program.

Background Notes

Where appropriate, background notes are provided in the Teacher's Manual to explain cultural and historical terms or concepts that appear in a reading selection. You can introduce these terms and concepts to students during a warm-up discussion, or you can use the notes as a reference if questions come up as students are reading.

Following the Background Notes is a list of vocabulary words and expressions that may be unfamiliar to students. Rather than pre-teaching these terms, you may wish to wait until students have finished reading. This allows students to focus on reading for general comprehension, building their reading fluency. See the section on vocabulary below for some ideas on how to respond to students' vocabulary questions.

Before You Read (5 minutes)

This pre-reading activity creates interest, elicits students' knowledge about the topic, and encourages students to make predictions about the reading.

Suggested Procedure for Before You Read
1. Have the class cover up the text and look at the illustrations.
2. Ask students to respond to the questions. Ask these questions in a conversational way, instead of reading them from the book.

Option A
- Have students work in pairs to read the questions and discuss their answers.
- Call on pairs to share their ideas with the class.

Option B
- Ask pairs of students to think about what they want to know about the topic and/or to prepare some questions they have about the topic.
- Call on pairs to share some of their questions and write them on the board.
- Have students try to find the information as they read.

Option C
- Have students work in groups of three.
- Each student chooses a question to memorize and, with books closed, ask their partners.
- Call on various groups to share their answers with the class.

Reading (15–20 minutes)

Depending on the needs of your class, have students complete the reading in class or at home (procedures for both options are given below). Whichever option you choose, encourage students (1) to read with a purpose; (2) to read the passage through once or twice without stopping for unknown words; and (3) to identify and deal with new vocabulary.

Comprehension questions and discussion topics are offered in the Unit-by-Unit Teaching Tips to supplement the grammar-focused activities of the Student Book.

Suggested Procedure for Reading

1. Play the audio and have students follow along in their books.
2. Write the comprehension questions from the Unit-by-Unit Teaching Tips on the board.
3. Have students read the passage again silently, looking for answers to the questions.
4. ⏱ Have students discuss their answers with a partner or in small groups.
5. Call on individuals to share their answers with the class.
6. Spend a few minutes going over any unfamiliar vocabulary terms. (See suggested procedures for Vocabulary.)
7. ⏱ Put students in pairs or small groups to discuss the reading. Invite them to respond to the reading in a way that is meaningful to them: What was most interesting? What did they learn? Refer to the Discussion Topics in the Unit-by-Unit Teaching Tips to help generate ideas for discussion.

Option A (At Home/In Class)

- Write the comprehension questions on the board for students to copy, or prepare them as a handout for students to take home.
- Have students read the passage and answer the questions at home.
- ⏱ Have students write a few additional questions about the reading.
- In class, have students work in pairs or small groups to discuss their answers.
- ⏱ Have students take turns asking and answering questions they prepared at home.
- Follow steps 5–7 in the Suggested Procedure for Reading above.

Option B (In Class)

- Have students work in pairs. Divide the reading in half, and have each student in the pair read one half.
- Have students summarize the information in their half of the reading for their partner.
- Follow steps 5–6 in the previous notes for Suggested Procedure for Reading.

Vocabulary

After students have read the passage and answered the comprehension questions, spend a few minutes going over any unfamiliar vocabulary terms. In addition to using the definitions provided in the Unit-by-Unit Teaching Tips, you may wish to use illustrations in the Student Book or pictures that you supply to illustrate the meaning of new words.

Suggested Procedure for Vocabulary

1. Have students make lists of the words in the reading they need help with.
2. Allow them to use their dictionaries or to work with other students to discuss, search for and find the meanings, or ask you for assistance.
3. ⏱ Write the new vocabulary items on the board, or have students write them, and provide definitions.
4. Encourage students to keep a record of vocabulary items by using a notebook or by making vocabulary cards. The entries should include a definition and an example sentence. Suggest that they be on the lookout for other examples of these items and add any new examples they find to their notebooks or cards.

Where appropriate, encourage students to draw pictures on the card or to record any information that helps them remember the vocabulary item. It may be helpful for students to include a translation of the new term in their own language.

Here's one way to do a vocabulary card:

```
                                    [front]



                thrill (n., v., adj.)



```

```
                                     [back]
(n) + (adj) a strong feeling of excitement
and pleasure; (v) to feel or make someone
feel strong excitement or pleasure
(n) My grandmother always gets a thrill
when I call her.
(v) The skaters thrilled their fans with their
high jumps.
(adj) I was thrilled to hear the good news.
```

Option A

- Write new vocabulary and definitions on the board, but do not write the definitions next to the corresponding words.
- Ask students to find the appropriate match.

Option B

- If classroom time is limited, allow students to consult their dictionaries as they are reading.
- Remind them that they will not necessarily need to know the meaning of every word in order to understand the meaning of the passage.

After You Read (5 minutes)

These post-reading questions help students focus on the meaning of the target grammar without explicitly presenting the grammar point.

Suggested Procedure for After You Read
1. Have students work individually to answer the questions.
2. Tell students to compare answers with a partner.
3. Call on volunteers to read their answers aloud.

Grammar Presentation

There are many ways to teach the material in the Grammar Presentation. As a general rule, the more varied and lively the classroom activities, the more engaged students will be— and the more learning will occur! Approaching grammar from different angles and trying out different classroom management options can help increase student motivation.

The Strategies for Teaching Grammar on page 11 provides some guidelines to keep in mind when presenting a new grammar point. In addition to these strategies and the procedures outlined below, you can find specific suggestions for presenting the unit's grammar in the Unit-by-Unit Teaching Tips.

Identify the Grammar (5–10 minutes)

This section in the Teacher's Manual provides support for you to help students identify the target grammatical structures embedded in the reading. This helps students learn the usage of the target grammar point and helps you make a smooth transition from Grammar in Context to the Grammar Presentation.

Suggested Procedure for Identify the Grammar
1. Choose an example of the target grammar from the reading and write it on the board. The Unit-by-Unit Teaching Tips provide examples that focus on specific features of that grammar point.
2. Point out that the target grammar is presented in boldfaced type in the reading for easy identification. Elicit more examples from students and write them on the board.
3. Find out what your students may already know about that grammar point. List the information you have elicited on the board. As students continue with the Grammar Presentation, encourage them to compare these notes with the information presented in the Grammar Charts and Grammar Notes.

After studying the target grammar in context, students should be ready to study the isolated forms, meanings, and usage. You can use the charts, notes, and examples to present and review the grammatical structures in a straightforward and comprehensive way.

Note that common grammatical terms are used throughout the Grammar Presentations because they help make the explanations clearer and because students often have learned them in their own language. If students are having trouble understanding the grammatical terms, encourage them to use the Glossary provided in the back of the Student Book.

Grammar Charts (5–10 minutes)

The Grammar Charts provide a clear reference of all the forms of the target grammar. Students also become familiar with grammatical terminology. The charts also enable you to pre-teach some of the Grammar Notes that follow. In addition to the charts in the Student Book, you may want to use the Focus on Grammar Transparencies (on the CD-ROM in the back of this Teacher's Manual) to help direct all of your students' attention to the same focus point.

Suggested Procedure for Grammar Charts

1. Using the examples you wrote on the board (see Identify the Grammar above) and/or Focus on Grammar Transparencies, draw students' attention to important features in the models by asking them questions or by pointing out the key features.
2. Confirm students' understanding by engaging them in some recognition activities. Try one or two activities from Strategies 3, 4, 5, or 6 (page 11).
3. Get students to manipulate the new structures through substitution or transformation drills. See Strategy 7 (page 11) for an example of a transformation drill.
4. Encourage students to make sentences that are personally meaningful using the new grammar.

Option A

- Have students study the Grammar Charts at home.
- In class, follow step 1 in the suggested procedure above.
- Move directly to the Grammar Notes section. Carry out steps 2, 3, and 4 in the suggested procedure above using the notes together with the charts.

Option B

- Assign individual students responsibility for presenting a topic to the class by combining the information in the charts and the relevant notes. Give them newsprint and a marker to prepare a display in class or at home.
- Ⓘ Meet with students individually. Allow them to rehearse their presentations and provide any coaching needed.
- Call on students to present their topics to the class. Encourage class questions.
- Choose appropriate practice activities from Strategies 4–8 (page 11) OR move directly to the Grammar Notes section.

Grammar Notes (20–30 minutes)

These notes provide helpful information about meaning, use, and form of the grammatical structures that students have encountered in the introductory reading selection and Grammar Charts. They include the following features to help students understand and use the forms.

- Where appropriate, time lines illustrate the meaning of verb forms and their relationship to one another.
- *Be careful!* notes alert students to common errors among English language learners.
- *Usage Notes* provide guidelines for using and understanding different levels of formality and correctness.
- *Pronunciation Notes* are provided when appropriate.
- Below the notes and examples, references to related structures are provided.

The Grammar Notes section includes cross-references to the Focused Practice exercises in the Student Book and to the Supplementary Activities in this Teacher's Manual. Have students complete the appropriate exercises after you present each note. This breaks up the grammar presentation into manageable chunks and allows students to check their understanding of the note.

Suggested Procedure for Grammar Notes

1. Have students read each note at home and/or in class.
2. For each note, write examples on the board and elicit from students the important features of the form (see Strategy 1, page 11, for suggestions) or point out the key features yourself.
3. If possible, demonstrate the meaning of the grammatical form(s) by performing actions (see Strategy 6, page 11).

4. Model the examples and have students repeat after you so that they become comfortable with the appropriate stress, intonation, and rhythm.

5. Engage students with the grammar point by choosing appropriate activities, for example:
  - Elicit examples of the target structure.
  - Confirm students' understanding by having them categorize examples or perform actions that illustrate structure. See Strategies 5 and 6 (page 11) for examples.
  - Provide controlled practice with quick substitution or transformation drills.
  - Encourage students to make personally meaningful sentences using the new grammatical forms.
  - Use the Focused Practice exercises in the Student Book and/or the Supplementary Activities starting on page 143 of this Teacher's Manual.

6. You may want to repeat steps 2–5 for each Grammar Note. Where appropriate, the Unit-by-Unit Teaching Tips give suggestions for presenting two or more notes simultaneously.

Option
  - Photocopy one set of Grammar Notes for each group of three or four students in your class. Cut them up so that the notes and their corresponding examples are not attached.
  - Divide the class into groups of three or four students and give a set of cut-up notes to each group.
  - Give students their task:
    1. Match the examples with the correct notes.
    2. Attach the notes and corresponding examples to a sheet of newsprint (a large piece of paper).
    3. Have students create more examples for each note.
  - Circulate to ensure that students are on the right track, and provide help as needed.
  - Have students post their results around the room, and invite groups to look at each other's work.
  - Regroup as a whole class to answer questions.

Focused Practice

The exercises in this section provide practice for the structures in the Grammar Presentation. You may wish to have students complete the corresponding exercise immediately after you have presented the relevant Grammar Note. Another option is for students to complete one

or more of the exercises at home, using the cross-references to the Grammar Note(s) for support.

If you decide to have students complete the exercises in class, you can keep them motivated by varying the order of the exercises and/or the way you conduct them. Following are various ways of conducting the exercises. In the Unit-by-Unit Teaching Tips, you will find definitions for potentially unfamiliar words and phrases that appear in the Focused Practice exercises.

Discover the Grammar (5–10 minutes)

This opening activity gets students to identify the target grammar structures in a realistic context. This recognition-only activity raises awareness of the structures as it builds confidence.

Suggested Procedure for Discover the Grammar
1. Go over the example with the class.
2. Have students complete the exercise individually or in pairs.
3. Elicit the correct answers from students.

Controlled Practice Exercises (5–10 minutes each)

Following the Discover the Grammar activity are exercises that provide practice in a controlled, but still contextualized, environment. The exercises proceed from simpler to more complex and include a variety of exercise types such as fill in the blanks, matching, and multiple-choice. Exercises are cross-referenced to the appropriate Grammar Notes so that students can review as necessary. Students are exposed to many different written formats, including letters, electronic bulletin boards, résumés, charts, and graphs. Many exercises are art-based, providing a rich context for meaningful practice.

Options
  - Have students work in pairs to complete the exercises.
  - If the exercise is in the form of a conversation, have students complete the exercise and then work in pairs to practice and perform the conversation for the class.
  - When going over answers with students, have them explain why each answer is correct.
  - Whenever possible, relate exercises to students' own lives. For example, if an exercise includes a time line, elicit from

students some important events that have happened in their own lives.

Editing (10 minutes)

All units include an editing exercise to build students' awareness of incorrect usage of the target grammar structures. Students identify and correct errors in a contextualized passage such as a student's composition, a journal entry, or an online message-board posting. The direction line indicates the number of errors in the passage.

Suggested Procedure for Editing

1. Have students read through the passage quickly to understand its context and meaning.
2. Tell students to read the passage line by line, circling incorrect structures and writing in the corrections.
3. Have students take turns reading the passage line by line, saying the structures correctly. Alternatively, read the passage aloud to the class and have students interrupt you with their corrections.
4. There are also usually examples of the correct usage of the structures in each editing exercise. After students have identified the errors, point out the correct usages and ask why they are not errors.

Communication Practice

These in-class exercises give students the opportunity to use the target structure in communicative activities. These activities help develop listening and speaking fluency and critical thinking skills, as well as provide opportunities for students to "own" the structures. As with the Focused Practice exercises, you may wish to vary the order of these activities to keep student motivation high.

Since there are many different exercise types in the Communication Practice section, specific ideas and guidelines are provided in the Unit-by-Unit Teaching Tips. Following are general suggestions for the three main types of exercises. (Note: See the FAQ on pages 12–14 for more information about setting up pair work and group work.)

Listening (10 minutes)

Each Communication Practice section begins with a listening and a comprehension exercise. Students hear a variety of listening formats, including conversations, television scripts,

weather forecasts, and interviews. After listening, students complete a task that focuses on the form or meaning of the target grammar structure. The listening exercises are included on the Student CD so that students may also complete these exercises outside of class.

Suggested Procedure for Listening

Before students listen
1. Explain the situation or context of the listening passage. Provide any necessary cultural information, and pre-teach any vocabulary students may need to know. Definitions are provided in the Unit-by-Unit Teaching Tips for words and phrases that may be unfamiliar to students. (Note that some of these words and phrases may appear in the listening, not in the exercise itself.)
2. Ask students to read the exercise questions first so that they know what to listen for.

Listening
1. Play the audio or read the audioscript aloud. If you choose to read:
   • Speak with a lot of expression and at a natural pace.
   • Change positions and tone of voice to indicate who the speaker is. Another method is to draw stick figures on the board and label them with the characters' names so that you can point to the appropriate character as you change roles.
2. Have students listen the first time with their pencils down.
3. Have students listen again and complete the task.
4. You may want to let students listen as many times as necessary to complete the task.

After students listen
1. Elicit answers for the exercise items and write them on the board. Answer any questions the students may have.
2. ⏱ Students listen a final time and review the passage.

Option A
• Make photocopies of the audioscript and hand it out to students.
• Play the audio recording and have students read along with it in chorus. Explain that this exercise will help them to hear and practice the rhythms, stresses, and clusters of English sounds.

Option B
Have students listen and complete the exercise at home or in a language lab.

Role Plays (10–20 minutes)

In these classroom speaking activities, students role-play a real-life encounter, such as a business meeting or an interview.

Advantages of Role Plays

- They are fun and motivating for most students.
- Role-playing characters often allows the more hesitant students to be more outgoing than if they are speaking as themselves.
- By broadening the world of the classroom to the world outside, role playing allows students to use a wider range of language than less open-ended activities.

Suggested Procedure for Role Plays

1. When possible, bring in props or costumes to add drama and fun.
2. Review the task so students understand what is required.
3. Perform a sample role play with a volunteer in front of the class.
4. Divide the class into the suggested groupings and give them a fixed time limit for completing the task.
5. Have students write a script for the role play. Then have them write key words on cards and perform the role play using the cards as prompts. OR Have students plan the action without a script and present it extemporaneously.
6. While students are working, circulate among the pairs or groups to answer students' questions and help them with the activity.
7. Have various pairs or groups perform their role plays in front of the class. If possible, tape-record or videotape the role plays for students' own listening or viewing. You may want to use the Speaking Rubric on page 158.

Information Gaps (10–20 minutes)

These games are designed to encourage communication between students. In these activities, each student has a different set of information. Students have to talk to their partners to solve a puzzle, draw a picture (describe and draw), put things in the right order (describe and arrange), or find similarities and differences between pictures.

Advantages of Information Gaps

- Like role plays, information gaps are motivating and fun.
- Information gaps are additionally motivating because there is a real need for

communication in order to combine the information to solve a problem and complete the task.
- Information sharing allows students to extend and personalize what they have learned in the unit.

Suggested Procedure for Information Gaps

1. Explain how the Student A and Student B pages relate to each other (how they are different or similar).
2. Refer students to the examples and to any language provided.
3. Divide the class into pairs (Student A and Student B) and have them position themselves so that they cannot see the contents of each other's books.
4. Tell the Student Bs what page to turn to, and circulate to check that they are looking at the correct page.
5. Have students read their separate instructions. Check comprehension of the task by asking each group, "What are you going to do?"
6. Remind students not to show each other the contents of their pages.
7. As students are working, circulate to answer individual questions and to help students with the activity.

Writing (15–25 minutes in-class time)

These activities give students the opportunity to develop their writing skills and provide additional practice using the target grammatical structures. There is a variety of realistic formats, including paragraphs, essays, letters, and journal entries. The themes are related to material covered in the unit so that students already have some preparation for the writing task.

A Scoring Rubric for Writing is included on page 159 so that you can assess students' general writing skills as well as their ability to apply the target grammar point within a written context. This rubric allows you to give students a holistic score from 1 to 5 that reflects how well students have responded to the topic, organized their ideas, and incorporated the new grammar points from the unit. It is best to hand out copies to students before they begin working on the assignment, so that they understand what competencies are required.

The rubric provided in this book is for classroom use. To see an example of a rubric used to evaluate writing in a formal assessment situation, you can look at the one used by raters of the writing section on the TOEFL® iBT. This is available to download at http://ftp.ets.org/pub/toefl/Writing_Rubrics.pdf.

Suggested Procedure for Writing

Pre-writing

1. Go over the requirements of the assignment to make sure students understand what they are expected to do.
2. Write some questions on the board, and have students work in pairs or small groups to brainstorm ideas for the writing assignment. The Unit-by-Unit Teaching Tips provide suggestions for questions you might write on the board.
3. Call on volunteers to answer the questions as you write key words and phrases on the board.
4. Remind students to include the grammar studied in the unit as they complete the assignment.

Composing and correcting

1. Have students compose a draft of the writing assignment at home and then submit it to you or share it with a partner in class.
2. Give students feedback on the following features:
   - Content: Has the student responded appropriately to the task? Are the main points well supported?
   - Organization: Is the flow of ideas logical and effective?
   - Accuracy: Are there any major errors in the grammar points taught in the unit? (At this stage, you may want to focus your comments on errors related to the target grammar point. Circle the errors, but let students make the corrections. If students are providing feedback to each other, encourage them to focus on content and organization.
3. 🕐 For longer assignments, have students complete a second draft. When you check these drafts, point out any further areas needing correction, concentrating especially on errors in the target grammar point or grammar points from a previous unit.
4. Have students prepare their final draft at home.

Presentation

1. In class, have students share their final drafts. There are a variety of ways to do this:
   - Post students' work on the class bulletin board.

- Publish it in a website or a magazine that the class creates.
- Exchange papers with others in the class.
- Read papers aloud.

2. 🕐 Have your students put all their corrected written work into a folder, or portfolio, which you can review at the end of the course. This will allow your students and you to see the progress they have made.

Internet Activity (20 minutes in-class time)

This activity gives students an opportunity to do research related to the content of the unit and to discuss or present their findings in class. The activity varies from unit to unit. In some cases students are given very specific questions to research, and the reporting task is brief. In other cases, the investigation is more open-ended, and there is potential for a more extensive presentation.

Suggested Procedure for Internet Activity

Before class

Try the activity yourself, and prepare a list of appropriate key words or specific websites. Note: some suggested website addresses are listed on the *Focus on Grammar* Companion Website (www.longman.com/focusongrammar).

In class: preparation

1. Go over the directions to be sure students understand them. Have students work in small groups to brainstorm ideas for their research.
2. For some projects, you may want to have students work in small groups to divide up the research tasks.
3. Ask students to think about how they would search for their topics. Discuss useful key words and/or write some suggested websites on the board. Remind students that they can find websites on the *Focus on Grammar* Companion Website (www.longman.com/focusongrammar).
4. Elicit language that students are likely to use when discussing their research results. Remind them to review language they have studied in the unit.

At home / language lab

1. Students research their topics and take notes.
2. Ask students to review the notes they made on each website and summarize the most important information.

In class: wrap-up
1. During the next class session, put students into small groups to discuss their research findings.
2. Call upon a spokesperson for each group to report what the group discussed and, if appropriate, what conclusions they came to.

Option (40–60 minutes in-class time)
- Follow the above procedure, but instead of having small group discussions, have students deliver more formal spoken presentations. You may wish to use the Speaking Rubric on page 158.
- When going over the directions to the activity, tell students that they should take notes as they do their research and prepare a short (5-minute) presentation.
- Talk with students about elements of successful spoken presentations, including the importance of making eye contact and using body language. Encourage them to practice at home and to bring in visuals if possible.
- Coach students as they present and provide feedback on their presentations. You may wish to have students complete feedback forms for other students' presentations.

Further Practice

One or more Further Practice activities (in the Teacher's Manual only) can be found at the end of every unit in the Unit-by-Unit Teaching Tips. These exercises offer additional communicative practice with the target structure of the unit. Most can be done in class with no before-class preparation.

This activity (in the Teacher's Manual only) offers ideas for how to bring "real life" into your grammar classroom. Using video, pictures, news articles, or other realia, these activities help students make the connection between the structures they learn in the classroom and their application in the real world.

From Grammar to Writing

The From Grammar to Writing section at the end of each Part of the Student Book includes a grammar point and relates this grammar point to the writing focus. Students first practice the teaching point in a controlled exercise such as fill in the blanks, identification, or editing. Following these exercises, students practice pre-writing strategies such as making charts, time lines, schedules, story maps, Venn diagrams, notes, and outlines. Finally, students apply the teaching point in a writing task. Text types include both formal and informal writing, such as personal letters, business letters, essays, summaries, and reports. The section concludes with peer review and editing.

Suggested Procedure for From Grammar to Writing
Pre-writing
1. Have students work individually to complete the controlled practice exercises. Then have them exchange books and compare answers.
2. Go over the answers as a class and answer any questions that students have at this point.
3. Explain the pre-writing task. Where appropriate, provide a model for students on the board or on an overhead.
4. Have students work in pairs or small groups to complete the pre-writing task. Circulate while they are working to answer any questions and to help them with the activity.

Composing and correcting
1. Go over the requirements of the assignment to make sure students understand what they are expected to do.
2. Have students complete the writing assignment at home.
3. In class, complete the peer review portion of the task. Circulate while students are working together to make sure they are on task and to provide appropriate feedback. (See Suggested Procedure for Writing on page 8 for examples of what kind of feedback to provide.)
4. ⏱ Have students revise their writing and turn in the second draft to you. You may wish to use the Scoring Rubric for Writing on page 159 to correct these drafts and to include the drafts as part of the students' writing portfolios.

Option

- Have students complete the controlled practice exercise(s) at home.
- In class, have students work in pairs to compare answers.
- Follow the suggested procedure, starting from step 4 in the pre-writing phase.

Review Test

The last section of each Part of the Student Book is a review feature that can be used as a self-test. These exercises test the form and use of the grammar content presented and practiced in that Part. They give students a chance to check their knowledge and to review any problematic areas before moving on to the next part. An answer key is provided at the back of the Student Book, with cross-references to units for easy review.

Suggested Procedure for Review Test

1. Have students complete the exercises at home and check their answers in the Answer Key.
2. During the next class, go over any remaining questions students may have.

Option

- Have students complete the exercises in class. Give them a time limit of 20–30 minutes and circulate as they work.
- Have students use the Answer Key to check and correct their answers in pairs. Or you can go over the answers as a class.

Strategies for Teaching Grammar

1. Develop awareness
- Ask questions that help students become aware of the form of the structure. For example, for the imperative (*FOG 3*, page 13), read the affirmative command, "Bend your knees," and ask the class to name the verb. *(Bend)* Ask students what form it is. *(the base form)* Ask students what "base" form means. *(the simple form without an ending)* Ask students, "Do you see a subject?" *(no)* Explain that in the imperative we understand that the subject is "you." Ask, "How do we form the negative in the imperative?" *(Add* Don't *before the base form.)*
- Compare information in the Grammar Charts. For example, for the simple past (*FOG 3*, pages 23–24) there are Grammar Charts for the past of *be* and for other verbs. Ask, "How many forms are there for the simple past of *be*?" *(two: was and* were) "How do you form the negative with *be* in the simple past?" *(wasn't, weren't)* "How many forms are there for the negative with other verbs?" *(one:* didn't + *base form)* Ask, "Do you use the base form for past *yes/no* questions with *be*?" *(no)* "Do you use the base form for past *yes/no* questions with other verbs?" *(yes)*

2. Present meaning
Show the meaning of a grammatical form through a classroom demonstration. For example, to illustrate the use of present perfect progressive, you could show a picture of a person carrying grocery bags full of food. *(He/She has been shopping.)*

3. Identify examples
Ask students to go back to the Grammar in Context section and label examples in the reading passage with the grammatical terms in the Grammar Charts.

4. Generate examples
Find examples from the reading or elsewhere that could fit into the Grammar Charts. An interesting way to do this is to photocopy and enlarge the Grammar Chart. White out the targeted structures and replace them with blank lines for each missing word. Make copies and distribute them to students in pairs or small groups. Have students fill in the blanks, using examples from the reading. Then generate more examples. Books can be open or closed, depending on the level of challenge desired.

5. Show understanding by categorizing
Check comprehension of a grammatical principle by asking students to label multiple examples appropriately. For example, students can label verbs "present" or "future" or they can label examples "correct" or "incorrect."

6. Show understanding by performing actions
Ask students to show their understanding of the meaning of a grammatical form by following instructions or devising a demonstration. Ask students, for example, to think of and perform a set of actions that they could describe using the present progressive.

7. Manipulate forms
Have students manipulate the examples in the Grammar Charts to practice the form. Drills such as substitution or transformation help students to build fluency. For example, in Unit 6 (*FOG 3*, page 54) you might put one form on the board *(He is going to leave soon.)* and then elicit other forms by saying, "Negative" *(He isn't going to leave soon.)*, "Yes/no question" *(Is he going to leave soon?)*, "Short answer, affirmative" *(Yes, he is.)*, "Wh- question, when" *(When is he going to leave?)*, and so on to get students to produce the other forms rapidly.

8. Personalize
Ask students to provide personal examples. For example, on page 357 of *FOG 3*, students see the example, "Eva enjoys going to the park. Eva wants to go to the park." Ask students what they enjoy or want to do. *(I enjoy playing soccer. I want to join a soccer team.)*

9. Repeat, reinforce
Students need to be exposed to new grammar many times in order to internalize it completely. You can first present a new structure on the board, then point it out in the book, then have students use it in an informal oral exercise, then do a written exercise in pairs, and finally review the same structure in homework. Varying the content and focus of these activities will keep students interested, and the grammar will be reinforced almost automatically.

Frequently Asked Questions (FAQ)

1. When should I have students work in pairs or groups rather than individually or as a whole class?

Varying your classroom organization to suit particular activity types will result in more effective and more interesting classes. Many students are not accustomed to working in pairs or groups, so it is important to use these groupings only when they are most beneficial.

- **Whole-class teaching** maximizes teacher control and is especially good for:
  —presenting information, giving explanations and instructions
  —showing material in texts and pictures or on audio or videotape
  —teacher-led drills (such as substitution or transformation) or dictations
  —reviewing answers or sharing ideas after students have completed an activity
  —enabling the whole class to benefit from teacher feedback to individuals
- **Students working individually** allows quiet, concentrated attention and is most effective for:
  —processing information or completing a task at students' own pace
  —performing writing tasks

For objective exercises such as fill-in-the-blank, matching, multiple choice, and editing, vary your class organization to keep student motivation high. Students can sometimes complete these exercises individually, and sometimes they can work with a partner.

- **Students working in pairs** maximizes student speaking time, breaks up the routine and "teacher talk," and is ideal for:
  —information-gap activities
  —role plays
  —writing and/or reading dialogues
  —predicting the content of reading and listening texts
  —comparing notes on what students listen to or see
  —checking answers
  —peer assessment

Pair work can also be very effective for completing objective exercises such as fill-in-the-blank, matching, multiple choice, and editing.

- **Students working in groups** creates ideal conditions for students to learn from each other and works well for:
  —generating ideas
  —pooling knowledge
  —writing group stories
  —preparing presentations
  —discussing an issue and reaching a group decision

2. How should I set up pair work and group work?

- **Streaming:** Grouping students according to ability or participation has certain advantages.
  —**ability:** Grouping weaker and stronger students together allows more able students to help their less fluent classmates.
  —**participation:** If you see that some students participate less than others, you could make a pair or group of weak participators. By the same token, you can also put especially talkative students together.
- **Chance:** Grouping students by chance has many benefits, especially if it results in students working with varied partners. You can group students by chance according to:
  —**where they sit:** Students sitting next to or near one another work in pairs or groups. This is the easiest option, but if students always sit in the same place, you will want to find other ways of grouping them.
  —**the "wheels" system:** Half the class stands in a circle facing outwards, and the other half stands in an outer circle facing inwards. The outer circle revolves in a clockwise direction, and the inner circle revolves in a counterclockwise direction. When you tell them to stop, students work with the person facing them. This is a very effective way to have students engage in meaningful repetition, such as asking the same question of many different partners.
  —**assigned letters:** Assign each student a letter from *A* to *E*. Then ask all the As to form a group, all the Bs to form a group, and so on.
  —**birthdays:** Students stand in a line in the order of their birthdays (with January at one end and December at the other). The first five students form one group; the second five students another group, and so on.

—**native language:** If possible, put students in groups or pairs with others who don't share a native language. This helps create an "English-only" classroom.

3. How can I make activities more successful?

Before the activity:

- **Motivate students and explain the purpose.** Make it clear that something enjoyable or interesting is going to happen. Explain the rationale for the activity. Making sure students understand the purpose of the activity is to practice what they learned and encourage them to participate.
- **Provide clear directions.** Explain what students should do in every step of the activity. Have students paraphrase or demonstrate the task to be sure they understand it.
- **Demonstrate.** Show the class what is supposed to happen in an activity. This might involve asking a student to demonstrate the activity with you or having two students role-play in the front of the room.
- **Provide a time frame.** It is helpful for students to know how much time they have and exactly when they should stop. Approximate times are given for all the activities in this Teacher's Manual.

For open-ended activities, such as the Internet Activity or writing exercises, you will also want to:

- **Stimulate thinking.** When there are choices for students to make, it is often helpful to set up small-group and/or whole-class brainstorming sessions to define the focus and/or content of their task.
- **Prepare language.** Review grammar and vocabulary that students may need to complete the task. This can be done as a follow-up to a brainstorming activity where you elicit ideas and write key language on the board.

During the activity:

- **Observe students.** Walk around the room watching and listening to pairs or groups.
- **Provide assistance as needed.** (See FAQ #5 for suggestions on giving feedback and correcting errors.)

After the activity:

- **Elicit student responses.** For some activities, you may ask for volunteers or call on students to share some of their ideas with the class. For other types of activities, a few pairs or groups can be asked to role-play their discussions to demonstrate the language they have been using.
- **Provide feedback.** In many cases, this is most conveniently done in a whole-class setting. It may be preferable, however, for you to meet with individuals, pairs, or groups. While the principal focus in a grammar class is language use, it is also important to acknowledge the value of students' ideas. See FAQ #5 below for suggestions on feedback and error correction.

4. What can I do to encourage students to use more English in the classroom?

It is perfectly natural for students to feel the need to use their first language in an English class. There are a number of actions that teachers can take to promote the use of English.

- **Set clear guidelines:** Some teachers in monolingual classes find that activities such as providing vocabulary definitions, presenting a grammar point, checking comprehension, giving instructions, and discussing classroom methodology are best done in the students' native language.
- **Use persuasion:** Walking among the students during speaking activities and saying things like "Please speak English!" or "Try to use English as much as possible." helps to ensure that students will speak English most of the time.

5. What's the best approach to giving feedback and correcting errors?

Be selective in offering correction. Students can't focus on everything at once, so concentrate first on errors relating to the target grammar point and grammar points from units previously studied, as well as any errors that interfere with communication. Whether you respond to other errors depends on your judgment of students' readiness to take in the information. If you see a teachable moment, seize it! Rather than correct every error individual students make in the course of activities, it is generally preferable to note commonly occurring mistakes and give a short presentation for the whole class at the end of the activity.

- **Recasting.** If a student makes an error—for example, "I *didn't came* to class yesterday because I was sick."—you can recast it as, "You *didn't come* to class yesterday because you were sick?" The student ideally notices the difference and restates the original sentence: "Right. I didn't come to class yesterday because I was sick." This process can be effective because the student has the opportunity to self-correct an error that is still in short-term memory. As a variation, you can restate but stop, with rising intonation, right before the potential error: "You didn't . . . ?"

6. What can I do to accommodate different learning styles?

Focus on Grammar recognizes different styles of learning and provides a variety of activities to accommodate these different styles. Some learners prefer an analytical, or rule-learning (deductive) approach. Others, especially younger learners, respond best to an inductive approach, or exposure to the language in meaningful contexts. Indeed, the same students may adopt different styles as they learn, or they may use different styles at different times.

As teachers, we want to help the students in our classes who prefer to follow rules become more able to take risks and to plunge into communicative activities. We also want to encourage the risk-takers to focus on accuracy. *Focus on Grammar* provides the variety to ensure that students achieve their goal: to learn to use the language confidently and appropriately.

Unit-by-Unit Teaching Tips

UNIT 1 · Present Progressive and Simple Present

Unit Overview

Unit 1 focuses on the meanings and uses of the present progressive and the simple present and on the comparison between them.
- The present progressive describes an action that is happening right now or in the extended present time.
- The simple present describes an action that happens regularly. It can also describe a scientific fact.

Grammar in Context (pages 2–3)

Background Note

A cross-cultural IQ measures a person's knowledge of other cultures and the ability to recognize and accurately interpret cross-cultural misunderstandings.

Vocabulary

cross-cultural: belonging to or involving two or more societies, countries, or cultures

IQ: intelligence quotient—the level of someone's intelligence, with 100 being the average level

misunderstanding: a failure to understand a question, situation, or instruction

uncomfortable: unable to relax because you are embarrassed

Comprehension Questions

- What's the misunderstanding (or problem) in situation 1? *(Tomás visits Claude without calling first. This is not something people do in Claude's culture.)*
- What's the misunderstanding (or problem) in situation 2? *(Nicole wants to kiss Sheila twice. This is not something people do in Sheila's culture.)*

Discussion Topics

- Ask students to discuss if it is important to learn about other cultures before traveling abroad. Encourage students to give reasons for their answers.
- Ask students to talk about cultural differences they know about that can cause misunderstandings.
- Ask students to discuss how the people in the cartoons could resolve their misunderstandings.

Grammar Presentation (pages 3–5)

Identify the Grammar

PRESENT PROGRESSIVE
Tomás is visiting Claude.
Nicole and Sheila are saying hello.

SIMPLE PRESENT
Claude looks very surprised.
. . . people often visit without calling first.

Grammar Charts

- Write two sets of contrastive sentences on the board:

Present Progressive	Simple Present
Nicole is visiting her friends now.	*She visits them every day.*
They are kissing goodbye.	*They always kiss twice.*

—Point to the examples of the present progressive and ask: "How many words are needed for the present progressive?" *(two)* "How do you form the present progressive?" *(form of* be + -ing *form of verb)*
—Point to the examples of the simple present and ask: "How many words are needed for the simple present?" *(one)* "How do you form the simple present?" *(base form of verb + s)*
—Point out that some verbs form the simple present by adding *es*. Write on the board:
kiss → kisses   watch → watches

- Write these examples on the board:

  They are not feeling   *People do not kiss*
    comfortable.   *more than once.*

  —Ask the class: "How do you form the negative present progressive?" *(form of* be *+ not + -ing form of verb)* "How do you form the negative simple present?" *(form of* do *+ not + base form of verb)*

  —Give an example of *does not.* You can say, "Sheila does not kiss people twice."

- Remind students of contractions by restating the examples of negative sentences. Say, "They aren't feeling comfortable. People don't kiss more than once."

- Point to the first set of examples on the board:

  —Ask a student to make the examples under Present Progressive negative, using contractions *(isn't visiting/aren't kissing).*

  —Ask another student to make the first two examples under Simple Present negative, using contractions *(doesn't visit/don't always kiss).*

- Write these examples on the board:

  Is Tomás visiting   *Do people call first?*
    Claude?

  —Ask the class: "How do you form *yes/no* questions in the present progressive?" *(form of* be *+ subject + -ing form of verb)* "How do you form *yes/no* questions in the simple present?" *(form of* do *+ subject + base form of verb)*

  —Have students provide an affirmative and a negative short answer for each question. *(Yes, he is./No, he isn't. Yes, they do./No, they don't.)*

- Write these examples on the board:

  What is Tomás doing?   *What do people do*
                                  in Sheila's culture?

  Ask the class: "How do you form *wh-* questions in the present progressive?" *(wh-word + form of* be *+ subject + -ing form of verb)* "How do you form *wh-* questions in the simple present?" *(wh- word + form of* do *+ subject + base form of verb)*

Grammar Notes

Before going over the notes, tell students that if they don't know or remember the meaning of a grammar term, they can refer to the Glossary on page G-1, which provides definitions of grammar terms and examples.

Note 1   *(Exercises 1–5, 7)*
- To review the present progressive, stand up and say, "Right now I'm standing." Then

address a student and ask, "What about you, are you sitting or standing?" Ask volunteers to say what the people in the class are doing. *(Brandon is looking out the window. Sam is holding a pen. Marian is talking with Carol. Sandra is smiling. Tony is looking at his watch.)*

- Write on the board:

  Pierre lives in Paris, but he's on vacation now, and he _____ (stay) with his brother in New York.

  Before students complete the sentence with the correct form of *stay,* ask the class: "Where does Pierre live?" *(in France)* "Is he in France now?" *(no)* "Where is he?" *(in New York)* "Why?" *(because he's on vacation)* Make sure students understand that *is staying* is the correct answer because the action is temporary.

- You can refer students to Appendix 21 on page A-10 for spelling rules on forming the present progressive.

→ For additional practice, see the Supplementary Activities on page 143.

Note 2   *(Exercises 1–7)*
- To review the simple present, ask students to say what they—or the people in their family—usually do after school or work in the evening. *(I watch TV. My sister walks the dog. My mother prepares dinner.)*

- Ask students to say other scientific facts they know. *(Oil floats in water. The sun rises in the east. Plants need light.)*

- You can refer students to Appendix 20 on page A-9 for spelling rules on forming the third person singular of the simple present, and Appendix 29 on page A-14 for pronunciation rules for the simple present.

Note 3   *(Exercises 1, 3–7)*
- To check comprehension, write two contrasting sentences on the board:

  Oliver is getting up early.   *Oliver gets up early.*

  Ask the class: "Which sentence expresses a routine—what Oliver always does?" *(Oliver gets up early.)* "Which sentence expresses a change in routine—what Oliver is doing these days?" *(Oliver is getting up early.)*

- Students take turns working in pairs saying what they are doing at school or at work this week or this month. *(In History we're studying the Egyptians. In Science we are working on a special project. At work I'm preparing the annual report. This week I'm organizing an office party.)*

Note 4 *(Exercises 1, 3–7)*

- Draw attention to the Be careful note. Then write on the board:
  I feel tired.   I am tired.
  Ask a volunteer to come to the front and rewrite the sentences inserting the adverb *always* in each. *(I always feel tired. I am always tired.)*
- Write on the board:
  How often do you . . . ?
    go to a movie   do sports
    eat out   give parties
    watch TV   other: _____
  How often are you . . . ?
    late to school/work, late to parties
  Have students think of their own ideas for the last item on the first list. Have students take turns in pairs asking and answering the questions on the board. Ask students to use frequency adverbs in their answers.

Note 5 *(Exercises 1, 3–7)*

- Write the verbs below on the board in two columns as shown:
  do   want
  buy   like
  Ask the class: "Which verbs express actions?" (do *and* buy) "Which verbs express states?" (want *and* like)
- Point out that non-action verbs are not usually used in the present progressive.
- Write these examples on the board:
  Steve is doing exercise because he wants to lose weight.
  Maria is buying a CD because she likes music.
  Point out that although both the actions (*do* and *buy*) and the states (*want* and *like*) exist at the moment of speaking, only the action verbs (*do* and *buy*) are used in the present progressive.
- Refer students to Appendix 2 on page A-2 for a list of non-action verbs.

Note 6 *(Exercises 1, 3–7)*

- Point out that the verbs *taste*, *smell*, and *look* can be used in the present progressive when they describe actions. Have students look at the examples in the book again. Ask: "What does *tastes* mean in the first sentence?" *(has a particular flavor)* "What does *is tasting* mean in the second sentence?" *(is trying)*
- Write two new examples on the board:
  The food smells nice.   She is smelling the roses.
  Have students discuss in pairs the meaning of the underlined verbs. *(smells: has a particular*

smell; is smelling: is putting her nose near the roses to discover what type of smell they have)

Focused Practice *(pages 6–10)*

Exercise 1
en route: on the way

seatmate: someone who sits next to you (on a plane)

host parent: the father or mother who invites a student to stay in his/her home

cute: attractive

nap: a short sleep during the day

Exercise 2
field trip: an occasion when students go somewhere to learn about a particular subject

sharp: exactly at a time

Exercise 3
down: sad

respectful: feeling or showing respect or admiration

date: to go out with someone in order to get to know them, or to have a romantic relationship with someone

Exercise 4
appear: to seem

Exercise 5
culture shock: the strange feelings that someone has when s/he visits a foreign country or a new place for the first time

routine: the usual or normal way in which you do things

go through: to have a very upsetting or difficult experience

stage: a particular state or level that something or someone reaches in a process before going to the next one

honeymoon: a vacation taken by two people who have just gotten married

rejection: the act of not accepting something

adjustment: a change in the way you behave or think

adaptation: the process of changing something so that it can be used in a different way or in different conditions

Exercise 6
improve: to become better, or to make something better

annoy: to make someone feel slightly angry about something

Exercise 7
homesick: feeling sad because you are away from your home

miss: to feel sad because you are not with a particular person, or because you no longer have something or are no longer doing something

analyze: to examine or think about something carefully in order to understand it

tardiness: being late

Communication Practice (pages 11–12)

Exercise 8
• To review answers as a class, ask students to make complete sentences using the simple present or the present progressive, as appropriate. *(She is speaking English right now. She usually speaks Spanish.)*

Exercise 9
• As a class [before students walk around the classroom] elicit a question for each item. *(Do you like visiting foreign countries? Are you wearing a watch? Do you speak more than two languages? Are you studying something besides English? Do you watch sports on TV? Are you planning to travel this year?)*
• Have students write their own question.
• Ask students to write notes as they interview their classmates. Encourage them to ask follow-up questions.
• Choose a few students to report back to the class. Circulate as students speak, listening to make sure students use correct verb forms.

Exercise 10
• To help students generate ideas, write the following questions on the board:
Where are the people?
Who are they addressing?
What are they saying?
• Go over the model. Point out *looks* to express what the man seems to be doing. Point out *maybe* to express possibility.
• Write on the board some useful language for students:

He/She	looks . . .	Maybe	he/she
	seems . . .	Perhaps	is . . .
	appears to be . . .		

• To review, have volunteers express their opinion of what the people in the photographs are doing.

Exercise 11
• Ask students to write *Yes* in front of appropriate questions and *No* in front of questions that they think are not appropriate.

Ask students to write notes explaining why some of the questions are inappropriate. Encourage students to use their notes as they discuss in groups.
• To review, have volunteers express their views about two of the questions.

Exercise 12
Questions to generate ideas and elicit vocabulary:
• What new experience are you having this week/month/year?
• How is this experience different from what you usually do?
• How do you feel?
Note: If some of your students find it difficult to come up with personal new experiences, have them write about the new experience(s) of someone they know.

Further Practice
Working in pairs, ask students to write a short description (30–60 words) of what the people do/are doing in a city or country of their choice, using the simple present to describe what the people usually do, and the present progressive to describe what the people are doing right now or in the extended present time. Then have students read their description aloud to another pair, who should guess the place. For example:
In this city, the people like music and dancing. They go to its wonderful beaches during the day and go out to restaurants and discos at night. At this time of the year, they are preparing spectacular costumes and parades. (Rio de Janeiro, Brazil)

Getting informed. Bring in newspapers. Give each group a newspaper. Each group member should get a page of the newspaper. Give students three or four minutes to skim through the newspaper page they have. Then have students tell their partners about the news they read using the present progressive (current events) and the simple present (habitual actions or scientific facts), as appropriate, for example: *In France, the police are looking for a man who robbed a bank. Scientists say that chocolate cures heart disease.*

UNIT 2 Imperative

Unit Overview

Unit 2 focuses on the uses of the imperative.
- The imperative is used to tell or ask someone to do something.
- It is often used in directions, instructions, orders, commands, suggestions, warnings, requests, and informal invitations.

Grammar in Context (pages 13–14)

Background Note

Kickboxing is a traditional martial art from Thailand. It uses the shins, knees, elbows, and wrists to position the body in different fighting moves.

Vocabulary

warrior: a soldier, especially an experienced and skillful one

workout: a series of physical exercises that you do to keep your body strong and healthy

jab: a sudden hard push or hit

raise: to move or lift something to a higher position or to an upright position

fist: a hand with all the fingers bent tightly in toward the palm

punch: to hit someone or something hard with your fist

lean: to move or bend your body in a particular position

kick: (n.): the act of hitting something with your foot; (v.): to hit something with your foot

weight: how heavy someone or something is

bend: to move a part of your body so that it is not straight or so that you are not standing upright

Comprehension Questions

- What's the kickboxing workout good for? *(feeling better, building your strength)*
- How often should you do it to get fast results? *(three times a week)*
- Which two exercises are explained? *(the jab and the power kick)*
- Which one is a strong punch? *(the jab)*
- What is the power kick? *(a strong kick to the side)*

Discussion Topics

- Ask students to talk about the benefits of doing exercise. Encourage students to discuss how exercise can help you stay fit, lift your spirits, relax, and reduce stress.
- Ask students to talk about the type of exercise—for example, martial arts, swimming, jogging, aerobics, weight lifting— they prefer. Encourage students to support their views.

Grammar Presentation (pages 14–15)

Identify the Grammar

AFFIRMATIVE IMPERATIVE
Get into the basic position.

NEGATIVE IMPERATIVE
Don't stand straight as you punch.

Grammar Charts

- Choose one of the examples on the board and write two contrastive sentences.

Affirmative Imperative	Negative Imperative
Stand straight.	Don't stand straight.

—Point to the example of the affirmative imperative and ask: "How do you form the affirmative imperative?" *(base form of verb)* "Does the imperative need a subject?" *(no)*
—Point to the example of the negative imperative and ask: "How do you form the negative imperative?" (don't + *base form of verb*)
- Ask volunteers to say some of the typical instructions you give in class. Encourage students to use both affirmative and negative imperatives. *(Listen carefully. Pay attention. Don't speak in [student's language]. Write this down. Don't cheat. Use a dictionary. Do exercise 3. Don't do exercise 4. Work in pairs. Work in groups. Don't forget to do your homework.)*

Grammar Notes

Note 1 *(Exercises 1–4)*
- Point out that the imperative is typically used to tell someone to do something, and that it has different uses.
- Write the following imperative statements and uses on the board in two columns, as shown:

Shut up!	warning
Watch out!	order
Take the escalator.	suggestion
Don't work so hard.	direction

Have students match the examples with the uses.

- To review as a class, connect the items on the board with arrows. (*Shut up!: order. Watch out!: warning. Take the escalator: direction. Don't work so hard: suggestion.*)
- Ask students in pairs to write down their own example for each use. To review, ask volunteers to read an example aloud withholding the use. Have the class guess the use.

→ For additional practice, see the Supplementary Activities on page 143.

Note 2 *(Exercises 1, 3–4)*
Draw attention to the Usage Note. Point out that using an imperative without *please* when extending an invitation will sound rude unless you know the person well.

Note 3 *(Exercises 1–4)*
Explain that it is rude to call out a person's name and then give an order. For example: *Sandra! Come here. You! Stand up!* People only speak like this when they have a great deal of power over someone else, such as in the military. However, it is possible to say the person's name if you want to make it clear who you are speaking to, but you should make it a point to sound polite and not authoritative. For example: *Alice, type this for me (please).* The fact that the imperative is the same in both the singular and the plural often makes it necessary to say the name of the person you are addressing. In this way, you make sure the right person gets the message.

Focused Practice (pages 15–18)

Exercise 1
warmly: in a way that makes you feel warm

pepper: a spicy black, pale yellow, or red hot-tasting powder, used in cooking

buckle: to fasten or join together two sides of something

Exercise 2
slice: to cut meat, bread, etc, into thin flat pieces

blend: to mix together two or more substances to form a single smooth substance

pour: to make a liquid or a substance such as salt or sand flow into something

blender: a small electric machine that you use to mix liquids together, or to make soft foods more liquid

Exercise 3
decrease: to become less in size, number, or amount, or to make something do this

increase: to become larger in number, amount, or degree, or to make something do this

focus: to pay special attention to a particular thing

trial: a short period during which you use something to find out whether it is satisfactory

membership: the state of being a member of a club, group, organization, or system

miss: to not go somewhere or do something, especially when you want to but cannot

Exercise 4
guilty: ashamed and sad because you have done something that you know is wrong

Communication Practice (pages 18–21)

Exercise 5
Before students listen, ask students to read over the items and use the context to figure out the meaning of any unknown words. Clarify the meaning of any words. Students might need help with some of the following words: *frying pan:* a round pan with a handle, used for frying (cooking in hot fat or oil) food. *melt:* to change something from solid to liquid by heating. *beat:* to mix food together quickly using a fork or a kitchen tool. *whole wheat:* made with every part of the wheat grain, including the outer layer. *flip over:* to turn over quickly, or to make something turn over. *thoroughly:* carefully and completely.

Exercise 6
- Write on the board the following abbreviations from the map:
  St   Rd   Ave   Exwy
  Elicit the full forms (*street, road, avenue, expressway*). If necessary, explain that an expressway is a wide road in a city on which cars can travel fast.
- Point out that these words are often left out in everyday speech. You can say, "Stay on Founders Street" or "Stay on Founders."
- Draw attention to the sentences in the box. Ask students to find in the box three ways to indicate that the person should not turn but continue on the same street. List them on the board:
  Go straight.
  Continue on 9th Street.
  Stay on Founders.

Then ask students to find in the box two ways to indicate that the person should turn. Write them on the board:

Turn right/left.

Make a right/left turn.

🕐 For further practice, have Student A mark a museum on the map, and Student B mark an art gallery. Then Student A asks Student B for directions to the art gallery, and Student B asks Student A for directions to the museum.

Exercise 7

- Go over the recipe given as an example. Encourage students to figure out the meaning of unknown words, and provide help as needed.
- You may want to have students underline the verbs in the imperative form in the instructions. Point out that students should use the imperative in their own recipe.
- Brainstorm and write on the board a list of useful kitchen verbs. Remind students of the verbs they learned in exercises 2 and 5. You can classify the verbs on the board as follows:

Adding and mixing	Cutting	Washing	Cooking	Others
add	cut	wash	heat	melt
pour	slice	rinse	simmer	top
mix	shred	drain	fry	flip over
beat	chop		boil*	spread*
blend			bake*	

*Verbs marked with an asterisk were not seen in previous exercises, but might be useful to students.

- Circulate as students write their recipes. Help students with any words they might not know in English. (If there is a dictionary in the classroom, encourage its use.)
- Choose a few students to read their recipes aloud to the class.

Exercise 8

- After working in groups, have students share their ideas with the class.
- Write students' answers in two columns on the board under the headings *Dos* and *Don'ts*.

Exercise 9

Questions to generate ideas and elicit vocabulary:
- Where am I going to direct the person?
- Is the person on foot or in his/her car?

Ask students to sketch a simple map of the area, and then draw the route from their school to the place they chose.

Further Practice

Have students give directions to places in the building they are in, for example, the restrooms, the library, or the cafeteria. You may want to write a list of useful vocabulary on the board. For example:

Go straight.
Turn right/left.
Go to the end of the hall.
Go up/down the stairs.
Take the elevator to the (second) floor.

GRAMMAR OUT OF THE BOX . . . . . .

Rules for road users. Bring in photocopies of *The Highway Code* or print out material from a highway code website. Give each group a different section of the code—for example, rules for pedestrians, rules about animals, rules for cyclists, rules for motorcyclists, rules for drivers. Ask each group to read the information they have and write down the five rules that they consider the most important. Then have each group report to the class on the rules they read. For example:

Rules for crossing the road
- Find a safe place to cross.
- Don't cross between parked cars.
- Stop and look both ways.
- Walk. Don't run.
- Keep looking while you cross.

UNIT 3 Simple Past

Unit Overview

Unit 3 focuses on the meanings and uses of the simple past. It covers the simple past of *be* and regular and irregular verbs.
- The simple past describes finished actions, states, or situations.
- It can be used with time expressions that refer to the past.

Grammar in Context (pages 22–23)

Background Note

Haiku is a traditional form of Japanese poetry, popular since the 17th century. It is a three-line poem of usually seventeen syllables in lines of five, seven, and five syllables each. It traditionally focuses on images of the natural world.

Vocabulary

biography: a book or an account of a person's life, written by someone else

establish: to start something such as a company, system, situation, etc., especially one that will exist for a long time

restless: not satisfied and wanting new experiences

Comprehension Questions

• What did Basho write? *(haiku/three-line poems)*
• What did he write about? *(nature, daily life, and human emotions)*
• Did he also teach how to write poems? *(yes)*
• How many students did he have by the end of his life? *(2,000)*

Discussion Topics

• Have students read Basho's poem again and give their opinion of it. You may want to write some questions on the board as a guide: *Do you like the poem? Is it effective? Is it fun? Why?* Then ask students to discuss why they think poems such as this one made Basho famous.
• Write on the board: *Where there's a will, there's a way.* Ask students to say what they think this expression means. *(When you really want to do something, you find a way to achieve it.)* Then ask students to say what Basho wanted to do and what he did to achieve it. Encourage students to mention other people they know who struggled to achieve what they wanted.

Grammar Presentation (pages 23–25)

Identify the Grammar

SIMPLE PAST
Basho . . . *was* restless.
. . . he *traveled* on foot . . .
. . . he *had* 2,000 students.

Grammar Charts

• Rewrite the first example on the board, and add a new one:
Basho <u>was</u> *restless.*
Basho's poems <u>were</u> *famous.*
—Ask the class: "What are *was* and *were* the simple past of?" *(be)* "Which subject

pronouns need *was*?" *(I, he, she, it)* "Which subject pronouns need *were*?" *(you, we, they)*
—Erase *was* and *were* in the examples and ask a student to make the sentences negative. Then ask the class: "How do you form the negative simple past of *be*?" *(was not* or *wasn't; were not* or *weren't)*
—Ask another student to turn the examples on the board into *yes/no* questions. Then ask the class: "How do you form *yes/no* questions with the simple past of *be*?" *(was* or *were + subject)*
• Rewrite the other two examples on the board, and add a new one:
He <u>traveled</u> *on foot.*
He <u>moved</u> *to Edo.*
He <u>had</u> *2,000 students.*
—Point to the examples, and ask the class: "Which verbs are regular?" *(traveled, moved)* "How do you form the simple past of regular verbs?" *(base form + -ed or base form + -d)* "Is *had* regular or irregular?" *(irregular)* "How do you form the simple past of irregular verbs?" *(There is no rule.)*
—Erase *traveled* and *had* and ask a student to make the sentences negative. Then ask the class: "How do you form the negative simple past of regular and irregular verbs?" *(didn't + base form of verb)*
—Do the same for *yes/no* questions.
• Write on the board:
Who was Basho?
What did he do?
—Ask the class: "How do you form simple past *wh-* questions?" *(wh- word + was/were + subject;* wh- *word + did + subject)*
—Call on different students to provide answers for the *yes/no* questions and *wh-* questions on the board.

Grammar Notes

Note 1 *(Exercises 1–7)*
• Remind students that the simple past is used for finished actions. Say, *"Basho* <u>was</u> *a poet. He's* <u>not</u> *a poet any longer."*
• To review simple past questions and statements, have students talk in pairs about members of their family who lived in past times. Encourage students to ask follow-up questions. For example:

A: My great-grandfather was Spanish.

B: Was he from Madrid?

A: No. He lived in the south of Spain.

Note 2 *(Exercises 1–7)*

- Elicit more time expressions and write them on the board. For example:

yesterday	*two weeks ago*
last month	*last summer*
in June	

- Point out that when time expressions come first in a sentence, they are usually followed by a comma. Have students compare the first two examples in the Student Book.
- Ask students to share in pairs important events in their lives. Point out that they should say when the events took place. *(I entered college last year. I traveled to Egypt in 2003. I met my girlfriend two months ago.)*

→ For additional practice, see the Supplementary Activities on page 143.

Note 3 *(Exercises 1–7)*

- Write on the board:

Base Form	Simple Past
want	*wanted*
live	*lived*

- Point to the verbs on the board and ask the class: "What kind of verbs are these?" *(regular)* "How is the past of *want* formed?" *(by adding -ed)* "How is the past of *live* formed?" *(by adding -d)*. If necessary, explain that when a verb ends in -*e*, you only need to add -*d*.
- Then write on the board:

Base Form	Simple Past
study	*studied*
play	*played*
hop	*hopped*
prefer	*preferred*
visit	*visited*

- Have students study the spelling changes in pairs. You can refer them to Appendix 22 on page A-10 for spelling rules of the simple past. To review as a class, have volunteers explain a verb each. (y *changes to* i *in* studied *because it is preceded by a consonant;* y *does not change to* i *in* played *because it is preceded by a vowel.*)
- Write new base forms on the board: (Do not erase the base forms and past forms already on the board.)

annoy	*stop*
trip	*try*
hurry	*control*
enjoy	*offer*
admit	

- Ask students in pairs to put these verbs in the past form, and group them with the other verbs on the board, according to the way in which their past form is formed. *(studied,*

hurried, tried; played, annoyed, enjoyed; hopped, tripped, stopped; preferred, controlled, admitted; visited, offered)

At this stage, you may want to refer students to Appendix 30 on page A-15 and review the pronunciation rules.

Note 4 *(Exercises 1–7)*

- Write on the board:

Base Form	Simple Past
do	*did*
eat	*ate*
cut	*cut*

Point to the verbs on the board and ask the class: "What kind of verbs are these?" *(irregular)* "Why are they irregular?" *(because their past tense is not formed by adding -d or -ed)* "Can a past form of an irregular verb be the same as its base form?" *(yes)*

- Write on the board:

Base Form	
write	*buy*
become	*put*
see	*grow*
meet	*find*

- Ask students to write in pairs the simple past form of the verbs on the board. Refer students to Appendix 1 (Irregular Verbs) on page A-1. Review as a class. *(wrote, became, saw, met, bought, put, grew, found)*

Have students use three of the verbs on the board in simple past statements of their own.

Focused Practice (pages 26–30)

Exercise 1

household: all the people who live together in one house

lord: a man who has a particular position in the aristocracy

success: something that has the result or effect that you intended, or the act of achieving this

loneliness: the state of being unhappy because you are alone

Exercise 2

theme: the main subject or idea in a book, movie, speech, etc.

lead: here, to have or live

recluse: someone who likes to live alone and avoids other people

Exercise 3

address: to write a name and address on an envelope

in print: writing that has been printed in books, newspapers, etc., and is available to buy

Exercise 4

bite: to cut or crunch something with your teeth. (In the poem the bird uses its beak.)

angle-worm: a small tube-shaped creature with a soft body and no legs that lives in the ground

fellow: a man. (In the poem *fellow* refers to the worm.)

raw: not cooked

dew: the small drops of water that form on outdoor surfaces during the night

convenient: useful to you because it makes something easier or saves you time

beetle: an insect with a hard round back

Exercise 6

neighborhood: a small area of a town

ethnic: relating to a particular race, nation, tribe, etc.

outgoing: wanting to meet and talk to new people, or showing this quality

Ph.D.: Doctor of Philosophy, the highest university degree that can be earned

Communication Practice (pages 31–33)

Exercise 8

To review answers as a class, have students say complete sentences. *(Veli was born in 1970.)*

Exercise 9

- Before students work in pairs, have them (quickly) read the biography to decide what kind of information is missing.
- Elicit *wh-* words that students will need to ask the questions. *(what, where, when, how)* You may want to write them on the board.
- As students compare their biographies, encourage them to use the negative simple past to talk about the differences, if any. *(They didn't have a baby in 2003. They had a baby in 2002.)*

Exercise 10

- Point out *both* in the example to express a similarity. Encourage students to use *both* in their sentences for common information.
- When students finish working, have volunteers read an idea aloud.

  ☺ As students say their ideas, put them on the board in note form. Then have students write a paragraph comparing the two poets, using the notes as a guide.

Exercise 11

- After students have generated rhyming past tense verbs, work as a class to compose a few rhyming lines. Point out that rhyming lines have the same number of syllables.
- You can use these prompts: "I knew the moment that he spoke" "Up the stairs she slowly crept"
- Then have students return to their partners to compose their own rhymes.

Exercise 12

Questions to generate ideas and elicit vocabulary:

- Where were you born?
- What were your favorite pastimes when you were a child?
- Where did you live?
- What school did you go to?
- What did you do when you finished school/college?
- What memorable experiences did you have?

Further Practice

Brainstorm some common verbs and their past forms with the class and write them on the board. Have students sit in a circle. Instruct the first student to begin a story using one of the verbs on the board. *(Yesterday I went to the store.)* Instruct the second student to repeat the phrase and add a new one to it. *(Yesterday I went to the store. I bought some strawberries.)* Continue until everyone has had a chance to contribute a sentence.

Poems. Bring in copies of a poem that uses the simple past. Have students read the poem individually. Then, in pairs, have them find the past form of the verbs and circle the rhyming words. Have pairs take turns reading the poem out loud by reading a stanza each. Briefly discuss the meaning of the poem as a class.

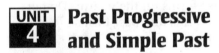

| UNIT 4 | Past Progressive and Simple Past |

Unit Overview

Unit 4 focuses on the meanings and uses of the past progressive and the simple past—specifically when these verb forms appear in sentences with two clauses.

- The past progressive describes an action that was in progress at a specific time in the past.

- When the simple past and the past progressive appear together in a sentence, the simple past describes the action that interrupts the action in progress.

Grammar in Context (pages 34–35)

Vocabulary

alibi: something that proves that someone was not where a crime happened and is therefore not guilty of the crime

burglary: the crime of going into a building, car, etc., to steal things

suspect: someone who may be guilty of a crime

blizzard: a long heavy storm with a lot of wind and snow

Comprehension Questions

- What happened at Ligo Diamonds last Friday? *(There was a burglary.)*
- Who is Officer Barker talking with? *(a man called Sal Sanders)*
- Why is he questioning him? *(because his wife works at Ligo Diamonds and they are suspects)*
- What does Officer Barker want to know? *(what Sanders and his wife were doing on Friday at the time of the burglary)*

Discussion Topics

- Ask students to discuss whether Sanders had a good alibi, and what they think happened next.
- Write on the board:
  "We had a perfect alibi, and the police let us go," Eve told her best friend.
  Have students work in groups and talk about what they think Eve's "perfect alibi" could have been.

Grammar Presentation (pages 35–37)

Identify the Grammar

Past Progressive	Simple Past
I was exercising in the basement	when you rang.

Past Progressive	Past Progressive
What were you doing	while your wife was talking?

Grammar Charts

- Write the following sentences on the board:
  We were staying at a ski lodge when it happened.

At 7:00, Eve was making a phone call, and I was watching TV.
- Ask the following questions: "How do you form the past progressive?" *(form of* be + -ing *form of verb)* "Which verb form is in the past progressive in the first example?" *(were staying)* "Which pronouns need *was* plus an *-ing* form?" *(I/he/she/it)* "Which pronouns need *were* plus an *-ing* form?" *(you/we/they)*
- Write the following cues on the board:
  Sanders / rang / was / when / exercising / Barker
  Have a student use the cues to write a *yes/no* question on the board. *(Was Sanders exercising when Barker rang?)*
  Then ask the class: "How do you form *yes/no* questions?" *(was/were + subject + -ing)*
  Call on a volunteer to come to the board to write the two possible answers to the question. *(Yes, he was. No, he wasn't.)*
- Ask another student to turn the question on the board into a *wh-* question. *(What was Sanders doing when Barker arrived?)*
  Then ask the class: "How do you form *wh-* questions?" *(wh- word + was/were + subject + -ing)*

Grammar Notes

Note 1 *(Exercises 1–5)*
- Write on the board:
  Sanders and his wife were eating dinner in their room at 7:00.
  Point out that the past progressive describes an action in progress over a period of time in the past: Sanders and his wife started eating dinner before 7:00, they were eating dinner at 7:00, and they may or may not continue eating dinner after 7:00.
- Ask several students what they were doing yesterday at 7:00. (You may want to change the time each time you address a new student.)
- Draw attention to the Be Careful note. Ask students to say other non-action verbs. If necessary, remind students of the verbs they saw in Unit 1 (pages 2–12).

Note 2 *(Exercises 1–5)*
- Say, "At 10:00 yesterday I was watching a horror movie." Draw a simple time line on the board:

watching a movie

Then say, "I was watching a movie when I heard a strange noise." Draw a cross on the line to indicate the interruption:

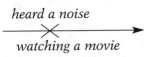

heard a noise

watching a movie

- Point out that there are two ways to express the same idea, and write two contrasting examples on the board:
  I was watching a movie <u>when</u> I <u>heard</u> a strange noise.
  <u>While</u> I <u>was watching</u> a movie, I <u>heard</u> a strange noise.
  Have the class study the examples, and ask: "What verb form follows *when*?" (simple past) "What verb form follows *while*?" (past progressive)
  To summarize, write on the board:
  past progressive + when + simple past
  while + past progressive + simple past
- Write cues on the board:
I walk the dog	*it start to rain*
You cross the street	*the light change*
She drive to work	*she see a UFO*
We study English	*the lights go out*
- Students take turns in pairs expressing the ideas on the board using *when* <u>and</u> *while*. *(A: I was walking the dog when it started to rain. B: While I was walking the dog, it started to rain.)* Make sure both students practice both ways.

→ For additional practice, see the Supplementary Activities on page 144.

Note 3 *(Exercises 1–5)*
- Point out that if two actions were in progress at the same time in the past, both actions are expressed in the past progressive. Give another example. You can say, "While I was reading, my brother was cooking."
- Write cues on the board:
I walk the dog	*you take out the trash*
You cross the street	*the cars wait*
She talk on the phone	*she drive to work*
He talk to his friend	*the teacher correct his paper*
- Students take turns in pairs expressing the ideas on the board starting with *while*. *(While I was walking the dog, you were taking out the trash.)*

→ For additional practice, see the Supplementary Activities on page 144.

Note 4 *(Exercises 1–5)*
- Write two time lines on the board:
  1. *she . . .   came in*

     he . . . working in the garden

2. *she . . . taking a shower*

he . . . answering his e-mails

Ask students to use the first time line to make a sentence with *when*, and the second time line to make a sentence with *while*. Point out they can use time clauses at the beginning or end of sentences.
- After students finish writing, have them compare sentences with a partner. *(When she came in, he was working in the garden. He was working in the garden when she came in. While she was taking a shower, he was answering his e-mails. She was taking a shower while he was answering his e-mails.)*

→ For additional practice, see the Supplementary Activities on page 144.

Note 5 *(Exercises 1–5)*
- To check comprehension, draw the following time line on the board.

On the left side of the board, write:	On the right side of the board, continue the time line:
the robber . . .	

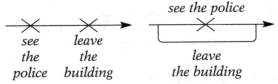

see the police

*see   leave   leave
the   the   the building
police   building*

- In pairs, ask students to write one statement about what happened for each time line. *(1. When the robber saw the police, he left the building. 2. When the robber saw the police, he was leaving the building.)*
- Write the following examples on the board:
  He was doing his homework when his mother came home.
  He did his homework when his mother came home.
  She was writing her essay when the lights went on.
  She wrote her essay when the lights went on.
  Have students study the examples on the board and restate them using *First . . .* and *Then . . . (First he started doing his homework. Then his mother came home.)*
- Have students compare answers with a partner, and review as a class.

Note 6 *(Exercises 1–5)*
- Write on the board:
  1. *The suspect was crossing the avenue.*
  2. *The suspect crossed the avenue.*
  To check comprehension, ask the class: "In example 1, do we know if the suspect actually

got to the other side?" *(no)* "Why?" *(because the past progressive does not indicate that the action is finished)* "In example 2, did the suspect get to the other side?" *(yes)* "Why?" *(because the simple past describes a finished action)*

Focused Practice (pages 38–40)

Exercise 2

pedestrian: someone who is walking instead of driving a car or riding a bicycle

brake: a piece of equipment that makes a vehicle go more slowly or stop

victim: someone who has been hurt or killed by someone or something

headphones: a piece of equipment that you wear over your ears to listen to a radio or recording

bleed: to lose blood, especially from an injury

wound: an injury, especially a deep cut made in your skin by something sharp

Exercise 3

shift: one of the periods during each day and night when workers in a factory, hospital, etc., are at work

flashlight: a small electric light that you carry in your hand

Exercise 5

pickpocket: someone who steals things from people's pockets or bags, especially in a crowd

Communication Practice (pages 41–42)

Exercise 6

• Before students listen, have pairs look at the pictures and take turns describing the scenes. *(A man is starting to cross the street. He is not paying attention to traffic.)*
• To review as a class, have students support their answers by saying what happened. *(Two men were starting to cross the street. A car was speeding and honking.)*

Exercise 7

• Have the class brainstorm questions to ask a witness. *(Was the car speeding? Was the driver a man or a woman? Was the driver speaking on her/his cell phone?)*
• After practicing their role play in groups, ask one group to perform their role play to the class.

Exercise 8

• As students compare their answers in pairs, ask them to discuss the differences. *(You put that the cat was eating, and I put that the cat*

was drinking milk. The little boy wasn't holding a teddy bear; he was holding a monkey.)

If students need further practice, say true and false statements about the picture. In pairs, have students consult their notes and each other before answering. Then have students check their answers by looking at the picture one last time.

Exercise 9

Questions to generate ideas and elicit vocabulary:
• What event did you witness?
• Where were you?
• What were you doing?
• What were the people doing?
• What happened?

Further Practice

Ask students to think of a time when they learned of some major event of personal or world significance. Can they recall exactly where they were and what they were doing at that time? Some possible world events can include the death of a public figure, the beginning of the new millennium, or a natural disaster. Students can write about what they were doing or describe it orally. Have volunteers report to the class on the event they remember and what they were doing at the time.

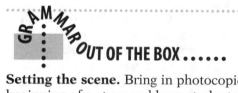

GRAMMAR OUT OF THE BOX . . . . . .

Setting the scene. Bring in photocopies of the beginning of a story and have students study how the past progressive and the simple past are used to set the scene. *(The past progressive describes the actions in progress at the moment when the story starts, and the simple past describes the sequence of events that take place.)* Then have students discuss why setting the scene for a story is important and what effect it has on the reader.

UNIT
5   *Used to*

Unit Overview

Unit 5 focuses on the meaning and use of *used to.*
• *Used to* describes a past action or situation that no longer exists in the present.

- It is often used in sentences that contrast the past and the present. Time expressions such as *now, no longer,* and *anymore* are often used to emphasize the contrast.

Grammar in Context (pages 43–44)

Background Note

"He-Man and the Masters of the Universe" was a TV cartoon in which He-Man, the most powerful man in the universe, fought the evil forces of Skeletor and other villains. "She-Ra Princess of Power" was created after He-Man for a new target audience—girls. She-Ra was He-Man's twin sister. As the cartoons became popular, action figures of the main characters from both series were manufactured and sold for children to play with. (Sources: http://www.he-man.org/cartoon/cmotu/index.shtml and http://www.he-man.org/cartoon/pop/index.shtml)

Vocabulary

blog: short for *Weblog,* a public website that is a personal journal for an individual, which is updated on a regular basis

awesome: extremely good

Comprehension Questions

- What time of her life does Sandra write about? *(her childhood/the time when she was a kid)*
- What does she remember doing in her childhood? *(watching cartoons, collecting the toys, and acting out the stories)*
- What did her sister use to do? *(play with a puzzle/a cube/Rubik's cube)*
- What did her brother use to do? *(practice with his rock band/play in a rock band)*
- Did her mother use to work? *(yes)*

Discussion Topics

- Ask students to compare what kids play with today with what kids used to play with in the past. Which toys require more imagination and creativity? Why?
- Ask students to compare their grandparents' lifestyles with their own. Is life better now or was it better then? Encourage students to support their views.

Grammar Presentation (pages 44–46)

Identify the Grammar

USED TO
. . . the Rubik's cube used to be very popular . . .
. . . we didn't use to play video games then!
Did you use to watch cartoons Saturday mornings?
What toys did you use to play with?

Grammar Charts

- Write the following examples on the board:
When I was a kid, I used to watch She-Ra.
My brother used to watch He-Man.
My sister didn't use to watch cartoons.
Did you use to watch cartoons when you were a kid?
—Ask the class: "How do you form affirmative statements with *used to?*" (used to + *base form of verb*) "Does *used to* change when the pronoun changes?" *(No. Used to is the same for all pronouns.)* "How do you form negative statements?" (didn't + use to + *base form of verb*) "How do you form *yes/no* questions?" (did + *subject* + use to + *base form of verb*)
—Call on a student to come to the front and write the two possible answers to the question on the board. *(Yes, I did. No, I didn't.)*
—Then ask the class: "How do you form *wh*-questions?" (wh- *word* + did + *subject* + use to + *base form of verb*)

Grammar Notes

Note 1 *(Exercises 1–4)*
- Draw a new time line on the board:

used to work in a bank

To explain the time line, point to the three crosses. Explain that *used to* indicates that an action or situation existed for some time in the past. Write below the time line on the board:
I used to work in a bank. = I worked in a bank for some time in the past.
Point out that there are no crosses on *NOW* or after *NOW.* This is because *used to* indicates that the action or situation no longer exists. Add a new sentence to the explanation on the board:

I used to work in a bank. = I worked in a bank for some time in the past. = I no longer work in a bank.

- Have students think about their childhood. Then call on students to say something they used to do and they no longer do. (*I used to live in a small town. I used to wear my hair long. I used to help my mother cook.*)
- Draw attention to the Be Careful note. Point out that in the present we say, "She loves cartoons." You may want to write two contrasting examples on the board:
  PAST: *I used to drive to school.*
  PRESENT: *I drive to school.* OR *I always drive to school.*

Note 2 *(Exercises 1–4)*

- Have students think in pairs about life 100 years ago, and write about what people used to do then.
- Elicit ideas from students and write them on the board. (*Men used to wear hats. Women used to stay at home all day. People used to wash their clothes by hand.*)
- Call on volunteers to read the sentences on the board aloud and contrast them with the present. Encourage students to use time expressions where appropriate. (*Men used to wear hats, but they don't wear them anymore. Women used to stay at home all day, but now most women work. People used to wash their clothes by hand, but now they use washing machines.*)

Note 3 *(Exercises 1–2, 4)*

- Write this example on the board:
  We <u>didn't use to play</u> video games.
  Point to *use* in the negative sentence and ask: "Why isn't there a *d* on *use*?" (*because* did *in* didn't *expresses the past*)

Note 4 *(Exercises 1, 2–4)*

- Write the following examples on the board:
  <u>Did you use</u> to watch cartoons?
  What <u>did</u> you <u>use to play</u>?
  Point to *use* in the first question and ask: "Why isn't there a *d* on *use*?" (*because* did *expresses the past*)
- Write the following verbs on the board:
  live   work   study   buy   have   shop
  In groups, have students take turns making three statements about their past habits using three verbs from the board. (*Some years ago, I used to shop at Green Mart. When I was a kid, I used to study Italian. Last year I never used to work late.*) Warn students to pay attention because they will be expected to remember

what their partners say. Then ask students to use the information about their partners to ask questions to one another. (*Where did [student's name] use to shop? What did [student's name] use to study when he/she was a kid? Did [student's name] use to work late last year?*)

→ For additional practice, see the Supplementary Activities on page 144.

Note 5

- Write on the board:
  I USED TO + BASE FORM =
  I no longer have a past habit
  I AM USED TO + -ING FORM =
  I no longer find something difficult or surprising
  I GOT USED TO + -ING FORM =
  I stopped finding something difficult or surprising
- To clarify the grammatical differences, point out that *used to* is followed by a base form and *be* and *get used to* by the *-ing* form of a verb. To clarify the semantic differences, point out that *used to* expresses a past habit that you no longer have. (*I used to wear glasses, but I don't wear them any longer. Now I wear contact lenses.*) *Get used to* indicates that you stopped finding something difficult or surprising. (*Although it was difficult at first, I finally got used to wearing contact lenses.*) *Be used to* indicates that you no longer find something difficult or surprising. (*Now I'm used to wearing contact lenses.*)
- Have volunteers talk about something they never used to do, but then they started doing, and, as a result, they got used to. (*I never used to eat vegetables, but when I started a diet, I soon got used to eating them.*)
- Draw students' attention to the pronunciation note. To provide practice, have students repeat simple sentences chorally after you. You can say: "I used to drive. I didn't use to drive. He used to work. He didn't use to work."

Focused Practice *(pages 46–48)*

Exercise 1

arcade: a special room or small building where people go to play video games

vinyl: a type of strong plastic

record: a round flat piece of vinyl on which music is stored

bother: to make someone feel slightly annoyed or upset

Exercise 2

reunion: a meeting of people who have not met for a long time

Exercise 3

shave: to cut off hair very close to the skin, especially from your face or legs, using a razor

Exercise 4

chateau: a castle or large country house

afford: to have enough money to buy or pay for something

stepfather: a man who is married to your mother but who is not your birth father

Communication Practice (pages 49–51)

Exercise 5

• To review answers, have students say full sentences and use *used to* where appropriate. *(They used to get up early without an alarm clock. Now they use an alarm clock.)*

Small groups. For further practice, have students share their own past and present habits in connection with getting up, having breakfast, and having energy.

Exercise 6

Write on the board:
She/He used to _____, but now _____.
In small groups, have students complete the statement on the board to describe a famous person, withholding the person's name. Point out that students can give more than one clue by saying more than once sentence—for example, one about the person's appearance and one about his/her habits. *(She used to have dark hair, but now she is blonde. She used to be a model, but now she is an actress.)* The other students in the group guess who the person is.

Exercise 7

• To set up the activity brainstorm topics students can talk about and write them on the board.

hairstyle	*tastes in music*
clothes	*hobbies*
eating habits	*free time activities*

• After students finish working in groups, have volunteers share with the class what their partners used to do or what their partners used to be like.

Exercise 8

Questions to generate ideas and elicit vocabulary:
• Where did you use to live?
• Who did you use to live with?
• What did you use to like/hate?
• How did you use to spend your time?

Further Practice

If your students are in the work force, have them talk in small groups about a past work experience they had. Encourage them to be specific and say the tasks they used to do at work. *(I used to answer the phone. I also used to address envelopes and mail out letters and notices.)* If your students are still in school, have them talk about elementary school. Encourage them to be specific and talk about the things they used to do in elementary school. *(On rainy days I used to play cards at recess. On sunny days I used to play baseball with my friends.)*

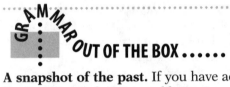

A snapshot of the past. If you have access to a lending library, borrow and bring in magazines from previous decades—for example, 1950s or 1960s. Divide the class into groups, and give each group at least one magazine. Have students flip through the magazine(s). Ask students to talk about what magazines used to be like and compare them with magazines today. (Some of the aspects students can compare are colors, illustrations, photographs, and advertisements.) Encourage students to also use the magazine(s) to find out what life used to be like, what people used to be interested in, what they used to worry about, etc.

 UNIT 6 **Future**

Unit Overview

Unit 6 focuses on different ways to talk about the future.
• *Be going to* and *will* express predictions or guesses about the future.
• *Be going to*, *will*, and the present progressive express future intentions or plans.
• The simple present expresses scheduled future events.

Grammar in Context (pages 52–53)

Background Note

SpaceshipOne, designed by Burt Rutan, was the first privately built spacecraft to reach an altitude of over 328,000 feet and carry passengers into space. Burton predicted that in the future, people will be able to experience sub-orbital space flights. They will go outside the atmosphere on large spacious ships, enjoy the view and the experience of floating around for a few minutes, and then fly back to Earth. The business will be competitive and hundreds of people will do it. However, people won't be spending their vacations in a hotel in orbit in the near future—or at least not until a safe way to send people into orbit is found. (Source: http://www.cnn.com/2005/TECH/space/05/11/visionary.rutan/index.html)

Vocabulary

lecture: a long talk to a group of people about a particular subject

be worth (doing) something: to be helpful, valuable, interesting, or good for you

claim: to state that something is true, even if it hasn't been proved

individual: one person, considered separately from the rest of the group or society that she/he lives in

entertainment: things such as television, movies, etc., that amuse or interest people

challenge: something that tests your skill or ability, especially in a way that is interesting

gravity: the force that makes objects fall to the ground

trainer: someone whose job is to train people or animals to do something

Comprehension Questions

• According to Collins, which business will create the most jobs in the future? *(space travel)*
• Why? *(because people will travel to space as tourists and the tourist industry will create new jobs in space)*
• Does everyone agree with Collins? *(no)*

Discussion Topics

• Ask students to discuss the advantages of space travel. Why would tourists be interested in a vacation in space? Write the following facts on the board:
In 2001, U.S. businessman Dennis Tito paid $20 million for a trip into space.

Some scientists predict that a trip into space will cost about $50,000 in the near future.
• Ask students to discuss how much they would be prepared to pay for a trip into space. Encourage them to support their views.

Grammar Presentation (pages 54–57)

Identify the Grammar

BE GOING TO
It's going to be full . . .

WILL
. . . people will travel to space as tourists . . .

PRESENT PROGRESSIVE
Professor Collins is speaking again at the space conference tomorrow . . .

SIMPLE PRESENT
It leaves at 9:00 A.M.

Grammar Charts

• Write these examples on the board:
I am going to take the next flight.
We are going to leave from Terminal B.
—Ask the class: "How do you form future statements with *going to?*" *(form of* be *+* going to *+ base form of verb)* "Is the future with *going to* the same for all pronouns?" *(no)*
—Erase "I am." Elicit the full conjugation of *be going to.* Have students say full sentences. *(You are going to take the next flight.)*
• Write the following examples on the board:
I will take the next flight.
We will leave from Terminal B.
—Ask the class: "How do you form future statements with *will?*" (will + *base form of verb*) "Does *will* change when the pronoun changes?" *(No.* Will *is the same for all pronouns.)*
• Write the following examples on the board:
I'm taking the next flight.
We're leaving from Terminal B.
—Ask the class: "Does the present progressive have present or future meaning in the first sentence?" *(future)* "How do you know?" *(because it says "next flight")* "Does the present progressive have present or future meaning in the second sentence?" *(future)* "How do you know?" *(because of the context/situation)*
• Write the following example on the board:
The next flight leaves at 9:00.

—Ask the class: "Does the simple present have present or future meaning in this sentence?" *(future)* "What future time expression is there in the sentence?" *(at 9:00)*

- Call on a student to turn the examples on the board into negative sentences. Then call on another student to turn them into yes/no and wh- questions. Have a third student answer the questions. Clarify any confusion about the formation of negative sentences or questions.

Grammar Notes

Note 1   *(Exercises 1, 6–7)*

- Draw a new time line on the board:

—Give examples related to the time line on the board. You can say, "I'm going to go to Cancun next week. I think I'll have fun. I'm catching a 5:00 flight. I come back at 8:00 on Sunday."

—Erase *Cancun* and write *Jungle Boys concert*. Then write the following prompts below the time line:

Jungle Boys / give / concert   (be going to)
Maybe / I / go   (will)
It / take place / Saturday   (Present
                                progressive)
It / start / 7:00 P.M.   (Simple present)

Have students write sentences using the prompts and the future forms indicated in parentheses. Then have them compare answers with a partner, and review as a class. *(The Jungle Boys are going to give a concert. Maybe I'll go. It's taking place on Saturday. It starts at 7:00 P.M.)*

Note 2   *(Exercises 1–2, 4, 6–7)*

- Have students work in pairs to predict what cars will be like in the future. Point out they can use either *will* or *going to*. Ask them to write down their predictions.
- Call on volunteers to tell the class what they think the car of the future will be like. Write a few ideas on the board. *(Cars will/are going to be small and fast. They will/are going to use solar energy. They won't/aren't going to cause pollution.)*
- Tell students to use *be going to* when they base their future prediction on a present fact. Give more examples. You can say, "I'm not feeling well. I think I'm going to be sick." "It's 5:55! We're going to miss the 6:00 train!"

- Write on the board:
  Look at that _____! _____ going to _____!
  Ask students to use the incomplete sentences on the board to make a prediction with *be going to.* You may want to write some examples on the board:
  Look at that car! It's going to crash!
  Look at that boy on that boat! He's going to fall into the water!

Note 3   *(Exercises 1, 3, 6–7)*

- To help clarify, summarize the information on the board.

  Intentions or plans →   *BE GOING TO /
                              WILL / PRESENT
                              PROGRESSIVE*

  *Decisions made at the
    moment of speaking* →   *WILL*
  *Plans that have been
    arranged* →   *PRESENT
                            PROGRESSIVE*

- Ask various students "What are you going to do this weekend?" For events that have been arranged, have students use the present progressive. *(I'm visiting my parents in Boston.)* For decisions made at the moment, have students use *will. (I don't have any plans. I think I'll stay home.)*
- Draw students' attention to the pronunciation note. Give examples of going to and gonna in sentences. You can say: "He's going to come. He's gonna come."

→ For additional practice, see the Supplementary Activities on page 144.

Note 4   *(Exercises 1, 5–7)*

- As a class, invent the name of a movie and a concert. Write the names on the board. Add a day of the week next to each name.
  Lost in the Dark—Friday
  Rock concert—Saturday
- Then ask students to say the time the movie and the concert start and end. Write the times on the board.
  Lost in the Dark—Friday 6:00 P.M.–7:45 P.M.
  Rock concert—Saturday 9:00 P.M.–10:30 P.M.
- Have students use the information on the board to make sentences. *(Lost in the Dark starts at 6:00 on Friday. The rock concert starts at 9:00 P.M. on Saturday. It finishes at 10:30.)*

Focused Practice (pages 57–62)

Exercise 1

exploration: a trip to a place you have not been, or a place where you are looking for something

outer space: the space outside the Earth's atmosphere where the stars and planets are

economy: the way that money, businesses, and products are organized in a particular country, area, etc.

resource: something such as land, minerals, or natural energy that exists in a country and can be used in order to increase its wealth

Exercise 3
economics: the study of the way in which money, goods, and services are produced and used

live: broadcast (sent out by radio or TV) as an event happens

Exercise 4
Q & A session: a period of time used for questions and answers by a group of people.

puffy: swollen (bigger than usual)

bump: to hit or knock against something, especially by accident

squeezable: something that can be squeezed

squeeze: to twist or press something in order to get liquid out of it

Exercise 5
Eastern Standard Time: the time that is used in the eastern United States for almost half the year, including the winter

shuttle: a space vehicle that can fly into space and return to Earth and be used more than once

Exercise 7
figure out: to understand something after thinking about it

screwdriver: a tool with a long thin metal end, used for turning screws (a thin pointed piece of metal that you push and turn in order to fasten pieces of wood or metal together)

Communication Practice (pages 63–64)

Exercise 8
• Have students listen a third time and write brief notes about what the people are talking about in each conversation.
• To review as a class, have students use their notes to support their answers. (*1. They are talking about the future—what he/she is doing tonight. 2. They are talking about what is happening now—what Pete is watching on TV.*)

Exercise 9
• Have students work individually to complete their schedules. Point out that they should write in note form. You may want to write a few examples on the board:

Buy gift for mom
Lunch with Jean at Rock Café
Meeting with Joe Pegs
• Brainstorm with the class ways to invite someone and ways to accept an invitation. Write students' ideas on the board.
Do you want to _____?   *I'd love to.*
Would you like to _____?   *That would be nice.*
Why don't we _____?   *Sounds great.*
• Have volunteers role play their conversations for the class.

Exercise 10
Follow up by asking each pair which events they will attend. Have students explain why they chose a particular event.

Exercise 11
Questions to generate ideas and elicit vocabulary:
• Where exactly is the vacation—on the Moon, on Mars, in a space station?
• How long will the vacation be?
• What kind of rooms are tourists going to stay in?
• What will they see from their room windows?
• What activities are they going to do?
• What type of foods are they going to eat?
• What kind of training are they going to get before the trip?
• When/What time does the shuttle leave?
• When/What time does the shuttle come back?

Further Practice
Ask students who have brought a personal organizer or a datebook to class to raise their hands. Have them form small groups by joining students who don't have one. (If half the class has a personal organizer or datebook, students should work in pairs.) Ask students to open their datebooks or turn on their organizers and talk about their plans for the coming weeks. Encourage students to ask follow-up questions. (Student A: *I'm going out for dinner on Friday.* Student B: *Who are you going with?* Student A: *I'm going to the movies on Saturday.* Student B: *What time does the movie start?*)

What do newspapers say about the future?
Bring in today's or yesterday's newspapers. Explain the game: Each group will get a newspaper and will be given 15 minutes to

circle in their newspaper three scheduled
events, three plans or arrangements, and three
predictions about the future, and write a
sentence about each on a separate sheet of
paper. Students should use the ways to express
the future they learned in this unit. If necessary,
give an example of each category: (scheduled
event) *The conference on globalization starts
at 8:00 A.M.* (arrangement) *The president is
traveling to Spain next week.* (prediction)
*Scientists say they will soon find a cure for
cancer.* When time is up, collect the sentences.
The group with a greater number of correct
sentences is the winner.

UNIT 7 Future Time Clauses

Unit Overview

Unit 7 focuses on the meanings and uses of
future time clauses.
• Future time clauses begin with time
  expressions such as *when, after, not . . . until,
  as soon as, before, until, by the time,* and *while.*
• The verb in future time clauses is normally in
  the simple present tense.
• Future time clauses can come at the beginning
  or end of sentences.

Grammar in Context (pages 65–66)

Vocabulary

degree: given to someone who has successfully
completed a program of study at a college or
university

goal: something that you hope to succeed in doing in
the future

achieve: to succeed in doing or getting something as
a result of your actions

journey: a trip from one place to another, especially
over a long distance

Comprehension Questions

• According to the article, what four steps
  should you take to change your dream into
  a goal? *(write down your dream, list your
  reasons, write down an action plan, and take
  your first steps)*
• Who does the article give as an example?
  (Latoya Jones)
• What is her dream? *(to be a successful
  businessperson)*

Discussion Topics

• Ask students to discuss what achieving a goal
  depends on. Does it only depend on yourself?
  Or does it also depend on luck? Can a goal be
  achieved in spite of the obstacles?
• Ask students to discuss which two steps from
  the article they consider more important.
  Encourage them to support their views. Ask
  them to also think about other steps that
  could have been included in the article.

Grammar Presentation (pages 66–67)

Identify the Grammar

FUTURE TIME CLAUSES
. . . *by the time you're 22?*
. . . *until we change them to goals.*

After you write a dream down, . . .
When things get difficult, . . .

. . . *when I am a successful businessperson.*
Before I apply to schools, . . .

Grammar Charts

• Write the following examples on the board:
  *I'm going to get my degree by the time I am 22.
  When I have my degree, I'll get a job with a big
  company.*
  —Ask the class: "How many clauses do the
    sentences have?" *(two)* "Which part of each
    sentence is the time clause?" *(the part that
    is underlined)* "How do time clauses start?"
    (with a time expression) "What time
    expressions are used in the examples?" *(by
    the time* and *when)*
• Write the following examples on the board:
  *I'll go to business school as soon as I save
  enough money.
  Before I apply to schools, I'm going to order
  some school catalogs.*
  —Point to the verb in the first time clause
    (save) and ask: "What verb form is this?"
    (simple present) "Does the other time clause
    also have a present verb form?" *(yes)* "What's
    the verb in the present in the other time
    clause?" *(apply)* "Do main clauses also have
    present verb forms?" *(no)* "What verb forms
    do they have?" *(future forms:* will *or* going to)
• Write the following example on the board and
  point out the subject-verb inversion in the
  question.
  *Will you start your own business before you
  turn 40?*

—Call on a volunteer to come to the front and turn all the affirmative sentences on the board into questions. *(Are you going to get your degree by the time you're 22? Will you get a job with a big company when you have your degree? Will you go to business school as soon as you save enough money? Are you going to order some school catalogs before you apply to schools?)*

—Call on another student to write the possible short answers. *(Yes, I am. No, I'm not. Yes, I will. No I won't.)*

—Have another student turn the *yes/no* questions on the board into *wh-* questions. *(What are you going to get by the time you're 22? Where will you work when you have your degree? What school are you going to go to as soon as you get enough money? What are you going to order before you apply to schools?)*

Grammar Notes

Note 1 *(Exercises 1–4)*

• Write the following sentences on the board:
  a. *Before I will turn 40, I will start my own business.*
  b. *I start my own business before I turn 40.*
  c. *I will start my own business, before I turn 40.*
  d. *Before I turn 40 I will start my own business.*
  To check comprehension, ask students in pairs to find the mistake in each sentence.

• To review as a class, have students explain the mistakes. *(a. A future form—will turn—is used in the time clause. b. The simple present—start—is used in the main clause. c. There is a comma after the main clause. d. There is no comma after the time clause.)* Ask students to write the two correct possibilities for the idea on the board. *(Before I turn 40, I will start my own business. I will start my own business before I turn 40.)*

• Call on volunteers to say what they will/are going to do before the year is over. *(Before the end of the year, I will take five exams.)*

Note 2 *(Exercises 1–4)*

• Write the following sentences on the board, leaving space above them:
  When Tom finishes his French course, he'll travel to Paris.
  Before Tom travels to Paris, he will finish his French course.
  Have students study the first example. Ask, "What will happen first?" *(Tom will finish his French course.)* Write 1 above the time clause

as shown below. Then ask, "What will happen next?" *(Tom will travel to Paris.)* Write 2 above the main clause as shown.

$$\overset{\displaystyle 1}{\boxed{}}$$
When Tom finishes his French course,

$$\overset{\displaystyle 2}{\boxed{}}$$
he'll travel to Paris.

Have students study the second example. Ask, "What will happen first?" *(Tom will finish his French course.)* Write 1 above the main clause. Then ask, "What will happen next?" *(Tom will travel to Paris.)* Write 2 above the time clause.

$$\overset{\displaystyle 2}{\boxed{}}$$
Before Tom travels to Paris,

$$\overset{\displaystyle 1}{\boxed{}}$$
he will finish his French course.

Then ask, "Does *when* introduce the first event or the second event? *(the first event)* "Does *before* introduce the first event or the second event? *(the second event)*

• Have students look at their books and say the time expressions that have the same meaning as *when*. Call on students to restate the examples on the board using the time expressions that have the same meaning as *when*, making any necessary changes. *(After Tom finishes his French course, he'll travel to Paris. Tom won't travel to Paris until he finishes his French course. As soon as Tom finishes his French course, he will travel to Paris.)*

• Have students look at their books and say the time expressions that have the same meaning as *before*. Write the following sentences on the board and have students complete them with *until* or *by the time*.
  _____ *Tom travels to Paris, he will know French.*
  Tom will study French _____ *he travels to Paris.*
  Review as a class. *(By the time Tom travels to Paris, he will know French. Tom will study French until he travels to Paris.)*

• Point out that *while* in a time clause indicates that something will happen at the same time as the event in the main clause. Give an example. Say "While Tom is in Paris, he will keep on learning French."

→ For additional practice, see the Supplementary Activities on page 145.

Focused Practice (pages 68–70)

Exercise 1

quit: to leave a job, school, etc., especially because you are annoyed or unhappy

retire: to stop working, usually because of reaching a certain age, or to make someone stop working

diploma: an official paper showing that someone has successfully finished a course of study (high school or college)

Exercise 2

worksheet: a piece of paper with questions, exercises, etc., for students

employment ad: an advertisement (set of words) that gives information about a job that is available

job notice board: a flat piece of wood, plastic, etc., where employment ads are shown

skill: an ability to do something very well, especially because you have learned or practiced it

résumé: a written list and description of your education and your previous jobs that you use when you are looking for a job

Exercise 3

raise: an increase in the money you earn

Exercise 4

word processing: using a small computer or computer software for writing

though: in spite of that

workshop: a meeting at which people try to improve their skills by discussing their experiences and doing practical exercises

Communication Practice (pages 71–72)

Exercise 5

- Before students listen, ask students to say what services an employment agency provides. *(They find jobs for people; they suggest additional training; they give people advice on the most suitable kind of work.)*
- If (some of) your students are in the workforce, you can draw on their previous experience by asking them if they ever got a job through an employment agency. Have them briefly describe their experience. After reviewing answers, ask students to combine two events from the list in a sentence containing a time clause. *(She will send a résumé before she has an interview.)*

Exercise 6

- Have students complete the sentences individually and then share them in small groups.

- Follow up by having a few students share their plans with the class.

Exercise 7

- Brainstorm possible questions to ask in an interview. Write them on the board.
  What will you do after you finish high school?
  What will you do as soon as you start college?
  Will you get a part-time job while you are in college?
  Will you go on a trip as soon as you graduate?
- Have students work in pairs. Set a time limit of ten minutes for the interview. Encourage students to take notes during the interview.
- After students write up their findings from the interview, have them return to their partner to check the accuracy of their summary.
- Have students submit their summary to you for final review.

Exercise 8

- Have students complete the worksheet individually. Point out that students should use future time clauses. Refer students to the reading on page 65 and to Exercise 2 on page 69, which illustrate how future time clauses can be used in this context.
- In small groups, have students share their plans with their partners. Encourage students to give their classmates any advice or information that can help them reach their goal.

Further Practice

Explain what a time capsule is (a container that is filled with objects from a particular time, so that people in the future will know what life was like then). Then ask students to predict the sequence of life events (marriage, homes, jobs, children) that they expect to experience in the next ten years. Ask students to write their predictions down. In small groups, students can discuss their predictions. Later, have students seal their predictions in an envelope and write on the front "Time Capsule: Open Ten Years From (today's date)." Suggest that they put it in a place where they will remember to look at it in 10 years.

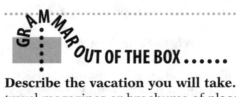

Describe the vacation you will take. Bring in travel magazines or brochures of places to go on vacation—for example, hotels, resorts, theme parks, etc. Hand out the magazines and/or brochures. Have students, working in pairs or small groups, imagine they will go on vacation to the place in their brochure or a place of their choice from the travel magazine. Ask them to plan their vacation by writing down notes of the things they will do in the order in which they will do them. Example:

1. Arrive at Heathrow airport.
2. Buy a camera at duty-free shop.
3. Get to hotel.
4. Take a nap!
5. Go sightseeing: visit the Tower of London.

After students finish writing their notes, have them join another pair or group and share their vacation plans. Ask students to use their notes as a guide. *(When we arrive at the airport, we'll buy a camera at the duty-free shop. As soon as we get to the hotel, we'll take a nap.)*

UNIT 8 Wh- Questions: Subject and Object

Unit Overview

Unit 8 focuses on the meanings and uses of *wh-*questions—specifically the comparison between questions about the subject and questions about the object.

- *Wh-* questions begin with *wh-* words—*who, what, where, when, why, which, whose, how, how many, how much,* and *how long.*
- They are used to ask specific information.
- *Wh-* questions that ask about the subject need statement word order.
- *Wh-* questions that ask about the object need *yes/no* question word order.

Grammar in Context (pages 73–74)

Background Note

In a criminal trial, the government makes an accusation of guilt and the accused (the defendant) defends himself or herself (usually with the help of a lawyer) against the accusation. Both sides present arguments, witnesses, and evidence. During the trial, a court reporter sits near the judge and records everything that is said and done during the trial. The record is called a transcript. After both sides have presented their case, a jury decides if the defendant is guilty or not guilty of the crime.

Vocabulary

courtroom: the room where a case is judged by a court of law

court: the people, such as judges, lawyers, and jury members, who decide whether someone is guilty of a crime; or the place where these judgments are made

defendant: the person in a court of law who has been accused of doing something illegal

lawyer: someone whose job is to advise people about laws, write formal agreements, or represent people in court

witness: someone who describes in a court of law what she/he has seen or knows about a crime

Comprehension Questions

- Where did the witness see the defendant? *(in a restaurant/at Al's Grill)*
- Who was he talking to? *(a woman)*
- What did the woman give him? *(a box)*
- Where did the man go after that? *(to the parking lot)*
- And what did he do then? *(He drove away.)*

Discussion Topics

- Ask students to discuss what they think there was in the box and what crime Harry Adams was accused of.
- In the United States, the jury (the people who listen to details of a case in court and decide whether someone is guilty or not) is usually a group of 12 people. These people are ordinary citizens who are selected from tax rolls or voting registers. Ask students to discuss whether they would like to be a member of the jury in a criminal case such as Harry M. Adams's. Encourage them to support their view.

Grammar Presentation (pages 74–75)

Identify the Grammar

QUESTIONS ABOUT THE SUBJECT
Who saw you?
What happened next?

QUESTIONS ABOUT THE OBJECT
Who did you see there?
Which one did you see?

Grammar Charts

- On the left of the board, rewrite the question: *Who saw you?*
 Add an answer:
 <u>Who</u> saw you?   *A woman saw me.*

—Direct attention to the answer. Ask the class: "Is *a woman* the subject or the object of the sentence?" *(the subject)* "Which is the object of the sentence?" *(me)*

—Underline the subject and the object, and write *subject* below *A woman* and *object* below *me*, as shown:

Who saw you?   <u>A woman</u> saw <u>me</u>.
      subject object

—Point to the question *(Who saw you?)* and ask: "Does this question ask about the subject or about the object?" *(the subject)*

—Draw an arrow from *Who* in the question to *A woman* in the answer, as shown:

       subject object
<u>Who</u> saw you?   <u>A woman</u> saw <u>me</u>.

—Then ask the class: "What is the word order of this type of question?" *(wh- word + verb + subject)*

- Do not erase the board. To the right of the board, rewrite the question:
Who did you see?

Add an answer:
<u>Who</u> did you see?   I saw a woman.

—Direct attention to the answer. Ask the class: "Is *a woman* the subject or the object of the sentence?" *(the object)* "Which is the subject of the sentence?" *(I)*

—Underline the subject and the object, and write *subject* below *I* and *object* below *a woman*, as shown:

Who did you see?   <u>I</u> saw <u>a woman</u>.
       subject object

—Point to the question *(Who did you see?)* and ask: "Does this question ask about the subject or about the object?" *(the object)*

—Draw an arrow from *Who* in the question to *a woman* in the answer, as shown:

       subject object
<u>Who</u> did you see?   <u>I</u> saw <u>a woman</u>.

—Then ask the class: "What is the word order of this type of question?" *(wh- word + auxiliary verb + subject + main verb)*

- To summarize, you may want to write on the board:
Subject questions: (wh- *word + verb + subject*)
Object questions: (wh- *word + auxiliary verb + subject + main verb*)

Grammar Notes

Note 1 *(Exercises 1–4)*

- Write a *yes/no* question and a *wh-* question on the board, with their answers:

Did he go to the parking lot? *Yes, he did.*
Where did he go?   *To the parking*
             lot.

Point out how the *yes/no* question seeks to confirm information *(yes or no)* and how the *wh-* question asks for specific information *(the parking lot)*.

- Write a list of four question words on the board:
Who
What
When
How many

Call on a student to make up a question with *who*. Write it on the board, making any necessary corrections. Call on another student to make up an answer. Continue in the same way with the other *wh-* words on the board.

Note 2 *(Exercises 1–4)*

- Write on the board:
Who gave him the box?
Ask students to say the pattern of the question on the board. Write the pattern to the right of the question:

 subject
 ⌐ ⌐
wh- word + verb (+ rest of the sentence)

Remind students that there is no change in word order when the question word refers to the subject of the sentence.

- Write below the question on the board:
Which witness
Whose witness *told lies?*
How many witnesses

Ask students to say the pattern of the questions on the board. Write the pattern to the right of the questions:

  subject
 ⌐ ⌐
wh- word + noun + verb (+ rest of the sentence)

- Ask students to work in pairs to make up three subject questions using a different *wh-* word in each. To review as a class, have volunteers read their questions aloud. You may want to write a few on the board.

Note 3 *(Exercises 1–4)*

- Write a new example on the board:

<u>Jay Bell</u> is <u>the witness</u>.
 subject   object

Who is Jay Bell?
Who is the witness?
- Ask students if both questions have the same word order. *(yes)*
- Point out that the word order never changes with the verb *be.*

Note 4   *(Exercises 1–4)*
- Write on the board:
What did the woman give Adams?
Ask students to say the pattern of the question on the board. Write the pattern to the left of the question:

object
┌─────┐
wh- word + auxiliary verb + subject + main verb (+ rest of the sentence)

- Write below the question on the board:
Which witness
Whose witness │ *did you question?*
How many witnesses │
Ask students to say the pattern of the questions on the board. Write the pattern to the left of the questions:

object
┌──────────┐
wh- word + noun + auxiliary verb + subject + main verb (+ rest of the sentence)

- Give examples with other auxiliaries: *Where do you work? Where have you been? What had she done? What can he do?*

→ For additional practice, see the Supplementary Activities on page 145.

Note 5   *(Exercises 1–4)*
- Write the following questions on the board.
a. *Whom did you meet?*
b. *Whom is at the door?*
c. *Whom gave it to you?*
d. *Whom did you interview?*
- Have students decide in pairs which questions are correct. *(a and d)* To review as a class, have students explain why b and c are incorrect. *(b is incorrect because you cannot use* whom *if the main verb is a form of* be. *c is incorrect because you cannot use* whom *when asking about someone as subject.)*

Note 6   *(Exercises 1–4)*
- Give more examples. You can say, "Where did he go? When did he call you? Why did he call?"
- Have pairs of students make up three *wh*-questions with *why, when,* and *where.*

Focused Practice (pages 76–78)

Exercise 2
cross-examination: questions about something someone just said to see if she/he has been telling the truth, especially in a court of law
ride: a trip in a car, train, or other vehicle

Exercise 3
testify: to make a formal statement of what is true, especially in a court of law
district attorney: (D.A.) a lawyer who works for the government in a particular district and brings criminals to court
verdict: an official decision that is made by a jury in a court of law about whether someone is guilty or not guilty of a crime
alibi: proof that someone was not where a crime happened and is therefore not guilty of the crime
trial: a legal process in which a court of law examines a case to decide whether someone is guilty of a crime

Communication Practice (pages 78–81)

Exercise 5
- If students disagree on the answers, play the segment in question again and have them write what they hear.
- Have students use what they wrote to support their answers. *(1. The correct question is "Who did you see at the restaurant?" The listener heard "I saw . . . at the restaurant." Nobody saw the speaker. The speaker saw someone.)*

Exercise 6
- Encourage students to use different *wh*-words, and to use both subject and object questions.
- Have students in pairs practice the conversation they created.
- Have pairs volunteer to perform their conversation for the class.

Exercise 7
- Before students work in pairs, have them read the models and look at the notes in the chart.
- Explain that the first column in the chart lists the people Mary Rogers saw. These people work at the same office and they are all suspected of committing a crime. The second and third column list when and where Mary Rogers saw the suspects, and the fourth column lists other people who saw the suspects at the same place and time.

- To review answers as a class, have a student ask a question and another student provide the answer. (A: *Who else saw Rick Simon?* B: *The janitor.*)

Exercise 8

- Model the format of the written interview for students. With the class, write an introductory paragraph for the interview.

    Sumalee Chonging is a ten-year-old girl. In many ways, she's like any ten-year-old, but in some ways, she's very special. Sumalee is a genius. She attends law school at Lincoln School. Recently, our reporter Max Lopez interviewed Sumalee about her life.

- Have students base their introductory paragraph on the one on the board.
- Have students type up and photocopy their interview to share it with other groups.
- ⏱ Have students vote for the most interesting interview.

Exercise 9

- After students have told each other their exciting or interesting story, have students work individually to write the questions they would like to ask their partner. When ready, have them interview each other.
- Have pairs volunteer to perform their interview for the class.
- ⏱ Have students write up their interviews in the format already introduced in Exercise 8, Star Reporters.

Further Practice

Tell students to imagine an interview with any person in history—for example, Leonardo da Vinci, Moses, Joan of Arc, or Lao Tzu. Have them write down ten questions they would like to ask this person. Have students share their questions in groups. You may then wish to have partners role-play the interviews.

 **OUT OF THE BOX** ......

A criminal case. Bring in articles from newspapers about criminal cases, and give each group one article. Have students imagine they will interview a witness of the crime in their article, and ask them to write down the questions they would ask the witness. Then have students report to the class on the crime they read and share the questions they prepared for the witness. You may want to have the class suggest other possible questions that might help solve the case. (Note: You can also bring in just one criminal case, and give each group a photocopy of the case. After writing the questions, students join another group and compare the questions they wrote.)

 UNIT 9

Reflexive and Reciprocal Pronouns

Unit Overview

Unit 9 focuses on the meanings and uses of reflexive and reciprocal pronouns.
- Reflexive pronouns (*myself, yourself,* etc.) are used when the subject and object of a sentence refer to the same people or things.
- Reciprocal pronouns (*each other, one another*) are used when the subject and the object of a sentence refer to the same people, and these have a two-way relationship.
- Reflexive pronouns can also be used to emphasize a person or thing.

Grammar in Context (pages 94–95)

Background Note

Recently, psychologists have been studying the effects of hope and optimism on people's lives. Studies indicate that positive attitudes have pervasive (existing or spreading everywhere) effects on many aspects of life, including physical and emotional health and success on the job. One study indicates that when college freshmen show a high degree of hopefulness, their grades are better than the grades of students who have similar ability but a more pessimistic outlook. Self-talk, one's dialogue with oneself, is an indicator of whether a person is optimistic or pessimistic. Optimists do not blame themselves, and they tell themselves that bad situations are temporary and limited. Pessimists, on the other hand, take the blame for bad outcomes and see them as permanent and pervasive. (Source: Daniel Goleman, "What hope can do for you," *Self,* June 1992, p. 112.)

Vocabulary

lay off: to stop employing someone, especially when there is not much work to do

keep fit: to stay healthy and strong

allow: to give someone permission to do something

gain: here, to increase in weight

helpless: unable to take care of or protect yourself

likely: something that is likely will probably happen

grumble: to complain in a quiet but slightly angry way

desperate: willing to do anything to change a very bad situation

Comprehension Questions

• What problem did Tom and Sara have? *(They lost their jobs.)*

• Who had a positive reaction to the problem? *(Sara)*

• What helped Sara have a positive reaction? *(the way she explained the problem to herself)*

Discussion Topics

• Ask students to think about who they identify with—Tom or Sara. Encourage them to give reasons for their choice.

• Ask students to talk about a problem they had and their reaction to the problem. Ask students to say what kind of self-talk they used. Was it positive or negative?

• Ask students to express their views on self-talk. Encourage them to say whether or not they think it is important and to give examples to support their views.

Grammar Presentation (pages 95–96)

Identify the Grammar

REFLEXIVE PRONOUNS

. . . we explain a problem to <u>ourselves</u>.
Tom saw <u>himself</u> as helpless . . .

RECIPROCAL PRONOUNS

Why were their reactions so different from
<u>one another</u>?
. . . they talked to <u>each other</u> . . .

Grammar Charts

• Write two examples on the board:

<u>Reflexive Pronoun</u>   <u>Reciprocal Pronoun</u>
She talked to herself.   *They talked to each*
                              other.

—Point to the first example and ask the class to: "Name the reflexive pronoun." *(herself)* "Name the subject of the sentence." *(She)* Draw an arrow from *herself* to *She*.

—Erase *She* and *herself*. Replace *She* with *John* and *herself* with a blank.
Ask students to say the missing reflexive pronoun. *(himself)* Write it in the blank on the board.
Say subject pronouns in random order, and ask students to say the corresponding reflexive pronouns.

—Point to the second example and ask the class to: "Name the reciprocal pronoun." *(each other)* "Name the subject of the sentence." *(They)*
Draw an arrow from *each other* to *They*.

• Point out that reciprocal pronouns are used with <u>plural</u> subject pronouns *(we, you, they)* because they indicate a reciprocal relationship between <u>two or more people</u>. (In the example on the board, A talked to B and B talked to A.)

Grammar Notes

Note 1   *(Exercises 1–5)*

• To help clarify, write two contrasting sentences on the board.
He felt proud of them.   *They felt proud of*
                                 themselves.
Ask the class in which sentence the subject and the object refer to the same people. *(They felt proud of themselves.)* Underline the subject *They* and the reflexive pronoun *themselves*.

• Drill the class on the use of reflexive pronouns saying incomplete sentences and having students complete them by adding the corresponding reflexive pronouns. *(She enjoyed . . . /She enjoyed herself; They blamed . . . /They blamed themselves; I cut . . . /I cut myself; You hurt . . . /You hurt yourself; We amused . . . /We amused ourselves.)*

• Point out that some verbs often take reflexive pronouns. Ask students to say the verbs that they remember from the previous activity, and write a list on the board. You can refer students to Appendix 3 on page A-2 for a list of such verbs.

• Have students, in groups of five or six, take turns saying things they taught themselves how to do. Encourage students to say as many sentences as they can.

A: I taught myself how to drive.

B: I also taught myself how to drive.

C: I taught myself how to play the guitar.

D: I taught myself how to ski.

Then, in turns, students address the partner to their right and say what they remember about one of the members of their group. *(Michael and Alex taught themselves how to drive. Brenda taught herself how to play the piano. You taught yourself how to ski.)*

• Draw attention to the example "My office light turns itself off." Point out that *itself* can be used with objects to express that objects do something automatically. Tell students that many people will just say "My office light turns off automatically."

Note 2   *(Exercises 1–3, 5)*

- To check comprehension, write two example sentences on the board:

  "Be yourself," Megan said.   *"Be yourselves," Steven said.*

  Ask the class: "How many people did Megan address?" *(one)* "How do you know?" *(because she used a singular reflexive pronoun:* yourself*)* "How many people did Steven address?" *(two or more than two)* "How do you know?" *(because he used a plural reflexive pronoun:* yourselves*)* "Why are *yourself* and *yourselves* the correct reflexive pronouns in imperative sentences?" *(because, although we don't say it, the subject of imperative sentences is always "you")*

→ For additional practice, see the Supplementary Activities on page 146.

Note 3   *(Exercises 1, 3, 5)*

- Write two pairs of example sentences on the board:

  The manager offered me a job.   *The manager himself offered me a job.*
  I myself made the cake.   *I made the cake.*

  Ask the class: "In which sentence is the speaker surprised that the manager—and not another person in the company—would have offered him/her a job?" *(in the second)* "How do you know?" *(because he/she used the reflexive pronoun "himself")* "In which sentence is the speaker particularly proud of having made the cake?" *(in the first)* "How do you know?" *(because he/she used the reflexive pronoun "myself")*
- Have students scan the reading for another example of a reflexive pronoun used for emphasis. *(She herself could change it.)*
- Ask pairs of students to create emphatic sentences using reflexive pronouns after nouns.

Note 4   *(Exercises 2–4)*

- To check comprehension, write two example sentences on the board:

  I'm going on vacation by myself.   *I decided to be myself.*

  Have pairs discuss the meaning of the underlined phrases. Review as a class.
- Ask volunteers to say if they ever lived or went on a trip by themselves, or if they ever did a difficult task by themselves. *(I went to Egypt by myself. I painted my room by myself.)*
- Ask volunteers to give situations in which it is advisable to be yourself. *(It's important to be yourself at a job interview. You should be yourself when you meet someone.)*

Note 5   *(Exercises 1–5)*

- Point to a student and to yourself and say, "We met each other (three months ago)." Write it on the board.

  We met each other three months ago.

  Explain that in this example, *we* refers to (name of the student you pointed to) and you. You may want to write below the example on the board:

  We = (student's name) + I
- Point to the entire class and to yourself, and say, "We met one another (three months ago)." Write it on the board.

  We met one another three months ago.

  Explain that in this example, *we* refers to all the students in the class, and yourself. You may want to write below the example on the board:

  We = the students + I
- Make sure students understand that some people also use *each other* for more than two people and *one another* for just two people.
- Have students turn to a classmate and find out about his/her best friend(s) by asking questions. Encourage students to use reflexive pronouns. *(Who is/are your best friend(s)? Where/How long ago did you meet each other/one another? Do you often see each other/one another? When do you give each other/one another gifts?)* Then have students change roles.
- To explain the difference between reflexive and reciprocal pronouns, write two contrastive sentences on the board:

  Diana and Ben take care of themselves.   *Diana and Ben take care of each other.*

  Point out that the second sentence expresses a reciprocal relationship.
- To clarify, write the following diagrams below the examples on the board:

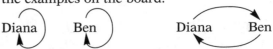

- To check comprehension, have pairs discuss the difference between the following sentences, which you may want to write on the board:

  We talked to ourselves.   *We talked to each other.*

Note 6

Call on volunteers to restate your sentences with possessive forms of reciprocal pronouns. Say, "Sam did Sonia's homework, and Sonia did Sam's homework." "Sam praised Sonia's work, and Sonia praised Sam's work." (Answers: *Sam and Sonia did each other's work. Sam and Sonia praised each other's work.*)

Focused Practice (pages 97–100)

Exercise 1

improve: to become better

performance: here, how well or badly you do an activity

pro: (informal) professional

shot: here, an attempt to hit the ball

mental movies: pictures that you form in your mind

Exercise 2

help yourself: to take something that you want, such as food, without asking permission

Exercise 3

run: here, to control or be in charge of

discipline: a way of training someone so that they learn to control their behavior and obey rules

interfere: to deliberately get involved when you are not wanted or needed

encourage: to help someone become confident enough to do something

give up: to stop trying to do something, especially something difficult

failure: something that is not successful

pride yourself on something: to be especially proud of something that you do well

satisfy yourself: to make someone happy by providing what she/he wants or needs

Exercise 5

be hard on yourself: to be strict or unfair with yourself

insulting: offensive to someone

forgive: to stop being angry with someone, although she/he has done something wrong

Communication Practice (pages 101–104)

Exercise 6

- Point out that both pronouns are possible in each context and that students must listen carefully to distinguish the correct pronoun.
- After completing and checking the exercise, ask students to interpret the two choices for each item.

Exercise 7

- Before students work in pairs, have them go over the situations individually, and think about what they would tell themselves in each of the situations. You may want to ask students to write a few notes for each.

- Point out the reflexive pronouns in the example, and encourage students to use as many reflexive pronouns as they can in their conversations.
- Elicit verbs which can be used with reflexive pronouns and will be useful for students while doing this activity. Write a list of verbs on the board: *tell yourself, talk to yourself, prepare yourself well, believe in yourself, (don't) blame yourself, imagine yourself, push yourself, remind yourself, see yourself.* If necessary, explain the meaning of *push yourself* (work hard).
- Choose a few students to report on what their partners said for a different situation each. As students speak, check the use of reflexive pronouns.

Exercise 8

- As students interview their partners, have them write notes about their partners' answers.
- Before students report to the class, have them reread the test and underline the verbs or expressions used reflexively. Encourage students to use these verbs and expressions as they report to the class.

Exercise 9

- To review answers, call on volunteers to read a sentence aloud. As students read the sentences aloud, write them on the board, making any necessary corrections.

Exercise 11

Questions to generate ideas and elicit vocabulary:

- What do you tell yourself when you have problems at school/work?
- How does it help?
- What do you tell yourself when you have problems with a boyfriend or girlfriend?
- How does it help?

Further Practice

Working in pairs, ask students to write three simple stories (15 to 35 words) combining two or three verbs or expressions used reflexively from Appendix 3 on page A-2. Ask students to underline the verbs and expressions they use. Encourage students to be creative!

When Sally was a child, she always <u>behaved herself</u> at school. She was at the top of the class, and she <u>was proud of herself</u>.

Last week Sam tried to underline{teach himself} how to ride a horse. He fell off the horse and underline{hurt himself} badly. He underline{blames himself} for the accident.

GRAMMAR OUT OF THE BOX......

Profiles. Bring in magazine interviews with famous people. Give groups of students one interview, and have them find in the interview the answers to some of the questions below, which you can write on the board, or enlarge and photocopy.

Find:
- something the person prides himself/ herself for
- something the person blames himself/ herself for
- an occasion when the person pushed himself/herself hard
- an occasion when the person enjoyed himself/herself
- who the person is living/going out with and when/where they met each other
- who the person works with and how they get along with each other/one another

---

After groups have finished working, ask one student from each group to describe the person they read about using reflexive and reciprocal pronouns. Challenge students to only say sentences that contain reflexive or reciprocal pronouns. *Steven Spielberg prides himself on making great movies. Spielberg and his wife, Kate Capshaw, met each other on the set of a film over 20 years ago.*

UNIT 10 Phrasal Verbs

Unit Overview

Unit 10 focuses on the meanings of phrasal verbs.
- Phrasal verbs consist of a verb and a particle which often changes the meaning of the verb.
- Many phrasal verbs have the same meaning as one-word verbs. Phrasal verbs are informal and more commonly used in everyday speech.
- Phrasal verbs can be transitive or intransitive. Many transitive phrasal verbs are separable.

Grammar in Context (pages 105–106)

Vocabulary

repellent: a substance that keeps insects away from you

chemistry: the science of studying substances and what happens to them when they change or combine with each other

major: here, someone who is studying a particular subject as his or her main subject at a college or university

anthropologist: a scientist who studies people, their societies, their beliefs, etc.

Comprehension Questions

- Who is Eloy Rodriguez? *(a famous scientist)*
- What was his childhood like? *(He was poor; he picked cotton to help support his family.)*
- Was he a good student? *(Yes. He did well in high school. He went to college and then to graduate school.)*
- Where does he go every summer? *(to the Amazon region in Venezuela)*
- What does he go there for? *(to search for medicinal plants)*
- What do Rodriguez and Wrangham study? *(how animals use plants as medicine)*

Discussion Topics

- Write on the board:
  If you had the chance to go anywhere in the world to do scientific research, where would you go? What would you study?
  Have students in small groups discuss the questions on the board. Encourage them to support their view.
- Have students list 10 important contributions that scientists have made. Then have them discuss their importance and rank them in order. Bring the class together, and ask students to say which contributions they discussed. As you get feedback from students, write a list of contributions on the board. Take a poll to find out which scientific contribution the class thinks is the most important.

Grammar Presentation (pages 106–107)

Identify the Grammar

TRANSITIVE PHRASAL VERBS
He also <u>picked up</u> an interest in plants.
. . . sick animals often <u>pick out</u> certain plants to eat.

INTRANSITIVE PHRASAL VERBS
Rodriguez <u>grew up</u> in Texas.
. . . he <u>went on</u> to college.

Grammar Charts

• Write the following examples on the board:

<u>Verb</u>	<u>Phrasal Verbs</u>
He picked cotton to earn some money.	*He <u>picked up</u> an interest in plants.*
	He <u>picked out</u> some plants to study.

—Have students look at the underlined phrasal verbs and ask: "How many words are necessary to form a phrasal verb?" *(two)*
—Point out that the two words are a verb and a particle. Write on the board:
phrasal verb = verb + particle
—Have students identify the verbs in the examples on the board. *(picked)*
—Have students identify the particles. *(up, out)*

• Point out that phrasal verbs have a meaning of their own, which is different from the meaning of the verb or the particle on their own.

—To illustrate your point, write on the board:

pick	*pull off from a plant (a flower)*
pick up	*select from a group (a present)*
pick out	*get (an interest)*

—Have students match the verb and phrasal verbs with their meanings. *(pick: pull off from a plant; pick up: get; pick out: select from a group)*

• Write the following examples on the board:

Transitive Phrasal Verb	*Intransitive Phrasal Verb*
He <u>took off</u> his sunglasses.	*The plane <u>took off</u>.*
He took them off.	

—Draw attention to the examples of a transitive phrasal verb. Point out that a transitive phrasal verb is a phrasal verb that takes a direct object (noun or pronoun). Have students say the objects. *(his sunglasses, them)*
—Point to the example of an intransitive phrasal verb. Ask students why this phrasal verb is intransitive. *(because it doesn't take an object)*

Grammar Notes

Note 1 *(Exercises 1–3, 6)*
• Provide an additional example of the change in meaning. Write on the board:
His office window looks over the park.
  (= faces)
He looks over the department report every morning. (= reviews)
Have students study the examples and ask: "Which example contains a phrasal verb?" *(the second)* "Is *over* in the first example a particle or a preposition?" *(a preposition)* "What is *over* in the second example?" *(a particle)*
• Write more examples on the board:
a. The firefighter helped the little boy out of the hole.
b. The teacher helps me out when I have a question.
c. The detective was looking into the cause of the fire.
d. The detective was looking into the microscope.
e. She was brought up to be honest and fair.
f. She brought up the books that I had left downstairs.
• Have students study in pairs the sentences and decide which ones contain phrasal verbs. Ask students to write the meaning of the phrasal verb to the right of each sentence. *(b. assist/help in a difficult situation; c. investigate; e. raise)*

Note 2 *(Exercises 1–3, 6)*
• Give two examples in context. You can say: " 'You should <u>return</u> this book on Friday,' the librarian told a student." " '<u>Give</u> her <u>back</u> her doll,' the mother told her daughter."
• Write more examples on the board:

come back	discuss
find out	return
go out	discover
talk over	exit

• Working in pairs, have students match the informal phrasal verbs with similar formal one-word verbs. *(come back = return; find out = discover; go out = exit; talk over = discuss)*

Note 3 *(Exercises 1, 4, 5–6)*
• To help clarify, write on the board:
Separable transitive phrasal verbs

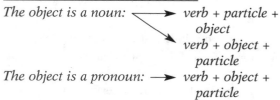

The object is a noun: → verb + particle + object
→ verb + object + particle

The object is a pronoun: → verb + object + particle

- To explain the information on the board, make the following points:
  —The summary on the board covers separable transitive phrasal verbs. (Point to the title.)
  —When the object is a noun, it has two possible positions. (Read the section about nouns aloud.)
  —When the object is a pronoun, it has only one position. (Read the section about pronouns aloud.)
- You may want to write an example next to each pattern:
  He took off his jacket.
  He took his jacket off.
  He took it off.
- Working in pairs, have students use the phrasal verb *put on* to write three different sentences.

→ For additional practice, see the Supplementary Activities on page 146.

Note 4   *(Exercises 1, 5–6)*
- Write more examples on the board:
  His family helped Rodriguez get by in life.
  When he came in we all stood up.
  Point out that intransitive verbs are always inseparable.

→ For additional practice, see the Supplementary Activities on page 146.

Focused Practice (pages 108–111)

Exercise 1
honors classes: classes that can be taken by honors students (students whose grades are good enough that their name is included in the honor roll)

role model: someone whose behavior, attitude, etc., people try to copy because they admire them

Exercise 2
hands-on: experience, training, etc., that you get by doing something rather than by studying it

Exercise 3
chimp: (informal) a chimpanzee (an African animal that is like a monkey without a tail)

furry: covered with fur, or looking or feeling as if covered with fur

swallow: to make food or drink go down your throat

antibiotic: a drug that is used in order to kill bacteria and cure infections

Exercise 4
generator: a machine that produces electricity

leftover food: food that remains at the end of a meal and is kept to be eaten later

ant: a common black or red insect that lives in groups

Exercise 6
major: (adj.) very large or important, especially when compared to other things or people of a similar kind

rash: a lot of red spots on someone's skin, caused by an illness or a reaction to food, plants, or medicine

cure: to make an injury or illness better, so that the person who was sick is well

stem: a long thin part of a plant, from which leaves or flowers grow

chew: to crush something with your teeth before swallowing it

pharmacology: the scientific study of drugs and medicines

major: (n.) here, the main subject that you study at a college or university

Communication Practice (pages 112–114)

Exercise 7
- Point out that both phrasal verbs are possible in each context and that students must listen carefully to distinguish the correct verb.
- After deciding if the statements are true or false, have students interpret the meaning of the phrasal verbs they didn't select in the previous exercise.
  Refer students to Appendices 4 and 5 on pages A-3 and A-4, or have them use a dictionary.

Exercise 8
- Draw on students' prior experience by asking them if they ever went on a field trip, and have them briefly describe their experience.
- After students finish working, have them share their lists with the class.

Exercise 9
- Before students discuss the pictures, remind them they should use as many phrasal verbs as they can as they describe them.
- As pairs read their stories aloud, have the class identify the sequence of pictures as they listen.

Exercise 10
- To help students get started, brainstorm and write on the board the names of famous people who are models to look up to.
- Before students write, point out that the person needn't be famous.

Further Practice
Have each student write one sentence using a phrasal verb from Appendix 4 or Appendix 5.

Review the sentences for errors. Then have each student copy the corrected sentence onto slips of paper, separating the phrasal verb between the verb and its particle.

The students took   off their lab coats. Have students put their two slips in a pile. Shuffle the pile and redistribute the slips of paper. Have students circulate around the room, looking for the matching half of sentence. Be sure students don't read each other's sentences but rather speak and listen to each other. When all the sentences are matched, have students read their matched sentences aloud to the class.

GRAMMAR OUT OF THE BOX ......

Phrasal verb search. Bring in any kind of authentic material—brochures, instruction manuals, handbooks, Internet print outs, magazines, novels, short stories, etc. Hand out the material, and have students, working in groups, scan the texts for phrasal verbs. Ask them to choose five phrasal verbs, write down the sentence they appear in, and figure out their meaning. Have students use a dictionary and/or Appendices 4 and 5 on pages A-3 and A-4 to check their guesses. Have students share their findings with the class.

UNIT 11 Ability: *Can, Could, Be able to*

Unit Overview

Unit 11 focuses on the uses of *can*, *could*, and *be able to* to express ability.
- *Can* and *can't* express present ability. They also express future ability when talking about plans or arrangements.
- *Could* and *couldn't* express past ability. *Could* can't be used for single past events—*was/were able to* should be used instead.
- Different forms of *be able to* express present, future, and past ability.

Grammar in Context (pages 124–125)

Vocabulary

nervous system: the system of nerves in your body, through which you feel pain, heat, etc., and control your movements

emotion: a strong human feeling such as love or hate

competition: a situation in which people or organizations compete (to try to win) with each other

audience: the people watching or listening to a concert, speech, or movie

hypnotize: to be so interesting or exciting that people cannot think of anything else

aspiration: a strong desire to have or achieve something

Comprehension Questions

- What dream did Verdi-Fletcher achieve? *(to become a dancer)*
- Why did people think she wouldn't be able to achieve her dream? *(because she couldn't stand or walk)*
- How did people react when she danced in her first competition? *(They stood and applauded.)*
- How has Verdi-Fletcher changed the definition of dancing? *(dancing does not have to be done standing up)*
- What does she want to show through her dance? *(that with hard work and dedication dreams can be achieved)*

Discussion Topics

- Have students discuss what questions they would ask Verdi-Fletcher if they had a chance to interview her.
- Have students share other achievements—big or small—of people with disabilities that they might know about. Have students talk about the kind of example these people set and what we can all learn from them.

Grammar Presentation (pages 125–127)

Identify the Grammar

ABILITY: *CAN*
You <u>can't walk</u> . . .
How <u>can</u> she <u>dance</u>?
You <u>can't take</u> your eyes off her.
. . . they <u>can achieve</u> their dreams . . .
. . . what people <u>can</u> or <u>cannot do</u>.

ABILITY: *COULD*
. . . she <u>could hypnotize</u> an audience . . .

ABILITY: *BE ABLE TO*
. . . she <u>wasn't able to stand</u> or <u>walk</u>.

Grammar Charts

* Write the following examples on the board:
  Ability: *Can*
  Verdi-Fletcher can't walk, but she can dance.
  You can't take your eyes off her.
  *She changed the perception of what we can or
    cannot do.*
  We can all achieve our dreams.
* Have students study the examples, and ask:
  —"How do you form affirmative statements
    with *can*?" (*can + base form of verb*)
  —"Does *can* change when the pronoun
    changes?" (*No. Can is the same for all
    pronouns.*)
  —"How do you form negative statements?"
    (*can not / cannot + base form of verb*)
  —"What is the contraction of *can not* and
    cannot?" (*can't*)
* Write the following examples on the board:
  Can she dance?
  How well can she dance?
  —Then ask the class: "How do you form
    yes/no questions?" (*can + subject + base
    form of verb*)
  —Call on a student to write the two possible
    short answers to the question on the board.
    (*Yes, she can. No, she can't.*)
  —Then ask: "How do you form *wh-*
    questions?" (*wh- word + can + subject +
    base form of verb*)
* Write on the board:
  Ability: *Could*
  *aff. statement: Mozart could write music at the
    age of five.*
  neg. statement:
  yes/no question:
  wh- question:
  Call on different students to come to the front
  and turn the affirmative statement with *could*
  into a negative statement, a *yes/no* question,
  and a *wh-* question.
* Write the following on the board, and follow
  the steps done for *could*.
  Ability: *Be able to*
  aff. statement: She was able to dance.
  neg. statement:
  yes/no question:
  wh- question:

Grammar Notes

Note 1   *(Exercises 1, 3, 5)*
* Write on the board:
  We can to swim.
  She cans type fast.
  He doesn't can drive.
  Do they can speak French?

Working in pairs, have students correct the
sentences. Review as a class.
* Write on the board:
  They can't write music.
  He could play the piano when he was five.
  Can she use a computer?
  Working in pairs, have students restate the
  statements on the board using *be able to*.
  Review as a class.

Note 2   *(Exercises 1–5)*
Point out that *can, could,* and *be able to* all
express ability. Give more examples. You can
say: "I could speak two languages when I was a
child." "I can understand Italian, but I can't
speak it." "After my trip to Italy, I will be able
to say a few things in Italian."

→ For additional practice, see the Supplementary Activities on
  pages 146–147.

Note 3   *(Exercises 1, 4–5)*
* Read the example in the Student Book aloud.
  Point out that in complete sentences the
  pronunciation of *can* is with a relaxed vowel
  /kən/ and is brief. The pronunciation of *can't*
  is with an open vowel /kænt/ and drawn out.
  Have students repeat the example in the
  Student Book chorally.
* Write a list of topics on the board:
  Driving and riding
  Languages
  Sports
  Music and dancing
  Give an example for each topic: *I can ride a
  motorbike. I can speak two languages. I can
  ski. I can't play any musical instruments.*
* Working in pairs, ask students to take turns
  asking and answering questions about the
  topics on the board. Encourage students to
  keep the conversation going as they talk
  about their abilities.

  A: Can you ride a bicycle?

  B: Yes, I can, and I can also ride a
     motorbike. Can you ride a motorbike?

  A: No I can't, but I can drive a car.

  Have volunteers report to the class on what
  their partners can do.

→ For additional practice, see the Supplementary Activities on
  pages 146–147.

Note 4   *(Exercises 1–5)*
* Point out that *can* expresses future ability only
  when talking about plans or arrangements. To
  talk about things we will learn in the future,
  we should use *will be able to*.

- Write on the board:
  I _____ call you after 6:00.
  The doctor said next month she _____ walk.
  I _____ (not) come to the party tonight.
  I only took two driving lessons—I _____
    (not) park yet, but by the end of next week, I
    _____ park.

  Have students work in pairs and complete the sentences with *can* or *be able to*. Students should use *can* wherever possible. Review as a class. (*I can call you after 6:00. The doctor said next month she will be able to walk. I can't come to the party tonight. I only took two driving lessons—I can't park yet, but by the end of next week, I will be able to park.*)

Note 5 *(Exercises 1–5)*

- Have students draw a time line and write information about things they could do at different ages in their childhood. You may want to write an example on the board:

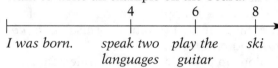

  To help students generate ideas, tell them to think about when they learned to ride a bike, tie their own shoelaces, cook a meal, get dressed, make their bed, play a sport, read, etc.

- Working in small groups, ask students to tell their partners what they could do when they were kids using *could*. Give an example: "When I was four, I could speak two languages."

- Give additional examples to establish the contrast between *could* and *was/were able to*. *Could* refers to a general ability but not to a single past event. You can write on the board:
  I could speak Spanish when I was a child.
  Tom knows very little Spanish, but he was able to make himself understood when he was in Spain.
  Jessica could run very fast when she was young. Once she was able to run to the store and back in five minutes.

- Write a list of single events on the board:
  pass an exam
  win a competition
  contact someone
  catch the bus
  Brainstorm and write on the board more single events to add to the list. (Students may say: *get a job, get a scholarship, finish a task on schedule, arrive on time, get tickets*)

Call on volunteers to make sentences with *was/were able to* using the ideas on the board. (*I was able to pass the history exam.*)

- Make sure students understand that *couldn't can* be used for single events. Call on volunteers to say single events they intended to do last week but they couldn't do in the end. Give examples. You can say, "I couldn't go shopping this morning because my car broke down." "I couldn't go out on Saturday because I had to study." You may want to point out that *wasn't able to* is also possible.

→ For additional practice, see the Supplementary Activities on pages 146–147.

Note 6 *(Exercises 1, 3–5)*

- Write more examples on the board:
  She is able to sing operas.
  I will be able to attend the meeting.
  The dentist wasn't able to see me yesterday.
  He wants to be able to play the guitar.
  I'd like to be able to ride a horse.
  Being able to walk is not necessary to become a dancer.

- Have students work in pairs. To provide practice with *be able to* for the future, write the To Do list below on the board. Tell students the following imaginary situation: "It's 7:00 A.M. and Sally just woke up with a fever." Have students say what they think Sally will/won't be able to do today. (*She won't be able to go to work. She will be able to call Tom. She won't be able to have lunch with Mary. She will be able to pay her telephone bill.*)
  To Do
  Work the morning shift (8–12)
  Call Tom for his birthday
  Have lunch with Mary at Al's Grill
  Pay telephone bill online

- Have students work in small groups. To provide practice with *to be able to* (infinitive), have students take turns saying the things they would like to be able to do. Encourage them to make relevant comments or ask follow-up questions:

  A: I'd like to be able to ski.

  B: Why don't you take lessons?

  A: That's what I'm planning to do this winter!

  Follow up by having a few students report to the class on what their partners would like to be able to do.

→ For additional practice, see the Supplementary Activities on pages 146–147.

Focused Practice (pages 128–131)

Exercise 1
keypunch: a machine that puts holes in special cards which are read by computers (no longer in use)

enroll: to officially join a school, university, etc., or to arrange for someone else to do this

disability: a physical or mental condition that makes it difficult for someone to do the things that most people are able to do

Exercise 2
sign up for: to put your name on a list because you want to take a class, belong to a group, etc.

waltz: a fairly slow dance with a rhythm consisting of patterns of three beats, or the music for this dance

Exercise 3
fox-trot: a type of formal dance with quick movements, or the music for this dance

Exercise 4
performance: an act of performing a play, piece of music, etc., or the occasion when something is performed

intermission: a short period of time between the parts of a play, concert, etc.

Exercise 5
perform: to do something to entertain people

background: here, the type of education or experience that someone has

athletic: physically strong and good at sports

gymnastics: a sport involving physical exercises and movements that need skill and control, often performed in competitions

recommend: to say that someone or something is good

Communication Practice (pages 132–134)

Exercise 6
• Before students listen, have them read the list of skills and abilities. Answer any questions about vocabulary. Students may need help with the following words: *design* (to make a drawing or plan of something that will be made); *newsletter* (a short written report of news about a club, organization, or particular subject that is sent regularly to people).

• Note: Students might not know some of the vocabulary in the conversation, but they should still be able to do the task successfully. After listening and reviewing answers, you can clarify the meaning of the following words.

word processing: using computer software for writing

spreadsheet: a document that contains rows and columns of numbers that can be used to calculate something

desktop publishing: the work of producing magazines, books, etc., with a computer that is designed to be used on a desk

• Point out that Karl talks about things he can do now and things he will be able to do soon. Students should only check the things he can do <u>now</u>.

• To review answers, have students say full sentences. *(Karl can answer the phones.)*

• After reviewing answers, ask students why Karl thinks he will soon be able to design a newsletter and dance *(Because he's taking a course in desktop publishing and he's applying for a job in a dance studio).*

Exercise 7
• Go over the example. Point out the use of present forms *(can)*, future forms *(will be able to)*, and past forms *(could)*.

• Follow up by asking students which dances from the schedule they can do and/or would like to be able to do.

Exercise 8
• Go over the list of skills and explain any unknown words.

• Before students get started, you may want to ask them to choose an imaginary topic for their presentation. This will help them generate ideas.

• Ask students to tell their group other skills they have which are useful to plan a presentation. Ask students to add these skills to the list.

• After assigning tasks, have a few students tell their class about their assignments. Encourage the class to ask follow-up questions.

  A: I can type fast, so I'm going to type on the computer.

  B: How fast can you type?

  C: I'm going to do research online.

  D: What are you going to do research on?

Exercise 9
Questions to generate ideas and elicit vocabulary:
• What did the person want to do or achieve?
• What kind of difficulty or problem did the person have?

- What did the person do to face the problem?
- What was this person's key to success?
- What can you learn from a story like this?

Further Practice

Have students choose a topic—for example, music, art, sports, computing, languages—to survey each other about skills and abilities they developed in their childhood, possess now, or plan for the future. Ask them to write four questions about the topic they chose. For example: *When you were a child, were you interested in music? Could you play a musical instrument? Can you play a musical instrument now? What (other) instrument would you like to be able to play?* Have students submit their surveys to you for correction. Then have students circulate around the room interviewing their classmates. Have students write up a report on their findings and submit it to you.

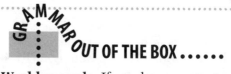

GRAMMAR OUT OF THE BOX ......

World records. If you have access to a lending library, bring in a copy of the book *Guinness World Records* or do an Internet search on **world records** and bring in printouts. (http://www.guinnessworldrecords.com). In small groups, have students browse the book—or read the printouts—and write notes about an achievement or special feat. Then have a student from each group report to the class on their findings. *(George Blair can water-ski barefoot. In 2002, he was able to break a record when he successfully skied barefoot on a lake in Florida at the age of 87!)*

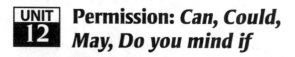

UNIT 12 — Permission: *Can, Could, May, Do you mind if*

Unit Overview

Unit 12 focuses on ways to ask permission and give and refuse permission.
- The modals *can, could,* and *may* are used in questions to ask permission. *May* is more formal.
- The word *please* makes permission requests more polite.
- Informal expressions such as *sure, certainly,* and *go ahead* are often used to give

permission. To refuse permission, we usually apologize and give an explanation.
- The expression *Do you mind if* is also used to ask permission.

Grammar in Context (pages 135–136)

Background Note

People normally know what is considered polite behavior in their own country. They know, for example, what they are expected to ask permission for, or what to say to sound polite. Rules of polite behavior are not the same in every country. Before traveling abroad, it is important to find out about etiquette in other countries. This will help avoid misunderstandings and embarrassing situations.

Vocabulary

hang out: to spend a lot of time at a particular place or with particular people

dorm: a dormitory (a large building at a college or university where students live)

counselor: someone whose job is to help and support people with problems

stuff: a number of different things, in this case, personal items

guidelines: rules or instructions about the best way to do something

Comprehension Questions

- Did Heather and Rema get along at first? *(yes)*
- What spoiled their relationship? *(They both did things that annoyed the other.)*
- What examples of annoying behavior does the article give? *(Rema ate Heather's cookies, and Heather invited friends without asking.)*
- Why is the title of the article "Always Ask First"? *(It's the advice the article gives. Heather and Rema had problems precisely because they didn't ask first.)*

Discussion Topics

- Have students discuss what they would do if they shared a room, and their roommate ate their cookies or invited friends without asking. How would they react? How would they try to resolve the problem?
- Have students discuss other guidelines a dorm counselor can give to help roommates get along with each other. Have students write a short list of guidelines and rank them in order of importance.

Grammar Presentation (pages 136–137)

Identify the Grammar

PERMISSION: *CAN, COULD, MAY, DO YOU MIND IF . . . ?*
Could I have one?
Hey, do you mind if they hang out here for a while?
May I use yours for a few hours?
Can Luis and Ming-Hwa work here tonight?

Grammar Charts

- Write the following examples on the board:
Permission: *Can, Could, May, Do you mind if . . . ?*
Can I work here tonight?
Could I have a cookie?
May I use your computer?
  —Have students study the examples, and ask: "How do you ask permission with *can, could,* and *may*?" (can/could/may + *subject* + *base form of verb*) "Which permission request from the board can be answered with 'Yes, you may'?" (*May I use your computer?*) "Which permission requests can be answered with 'Yes, you can'?" (*Can I work here tonight? Could I have a cookie?*)
  —Point out that *could* cannot be used in short answers. *Can* is used instead.
- Write below the other three questions on the board:
Do you mind if they hang out here for a while? Then ask: "How do you ask permission with *do you mind*?" (do you mind + if + *subject* + *simple present tense*) "What's the affirmative short answer?" (*Yes, I do.*) "Does *Yes, I do* give or refuse permission?" (*It refuses permission because you mind if the person does what he/she asked permission for.*) "What's the negative short answer?" (*No, I don't.*) "Does *No, I don't* give or refuse permission?" (*It gives permission because you do not mind if the person does what he/she asked permission for.*)
- Write below the questions on the board:
Sure.   Not at all.
Then ask the class: "Which questions from the board can be replied with *Sure*?" (*the first three*) "Does *Sure* give permission?" (*yes*) "Which question can be replied with *Not at all*?" (*Do you mind if they hang out here for a while?*) "Does *Not at all* give or refuse permission?" (*give permission*) "Why?" (*because it means that you don't mind at all*

if the person does what he/she asked permission for)
- To summarize, you may want to add the responses next to the questions on the board:

Permission	Given	Refused
Can Luis and Ming-Hwa work here tonight? *Could I have one?*	*Yes, . . . can/ may.*	*No, . . . can't/ may not.*
May I use yours for a few hours?	*Sure.*	
Do you mind if they hang out here for a while?	*No, I don't.* *No, not at all.*	*Yes, I do.*

- Point out that other expressions are also possible. Refer students to the grammar charts and elicit more expressions with the same meaning as *Sure* (*Certainly, Of course, Why not?*) and *Not at all* (*Go right ahead*).

Grammar Notes

Note 1 *(Exercises 1–4)*
- Emphasize that *could* does not have a past meaning in questions asking permission. To help clarify, write on the board:
Can I use this book? = Could I use this book?
- Point out that *can* is less formal than *could,* and *could* is less formal than *may.* Direct students' attention to the vertical arrow in their book which illustrates this point.
- Ask students to say questions they normally use in class to ask permission. Encourage students to use different modals. (*May I borrow your pen? Could I use your book? Can we leave now? May I leave earlier today? Can I use a dictionary? May I ask a question? Can we do this exercise with a partner? Could I finish this exercise for next class?*)

→ For additional practice, see the Supplementary Activities on page 147.

Note 2 *(Exercises 1, 3–4)*
- Point out that *please* may be placed just before the main verb or at the end of a question.
- Write the questions below on the board, and have students rate them from 1 to 4, with 4 being the most polite form.
Can I take a photograph?
May I please take a photograph?
Could I take a photograph?
May I take a photograph?

Note 3 *(Exercises 1–4)*

• Write on the board:

Can		Sure.
Could	I close the door?	Certainly.
May		Go ahead.

Make sure students understand that requests with *can*, *could*, and *may* can be replied to with any of the four expressions on the board. These expressions are more common than answers with modals.

• Point out that only the modals *can* and *may* can be used in responses. To help clarify, write examples on the board:

Can I borrow this pen? ⎤ *Yes, of course*
Could I borrow this pen? ⎦ *you can.*

May I borrow this pen? ⎤⎦ *Yes, you may.*

• Have students practice responding rapidly to requests. You can say:
"Can I use the phone?"
"Could I ask a question?"
"Can I use your pen?"
"May I pay by check?"
"Could I have some water, please?"

• Point out that when permission is refused, an apology and a brief explanation are expected. Brainstorm with the class possible explanations to the permission requests below. (Possible explanations are given in parentheses.)
Can I make a phone call? (I'm sorry. This phone is for employees only.)
May I sit here? (I'm sorry. That seat is already taken.)
Can I use your cell phone? (I'm sorry. The battery is dead.)
Can I take a look at your magazine? (I'm sorry. It's not mine.)
Could I smoke? (No, please don't. I'm allergic to smoke.)

→ For additional practice, see the Supplementary Activities on page 147.

Note 4 *(Exercises 1–4)*

• To help clarify, you can say, "If your roommate is studying and you want to turn up the TV, you would say, *Do you mind if I turn up the TV?* because you can anticipate that it will disturb him/her."
Write two examples on the board and point out the simple present tense after *if* (*turn up* after *I* and *stays* after *Lorna*).
Do you mind if I turn up the TV?
Do you mind if Lorna stays here?

• Ask the class: "How can you reply to give permission?" *(Not at all.* OR *No, I don't.)*
"How can you reply to refuse permission?" *(Yes, [actually] I do + an explanation)*

• Have students practice responding rapidly to different kinds of requests. You can say:
"Can I use your dictionary?"
"Do you mind if I use your dictionary?"
"Do you mind if I leave class early tonight?"
"Could I leave early tonight?"
"Can I use your computer?"
"Do you mind if I use your computer?"

Focused Practice (pages 138–141)

Exercise 1
overnight: for or during the night

Exercise 2
earplug: a small piece of rubber that you put into your ear to keep out noise or water

Exercise 3
lounge: a room in a public building where people can relax, sit down, or drink
available: able to be used or obtained

Communication Practice (pages 141–143)

Exercise 5
• To review answers, for each conversation, ask, "Who was speaking? Was permission given?" If students disagree, play the segment in question again.
⏱ After reviewing answers, have students listen to the conversations again, and write down the permission requests they hear. Working in pairs, have students role-play the conversations. Have them take turns asking permission and responding.

Exercise 6
• Review the first situation and the examples. With the class, brainstorm other possible questions for this situation. *(Do you mind if they use the phone? Can Zoe use the kitchen to bake a cake for Larry's birthday? Can they put their bags in this closet?)*
• Encourage students to use their imagination and ask as many questions as they can think of.
• Have groups share with the class their ideas for each situation, as you take notes on the board. For each situation, you can ask, "What are the possible responses to these requests? How polite is each request? In this situation, which request would you be most comfortable making?"

Exercise 7

- Review the first situation and the examples. Ask volunteers to say other possible ways to make the same requests. (*Can I copy your notes from class yesterday? Could I please copy your notes from class yesterday? May I call you tonight if I have any questions? Do you mind if I call you tonight if I have any questions?*)
- As students work in pairs, make sure they take turns being Student A and Student B. To add a dramatic element to the exercise, you may want to have students read only their own role information, not that of their partners.
- After students have worked in pairs, have volunteers role-play their conversations for the class.

Exercise 8

- With the class, brainstorm other situations in which someone might need to write a note asking permission. Write students' ideas on the board.
  - —to borrow a bicycle
  - —to use someone's computer
  - —to borrow money
  - —to invite a friend to stay overnight
  - —to have a party
  - —to borrow clothes
- Before students trade notes, have students submit their notes to you, and review them for accuracy.

Further Practice

Have groups develop and write out their own situations relating to asking permission to do something (as in Exercise 6 on page 142). Then have groups exchange situations and plan how *they* would respond.

 OUT OF THE BOX . . . . . .

FAQs. Have students work in small groups. Bring in enough copies of a FAQs web page for a museum (Keyword: museum) for each group. You can give each group different or the same material. Many FAQs are framed starting with *Can I . . . ?* (*Can I bring a stroller into the museum?*) Make sure *can* is used for asking permission in some of the questions of the web page you select. Have students read the questions and answers and make up at least four new questions for the web page starting *Can I . . . ?* Follow up by asking students from

each group to read their questions aloud. You may want to write some of the questions on the board.

Requests: *Can, Could, Will, Would, Would you mind*

UNIT 13

Unit Overview

Unit 13 focuses on ways to make requests and respond to them.

- The modals *can, could, will,* and *would* are used in questions to make polite requests.
- The modals *could* and *would* make requests more polite.
- *Sure, certainly, of course,* and *no problem* are often used to reply positively to a request. To say *no,* we usually apologize and give an explanation.
- *Would you mind* plus a gerund is also used to make a polite request.

Grammar in Context (pages 144–146)

Background Note

E-mail, or electronic mail, has become a very popular method of communication in recent years. It's quicker than sending letters, and a little less personal. The style is much less formal than handwritten personal letters.

Vocabulary

pick up: to buy something

sales: the total number of products that are sold during a particular period of time

Comprehension Questions

- What does Marcia's mother ask her daughter to do? (*to drive her to the Burtons and pick up dessert at the bakery*)
- What does Marcia ask Ann to do? (*to make copies of the sales report and deliver them to her*)
- What will Marcia ask her husband to do? (*to drive her mother to the Burtons*)

Discussion Topics

- Have students discuss different methods of communication—for example, letters, e-mails, phones, cell phones, fax machines, pagers. Ask students to talk about the different ways they communicate with the different people in their lives. Encourage students to explain why they use different methods for different situations.

- Have students talk about situations in which it is particularly important to be polite when making requests. Have them also talk about situations in which politeness is not so important. Encourage students to give examples from their everyday life.

Grammar Presentation (pages 146–147)

> ## Identify the Grammar
>
> REQUESTS
> _<u>Can</u> you <u>drive</u> me to the Burtons . . . ?_
> _. . . <u>will</u> you <u>pick up</u> something special at the bakery . . . ?_
> _<u>Would</u> you please <u>photocopy</u> the monthly sales report . . . ?_
> _<u>Could</u> you <u>make</u> 25 copies?_
> _. . . <u>would you mind delivering</u> them to me . . . ?_

Grammar Charts

- Write the following examples on the board:
  Requests
  Can you drive me to the Burtons?
  Could you make 25 copies?
  Will you pick up dessert?
  Would you photocopy this report?
  Would you mind delivering it to me?
  Point to the first four examples, and ask: "How do you form requests with _can, could, will,_ and _would_?" (can/could/will/would + you + _base form of verb_)
  —Point to the last example on the board, and ask: "How do you make requests with _would you mind_?" (would you mind + -ing _form of verb_)
  —Write below the questions on the board:
  Certainly.   No, not at all.   I'm sorry, but I can't.
  —Ask the class:
  "Which questions from the board can be replied with _Certainly_?" (the first four)
  "Does _Certainly_ mean you will do what the person asked you to do?" (yes)
  "Which question can be replied with _No, not at all_?" (Would you mind delivering it to me?)
  "Does _No, not at all_ mean you will do what the person asked you to do?" (yes)
  "Why?" (because it means that you don't mind doing it)

"Which questions can be replied with _I'm sorry, but I can't_?" (all of them)
"What does this reply mean?" (that you can't do what the person asked you to do)

- To summarize, you may want to add the replies to the questions on the board:

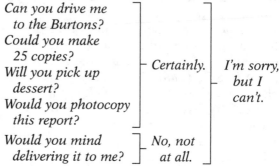

Can you drive me to the Burtons?
Could you make 25 copies?
Will you pick up dessert?
Would you photocopy this report?
] Certainly.   ] I'm sorry, but I can't.
Would you mind delivering it to me?] No, not at all.

Grammar Notes

Note 1 _(Exercises 1, 3–4)_

- Point out that requests with _could_ and _would_ are more formal and polite than requests with _can_ and _will_.
- Call on students to say typical requests they make at home or at work. (Will you answer the phone? Could you pass the salt? Can you pick up something to eat on your way home? Would you photocopy this report for me? Could you mail this package?)

→ For additional practice, see the Supplementary Activities on page 147.

Note 2 _(Exercises 1, 3–4)_

- Point out that _please_ may be placed just before the main verb or at the end of a question.
- Write the requests below on the board, and have students rate them from 1 to 4, with 4 being the most polite form.
  Would you call me after 5:00?
  Call me after 5:00.
  Can you call me after 5:00?
  Could you please call me after 5:00?

→ For additional practice, see the Supplementary Activities on page 147.

Note 3 _(Exercises 1–2, 4)_

- Write on the board:

Can		Sure.
Could	you open the door?	Certainly.
Will		Of course.
Would		No problem.

Make sure students understand that requests with _can, will, could,_ and _would_ can be replied with any of the four expressions on the board.

- Point out that only the modals *can* and *will* can be used in replies. To help clarify, write examples on the board:

Can you answer the phone?
Could you answer the phone? } Sure I can.

Will you type this letter?
Would you type this letter? } Sure I will.

- Have students practice responding rapidly to requests. Point out they can use the expressions with or without *I* plus *can* or *will* (*Sure* OR *Sure I can*). You can say: "Could you close the window?" "Can you clean the board?" "Will you lend me your dictionary?" "Would you spell that for me?"
- Point out that in English-speaking cultures, when someone cannot help with a request, an apology and a brief explanation are expected. Brainstorm with the class possible excuses to the following requests. You can ask: "Could you lend me a pen?" "Could you stay after class today?" "Would you mind giving me a ride home?" "Could you pick up a class snack on the way to class tomorrow?"

→ For additional practice, see the Supplementary Activities on page 147.

Note 4 *(Exercises 1–4)*

- Write the structure of the question on the board and point out the gerund (verb + *-ing*) after *mind*.
  Would you mind + gerund . . . ?
  Add an example and its reply:
  Would you mind calling back later? Not at all.
  Ask the class: "Does *Not at all* mean the person will call back later?" (*yes, because* Not at all *means the person doesn't mind calling back later at all*) "What should the person say if he/she can't call back later?" (*I'm sorry, I can't.*)
- Have students practice responding rapidly to different kinds of requests. You can say: "Can you take this to the post office?" "Would you please take this to the post office?" "Would you mind answering the phone for me?" "Would you please answer the phone for me?" "Would you mind giving me a ride home?" "Could you give me a ride home?"

→ For additional practice, see the Supplementary Activities on page 147.

Focused Practice (pages 148–151)

Exercise 3
file: to store papers or information in a particular order or a particular place

Exercise 4
extend: to continue for a longer period of time or make something last longer

Communication Practice (pages 152–153)

Exercise 5
(!) After reviewing answers, divide the class into two groups, A and B. Have students listen to the conversations again. Students in group A should write down the requests they hear; Students in group B should write down the replies to requests that they hear.
Have students pair up, A and B, to match the requests they wrote down with possible replies. Then ask students to role-play similar conversations using their notes as a guide.

Exercise 6
After students have completed their schedules, brainstorm the types of requests they might ask of each other (*give a ride, pick up the kids, return a book to the library, pick up some groceries, stop at the post office, buy a gift, bake a cake, prepare dinner, cancel an appointment, etc.*).

Exercise 7
- Review the first situation and the note. Point out that although the bike is not mentioned in the situation, it appears in the note. Explain that students are expected to use their own ideas when writing the notes.
- Encourage students to use the different ways of making requests they learned in this unit.
- After students have written their notes, have them exchange notes with a partner and write replies.

Further Practice
Divide the class into groups of four. Have students make polite requests of each other. The student who receives the request must either perform the action or apologize and explain why he or she is refusing.

A: Kenno, can you open the door?
B: I'm sorry. I can't get up right now. I have too many papers on my desk.
C: Andrew, could you please open the door?
D: No problem!

GRAMMAR OUT OF THE BOX......

A two-person job. Bring in home decorating magazines that include do-it-yourself sections to improve one's home. Hand out the magazines and have each student choose a remodeling or decoration project. Point out that students will need help from a friend to complete the project. Write the following questions on the board:

What are you going to remodel/redecorate?
What do you need to borrow from your friend?
What do you need to buy?
What are you going to ask your friend to get for you?
When are you going to ask your friend to come to your place to help you?
What else are you going to ask your friend to do?

Have students answer the questions in note form individually, and think about the requests they will need to make. Pairs of students take turns making requests and replying to them. The student who receives the request should either accept to help or apologize and explain why he or she is refusing.

UNIT 14 Advice: *Should, Ought to, Had better*

Unit Overview

Unit 14 focuses on ways to give and ask for advice.
- *Should* and *ought to* are used to say something is advisable.
- *Had better* is used to give strong advice. It expresses that something bad will happen if the person does not follow the advice.
- *Should* is used in questions. *Ought to* and *had better* are not normally used in questions.

Grammar in Context (pages 154–155)

Vocabulary

cyber: relating to computers, especially to the messages and information on the Internet

Comprehension Questions

- What kind of advice does the article give? *(about how to be polite when using the Internet)*

- What should you do before posting your own ideas? *(read old messages and/or FAQs)*
- Why shouldn't you use capital letters? *(because they seem like shouting)*
- Why should you count to ten before replying to a message that made you angry? *(to avoid sending a reply that can hurt someone)*
- What do emoticons show? *(the feelings of the person who is writing a message)*
- Why shouldn't you use your real name on the Internet? *(because of safety reasons)*

Discussion Topics

- Have students discuss the following questions: "Why is netiquette important?" "Which rules from the article do you follow?" "What problems might you have if you don't know or follow the rules of netiquette?" If students have had any problems when using the Internet, have them share their experiences.
- Ask students to list other rules of netiquette that could have been included in the article. Have them discuss their importance.

Grammar Presentation (pages 156–157)

Identify the Grammar

ADVICE: *SHOULD, OUGHT TO, HAD BETTER*
. . . *you should know these simple rules of netiquette.*
When should you post to a bulletin board or chat room?
Newbies shouldn't jump in right away . . .
. . . they ought to lurk a little first.
You'd better not reply right away.

Grammar Charts

- Write the following examples on the board:
Advice: *Should*
They should learn the rules of netiquette.
Should he use capital letters?
You shouldn't forget that people have feelings.
When should we post to the bulletin board?
—Have students study the examples, and ask: "How do you give advice with *should*?" (should + *base form of verb*) "Does *should* change when the pronoun changes?" (no— should *is the same for all pronouns because it is a modal*) "How do you form the negative of *should*?" (shouldn't OR should + not + *base form of verb*) "How do you form *yes/no* questions?" (should + *subject + base form of verb*) "How do you form *wh-*

questions?" (wh- *word* + should + *subject* + *base form of verb*)

—Call on a volunteer to provide the two possible short answers. (*Yes, they should. No, they shouldn't.*)

• Write the following example on the board:
  Advice: *Ought to*
  You ought to lurk a little first.

  —Ask the class: "How do you give advice with *ought to*?" (ought to + *base form of verb*) "Does *ought to* change when the pronoun changes?" (*No—*ought to *is the same for all pronouns because it is a modal.*)
  —Point out that negative statements and questions with *ought to* are not common.

• Write the following examples on the board
  Advice: *Had better*
  You'd better use a screen name.
  You'd better not reply right away.

  Have students study the examples and ask: "What does the *d* in *you'd* stand for?" (*had*) "How do you give advice with *had better*?" (had better + *base form of verb*) "How do you form the negative of *had better*?" (had better + not + *base form of verb*)
  —Point out that *had better* does not change when the pronoun changes. *Had better* is not a modal but it behaves like a modal.
  —Point out that *had better* is often contracted in everyday speech and that questions with *had better* are not common.

• Write on the board:
  You / be polite

• Have students use the cues on the board to give advice with *should, ought to,* and *had better.* (*You should be polite. You ought to be polite. You'd better be polite.*) As students say the statements, you may want to have a volunteer come to the front and write the statements on the board.

Grammar Notes

Note 1   *(Exercises 1–2, 4–5)*
• To help clarify, write on the board:
  (+) *You should remember the rules. = You ought to remember the rules.*
  (−) *You shouldn't forget the rules.*
  Make sure students understand that although *ought not to* is not common in American English, it is used in British English.
• Have students write a sentence with *shouldn't* and a sentence with *ought to* describing the responsibilities of students in an English class. (*Students shouldn't be late to class.*

Students ought to do their homework.) Have students share their ideas with the class.
• Point out that when we give advice, we often use *maybe, perhaps,* or *I think* in order to sound gentler.
• Working in pairs, have students think of an imaginary problem to share with their partners and receive advice. Ask students to soften their advice using *maybe, perhaps,* or *I think.* (Student A: *My computer got infected by a virus.* Student B: *Maybe you should update your virus protection.*)

→ For additional practice, see the Supplementary Activities on pages 147–148.

Note 2   *(Exercises 1–2, 4–5)*
• Emphasize that *had better* is used when you believe something bad will happen if the person does not follow the advice. Point out that the undesired consequence is often said, and it is introduced by *or.* Write examples on the board:
  You'd better keep your post short, or no one will read it.
  You'd better write a polite reply, or you might offend him.
• Point out that the contraction of *had better* is normally used in everyday speech. Say the following statements one by one, and have students restate them chorally using the contraction. "You had better learn the rules." "You had better stop chatting and get down to work." "You had better change your attitude."
• Point out that the negative form of *had better* is *had better not* (NOT ~~Had not better~~).
  Write the following examples on the board, and have students turn them into the negative.
  You'd better give your real name.
  You'd better use capital letters.
  You'd better reply right away.
• Write on the board:
  _____, or she'll be late.
  _____, or he'll lose his job.
  _____, or they'll get angry.
  _____, or you'll catch a cold.

  Have students work in pairs to complete the statements on the board using *had better* or *had better not.* To review, have several students read their statements aloud.

Note 3   *(Exercises 1, 3, 5)*
• Give more examples. You can say, "Should I post my opinion?" "Should I get virus protection?" "Should I tell her my password?"

- Have volunteers make up and say their own questions with *should*.

Focused Practice (pages 158–161)

Exercise 1
debate team: a group of people who discuss a subject formally so that they can make a decision or solve a problem

burn out: to work at something over a period of time to the point of becoming very tired of it

get a life: here, to enjoy life

Exercise 2
remote: a piece of equipment that you use to control a television, video, etc., from a distance

subtitles: words that translate what the actors in a foreign movie are saying that appear on the bottom of the screen

rewind: to make a tape go back to the beginning or to an earlier place

Groundhog Day: February 2, according to American stories, the first day of the year that a groundhog (a small North American animal that has thick brown fur and lives in holes in the ground) comes out of its hole. If it sees its shadow, there will be six more weeks of winter; if it does not, good weather will come early

plot: the events that form the main story of a book, movie, or play

Exercise 3
dependable: someone or something that is dependable will always do what you need or expect him, her, or it to do

Exercise 5
LOL: a written abbreviation of "laughing out loud" used by people communicating in chat rooms on the Internet to say that they are laughing at something that someone else has written

Communication Practice (pages 162–164)

Exercise 6
- Before students listen, have them look at the sentences and predict the advice the radio show host will give.
- After reviewing answers, ask students to say if they were right in their predictions.
- ⏱ Ask students if they have any other advice for buying a computer. Have them brainstorm in small groups and then share their ideas with the class.

Exercise 7
- Go over the list of topics. As a class, brainstorm other topics and write them on the board.
  dressing for work
  punctuality at work
  office schedules
  socializing after work with colleagues
  gift giving
- Before students interact, have them choose two topics from the board and add them to their list.
- Follow up by having volunteers share with the class the advice they gave. You may want to write a few statements on the board.

Exercise 8
- Point out that every student should receive advice from his/her group partners.
- After all groups have finished the discussion, ask each group to present one problem and their advice to the class. Invite the class to offer additional advice for each problem posed.

Exercise 9
- To help students with unknown vocabulary, have the class name the objects that need repairing, cleaning, or arranging. Provide any unknown words. Write a list on the board.

ceiling	*notice board*
panel	*radiator*
wallpaper	*photocopier*
window pane	*computer desk*
floor	*chair*
blackboard	*wastepaper basket*

- To help students generate ideas, ask the class what the people in the line could be complaining about. (*The man at the computer is taking too long. He is wasting time as he drinks coffee and eats snacks. The computer desk is messy. There is only one computer in the classroom.*)
- Have each pair assign a scribe. Encourage students to write as many sentences as they can think of.
- After each pair has compared their list with another pair, follow up with a class discussion about what should be done to improve the institute.

Exercise 10

- Draw the format of a formal letter on the board:

April 12, 2005
13 Apple Lane
Newtonville, MA 02166

Mr. Thompson
EFL Computer Training Institute
10 Ferry Street
Newbury, MA 01951

Dear Mr. Thompson:
(body of letter)

Sincerely,
(your signature)

- Tell students that Mr. Thompson is the owner of the institute. (Students can use another name.) Point out the date, the address of the person who is writing the letter, the address of the institute, the closing, and the signature.
- Questions to elicit vocabulary and generate ideas:
  —What should they repair?
  —What should they clean?
  —What should they put in order?
  —What new equipment should they buy?
  —What rules should there be for computer use?
  —What signs should they put up on the walls?

Further Practice

Have students discuss the following questions in small groups:
- Have you ever been on a job interview?
- Was it a good interview? Why or why not?
- What advice would you give to someone interviewing for the first time?

Follow up with a class discussion. Encourage students to add other suggestions for the job interviews, such as what to wear, how to greet and say good-bye to the interviewer, what to say and not to say, and how to follow up appropriately. Write students' ideas on the board.

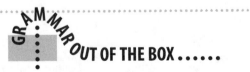

Advice columns. Bring in magazines that have advice columns. (Make sure that the topics covered are appropriate for your group. If

necessary, select questions and answers, and photocopy them for each group.) Ask students, working in small groups, to choose and discuss a problem from the advice column—or the problem in their photocopy—and the advice given by the expert. Also ask students to write down a few statements giving their own advice. Follow up by asking each group what problem they discussed. Ask students to give their opinion of the advice given by the expert and share their own advice.

Suggestions: *Let's, Could, Why don't, Why not, How about*

UNIT 15

Unit Overview

Unit 15 focuses on ways to make suggestions and ways to agree or disagree with them.
- *Let's, (Maybe) . . . could, Why don't,* and *Why not* are used to make suggestions and are followed by the base form of a verb. *How about* is also used for suggestions and is followed by a noun or gerund.
- To agree with a suggestion, we use informal expressions such as *Good idea, Great, I'd like that, OK,* or *Sure.* To disagree, we often give an explanation and make a new suggestion.

Grammar in Context (pages 165–166)

Background Note

Youth hostels are run by the International Youth Hostel Association. They offer inexpensive accommodations for travelers, and they are very popular with students. However, older people and non-students also use them.

Vocabulary

youth hostel: a place where people, especially young people who are traveling, can stay very cheaply for a short time

volcano: a mountain with a large hole at the top out of which rocks, melted rock, and ash sometimes explode

lodge: a building in the country where people can stay for a short time, especially in order to do a particular activity

lava: hot melted rock that flows from a volcano

overlook: to have a view of something from above

harbor: an area of water next to the land, where ships can stay safely

rock: to move gently, leaning from one side to the other, or to make something do this

Comprehension Questions

- Why are youth hostels a good choice for students? *(because they are cheaper than hotels and friendly people from all over the world stay in them)*
- What is special about each of the hostels on the web site? *(The lodge in Costa Rica is near a volcano in the rainforest, the hostel in Hong Kong overlooks the harbor and is near the city center, and af Chapman in Stockholm is a sailing ship.)*

Discussion Topics

- Have students discuss the advantages and disadvantages of staying at a youth hostel. If some students have stayed at youth hostels, have them share their experiences.
- Have students talk about which of the five hostels described on the website they would like/wouldn't like to stay at. Encourage students to support their views.
- Staying at a youth hostel will make your vacation cheaper. Have students discuss what else can be done to reduce the cost of a vacation.

Grammar Presentation (pages 166–168)

Identify the Grammar

SUGGESTIONS: LET'S, COULD, WHY DON'T, WHY NOT, HOW ABOUT
Let's travel!
. . . why don't you travel and stay at youth hostels?
In the evening, maybe you could watch red-hot lava . . .
Why not stay at the Jockey Club Mt. Davis Youth Hostel . . . ?
How about a room on the af Chapman . . . ?

Grammar Charts

- Write the following examples on the left side of the board:
  Suggestions: *Let's, Could, Why don't, Why not, How about*
  Let's travel.
  Maybe we could spend the night here.
  Why don't we stay at a youth hostel?
  Why doesn't she come with us?

Why not stay in a city?
How about staying near the harbor?
How about a room on the af Chapman?
—Point to the example with *Let's*, and ask: "How do you form suggestions with *let's*?" (let's + *base form of verb*)
  Write on the right side of the board:
  Let's + base form of verb
—Continue in the same way with:
  Maybe . . . could
  Why don't/doesn't
  Why not
  How about
—When you're finished, the following structures should be written on the board:
  Let's + base form of verb
  Maybe + subject + could + base form of verb
  Why + don't/doesn't + subject + base form of verb?
  Why not + base form of verb?
  How about + noun/gerund?
- Make a suggestion and have students restate it using the structures on the board. You can say, "Let's go to Scotland." Students should say, *Maybe we could go to Scotland. Why don't we go to Scotland? Why not go to Scotland? How about Scotland/going to Scotland?* As students restate your example, you may want to have volunteers come to the front and write a suggestion on the board each.

Grammar Notes

Note 1   *(Exercises 1–2, 4)*
- Point out that *maybe* is optional. Write on the board:
  Maybe we could take the train. = We could take the train.
- Have students work in pairs and imagine it is lunchtime. Ask them to decide what and/or where to eat. Ask them to write four or five suggestions using different ways to make suggestions. *(Let's eat a sandwich. Maybe we could go out for lunch. Why don't we go to Pizza Palace? Why not get takeout? How about getting Chinese takeout?)*

→ For additional practice, see the Supplementary Activities on page 148.

Note 2   *(Exercises 1–2, 4)*
- Emphasize that a suggestion with *let's* includes the speaker. Give more examples. As you speak, indicate with your hand that you are including the class and yourself in the suggestion. You can say, "Let's take a break." "Let's get a cup of coffee." "Let's look at the examples again."

- Point out that you can use *Let's not* to suggest not doing something. Give more examples. You can say, "Let's not take a break now." "Let's not waste time."

→ For additional practice, see the Supplementary Activities on page 148.

Note 3 *(Exercises 1–4)*
- Write on the board:
  Let's not go out in the rain.
  Maybe we could watch TV.
  Why don't we do it tomorrow?
  How about taking a break?
  Why not finish first?
  How about a cup of coffee?
- Elicit from students the base forms of verbs. Underline the verbs on the board as students say them. *(go, watch, do, finish)*
- Ask students what a gerund is. *(-ing form of a verb)* Ask students to say which example contains a gerund. *(How about taking a break?)* Elicit the gerund and underline it. *(taking)*
- Ask students which example contains a noun *(How about a cup of coffee?)* and follow the same procedure. Direct attention to the examples with *How about*. Point out that *about* is a preposition and that prepositions are typically followed by nouns or gerunds.

→ For additional practice, see the Supplementary Activities on page 148.

Note 4 *(Exercises 1–4)*
- Write several suggestions without punctuation on the board and have students add to it. You can write:
  Why don't you call her
  Let's leave now
  How about going to the movies
  Why not rent a video
  Maybe we could go shopping
- Point out that the intonation of statements and *wh-* questions is the same. Both fall at the end. *(Yes/no* questions, in contrast, end on a high note.)* Read the examples on the board one by one, and have students repeat them chorally.

→ For additional practice, see the Supplementary Activities on page 148.

Note 5 *(Exercises 1, 4)*
- Point out that when we disagree with a suggestion, not giving an explanation may sound impolite. Also point out that after disagreeing with a suggestion, a new suggestion is usually made.

- Have students work in pairs and take turns making suggestions and agreeing or disagreeing.

Focused Practice (pages 168–171)

Exercise 1
the races: an event at which horses are raced against each other

dim sum: Chinese food that consists mainly of a variety of small dumplings filled with vegetables, meat, or shrimp

bargain: something bought for less than its usual price

rooftop: the top surface of a building

racecourse: a track around which runners, cars, horses, etc., race

double-decker: having two floors or decks

download: to move information from one part of a computer system to another

Exercise 4
sheet: a large piece of thin cloth that you put on your bed to lie on or under

convenience: a service, piece of equipment, etc., that is useful because it saves you time or work

Internet access: the right or ability to use the Internet

Communication Practice (pages 172–173)

Exercise 5
- Before students listen to the tape, have them look over the map and practice pronouncing the names of the places so they can recognize the names while listening to the tape. (Tian Tan /tin tan/, Po Lin /boʊ lɪŋ/, Lantau /læm taʊ/)
- After reviewing answers, have students say what is special about each of the things Emily and Megan decide to do or see.
  ⏱ Have students listen to the conversation again and write down the suggestions they hear. Have students work in pairs to compare their notes. Walk around the room and clarify any doubts. Then have students role-play a similar conversation using their notes as a guide.

Exercise 6
- Go over the example. As a class, brainstorm possible responses A could give. Encourage the class to provide responses in which A agrees, and responses in which A disagrees. You may want to write students' ideas on the board.
- Follow up by asking volunteers to role-play their conversations for the class.

Exercise 7

- To ensure that all students don't select the same tourist sights, brainstorm different types of trips. *(class field trip, summer mini-vacation, winter mini-vacation, family day out, romantic weekend, athletic weekend, arts weekend, cultural tour)*
- Give the groups a time limit of 15 minutes to plan. Circulate as students plan and encourage them to use the language they learned in this unit.
- Follow up by having students share their ideas with the class. You may want to write students' ideas in note form on the board.

Exercise 8

- Go over the example and point out the suggestions.
- Encourage students to use the different ways of making suggestions they learned in this unit.
  ⏲ After students have written their letter, have them exchange letters with a partner and write replies.

Further Practice

Tell students you will give them the opportunity to decide what to do the first 15 minutes of next class. Point out that suggestions such as taking a break or not working are not valid! Have students spontaneously make suggestions about what they would like to do. *(Why don't we read a story? Maybe we could listen to a song. How about reviewing this unit? Why not play a game?)* Encourage a friendly exchange of ideas and the use of the language students learned in this unit. As students discuss, write students' ideas on the board. At the end of the discussion, have students vote for one of the suggestions on the board. Don't forget to keep your word next class!

GRAMMAR OUT OF THE BOX . . . . . .

Going out. Bring in the entertainment section of several newspapers (or several photocopies of an entertainment section). Working in small groups, give each group a newspaper page, and have students make plans for the weekend. Point out that students should use the language they learned in this unit as they make suggestions and discuss what they will do. Follow up by having a student from each group share with the class what his/her group has decided to do.

UNIT 16 Present Perfect: *Since* and *For*

Unit Overview

Unit 16 focuses on the uses of the present perfect with *since* and *for*.
- The present perfect describes something that began in the past and continues into the present (and may continue into the future).
- It is used with *since* to show when something started and with *for* to show how long a present condition has lasted.

Grammar in Context (pages 182–183)

Vocabulary

contest: a competition, usually a small one
individuality: the quality that makes someone or something different from all others
support: to provide enough money for someone to live
dual: having two of something, or two parts

Comprehension Questions

- Why did Bob Burnquist's life change when he was eleven years old? *(because he started skating and he has never stopped since then)*
- Did he turn pro soon after that? *(yes, four years later)*
- How does he support himself? *(doing his favorite sport—skateboarding)*
- What other sports does he do? *(snowboarding, surfing, mountain biking)*

Discussion Topics

- Bob Burnquist supports himself doing what he loves the most. Have students share with their partners what they love to do the most, and whether they would like to support themselves doing that. Encourage students to support their views.
- Have students discuss the advantages and disadvantages of being a professional sportsperson. Have students consider such aspects as fame, ups and downs, etc.

Grammar Presentation (pages 183–185)

Identify the Grammar

PRESENT PERFECT: *SINCE* AND *FOR*
He *hasn't stopped* since then.
Bob *has lived* in California since 1995 . . .
He's had dual citizenship (Brazil and the United States) for many years.

Grammar Charts

- Write the following examples on the board:
Present Perfect: *Since* and *For*
Bob has lived in California since 1995.
His friends have lived in Brazil for about 30 years.
  - —Have students study the examples, and ask: "How many words are needed for the present perfect?" *(two)* "How do you form the present perfect?" *(form of* have + *past participle)*
  - —Underline *since 1995* and *for about 30 years* in the examples, and ask the class: "What does *since 1995* express?" *(the moment when Bob started living in California)* "Does Bob still live in California?" *(yes)* "What does *for about 30 years* express?" *(how long Bob's friends have lived in Brazil)* "Do Bob's friends still live in Brazil?" *(yes)*
  - —Emphasize that the present perfect with *for* and *since* expresses things that began in the past and continue into the present.
  - —Erase *Bob has* and *His friends have,* and replace them with *He's* and *They've.* Point out that *have* and *has* are contracted in everyday speech—especially after pronouns. Point out that the contraction for *has* is the same as for *be: he's, she's, it's.* Use of the past participle marks the present perfect.
- Write two sets of example sentences on the board:

  Bob and Jen have not married. *Bob has not stopped since then.*
  They haven't married. *He hasn't stopped since then.*

  - —Ask the class: "How do you form the negative present perfect?" *(form of* have + not + *past participle)* "What are the contractions?" *(haven't or* hasn't + *past participle)*
- Write these questions on the board:
  Has he won any prizes?
  How long has he been a skater?
  - —Ask the class: "How do you form *yes/no* questions?" *(form of* have + *subject* + *past participle)* "How do you form *wh-* questions?" *(wh-* word + *form of* have + *subject* + *past participle)*
  - —Call on a volunteer to write on the board the two possible answers to the *yes/no* question. *(Yes, he has. No, he hasn't.)*
  - —Call on another volunteer to provide the two possible short answers for the *wh-* question. *(Since 1991. For [number of years].)*

Grammar Notes

Note 1 *(Exercises 1–2, 4–6)*
- Remind students that the present perfect with *since* and *for* expresses something that started in the past and continues into the present. To illustrate your point, draw a time line on the board with information about yourself:

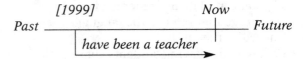

Say, "I have been a teacher since [1999]. I started being a teacher in [1999], and I'm still a teacher."
- Choose different students and ask: "How long have you studied English?" "How long have you lived here?" Personalize the questions with information you already know about your students. For example, if you know that a student owns a car, ask him/her, "How long have you had your car?" Encourage full answers.

→ For additional practice, see the Supplementary Activities on page 149.

Note 2 *(Exercises 1–2, 4–6)*
- Point out that *since* is used plus a point in time. Write more examples on the board:
since July
since spring
since I graduated
since last week
since they were born
since my parents moved here
Explain that the point in time can be expressed with a time clause. Ask students to say which examples from the board contain time clauses. *(since I graduated, since they were born, since my parents moved here)*
- Call on volunteers to say true statements about themselves using *since.* *(I have worked in a bank since 1997/since I finished school.)*

→ For additional practice, see the Supplementary Activities on page 149.

Note 3 *(Exercises 1–2, 4–6)*
- Point out that *for* is used plus a length of time. Write more examples on the board:
for three hours
for several weeks
for two months
for a year
Point out that *for* plus a length of time can express the same idea as *since* plus a point in time. Write two contrasting examples on the board:

I have lived here since 2003. = I have lived here for [insert correct number of years].

- Say statements with *since*, and have students restate them using *for*. You can say, "He has worked here since last Monday. She has lived in Tokyo since January. They have been in medical school since 2004. I have had this watch since yesterday."

→ For additional practice, see the Supplementary Activities on page 149.

Note 4 *(Exercises 1, 3–6)*
- Write two examples on the board:
  They <u>have worked</u> for a big company for several years.
  They <u>have been</u> here for two hours.
  —Ask the class: "Is *work* regular or irregular?" *(regular)* "Why?" *(because it forms the past form and the past participle by adding -ed)* "Is *be* regular or irregular?" *(irregular)* "Why?" *(because neither the past form nor the past participle are formed by adding -ed)*
- Write examples on the board:

<u>Base Form</u>	<u>Simple Past</u>	<u>Past Participle</u>
work	worked	worked
live	lived	lived
decide	decided	decided

  —Point out that the past participle of regular verbs is the same as the past form.
  —Draw a horizontal line below *decide*, and add more verbs in each column:

spend	spent	spent
meet	met	met
pay	paid	paid

  —Point out that the past participle of some irregular verbs is the same as the past form.
  —Draw another horizontal line below *pay*, and add more verbs in each column:

come	came	come
go	went	gone
give	gave	given

  —Point out that the past participle of some irregular verbs is <u>not</u> the same as the past form.
- Have students look at the article about Bob Burnquist and find regular and irregular past participles. Have students write them in two lists. Review as a class. *(regular past participles: stopped, earned, lived; irregular past participles: taken, had, been)*
- Refer students to Appendix 1 on pages A-1–A-2 for a list of irregular past participles.

→ For additional practice, see the Supplementary Activities on page 149.

Focused Practice (pages 186–190)

Exercise 1
championship: a competition to find the best player or team in a particular sport

Exercise 4
injury: physical harm or damage that is caused by an accident or attack, or a particular example of this

Exercise 5
M.A.: (Master of Arts) a university degree in a subject such as history or literature that you can get after you have your first degree

Communication Practice (pages 191–192)

Exercise 7
- Before students listen to the tape, point out that there may be more than one way to complete each sentence. To give an example, say, "*Since Monday* is the same as *for [number] days.*"
- Follow up with a brief discussion. Ask, "Is Antonio Serrano a good candidate for the job?" Encourage students to support their answers.

Exercise 8
- Brainstorm with the class several job openings that would interest them. Write a list on the board.
- Tell students that they are going to write a résumé and then interview each other for one of the jobs on the board.
- Have students choose a job and write their résumé individually. Then have them submit their résumé to you for correction.
- Before students conduct the interview, have them tell their partner the job they are interested in. Refer students to the script as they conduct their interviews.
- Once students have interviewed each other, have them complete the script using the interviews they conducted as a guide.

Exercise 9
- Elicit from the class what a résumé is (a written list and description of your education and your previous jobs, usually in chronological order with the most recent experience first)
- Go over the résumés with the class and clarify any confusion. If necessary, remind students that Ph.D. means Doctor of Philosophy, the highest university degree that can be earned.

NYC is the written abbreviation of New York City, and UCLA is the written abbreviation of University of California, Los Angeles. You may also want to point out that a publication is something that the person has written and has appeared in a magazine, journal, etc.

- After groups have finished discussing, have each group present their decision and explain their choice to the class.

Exercise 10

Questions to generate ideas and elicit vocabulary:

- How long has the person been a/an [job or profession]?
- How long has the person worked in/for [company or person]?
- How many prizes/awards has the person received since _____?
- How many books has the person written since _____?
- How many times has the person appeared on TV since _____?
- What important things has the person achieved since _____?
- How long has the person been a member of [institution]?

Further Practice

Ask students to write three statements with *since* or *for* about themselves. Give examples. You can say, "I've lived in this city since 1999. I've been a teacher since 1998. I've been married since I graduated from college." Point out that they should write each sentence on a separate slip of paper. Collect the slips, shuffle, and redistribute them. Have students read the statements and identify the person.

Up to now since then. Have students work in small groups. Bring in biographies of contemporary people from magazines or websites. Give each group a biography. Have students find in the biography things about the person's life that started in the past and continue into the present. Ask students to write at least four sentences with *since* and *for* using the information they found. You may want to write the following on the board, for students to use as a guide as they write their sentences:

He/she has	been a lived in had studied won been married to worked in/for/as liked	_____ since _____. _____ for _____.

Have students from each group report to the class on the biography they read. Point out that students should only say sentences that use the present perfect with either *since* or *for.*

UNIT 17 Present Perfect: *Already* and *Yet*

Unit Overview

Unit 17 focuses on the uses of the present perfect with *already* and *yet.*

- Affirmative present perfect statements with *already* express something that has happened before now.
- Negative present perfect statements with *yet* express something that has not happened before now.
- Present perfect questions with *yet* ask whether something has happened before now.

Grammar in Context (pages 193–194)

Vocabulary

take the plunge: to decide to do something risky, usually after delaying or worrying about it

don't panic: stay calm

handy: useful, or simple to use

take a deep breath: to breathe a lot of air into your lungs at once

Comprehension Questions

- According to the article, is giving a party a very difficult task? *(no)*
- Who is Patty Cake? *(a professional party planner)*
- Does she think giving a party requires a lot of new skills? *(no)*
- What skills do we already have? *(shopping for food, putting food on plates, introducing friends to one another)*

- What kind of help can you find on Patty Cake's website? *(free advice, handy lists to check out what you have done/haven't done)*

Discussion Topics

- Have students talk about how they feel about parties. You may want to write some questions on the board as a guide:
  Do you enjoy going to parties?
  Do you also enjoy giving parties?
  What would you rather be—the host or a guest?
- Have students imagine that they will give a party for their next birthday. Have them tell their classmates what kind of party they would give and if they would hire a party planner. Encourage students to support their views.

Grammar Presentation (pages 194–195)

Identify the Grammar

PRESENT PERFECT: *ALREADY* AND *YET*
. . . *you've already been* to several parties . . .
. . . you *haven't given* one yet.
Have you *chosen* the day *yet*?
You've already chosen the day and the time . . .
. . . you *haven't decided* on the menu *yet* . . .

Grammar Charts

- Write two contrasting sentences on the board:

Present Perfect: *Already*	Present Perfect: *Yet*
I've already sent the invitations.	I haven't decided on the menu yet.

  —Point to the first example and ask the class: "How do you form present perfect statements with *already*?" *(form of* have + already + *past participle)* "Is *already* used in affirmative or in negative statements?" *(affirmative statements)* "In what position does *already* normally go?" *(between a form of* have *and the past participle)*
  —Point to the second example and ask the class: "How do you form present perfect statements with *yet*?" *(form of* have + not + *past participle* + yet) "Is *yet* used in affirmative or in negative statements?" *(negative statements)* "In what position does *yet* normally go?" *(at the end of a clause)*
- Write on the board:
  Have you chosen the date yet?
  Has Patty Cake replied to your e-mail yet?
  —Have students study the examples, and ask: "How do you form present perfect questions with *yet*?" (*form of* have + subject + *past participle* + yet)

—Call on a student to come to the front and write the two possible short answers to the first question on the board. *(Yes, I have. No, I haven't.)* Do the same for the second question. *(Yes, she has. No, she hasn't.)*
—Point out that *yet* can also be used in negative short answers. Write on the board:
No, I haven't. = No, not yet.
No, she hasn't. = No, not yet.

Grammar Notes

Note 1   (Exercises 1–4)
- Write an example on the board and draw a time line to help clarify:
  I've already hired a party planner.

Point out that the present perfect with *already* expresses that something has happened some time before now. (Some time before now the person hired a party planner.)
- Direct attention to the Be Careful note. Point out that the simple past—not the present perfect—is used with past time expressions. To clarify, write on the board:
  Unspecified time in the past: present perfect + already
  Specific time in the past: simple past + time expression
- To illustrate the patterns on the board, write two contrasting examples:
  I've already bought the decorations.   I bought the decorations yesterday.

→ For additional practice, see the Supplementary Activities on page 149.

Note 2   (Exercises 1–4)
- Write on the board:
  have/has + already + past participle + (. . .)
  have/has + past participle + (. . .) + already
  Point out that the usual placement of *already* is between a form of *have* and the past participle. The end position is usually emphatic.
- Write on the board:
  She's sent the invitations.
  She's spoken to a party planner.
  She's decided on the menu.
  Have students read each sentence aloud twice, inserting *already* in its two possible positions.

→ For additional practice, see the Supplementary Activities on page 149.

Note 3 *(Exercises 1–4)*
- To point out the difference with *already*, give contrasting examples. You can say, "We've already finished unit 16, but we haven't finished unit 17 yet." "We've already read notes 1, 2, and 3, but we haven't read note 4 yet."
- Emphasize that the present perfect with *yet* usually indicates that something we expected to happen did not happen, and it may happen in the future.
- To practice the contrast between *already* and *yet*, write a daily schedule on the board, for example:
  Patty Cake
  7:00 gets up and eats breakfast
  8:30 takes a shower and gets dressed
  9:00 leaves home
  9:30 gets to her office
  Make statements with *already* and *yet*, and have students tell you whether they are true or false. For example:
  TEACHER: It's 7:30. Patty has already taken a shower.
  STUDENT: False.

→ For additional practice, see the Supplementary Activities on page 149.

Note 4 *(Exercises 1–4)*
- Write on the board:
  haven't/hasn't + past participle + (. . .) + yet
  haven't/hasn't + yet + past participle + (. . .)
  Point out that the usual placement of *yet* is at the end of a clause.
- Write on the board:
  I haven't chosen the day.
  I haven't done the shopping.
  I haven't bought the invitations.
  Have students read each sentence aloud twice, inserting *yet* in its two possible positions.

→ For additional practice, see the Supplementary Activities on page 149.

Note 5 *(Exercises 1–2, 4)*
To exemplify further, write two contrasting conversations on the board:

LYNN: I'm giving a party next month.
MAX: <u>Have you mailed the invitations yet?</u>
LYNN: Yes, I have.

LYNN: I'm giving a party for my birthday. I mailed the invitations this morning.
MAX: <u>Have you already mailed them?</u> Your birthday is three months away!

Have students compare the conversations and ask: "In which of the two conversations is Max

surprised?" *(in the second)* "Why?" *(because Lynn's birthday is three months away and she has already sent the invitations)*
- Refer students to Appendix 1 on pages A-1–A-2 for a list of irregular past participles.

→ For additional practice, see the Supplementary Activities on page 149.

Note 6 *(Exercises 1–2, 4)*
- Write the following questions on the board:
  Have you prepared the food yet?
  Has Luis arrived yet?
  Have they eaten yet?
- Have students answer the questions with negative short answers. Point out that for each question they should provide the three possible negative short answers. ("No, I haven't." OR "No, not yet." OR "Not yet.")
- You may want to point out that when answering questions with "yet" in the negative, "Not yet" by itself is very commonly used.

Communication Practice *(pages 198–201)*

Exercise 5
- To review answers, have students say complete sentences using *already* or *yet*. *(They've already found a place.)*

Exercise 6
- Before students interact, go over Helmut and Gisela's To Do lists, and elicit from students the past participles of the verbs on the lists. You may want to write them on the board as students say them. For example:

Base Form	Past Participle
bake	baked
put	put
mop	mopped

- To provide practice pronouncing the past participles, read them aloud, and have students repeat them chorally. You may want to leave the lists on the board for students to refer to as they interact.
  ⏲ After students have finished interacting, have them close their books and play a memory game. Call on students to say a sentence each about the things Helmut and Gisela have already done and haven't done yet.

Exercise 7
- Brainstorm with the class possible items for students to put on their lists. Write a list on the board.

buy a new computer
plan my birthday party
get a gift for Mom
take driving lessons
choose a college .
plan my vacations
save money for a car

- Then have students write their own lists individually. Point out they can use some of the ideas on the board.

Exercise 8

- Write the following column headings on the board and brainstorm with the class items for each column. Write the items on the board as students bring them up.

Things to buy	*Things to choose*	*Things to do*
soda	place	write a guest list
potato chips	date	bake the cake
flowers	time	send the invitations
balloons	music	hang the balloons/decorations
napkins	the menu	
invitations	theme for the party	borrow extra chairs
		clean the house

- As students write, have them refer to the lists on the board for ideas.

Further Practice

Have students think of a homework assignment or task at work, and ask them to write down the things they have already done and the things they haven't done yet, for example:
For geography, I must write a paragraph about a big city and include a picture.
I've already chosen the city.
I've already done a search on the Internet.
I've already selected the picture.
I haven't written the paragraph yet.
I haven't chosen a title for my paragraph yet.

GRAMMAR OUT OF THE BOX ......

The development of a project. Bring in newspapers. Have students work in small groups. Give each group a newspaper. Have students browse the newspaper in search of a project, and ask them to write four to six statements to describe the development of the project using *already* and *yet*, for example:

They are going to build a dam in India:
They have already chosen the place.
They have already told the villagers about the project.
They haven't started building the dam yet.
The villagers haven't moved somewhere else yet.

UNIT 18 **Present Perfect: Indefinite Past**

Unit Overview

Unit 18 focuses on the use of the present perfect to express what happened at an indefinite time in the past.
- The present perfect is used for repeated actions at some indefinite time in the past with adverbs like *twice, always, often,* and *many times.*
- It is used for actions in the very recent but still indefinite past with *just, recently,* and *lately.*

Grammar in Context (pages 202–203)

Vocabulary

the globe: the world

come out: if a book, movie, etc., comes out, it is available for people to buy or see

safari: a trip through the country areas of Africa in order to watch wild animals

affordable: not expensive

Comprehension Questions

- Why are people looking for new places to see and new things to do? *(because they've already traveled the globe/been to typical vacation places)*
- What is the *Travel Today* survey about? *(what people would like to do that they've never done before)*
- What did some of the people who took the survey answer? *(that they'd like to ride a camel, go hot-air ballooning, and go ice-climbing)*
- Are those activities expensive? *(yes)*
- What other less expensive activities are suggested in the article? *(walking in the woods, watching the sun set over the ocean)*

Discussion Topics

- Have students discuss their ideal vacation. Would they rather go sightseeing to traditional places or try new experiences? Encourage students to also discuss whether

they would like to do any of the activities mentioned in the article—riding a camel, hot-air ballooning, and ice climbing—and explain their views.
- Brainstorm ideas about how to have a great vacation without spending much money. List students' ideas on the board.

Grammar Presentation (pages 203–204)

Identify the Grammar

PRESENT PERFECT: INDEFINITE PAST
They've been to Rome.
They've seen the ancient pyramids of Egypt.
Travel Today has just come out . . .
. . . I've never ridden a camel.
Have you ever spent the day walking in the woods . . . ?

Grammar Charts

- Write the following example on the board:
Present Perfect: *Indefinite Past*
They've been to Rome.
  —Point to the example and ask the class: "What tense is this?" *(present perfect)* "Is the action past, present, or future?" *(past)* "Do we know exactly when the action happened?" *(no)*
  —Emphasize that the present perfect describes things that happened at an indefinite past time.
- Write two new examples on the board:
He hasn't been to Egypt.
He's never ridden a camel.
  —Have students study the examples, and ask: "What tense do we use for something that did not happen at an indefinite time in the past?" *(present perfect)* "What two ways are there to express this?" *(form of* have + not + *present perfect* OR *form of* have + never + *present perfect)*
- Write the following examples on the board:
She has just gotten back from a trip.
She has recently made a trip.
She has made a trip recently.
She has made several trips lately.
  —Have students study the examples and ask: "What adverbs can be used with the present perfect?" *(just, recently, lately)* "What do the adverbs *just, recently,* and *lately* express?" *(that the action happened in the recent past)* "Do we know exactly when the action happened?" *(no)*

—Have students look at the examples again, and ask students to find:
  - an adverb that goes between a form of *have* and the past participle OR at the end of the sentence *(recently)*
  - an adverb that goes between a form of *have* and the past participle *(just)*
  - an adverb that goes at the end of the sentence *(lately)*
- Write these questions on the board:
Have you ever climbed a mountain?
How often have you been on safari?
  —Have students study the questions and ask: "Which question seeks to find out if something happened?" *(the first)* "Which question seeks to find out if something happened several times?" *(the second)*
  —Call on a volunteer to provide the two possible short answers to the first question. *(Yes, I have. No, I haven't.)*
  —Point out that *never* can also be used in short answers. Write on the board: *No, I haven't. = No, never.*
  —Call on another student to provide an answer to the second question. *(Twice.)*

Grammar Notes

Note 1 *(Exercises 1–6)*
- Draw a time line on the board, and write an example:

I've visited the Metropolitan Museum in New York.
Point out that the present perfect expresses that something happened at an indefinite time in the past. The time is not important. What matters is the action. (Note: If necessary, point out that when the time is important, the simple past should be used.)
- Have students share with the class interesting places they've been to or interesting things they've seen. Students should use the present perfect. *(I've been to Australia. I've been to an interesting museum in Berlin. I've seen the* Mona Lisa *at the Louvre Museum.)* (Note: Make sure students don't say *I've been ~~in~~ Australia* instead of *I've been to Australia.*)

→ For additional practice, see the Supplementary Activities on pages 149–150.

Note 2 *(Exercises 1–2, 4–6)*
- Write these contrasting examples on the board.

I've | always / often / never | traveled by plane.

I've traveled by plane | once. / twice. / many times.

Point out that we use the present perfect for something that happened several times at an indefinite past time. We also use it with *never* for something that did not happen before now. Have students study the examples on the board and ask: "Where do frequency adverbs go?" *(between a form of* have *and the past participle)* "Where do adverbs like *once, twice,* or *many times* go?" *(at the end of the sentence)*

• Write on the board:
Something I've never done: _____
Something I've often done: _____
Something I've done only once: _____
Have students complete each item with notes. Working in small groups, have students take turns using their notes as a guide to talk about themselves. Point out that students should use the present perfect.

→ For additional practice, see the Supplementary Activities on pages 149–150.

Note 3 *(Exercises 1–2, 4, 6)*
• Point out that when we answer positively, we normally add more information. To answer negatively, we normally use *never*. Write a question and different possible answers on the board:

Have you ever ridden an elephant?
]
Yes, once.
Yes, I once rode an elephant in India.
No, never.
No, I've never ridden an elephant.

• Brainstorm interesting adventures or experiences. Write a list on the board, for example:
touch a snake
swim with dolphins
hunt an animal
go snorkeling
fly in a helicopter
Have students work in pairs and ask each other questions starting with "Have you ever" using the information on the board.

Note 4 *(Exercises 1–2, 4, 6)*
• Write the following sentences on the board:
a. *I've just finished packing.*
b. *We haven't lately been there.*
c. *He just booked a ticket.*
d. *She hasn't traveled lately.*
e. *They've boarded the plane just.*
f. *We've recently been on vacation.*
g. *They have met each other recently.*
h. *They recently climbed a mountain.*
To check comprehension, have students identify the correct statements. Review as a class. (Correct statements: a, c, d, f, g) Have students explain why the incorrect statements are wrong.
• Refer students to Appendix 1 on pages A-1–A-2 for a list of irregular past participles.

→ For additional practice, see the Supplementary Activities on pages 149–150.

Focused Practice (pages 205–209)

Exercise 3
parachute: a large piece of cloth that is attached to your back to make you fall slowly when you jump out of a plane

Exercise 5
souvenir: an object that you keep to remind yourself of a special occasion or a place that you have visited

Exercise 6
client: someone who pays a person or organization for a service

heights: a high position or high places

disappointed: unhappy because something you hoped for did not happen, or because something or someone was not as good as you expected

Communication Practice (pages 210–211)

Exercise 7
• Write the following list on the board:
sky diving
snow mobiling
hang gliding
shark diving
white water rafting
relaxing
To help students familiarize themselves with the vocabulary before they listen, have them match the items on the board with the pictures. Review as a class.
• To review answers, ask students to say full sentences. *(She's tried white water rafting. She has never tried sky diving.)* Have students support their choice of the best vacation for Olivia.
Working in pairs, have students take turns saying which activities in the pictures they have done/have never done.

- Encourage students to ask follow-up questions. Point out that they should use the simple past to find out more. Write an example on the board:

  A: *Have you ever climbed a mountain?*
  B: *Yes, I have.*
  A: *Where was that?*
  B: *In the Andes.*
  A: *Did you reach the top?*

- After students have finished asking one another, have volunteers choose an interesting activity a classmate has done, and share the story with the class.

Exercise 9

Some more questions to generate ideas:

- What did you like about the place(s) where you have been?
- Why would you like to go to [the place you chose that you have never been to]?
- What have you heard/read about it?
- Do you think you will ever be able to go? If so, when?
- Who would you like to go with?
- After students finish writing, have them share with the class the places they have never been to that they would like to go to. Write a list of places on the board. Is there a place that several students would like to visit?

Further Practice

Write the following chart on the board:

Something I've never done that I hope to be able to do: _____
Something I've never done that I don't think I'll ever do: _____
Something I've done that I don't want to try again: _____
Something I've done that I hope to be able to do again: _____

Have students complete the chart with information about themselves. Then have them use the present perfect to talk about the information in their chart. Encourage students to explain why they would like/wouldn't like to do the activities.

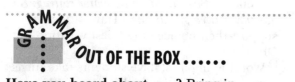

GRAMMAR OUT OF THE BOX . . . . . .

Have you heard about . . . ? Bring in magazines of science and technology. Have students work in small groups. Give each

group a different magazine. Have students browse the magazine and choose two latest developments in different fields—for example, cars, aviation, electronics, space exploration, or communications—and read about them. Ask students to write a few notes about the developments. Have each group join another group. Students from groups A and B take turns asking each other if they have ever heard about the developments they read about. (Student A: *Have you ever heard about the Five-Billion-Star Hotel?* Student B: *No. What's that?* Student A: *A prototype space hotel. It was designed by a former NASA engineer.*) If the magazines include pictures of the developments, encourage students to show the pictures to their classmates as they talk about them.

Present Perfect and Simple Past

Unit Overview

Unit 19 focuses on the comparison between the present perfect and the simple past.

- Present perfect statements with *for* express things that started in the past and continue into the present. Simple past statements with *for* express things that started and finished in the past.
- Present perfect statements express things that happened at an unspecified time in the past. Simple past statements express things that happened at a specific time in the past.
- Present perfect statements express things that happened in a period of time that is not finished. Simple past statements express things that happened in a period of time that is finished.

Grammar in Context (pages 212–213)

Background Note

Commuter marriages have become more common as women have entered professional careers. Advances in technology—specifically in the fields of transportation and communications—have made this kind of marriage possible.

Vocabulary

commuter: someone who regularly travels in order to get someplace, usually to work *back and forth:* in one direction and then in the opposite direction several times

sociologist: someone who studies societies and the behavior of people in groups

sky high: extremely high or expensive

expense: the amount of money that you spend on something

pay off: if something that you try to do pays off, it is successful after a long time

Comprehension Questions

- Why did Joe move to Los Angeles? *(because he got a great job offer there)*
- Why did Maria move to Boston? *(because her company moved there)*
- What are some of the disadvantages to this arrangement? *(infrequent visits, high cost of air flights and long-distance telephone calls)*
- What are some of the advantages to the arrangement? *(They are happy with their work, and they are much closer emotionally.)*

Discussion Topics

- In the past commuter marriages were not common. Have students discuss why they think commuter marriages have become more common. What causes them? What makes them possible?
- Have students discuss the advantages and disadvantages of commuter marriages, and what they would have done if they had been in Joe and Maria's shoes.

Grammar Presentation (pages 213–214)

Identify the Grammar

PRESENT PERFECT AND SIMPLE PAST
Joe and Maria <u>married</u> in June 2000.
They <u>lived</u> in Detroit for three years.
. . . they <u>have lived</u> apart ever since.
Last month I <u>saw</u> Joe three times . . .
. . . this month I've only <u>seen</u> him once.
. . . they <u>started</u> to communicate more by e-mail . . .

Grammar Charts

- Write two sentences on the board:

Present Perfect	Simple Past
Maria has lived in Boston for three years.	Maria lived in Detroit for three years.

Have students study the examples, and ask: "Which example describes something that has no connection with the present?" *(Maria lived in Detroit for three years.)* "What tense does it

use?" *(simple past)* "Which example describes something that continues up to the present?" *(Maria has lived in Boston for three years.)* "What tense does it use?" *(present perfect)* "From which example do we learn where Maria lives now?" *(the one that uses the present perfect)*

- Write two new contrasting sentences on the board:

Present Perfect	Simple Past
They've found new jobs.	They changed jobs in 2003.

Have students study the examples, and ask: "Which example describes something that happened at a specific time in the past?" *(They changed jobs in 2003.)* "What tense does it use?" *(simple past)* "Which example describes something that happened at an unspecified time in the past?" *(They've found new jobs.)* "What tense does it use?" *(present perfect)* "Which example focuses on <u>what</u> happened and <u>when</u> it happened?" *(the one that uses the simple past)* "Which example focuses on <u>what</u> happened only?" *(the one that uses the present perfect)*

- Write two new contrasting sentences on the board:

Present Perfect	Simple Past
This month they've seen each other twice.	Last month they saw each other once.

Have students study the examples, and ask: "Which example expresses what happened in a time period that is finished?" *(Last month they saw each other once.)* "What tense does it use?" *(simple past)* "Which example expresses what happened in a time period that is <u>not</u> finished?" *(This month they've seen each other twice.)* "What tense does it use?" *(present perfect)*

Grammar Notes

Note 1 *(Exercises 1–6)*

- Write the following sentences on the board. You may want to use true information about yourself.
  I <u>lived</u> in Brasilia for 10 years. Then I moved to São Paulo. I've <u>lived</u> here for 6 years.
  Draw a time line to clarify the information on the board.

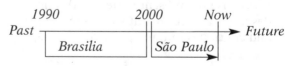

- Have students draw their own time line about the last two places where they lived, worked, or studied.

In small groups, have students look at their time line and tell their partners about themselves. Follow up by having a few volunteers share with the class information about a partner.

Note 2 *(Exercises 1–6)*
- To help clarify, say, "Use the present perfect to say <u>what</u> happened. Use the simple past to say <u>what</u> happened and <u>when</u> it happened." Point out that the present perfect is used when the specific time in the past is either not known or not important. Write on the board:
present perfect = what happened
simple past = what happened + when it happened
- Draw the following chart on the board:

	Unspecified past time	Specific past time
They married in 2000. They changed jobs in 2003. Life hasn't been easy. They've grown a lot closer.		

Have students check the correct column for each example. *(They married in 2000: Specific past time. They changed jobs in 2003: Specific past time. They've grown a lot closer: Unspecified past time. Life hasn't been easy: Unspecified past time.)*
- Have students think about an interesting experience they had. Have students write two sentences about it, one using the present perfect, and the other using the simple past plus the specific past time. Write some examples on the board:

I've been to Paris.	*I was in Paris in 2004.*
I've met Tom Cruise in person.	*I met Tom Cruise in a restaurant last month.*
I've done a parachute jump.	*I did a parachute jump when I was on vacation.*

- Point out that the present perfect can be used with *since* with a specific point in time. This is because the present perfect with *since* describes an action that started in the past and continues into the present.

Note 3 *(Exercises 1–3, 5–6)*
- To help clarify, write on the board:
present perfect + unfinished time period
simple past + finished time period
Write two contrasting examples on the board:
Today I've received twenty e-mails.
Yesterday I received ten e-mails.
- Working in pairs, have students take turns asking and answering the following questions, which you may want to write on the board:
What are some of the things you've done this month?
What are some of the things you did last month?

→ For additional practice, see the Supplementary Activities on page 150.

Focused Practice (pages 215–218)

Exercise 1
uncomfortable: not making you feel physically relaxed

Exercise 2
due: to be expected to happen or arrive at a particular time
exhausted: extremely tired
get someone down: to make someone feel unhappy

Exercise 3
catch up: to do something that needs to be done that you have not had time to do in the past
rough: a rough period of time is one when you have a lot of problems and difficulties

Exercise 4
clean shaven: a man who is clean shaven does not have a beard or mustache (hair on his face)

Exercise 6
talk show: a television show in which famous people answer questions about themselves
host: someone who introduces and talks to the guests on a television or radio show
worthwhile: if something is worthwhile, it is important or useful, or you gain something from it

Communication Practice (pages 219–221)

Exercise 7
- Before students listen, explain what a faculty member is: a teacher in a school or college, or in a particular department of a school or college.

⏱ After reviewing answers, have students listen again and write down the length of time for each item. *(1. for ten years. 2. for almost ten years. 3. for a year. 4. for six years. 5. for a year. 6. for a month.)* Then have students write a sentence for each item. Point out that students should use the present perfect for the items that are still true and the simple past for the items that happened in the past. *(1. They've been married for ten years. 2. They lived in different cities for almost ten years. 3. They've been at the same university for a year. 4. They lived in Boston for six years. 5. They've been in Austin for a year. 6. They've had a house for a month.)*

Exercise 8

- Review the boxed vocabulary. Point out that the words in the same column are synonyms.
- Go over the example. Point out the present perfect with *since* plus a point in time, and the simple past with specific past times.
- After students work in pairs, you may want to have students write five sentences.
- Have students share their statements with the class.

⏱ Follow up with a brief discussion. Ask: "Why do you think the number of marriages has decreased since 1980?" "Why do you think half of the marriages end in divorce?" "Why do you think people wait longer before getting married?" "Why do you think women usually marry at a younger age than men?"

Exercise 9

- Brainstorm with the class areas in which students have observed changes in their culture, and write a list of areas that may undergo changes on the board. For example:
  employment
  standard of living
  prices
- Have students refer to the list as they speak in small groups. Encourage students to use the present perfect, for example: *The number of new jobs has increased. The standard of living has improved. Prices have increased.*
- To follow up, have students share their ideas with the class. Ask: "What things have changed in your country?" "What things have not changed and you would like to see changed?"

Exercise 10

- Briefly go over the chart with the class. Make sure students understand the symbols (x = time; L.A. = Los Angeles).

- Go over the example. Remind students that they should use the simple past to talk about last year and the present perfect for this year so far.
- Follow up by having students share their sentences with the class.

⏱ Have students write similar records about themselves and discuss them in small groups.

Exercise 11

Questions to generate ideas and elicit vocabulary:

- Where did you live _____ years ago? Where have you lived since then?
- Who did you live with _____ years ago? Who have you lived with since then?
- What was life like _____ years ago? Has life been easy or difficult lately?
- What important changes have there been in your life?
- What important decisions have the people in your family made? Have they moved, graduated, changed jobs, married?

Further Practice

If possible, have students bring to class photographs of themselves when they were young. Mix the photographs up and put them on display for a few minutes. Have students look at the display and try to identify their classmates. Then select a picture and ask the class, "Who is this?" Once the person has been identified, have that student describe him/herself as a child and then describe how he/she has changed. (Note: If necessary, refer students to exercise 4 on page 217 to see how descriptions are given using the simple past and the present perfect.) Encourage the class to ask questions about the student's childhood.

Lifestyles. Bring in magazines that have a section about lifestyles. Have students work in small groups. Give each group a magazine. Summarize on the board the uses of the present perfect and the simple past that students learned in this unit. Ask students to find in the article examples that match (some) of the uses in the list.

1.a. Present perfect + *for:* action that continues into the present
  b. Simple past + *for:* action that started and finished in the past

2.a. Present perfect + past action at an indefinite past time

  b. Simple past + past action at a specific past time

3.a. Present perfect + time period that is not finished

  b. Simple past + time period that is finished

UNIT 20
Present Perfect Progressive and Present Perfect

Unit Overview

Unit 20 focuses on the comparison between the present perfect progressive and the present perfect.

- The present perfect progressive often shows that an action is unfinished. The present perfect often shows that an action is finished.
- The present perfect progressive is often used to talk about how long something has been happening. The present perfect is often used to talk about how much someone has done, how many things someone has done, or how many times someone has done something.
- Both the present perfect progressive and the present perfect are used with *for* or *since* for an action that started in the past and continues into the present.

Grammar in Context (pages 222–223)

Vocabulary

trunk: the very long nose of an elephant

tusk: one of the two very long teeth that stick out of an animal's mouth, for example an elephant's

life span: the average length of time that someone will live

ancestor: a member of your family (in this case the elephant family) who lived in past times

survive: to continue to live, especially after a difficult or dangerous situation

environment: the land, water, and air in which people, animals, and plants live

grassland: a large area of land covered with wild grass

extinct: an extinct plant or animal no longer exists

ivory: the hard smooth yellow-white substance from the tusk of an elephant

Comprehension Questions

- How long have elephants been living on this planet? *(for 5 million years)*

- Why are they almost extinct? *(because poachers kill them)*
- What are they killed for? *(the ivory of their tusks)*
- What action have governments taken to protect them? *(They banned the trade of ivory./ They declared that it is illegal to sell ivory.)*
- Why is the elephant population still dropping then? *(because governments have lost control of poachers)*

Discussion Topics

- Governments seem to have lost control of poachers. Have students discuss what can be done to stop poaching and save the elephant. Write students' ideas on the board in note form.
- Have students share with the class what they know about other endangered animals. Ask students to say why the animals are endangered and what is being done to save them.
- Have students discuss why it is important to protect endangered animals. What happens when a species becomes extinct?

Grammar Presentation (pages 223–225)

Identify the Grammar

PRESENT PERFECT PROGRESSIVE AND PRESENT PERFECT

Elephants and their ancestors <u>have been living</u> on this planet for 5 million years.

Scientists <u>have found</u> their bones in many places . . .

. . . elephants <u>have</u> also <u>survived</u> in many different kinds of environments . . .

. . . elephants <u>have</u> always <u>fascinated</u> humans.

. . . it <u>has been dropping</u> again.

Grammar Charts

- Write two pairs of contrasting sentences on the board:

Present Perfect Progressive	Present Perfect
Elephants have been living on this planet for years.	*They have lived in many places.*
The elephant population has been dropping again.	*It has dropped to very low levels.*

  —Have students study the examples, and ask: "How many words are needed for the present perfect?" *(two)* "How do you form the present perfect?" *(form of* have + *past participle)* "How many words are needed for

the present perfect progressive?" *(three)*
"How do you form the present perfect
progressive?" *(form of* have + been + *present
participle)*
- Write a negative present progressive
statement on the board:
  *Governments have not been taking effective
  measures to protect the elephant.*
  Have students study the example, and ask:
  "How do you form the negative present
  perfect progressive?" *(form of* have + not +
  been + *present participle)*
- Point to the second example under Present
  perfect progressive *(The elephant population
  has been dropping again.),* and ask students to
  turn it into a *yes/no* question. Have a volunteer
  write the question on the board. *(Has the
  elephant population been dropping again?)*
  —Ask the class: "How do you form *yes/no*
    questions?" *(form of* have + *subject* + been
    + *present participle)*
  —Elicit from the class the two possible short
    answers to the question on the board. *(Yes,
    it has. No, it hasn't.)* Have a student write
    them on the board.
  —Point to the first example under *Present
    perfect progressive (Elephants have been
    living on this planet for years.),* and ask
    students to turn it into a question starting
    with *How long.* Have a volunteer write the
    question on the board. *(How long have
    elephants been living on this planet?)*
  —Ask the class: "How do you form *wh-*
    questions?" (wh- *word* + *form of* have +
    subject + been + *present participle)*

Grammar Notes

Note 1   *(Exercises 1–4, 6)*
- To help clarify, write two new contrasting
  examples on the board:
  Poachers have been hunting *elephants for years.*
  Jane Owen has written *an article for* Science
    Today.
  Ask the class: "Are poachers still hunting
  elephants?" *(yes)* Write at the end of the first
  example:
  = *unfinished action*
  Then ask the class: "Is Jane Owen still writing
  the article?" *(No. She has already written it.)*
  Write at the end of the second example:
  = *finished action*
  Note: Students learned in previous units that
  the present perfect is used for actions that are
  not finished: actions that started in the past
  and continue into the present. If necessary,

clarify that for the present perfect to describe
an unfinished action it must be used with *for*
or *since.*
- Draw attention to the Be Careful note. Elicit
  non-action verbs from the students. If
  necessary, refer students to Appendix 2 on
  page A-2. Write some verbs on the board as
  students say them. Have students use some of
  the verbs in present perfect statements.
- Write on the board:
  *A book/task I started reading/doing and I
    haven't finished yet: _____*
  *A book/task I started and finished
    reading/doing: _____*
  Ask students to complete each item with
  information about themselves.
- Working in pairs, have students take turns
  using their notes as a guide to talk about
  things they have done and things they have
  been doing.
  A: I've been reading *The Bourne Identity.*
  B: Is it good?
  A: Yes. It's great!

  A: I've read a nice book by Charles Dickens.
  B: What's it called?
  A: *A Christmas Carol.*

→ For additional practice, see the Supplementary Activities on
  page 150.

Note 2   *(Exercises 1–2, 4–6)*
- To summarize, write on the board:
  <u>Present perfect progressive:</u> *how long +
    unfinished action*
  <u>Present perfect:</u> *how much, how many things,
    or how many times + finished action*
  Point to the first summary and give more
  examples: "I've been studying for three
  hours." "He's been cooking for an hour."
  "They've been working all day." Point to the
  second summary and give more examples:
  "I've talked to a lot of people." "He's called me
  twice." "I've mailed three packages."
- Write the following sentences on the board:
  a. Tom _____ (reply) to e-mails all morning
    and he still hasn't finished!
  b. Sue _____ (reply) to ten e-mails this
    morning.
  c. Tom _____ (read) Owen's book about
    elephants twice.
  d. Sue _____ (read) a book by Owen and she
    hopes to finish it tonight.
  Have students complete the sentences with
  the present perfect progressive or the present
  perfect. Have students compare answers with

a partner, and review as a class. *(a. has been replying, b. has replied, c. has read, d. has been reading)*

→ For additional practice, see the Supplementary Activities on page 150.

Note 3   *(Exercises 1–2, 4, 6)*
• Write on the board additional examples of the same meaning:
She has been working in Africa for a year. =
   She has worked in Africa for a year.
Point out that with verbs such as *live, study, teach,* and *work* plus *since* or *for* the present perfect progressive and the present perfect have the same meaning.
• Write on the board additional examples contrasting temporary with permanent actions:
She's been teaching French since she got her degree. (She hasn't always taught French. = temporary)
She's always taught Spanish. (She has taught Spanish since she started teaching. = permanent)
• Use the examples on the board to point out how the present perfect progressive can show that something is temporary and how the present perfect can show that something is permanent.
• Have students write two examples of their own, one using the present perfect progressive for something that is temporary, and the other using the present perfect for something that is permanent. Have students share their sentences with the class.

Focused Practice *(pages 225–229)*

Exercise 1
supplies: food, clothes, and things that are necessary for daily life, especially for a particular period
environmental: relating to or affecting the air, land, or water on Earth

Exercise 2
preservation: the act of keeping something unharmed or unchanged
endangered: here, that soon might not exist
spotted owl: a dark brown owl (bird that hunts at night and has large eyes and a loud call) with white spots on its chest
chairperson: someone who is in charge of a meeting or directs the work of a committee or organization
environmentalist: someone who is concerned about protecting the environment

Exercise 3
in the field: a work or study that is done in the field is done in the real world or in the area where something is happening, rather than in a classroom or laboratory

Exercise 4
tusker: an animal, in this case, an elephant, with long tusks
countless: very many
threat: someone or something that is a danger to something else, or may cause damage or harm to another person or thing
courage: the ability to be brave when you are in danger, a difficult situation, etc.

Exercise 5
fieldwork: the study of scientific or social subjects that is done outside the school or laboratory
Note: *Proboscidea, elephantidae,* and *loxodonta africana* are scientific names.

Exercise 6
roam: to walk or travel for a long time with no clear purpose

Communication Practice *(pages 229–231)*

Exercise 7
After reviewing answers, have students listen again carefully and write *Finished* or *Unfinished* next to each of the letters they circled. Then write on the board:
1. cut down
2. pack
3. rain
4. write
5. eat
Have students work in pairs and use the verbs on the board plus the present perfect or the present perfect progressive to describe each picture. Review as a class. *(1. They've cut down the tree. 2. They've packed their things. 3. It has rained. 4. She's been writing a book about elephants. 5. The elephant has been eating all morning.)*

Exercise 8
• Begin by having students brainstorm topics related to a city or town. Write students' ideas on the board, for example:
traffic
public transportation
pollution
entertainment
shopping facilities

cultural events
public works
housing

- Go over the example. Have students underline examples of the present perfect progressive and the present perfect.
- As students discuss, take down on a sheet of paper some of the present perfect progressive and present perfect statements that students make.
- After students have finished discussing, write their statements on the board.

Exercise 10
Questions to generate ideas and elicit vocabulary:
- What is the animal like?
- How long has it been living on this planet?
- Why has it become endangered?
- What have governments done to protect it?
- What projects have environmental groups been working on lately?
- How long have governments or environmental groups been taking action to save it?
- Has their action been effective?
- What has been happening recently—has the animal population been rising or dropping?

Further Practice
Address different students and ask the questions below. You can ask some of the questions to more than one student. Encourage full answers so that students practice the present perfect progressive and the present perfect.

How long have you been studying English?
How many English teachers have you had?

How long have you been reading in English?
How many books have you read in English?

How long have you been using Focus on Grammar?
How many units have you done so far?

How long have you been studying the perfect tenses?
How much have you learned about the present perfect?

Have you traveled to any English-speaking countries?
How many English-speaking countries have you visited?

Then have students write a short paragraph using the questions as a guide about their English studies.

GRAMMAR OUT OF THE BOX . . . . . .

People and nature. Bring in Internet printouts about the work of nature photographers or conservationists such as David Doubilet, Frans Lanting, or Jenny Daltry. Have students find in the printout the answers to some of the following questions:
- How long has he/she been working as a nature photographer/conservationist?
- What animals has he/she photographed?
- What animal(s) is he/she concerned about?
- Has he/she published any books?
- Has he/she given any lectures?
- What has he/she been doing lately?

UNIT 21 Nouns and Quantifiers

Unit Overview

Unit 21 focuses on the uses of nouns and quantifiers.
- Proper nouns are names of people, places, or things. Common nouns refer to people, places, and things, but are not names.
- Common nouns can be either count or non-count. Count nouns can be singular or plural, and they take singular or plural verbs. Non-count nouns have no plural forms, and they take singular verbs.
- Some quantifiers (e.g., *some, enough, a lot of*) can be used with both count nouns and non-count nouns. Some quantifiers (e.g., *few, several, many*) are only used with plural count nouns, and other quantifiers (e.g., *a little, a great deal of, much*) are only used with non-count nouns.

Grammar in Context (pages 240–241)

Background Note
Christopher Columbus (1451–1506) was an Italian-born navigator who sailed across the Atlantic and reached America in 1492. He agreed with other navigators of his day that the Earth was round and smaller than previously thought. He searched for a new route to India by sailing west and reached the Caribbean Sea.

Vocabulary

explorer: someone who travels to places that people have not visited before

ancient: happening or existing very far back in history

reed: a tall plant like grass that grows near water

pot: here, a container made of clay, used to hold food

expedition: a long and carefully organized trip, especially to a dangerous place

head: to go or make something go in a particular direction

fall apart: to separate into many pieces

civilization: a society that is well organized and developed

Comprehension Questions

- What did Heyerdahl believe? *(that Columbus was not the first explorer to discover America)*
- What kind of boat did Heyerdahl build? *(a copy of the boat pictured in ancient Egyptian paintings)*
- What did he build the boat for? *(to sail across the Atlantic and prove that ancient people could cross oceans)*
- Was his first expedition a success? *(No. The boat fell apart just before it reached Barbados.)*
- Did he try again? *(Yes. Ra II successfully crossed the Atlantic in 1970.)*

Discussion Topics

- An international group of sailors crossed the Atlantic with Heyerdahl. Have students discuss whether they would have liked to join Heyerdahl on his expedition. Encourage students to support their view.
- Who really discovered America is a mystery of history. Have students share with the class other interesting mysteries of history about which there are several theories, for example: How were the pyramids in Egypt built? Why did dinosaurs become extinct? When did the universe start?

Grammar Presentation (pages 241–243)

Identify the Grammar

NOUNS AND QUANTIFIERS

Was *Christopher Columbus* really the first *explorer* to discover the *Americas*?
He believed that ancient *people* were able to build *boats* that could cross *oceans*.
. . . dried *fish, honey, oil, some eggs* and *nuts,* and *a little* fresh *fruit.*

Grammar Charts

- Write the following example on the board:
  Proper Nouns
  Was *Columbus* the first explorer to discover *America*?
  —Have students find in the example: the name of a person *(Columbus),* the name of a place *(America)*
  —Point out that the names of people, places, and things are proper nouns. Then ask the class: "Do *Columbus* and *America* start with a small letter or a capital letter?" *(with a capital letter)*
- Write a new example sentence on the board:
  Common Nouns
  The *sailors* crossed the *ocean* on a small *boat*.
  —Have students find in the sentence: a noun that refers to people *(sailors),* a noun that refers to a thing *(boat),* a noun that refers to a place *(ocean)*
  —Point out that nouns that are not names and refer to people, places, and things are common nouns. Then ask the class: "Do common nouns start with a small letter or a capital letter?" *(with a small letter)*
- Write a new example on the board:
  They took three pots filled with honey.
  —Have students study the example, and ask: "Is it correct to say 'a pot,' 'two pots,' 'three pots'?" *(yes)* "Is it correct to say 'a honey,' 'two honeys,' 'three honeys'?" *(no)*
  —Point out that some common nouns are count nouns: they can be counted and they can be singular or plural. Other common nouns are non-count nouns: they can't be counted and they have no plural forms. Then ask: "Is *pot* count or non-count?" *(count)* "Does the example on the board use the singular or the plural form of *pot*?" *(the plural form)* "Is honey count or non-count?" *(non-count)* "Does it have a plural form?" *(no)*
- Write a new example on the board:
  They ate some eggs, some fish, a few nuts, and a little honey.
  —Have students study the example and ask: "Is *egg* count or non-count?" *(count)* "Is *fish* count or non-count?" *(non-count)* "What word comes before *fish* and *eggs* in the example?" *(some)*
  —Point out that *some* is a quantifier, and that some quantifiers can be used with both count and non-count nouns. Then ask: "Is *nut* count or non-count?" *(count)* "Is *honey* count or non-count?" *(non-count)* "What word comes before *nuts* in the example?"

(a few) "What word comes before *honey*?" *(a little)*

—Point out that *a few* and *a little* are quantifiers, and that *a few* is used with count nouns, and *a little* with non-count nouns. There are more quantifiers that are used in this way.

• To summarize, you may want to draw the following diagram on the board:

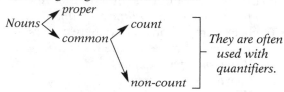

Grammar Notes

Note 1 *(Exercises 1, 4)*

• Write on the board the following column headings and one example under each:

People	Places	Months	Nationalities	Seasons
Sarah	Mexico	April	Japanese	winter

Have students say more nouns for each category. Write the nouns on the board as students say them.

• Point out that the nouns on the board are proper nouns. Then ask: "Are all proper nouns capitalized?" *(no)* "Which are not capitalized?" *(names of seasons)* Then write on the board:
Sarah traveled to Mexico in April.
Have students study the example and ask: "Do we usually use articles *(a/an/the)* before proper nouns?" *(no)*

• Working in pairs, have students combine the proper nouns on the board into sentences of their own. Ask students to write down the sentences. Remind students to capitalize proper nouns, and not to use articles before them.

• You may want to point out that seasons are often preceded by *the*. Write two contrasting examples on the board:
It's <u>winter</u>.   *We went there in* <u>the winter</u>.
Refer students to Appendix 8 on page A-5 for categories of proper nouns.

→ For additional practice, see the Supplementary Activities on page 151.

Note 2 *(Exercises 1–2, 4)*

• Write on the board the following column headings and one example under each:

People	Places	Things
student	street	car

Have students say more nouns for each category. Write the nouns on the board as students say them.

Point out that the nouns on the board are common nouns. Then ask: "Are common nouns capitalized?" *(no)*

• Write on the board a list of proper nouns that you think your students will be familiar with.
Himalayas
Amazon
New York
Robbie Williams
Africa
Ferrari
Working in pairs, have students write next to each proper noun a common noun that refers to it. (Examples: *Himalayas: mountains; Amazon: river; New York: city; Robbie Williams: singer; Africa: continent; Ferrari: car*)

• Refer students to Appendix 25 on page A-11 for spelling rules for regular plural nouns, and to Appendix 6 on page A-4 for a list of irregular plural nouns.

→ For additional practice, see the Supplementary Activities on page 151.

Note 3 *(Exercises 1–2, 4)*

• Write on the board nouns in a context:
Eight sailors crossed the ocean in 57 days on a boat named Ra II.
The boat is exhibited in a museum in Norway.
Other boats are exhibited there too.
To check comprehension, have students work in pairs and find in the sentences: singular count nouns *(ocean, boat, museum)*; plural count nouns *(sailors, days, boats)*; common nouns preceded by *a (a boat, a museum)*; common nouns preceded by *the (the ocean, the boat)*; a common noun that takes a singular verb *(The* <u>boat</u> <u>is</u> *exhibited . . .)*; a common noun that takes a plural verb *(Other* <u>boats</u> <u>are</u> *exhibited . . .)*

Note 4 *(Exercises 1–2, 4)*

• Write on the board the following column headings and one example under each:

Abstract words	Activities	Fields of study	Foods
love	dancing	biology	meat

Elicit from students more nouns for each category. Write the nouns on the board as students say them.

• Write the following sentences on the board:
I thanked her for her advices.
Heyerdahl needed a courage for his expeditions.
Reading are going to help you improve your English.
I don't like fish—they have a strong smell.
I need an information about the Egyptians.
To check comprehension, have students work in pairs to find the mistake(s) in each

sentence. To review as a class, have students explain the mistakes. (*I thanked her for her advice. Heyerdahl needed courage for his expeditions. Reading is going to help you improve your English. I don't like fish—it has a strong smell. I need (some) information about the Egyptians.*)
- Refer students to Appendix 7 on page A-4 for a list of common non-count nouns.

Note 5   (*Exercises 1, 3–4*)
- Write on the board:

Count nouns

There are | some / enough / a lot of | eggs.
There aren't any eggs.
Are there any eggs?

Non-count nouns

There is | some / enough / a lot of | honey.
There isn't any honey.
Is there any honey?

Have students look at the board and ask: "Which quantifiers can be used with both count nouns and non-count nouns?" (*some, enough, a lot of, any*) "Which quantifier is used in negative sentences and questions?" (*any*)
- You may want to point out that *enough* and *a lot of* can also be used in negative sentences and questions. *Some* can also be used in questions. Write these additional sentences on the board: *There isn't enough food. Are there enough chairs? Do you want some coffee?*

Note 6   (*Exercises 1, 3–4*)
- Write on the board:

Count nouns

There are | a few / several / many | nuts.

Non-count nouns

There is | a little / a great deal of | food.

Have students look at the board and ask: "Which quantifiers are used with count nouns?" (*a few, several, many*) "Which quantifiers are used with non-count nouns?" (*a little, a great deal of*)

- Write on the board:

There are *a few* nuts.   There is *a little* food.
                    → some ←
There are *few* nuts.   There is *little* food.
            → not enough ←

Direct attention to the examples on the board, and point out the different meanings of *a few* and *few*, and *a little* and *little*.
- To check comprehension, write two pairs of contrasting sentences on the board:
1a. They took a few supplies.
1b. They took few supplies.
2a. They had a little water.
2b. They had little water
Working in pairs, have students compare the sentences. Review as a class. (*1a. They didn't take a lot of supplies, but they probably took enough. 1b. They didn't take enough supplies. 2a. They didn't have a lot of water, but they probably had enough. 2b. They didn't have enough water.*)

Note 7   (*Exercises 1, 3–4*)
- Write on the board:

Count nouns	*Non-count nouns*
How many sandwiches are there?	How much milk is there?
There aren't many.	There isn't much.

Have students look at the examples and ask: "Which quantifier is used with count nouns?" (*many*) "Which quantifier is used with non-count nouns?" (*much*) "Can *many* and *much* be used in negative sentences and questions?" (*yes*)
- Point out that although *much* is formal in affirmative statements, it is <u>not</u> formal in negative sentences and questions.

Focused Practice (pages 244–247)

Exercise 1
navigate: to find the way to a place

Thanksgiving: a holiday in the United States and Canada in the fall when families have a large meal together to celebrate and be thankful for good health, families, etc.

Exercise 2
chilly: cold enough to make you feel uncomfortable

bother: to annoy someone, especially by interrupting what she/he is doing

Exercise 3

roaring fire: a fire that burns with a lot of flames and heat

treat: something special

beverage: a drink

blast: an enjoyable and exciting experience

inconvenience: something that causes you problems or difficulties, or the state of having problems or difficulties

campsite: a place where you can camp

Exercise 4

thunder: the loud noise that you hear during a storm, usually after a flash of lightning (a bright flash of light in the sky that happens during a storm)

Communication Practice (pages 247–248)

Exercise 5

⏱ After reviewing answers, have students use the list of ingredients to write sentences about what Jason is/isn't going to buy. Point out that they should give reasons why he is/isn't going to buy each ingredient on the list. Write two examples on the board:

Jason is going to buy some butter because they don't have much.

They have a lot of sugar, so he's not going to buy any.

- Have students compare their sentences with a partner. To review as a class, have volunteers read their sentences aloud. (Example sentences: *They have only a little oatmeal, so he's going to buy some. He's going to buy flour because there isn't enough. He's not going to buy any cornflakes because they have a lot. He's going to buy some eggs because they only have four. They have a lot of raisins, so he's not going to buy any. They don't have any chocolate chips, so he's going to buy some.*)

Exercise 6

- Go over the example and point out the quantifiers.
- After students have finished discussing in groups, have students write down what they agreed to take and explain the reasons. Students can either choose a scribe or contribute a sentence each. Encourage the use of quantifiers.
- Have all groups present their decisions and rationales to the class. (Note: Students were asked to write down what they decided to take in order to round off their discussion, but they are not meant to read their notes as they present their choices to the class.)

Exercise 7

Before students write, brainstorm with the class a list of things we normally take on a trip. Write students' ideas in two columns on the board under the headings *Count nouns* and *Non-count nouns*. Have students refer to these lists as they write.

Count nouns	*Non-count nouns*
camera	film
guidebook	suntan lotion
credit card	cash
travelers checks	local currency
sweaters	fresh water

Further Practice

Ask students to share a favorite recipe with the class. With students, brainstorm the major categories of foods. Show several examples of the way recipes are written. Discuss measurements and terms commonly used. (Remind students of the language they learned in Unit 2.) Then ask students to write their recipes on index cards, listing the ingredients and quantities first, and then describing the steps in making the recipe. Tell students to note which category of food dishes the recipe belongs in. Students may want to enter the recipes into a computer and make a class recipe book.

 GRAMMAR OUT OF THE BOX ......

More about Thor Heyerdahl. Bring in Internet printouts from *The Kon-Tiki Museum* website. This museum exhibits vessels and objects from Thor Heyerdahl's expeditions. You can print out information about the museum, Heyerdahl's expeditions, and Heyerdahl himself. Alternatively, print out information from an online encyclopedia about Thor Heyerdahl or Kon-Tiki, the raft Heyerdahl used to cross the Pacific Ocean from Peru to Polynesia to prove that South Americans could have migrated to the Pacific Islands. Hand out the material. Have students, working in small groups, read the material and find proper and common nouns and quantifiers. Ask students to choose two brief pieces of information that contain proper nouns and/or quantifiers plus common nouns to share with the class.

(Note: *Kon-Tiki* is also the name of an Academy award-winning documentary about Heyerdahl's expedition, released in 1951.)

UNIT 22 — Articles: Indefinite and Definite

Unit Overview

Unit 22 focuses on the uses of indefinite and definite articles.

- Indefinite articles *(a, an)* are used with singular count nouns that are indefinite. (A noun is indefinite if it does not refer to a specific person, place, or thing.)
- The definite article *the* is used with singular and plural count nouns and non-count nouns that are definite. (A noun is definite if it refers to a specific person, place, or thing.)
- Use no article or *some* with plural count nouns and non-count nouns that are indefinite.

Grammar in Context (pages 249–250)

Background Note

Aesop was an ancient Greek writer, about whom little is known. He is said to have lived from about 620 to 560 B.C. and to have been a slave who was then freed. He is credited for the creation of over 600 fables, most of which deal with animals. His fables are often told to children because of the valuable lessons they teach.

Vocabulary

fable: a traditional story, often about animals, that teaches a moral lesson

dove: a type of small white bird often used as a sign of peace

struggle: to move somewhere with a lot of difficulty

leftovers: food that remains at the end of a meal and is kept to be eaten later

enormous: extremely large in size

fear: (n.): the feeling that you get when you are afraid or worried that something bad will happen; (v.): to be afraid of someone because she/he is very powerful

Comprehension Questions

The Ant and the Dove
- What problem did the ant have? *(He fell into the river when he went to drink water.)*
- What did the dove do to help him? *(It picked a leaf from the tree and dropped it in the river.)*
- What problem did the dove have after that? *(A hunter came to catch birds.)*

- What did the ant do to help the dove? *(He bit the hunter's foot. The hunter shouted in pain, and the noise made the dove fly away.)*

The Town Mouse and the Country Mouse
- What did the country mouse serve the town mouse? *(the only food he had—some beans and some bread)*
- Did the town mouse enjoy the meal? *(Yes. He ate and laughed.)*
- What did the town mouse serve the country mouse? *(the leftovers of a wonderful dinner—jelly, cake, and many nice things)*
- Did the country mouse enjoy the meal? *(No. A dog ran in and they both had to run away.)*

Discussion Topics

- A fable is a story that teaches a moral lesson. Have students discuss what moral lesson is taught by each of the fables.
- Have students share other fables they know and discuss their moral lessons.

Grammar Presentation (pages 251–253)

Identify the Grammar

ARTICLES: INDEFINITE AND DEFINITE
An ant lived next to a river.
. . . the ant went to the river to drink . . .
. . . a hunter came to the river to catch birds.
. . . some beans and some bread.
The moon was shining brightly that night . . .
. . . the mice left immediately.
. . . I'd rather eat bread in peace than cake in fear.

Grammar Charts

- Write the following examples on the board:
Indefinite Articles
a dove
a river
an ant
an idea
Have students study the examples and ask: "Do you use *a* before a vowel sound or a consonant sound?" *(before a vowel sound)* — [correction] "Do you use *a* before a vowel sound or a consonant sound?" *(before a consonant sound)* "Do you use *an* before a vowel sound or a consonant sound?" *(before a vowel sound)* "What kind of nouns use *a* or *an*—count nouns or non-count nouns, singular nouns or plural nouns?" *(singular count nouns)*
- Point out that the definite article *the* is used with most nouns. To illustrate this point, write on the board:

Definite Article

the ant	*plural count noun*
the food	*singular count noun*
the mice	*non-count noun*

Have students match the examples with the nouns. Connect the items on the board with arrows as students give their answers.

- Write two example sentences on the board:

  <u>An ant</u> lived next to <u>a river</u>.

  <u>The ant</u> went to <u>the river</u> to drink.

  —Point to the first sentence and ask: "Do we know exactly what ant or river this sentence refers to?" *(no)*

  —Explain that *ant* and *river* are indefinite nouns in this sentence because they do not refer to a specific ant or a specific river. This is why the indefinite articles *an* and *a* are used before them.

  —Point to the second sentence and ask: "Do we know what ant this sentence refers to?" *(yes—the one that lives next to the river)* "Do we know what river this sentence refers to?" *(yes—the one that is near the ant's home)*

  —Explain that *ant* and *river* are definite nouns in this sentence because they refer to a specific ant and a specific river. This is why the definite article *the* is used before them.

- Write new example sentences on the board:

  The mouse ate <u>beans</u> and <u>bread</u>.

  The mouse ate <u>some beans</u> and <u>some bread</u>.

  Have students study the examples, and ask:

  —"Is *bread* in either sentence a definite or indefinite non-count noun?" *(an indefinite non-count noun)*

  —"Is *beans* in either sentence a definite or indefinite plural count noun?" *(an indefinite plural count noun)*

  —"Are *beans* and *bread* preceded by any articles in the first example?" *(No. They are used without articles.)*

  —"What comes before *beans* and *bread* in the second example?" *(some)*

  —Explain that indefinite plural count nouns or indefinite non-count nouns can be used with no article or with *some*.

- If necessary, write the following summary on the board:

  Indefinite singular count nouns ⊣ *a/an*

  Indefinite plural count nouns
  Indefinite non-count nouns ⊣ *no article or some*

  Definite singular count nouns
  Definite plural count nouns ⊣ *the*
  Definite non-count nouns

Grammar Notes

Note 1 *(Exercises 1–6)*

- To help clarify, write a new example on the board:

  "I saw <u>a hunter</u> in <u>the forest</u>," Kim told Joe.

  Have students study the example and ask:

  —"Does Kim know the hunter?" *(no)*

  —"Is she talking about a specific hunter?" *(no)*

  —"Is Kim talking about a specific forest?" *(yes, probably the one in the area)*

  —"Does Joe know what forest Kim is talking about?" *(yes)*

  —"Is *hunter* a definite or indefinite noun in the sentence on the board?" *(an indefinite noun)*

  —"Is *forest* a definite or indefinite noun?" *(a definite noun)*

Note 2 *(Exercises 1–3, 5–6)*

- To help clarify, write on the board contrasting examples of the use of *a* and *an*:

a horse	*an honest man*
a union	*an umbrella*
a European writer	*an excellent book*
a house	*an hour*

  Read the examples so that students can compare and contrast the beginning sound of each word. Then have students repeat chorally after you.

- Write on the board:

a	
an	*singular count nouns*
some	*plural count nouns*
no article	*non-count nouns*

  To check comprehension, have students connect the items with arrows, according to what can come before each type of noun. As students give their answers, connect the items on the board with arrows. *(a: singular count nouns; an: singular count nouns; some: plural count nouns and non-count nouns; no article: plural count nouns and non-count nouns)*

- Then write on the board:

_____ *apple*	_____ *bread*	_____ *oranges*
_____ *university*	_____ *story*	_____ *mouse*
_____ *island*	_____ *music*	

  Working in pairs, have students fill in the blanks with *a*, *an*, or *some*. (You may want to point out that where *some* is correct no article is also correct.) Review as a class. *(an apple, some bread, some oranges, a university, a story, a mouse, an island, some music)*

  Refer students to Appendix 7 on pages A-4–A-5 for a list of common non-count nouns.

→ For additional practice, see the Supplementary Activities on pages 151–152.

Note 3   *(Exercises 1–6)*

- To practice identification, point to different items in the classroom, and ask students to say what they are, using *a, an,* or no article as appropriate. Ask: (pointing to a window) "What's this?" *(It's a window.)* (pointing to a piece of chalk) "What's this?" *(It's chalk.)* (pointing to the posters in the classroom) "What are those?" *(They are posters.)*
- To practice generalizations, write additional examples of likes and dislikes on the board, and elicit other examples from students. *I like football but not basketball. I like opera. I don't like heavy metal.*

⏱ Have students working in pairs write their own general statements, and then share them with the class. Write two examples on the board:
Cats drink milk.
Fruit is good for your health.

→ For additional practice, see the Supplementary Activities on pages 151–152.

Note 4   *(Exercises 1–6)*

- Write the following sentences on the board:
  Can you close the window?
  The sun rises in the east.
  There are a man and a woman at the door.
    The man wants to talk to you.
  Sam, please clean the board.
  I didn't buy the right size.
  A cat and a dog were on the doormat. The cat was sleeping, and the dog was eating a bone.
  This is the only book I have.
  There are many undiscovered places in the world.
- To check comprehension, have students work in pairs and match the underlined phrases to the uses of *the* above. Review as a class. *(Can you close the window (b)? The sun (a) rises in the east (a). There are a man and a woman at the door (b). The man (c) wants to talk to you. Sam, please clean the board (b). I didn't buy the right size (d). A cat and a dog were on the doormat (b). The cat (c) was sleeping, and the dog (c) was eating a bone. This is the only book (d) I have. There are many undiscovered places in the world (c).)*

→ For additional practice, see the Supplementary Activities on pages 151–152.

Note 5   *(Exercises 1–6)*

- To summarize, write on the board:
  a/an + adj. + noun
  the + adj. + noun
  some + adj. + noun

Point to each pattern and give examples. You can say: "a wonderful dinner, the best food, some fresh bread."

- Working in pairs, have students write two examples for each pattern. Follow up by having volunteers share their examples with the class.

→ For additional practice, see the Supplementary Activities on pages 151–152.

Focused Practice (pages 253–257)

Exercise 1

I bet: said when you think something is true or likely to happen

close: said when something someone said is almost correct

Exercise 2

scholar: someone who studies and knows a lot about a particular subject

slave: someone who is owned by another person and works without pay for him/her

wisdom: good judgment and the ability to make wise decisions based on your knowledge and experience

master: a man who has authority over people or animals

convince: to make someone feel certain that something is true

disgusted: feeling or showing dislike and disapproval

greed: a strong desire to have more money, power, possessions, etc., than you need

sculptor: an artist who makes sculptures (a work of art made from stone, wood, clay, etc.)

Exercise 4

trivia: detailed facts about history, famous people, sports, etc.

Exercise 5

rule: to have the official power to control a country and its people

Exercise 6

plumber: someone whose job is to repair pipes, sinks, toilets, etc.

ape: a large monkey without a tail or with a very short tail, such as a gorilla

kidnap: to take someone away illegally and demand money for returning him/her

chase: to quickly follow someone or something in order to catch him, her, or it

Communication Practice (pages 258–261)

Exercise 7

- Before students listen, point out that both articles are possible in each context, and that students must listen carefully to distinguish the correct article.
- After students listen, have them decide which statement best describes each conversation. If necessary, have students discuss the conversations with a partner.
- To review as a class, have students support their answers.

Exercise 8

- Explain that the illustrations are the same, but each is lacking certain information.
- Go over the examples and point out the definite and indefinite articles.

Exercise 9

- Go over the example and point out the indefinite and definite articles.
- Before students write, you may want to write three clues on the board, for students to guess as a class. For example:

  It's a yellow-white substance. Hunters kill a large animal to get this substance. The animal is now in danger of extinction. (ivory)

- Circulate as students write the clues, providing help as needed. Point out that students should pay particular attention to the use of articles in their sentences.
- Have students submit their clues to you before they give their clues to another group.
- Follow up by having each group share a set of clues with the class. Have students who were not given those clues before guess the thing.

Exercise 10

- Go over the example.
- Have students discuss the list of morals in groups.
- As students discuss, have them write notes at the end of each moral about what they think it means. Also ask them to decide which moral from the list could be the moral of *"The Ant and the Dove."*
- Follow up by asking volunteers to say the meaning of a moral each.

Exercise 11

- To help students plan their ideas, draw the following diagram on the board and have students complete it with notes:

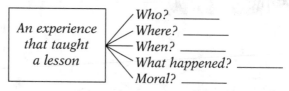

- After students have finished their first draft, have them submit it to you for correction. Correct any mistakes, but don't correct wrong articles. Just underline the article or noun in question, and have students correct the mistakes. As students revise their work, clarify any confusion.
- Follow up by having volunteers share the experience they wrote about with the class.

Further Practice

Have students work in pairs to write a short fable. Students can either invent a fable, or write a version of a fable they know. Point out that students can also write a fable that teaches a moral from the list in Exercise 10. After students have written their fable, have them go over the nouns and articles to make sure they used *a, an, the, some,* or no article, as appropriate. You may want to have a few volunteers read their fables aloud to the class.

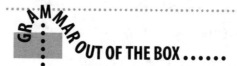

Book reviews. Have students work in small groups. Bring in book reviews from newspapers or magazines. Give each group member a book review. Have students read the review and tell their partners about the book whose review they read. (*I read a review of a suspense book called "Night Chase." It is the story of a detective who is chasing a criminal on a dark stormy night. The criminal is very dangerous and . . .*) After listening to all the reviews, students decide which book they would like to read and tell their partners about their choice. (Note: If possible, instead of reviews, bring in different kinds of books, and have students read the information on the back cover.)

UNIT 23 Adjectives and Adverbs

Unit Overview

Unit 23 focuses on the uses of adjectives and adverbs.

- Adjectives describe or give more information about nouns.
- Adverbs describe or give more information about verbs, adjectives, or other adverbs.
- Adverbs of manner describe or give more information about action verbs.
- Adverbs of frequency express how often something happens.
- Participial adjectives (adjectives ending in *-ing* or *-ed*) often describe feelings.

Grammar in Context (pages 268–269)

Vocabulary

residential: a residential area consists of private houses, with no offices or businesses

charming: very pleasing or attractive

furnished: a room, house, etc., that has furniture in it

rent: to let someone live in a place that you own in return for money

tenant: someone who lives in a house, room, etc., and pays rent to the person who owns it

Comprehension Questions

- Are the apartments in the advertisement for rent or for sale? *(for rent)*
- Where are the apartments located? *(in Wakefield House near Lake Forest Park)*
- What is the area like? *(the neighborhood is nice; the streets are safe and quiet; it's a peaceful, residential area)*
- What are the apartments like? *(They have big sunny rooms with high ceilings and modern appliances.)*
- Is the rent expensive? *(No. It's affordable.)*

Discussion Topics

- Have students discuss whether they would be interested in renting one of the apartments in the advertisement. Have students support their views.
- Have students share with their partners their views on the ideal place to live. As you get feedback from students, write a list of "ideal places" on the board.

Grammar Presentation (pages 269–271)

Identify the Grammar

ADJECTIVES AND ADVERBS
Are you looking for a <u>nice</u> neighborhood with <u>safe</u>, <u>quiet</u> streets?
Here's your place to relax <u>completely</u> . . .
We have two <u>beautifully</u> <u>furnished</u> apartments . . .
Our apartments rent <u>very</u> <u>quickly</u>.
This place is <u>absolutely</u> <u>perfect</u>.

Grammar Charts

- Write the following examples on the board:
  <u>Adjectives</u>
  Maggie lives in a residential area with safe, quiet streets.
  —Ask the class: "What is the area where Maggie lives like?" *(residential)* "What are the streets like?" *(safe and quiet)*
  —Remind students that the words that describe or give information about nouns are called adjectives.
  —Ask students to name the adjectives in the example. *(residential, safe, quiet)* Underline the adjectives as students say them. Then ask: "Do adjectives come before or after the nouns they describe?" *(before the nouns they describe)*
  —Summarize by adding the following to the example on the board:

  adj.   noun
  Maggie lives in a <u>residential</u> area with

  adj.   adj.   noun
  <u>safe</u>, <u>quiet</u> streets.

- Write the following examples on the board:
  The place is perfect.
  The people seem friendly.
  —Ask the class: "What is the place like?" *(perfect)* "What are the people like?" *(friendly)*
  —Ask students to name the adjectives in the examples. *(perfect, friendly)* Underline the adjectives in the examples as students say them. Then ask: "Do *perfect* and *friendly* come before nouns in the examples?" *(no)* "Where do they come?" *(after the verbs)*
  —Point out that adjectives can also come after *be* or other non-action verbs such as *seem* or *look*.
  —Summarize by adding the following to one of the examples on the board:

noun   adj.
The people seem friendly.

- Write the following example on the board:
  Wakefield House apartments rent quickly.
  —Ask the class: "How do Wakefield apartments rent?" *(quickly)*
  —Point out that words that give information about a verb are called adverbs.
  —Ask students to name the adverb in the example. *(quickly)* Underline *quickly.* Then ask: "Does *quickly* come before or after the verb?" *(after the verb)*
  —Summarize by adding the following to the example on the board:

  verb   adv.
  Wakefield House apartments rent quickly.

- Write below the example on the board:
  Wakefield House apartments rent very quickly.
  —Ask the class: "How quickly do Wakefield apartments rent?" *(very quickly)*
  —Point out that an adverb can also give more information about another adverb.
  —Ask students to name the two adverbs in the example. *(very quickly)* Underline both adverbs.
  —Summarize by adding the following to the example on the board:

  adv.   adv.
  Wakefield House apartments rent very quickly.

- Write a new example on the board:
  We offer two beautifully furnished apartments.
  —Ask the class: "Are the apartments furnished?" *(yes)* "How are they furnished?" *(beautifully)*
  —Point out that an adverb can also give more information about an adjective.
  —Ask students to name the adjective and the adverb in the example. *(furnished, beautifully)* Underline both words.
  —Summarize by adding the following to the example on the board:

  adv.   adj.
  We offer two beautifully furnished apartments.

Grammar Notes

Note 1   *(Exercises 1–2, 5)*
- Write new examples on the board:
  It's in a residential area.
  The rooms are sunny.
  The place seems quiet.

Have students study the examples and ask students to: "Name the adjectives." *(residential, sunny, quiet)* "Say the two possible positions of adjectives." *(before nouns or after non-action verbs)*
- Write the following incomplete sentences on the board:
  The building has ____ windows.
  It has ____ roofs.
  It has a ____ porch.
  It looks ____.
  The area seems ____.
  The trees are ____.
  To provide practice, have pairs look at the photo of Wakefield House on page 268, and ask them to complete the blanks with adjectives. Review as a class. (Possible answers: *The building has big windows. It has red roofs. It has a wide porch. It looks old. The area seems quiet. The trees are tall.*)
- Refer students to Appendix 2 on page A-2 for a list of non-action verbs.

Note 2   *(Exercises 1–3, 5)*
- Write on the board:

They repaired the building extremely quickly.	verb + adverb
The rent is surprisingly affordable.	adverb + adjective
You can walk safely through the park.	adverb + adverb

  To check comprehension, have students work in pairs to match the underlined words with the patterns. Review as a class.
  (!) Have pairs write their own examples for each pattern.

Note 3   *(Exercises 1–2, 5)*
- Point out that if a verb has no object, the adverb of manner goes right after the verb. If a verb has an object, the adverb of manner goes after the object. To illustrate your point, write two contrasting examples on the board:
  Maria sings beautifully.   *They decorated the room beautifully.*
- Write on the board:
  a. They called immediately.
  b. They called immediately the owner.
  c. They called the owner immediately.
  To check comprehension, have students working in pairs decide which statements are correct. *(a and c)* Review as a class.

Note 4   *(Exercises 1–3, 5)*
- Write the following adjectives on the board:

beautiful	nice	absolute
surprising	complete	quick

Have students change the adjectives into adverbs by adding -ly. (*beautifully, surprisingly, nicely, completely, absolutely, quickly*)
• Say the following statements, and have students give the informal equivalents: "Come quickly." "Don't walk so slowly." "Don't play the music so loudly." (*Come quick. Don't walk so slow. Don't play the music so loud.*) Refer students to Appendix 24 on page A-11 for spelling rules for forming *-ly* adverbs.

Note 5 (*Exercises 1–2, 5*)
• Write the following on the board:
She's a good dancer. She dances _____.
He's a fast runner. He runs _____.
It was hard work. We worked _____.
It was early. We arrived _____.
It was late. We arrived _____.
Working in pairs, have students underline the adjectives in the first sentences and complete the second sentences with adverbs. Review as a class. (*She's a <u>good</u> dancer. She dances well. He's a <u>fast</u> runner. He runs fast. It was <u>hard</u> work. We worked hard. It was <u>early</u>. We arrived early. It was <u>late</u>. We arrived late.*)

Note 6 (*Exercises 1–2, 5*)
• Write the following examples on the board:
She always walks to school.
She walks slowly.
She is often late.
Ask students to find in the examples: an adverb of manner (*slowly*) and two adverbs of frequency (*always, often*). Then ask: "Where does the adverb of manner come?" (*after the verb*) "Where does the adverb of frequency come?" (*before the main verb but after a form of be*)
• Refer students to Unit 1 on page 5 for a discussion of adverbs of frequency.

Note 7 (*Exercises 1–2, 4–5*)
• Write the following on the board:
INTEREST
The book is _____.
I'm _____ *in the book.*
ANNOY
He is _____ *by the smoke.*
The smoke is _____ *him.*
BORE
The movie is _____ *her.*
She is _____ *by the movie.*
Working in pairs, have students complete the sentences with a participial adjective

derived from the word in capital letters. Review as a class.
• Refer students to Appendix 11 on page A-6 for a list of participial adjectives.

→ For additional practice, see the Supplementary Activities on page 152.

Focused Practice (pages 272–274)

Exercise 2
gorgeous: very beautiful or pleasant

Exercise 3
accurate: correct in every detail

Exercise 4
mood: the way you feel at a particular time

Communication Practice (pages 274–276)

Exercise 6
• Elicit from students what the abbreviations in the ads stand for. As students name the words, make a list on the board.

bed	bedroom
ext	extension
bldg	building
nr pub transport	near public transportation
mod	modern
ba	bathroom
excel	excellent

• To review as a class, have students support their answers by saying the information the woman mentioned. (*The first ad they discuss is in Smithfield. The woman says the apartment is large, in a new building, near public transportation.*)

Exercise 7
• Go over the example with the class, and have students say the adjectives included in the example. (*disappointed, small*)
• Write the following column headings on the board:
The area   The apartment   Feelings
• Brainstorm with the class adjectives—or phrases—to describe the nouns on the board. If students need ideas, have them look at the ads in the previous exercise and the reading on page 268.
• Write students' ideas under the corresponding heading.

The area
busy
quiet
safe
peaceful
residential
near stores
near schools
near public transportation

The apartment
recently redecorated
beautifully furnished
newly painted
in excellent condition
cute and cozy
sunny and spacious
light and bright
fully equipped

Feelings
(terribly) disappointed
(extremely) confused
(absolutely) fascinated
(very) surprised
(very) pleased
(really) excited
(really) interested
satisfied

• Follow up by having each student report to the class on another classmate's home. Give the reports a time limit of one minute each.

Exercise 8

• Encourage students to list a few adjectives or adverbs plus adjectives to describe each type of housing. Point out that students can extract these adjectives from dictionary definitions or think them up on their own.
• Have students share their descriptions of the types of housing with the class. As students speak, they can use their lists as a guide.

Exercise 9

• After students have finished discussing, write the following questions on the board:
How similar are your ideal neighbors?
Is there one ideal neighbor for everyone?
• Have students from different groups report to the class on their discussion using the questions on the board as a guide.

Exercise 10

Questions to generate ideas and elicit vocabulary:

• Where is the home located?
• What is the area like?
• What is the apartment/house/room like?
• What are the neighbors like?

Further Practice
Divide the class into two teams. To alternating teams, call out an adjective or adverb and have the team come up with its opposite within fifteen seconds. If the team is unable to name an opposite, give the other team a chance to try. Each time a team successfully identifies an opposite, it wins one point. The team with the most points wins.

Classifieds. Have students work in small groups. Bring in newspaper house and/or apartment ads. Give each group a newspaper page or a photocopy containing ads. Have students read the ads and figure out the meaning of abbreviations. Then have students share with their partners which apartment or house they would be interested in buying or renting. Have students support their views.

UNIT 24 Adjectives: Comparison with *As . . . as* and *Than*

Unit Overview

Unit 24 focuses on the uses of adjectives to make comparisons—specifically comparisons with *as . . . as* and comparative adjectives with *than*.

• *As* + adjective + *as* is used to compare people, places, or things, and show how they are the same or equal.
• *Not as* + adjective + *as* is used to compare people, places, or things, and show how they are not the same or equal. Similarly, comparative adjectives + *than* show how people, places, or things are different.
• Comparative adjective + *and* + comparative adjective shows how something is increasing or decreasing.
• *The* + comparative adjective + *the* + comparative adjective shows cause and effect.

Grammar in Context (pages 277–278)

Vocabulary

chain: a group of stores, hotels, etc., that are owned by the same person or company

staff: the people who work for an organization

professional: showing that someone has been well trained and is good at his/her work

mushroom: one of several kinds of fungus with stems and round tops, some of which can be eaten, and some of which are poisonous

varied: including many different types of things

mashed potatoes: a type of potato dish in which boiled, skinned potatoes are crushed then mixed together with milk, butter, and other seasonings

garlic: a small plant like an onion with a very strong taste, used in cooking

eatery: a restaurant, especially an informal one

Comprehension Questions

- What has just opened on Main Street? *(a new Pizza Place restaurant)*
- Did Pete Tsa eat there himself? *(yes)*
- What does he say about the service? *(It was not as good as at other Pizza Place restaurants. The staff needs to become more professional.)*
- What does he say about the food? *(The pizza was incredible. It seemed bigger and better than at other Pizza Place restaurants.)*
- Is the new restaurant larger or smaller than other Pizza Place restaurants? *(It's larger.)*
- Why is it more crowded, then? *(because students love it)*
- What should you do for a quieter, more relaxed meal? *(go early)*

Discussion Topics

- Have students tell their partners about the best restaurant they have ever been to. Encourage students to briefly describe the place and explain their choice.
- Have students discuss why they would/wouldn't like to go to the restaurant in the review.

Grammar Presentation (pages 278–280)

Identify the Grammar

ADJECTIVES: COMPARISON WITH *As . . . As*
. . . the service was <u>not as good as</u> at the other Pizza Place restaurants . . .
The ingredients at the new Pizza Place are <u>as fresh as</u> you can get . . .

continued

ADJECTIVES: COMPARATIVES WITH *Than*
It seemed <u>bigger</u> and <u>better than</u> at the other six locations.
The one on Main Street is <u>larger</u> (and <u>louder</u>) <u>than</u> the others.
. . . the choices are much <u>more varied than</u> at their other restaurants.
It's also <u>more crowded</u> because students love it.

Grammar Charts

- Write the following example on the board:
  Comparison with As . . . as
  The new Pizza Place is as interesting as the other Pizza Place restaurants.
  —Have students study the example, and ask: "How can you make comparisons to show that two things are the same?" (as + *adjective* + as)
  —Write a new example on the board:
  The service is not as good as at the other locations.
  —Then ask: "How can you make comparisons to show that two things are *not* the same?" (not + as + *adjective* + as)
- Write the following example on the board:
  Comparatives with Than
  The new Pizza Place is bigger and louder than the other Pizza Place restaurants.
  —Ask students to name the two comparative adjectives in the example *(bigger, louder),* and underline them. Then ask: "How do you form the comparative of short adjectives such as *loud*?" *(short adjective + -er)* "What comes after *louder*?" (than + *the other place being compared*) "What spelling change is there in *bigger*?" *(the final g is doubled to form the comparative)*
  —Point out that spelling changes are sometimes necessary to form the comparative of short adjectives. Write additional examples on the board:
  busy—busier
  hot—hotter
- Write new examples on the board:
  At the new Pizza Place the choices are more varied than at the other locations.
  The new Pizza Place is less crowded before 1:00 P.M.
  Ask students to name the comparative adjectives in the examples *(more varied, less crowded)* and underline them. Then ask: "How do you form the comparative of long adjectives such as *varied* or *crowded*?" (more OR less + *adjective*)

• Write a new example on the board:
At the New Pizza Place the pizza is better than at other locations.
  —Ask students to name the comparative adjective in the example *(better)* and underline it. Then ask: "What is *better* the comparative of?" *(good)*
  —Point out that some adjectives such as *good* have irregular comparative forms. Write a new example on the board: *bad—worse*

Grammar Notes

Note 1   *(Exercises 1–2, 5)*
• Write the following example on the board:
<u>Comparison with As . . . as</u>
The new Pizza Place is as good as the one on Knight Street.
Have students study the example, and ask: "Is the restaurant on Knight Street good?" *(yes)* "Is the new Pizza Place equally good?" *(yes)* Insert *just* between *is* and *as.* Then ask: "Is the comparison weaker or stronger now?" *(stronger)*
To summarize, write on the board:
A is (just) as good as B. = A and B are equally good.
• Write a new example on the board:
The new Pizza Place is not as quiet as the one on Knight Street.
Then ask: "Is the Pizza Place on Knight Street quiet?" *(yes)* "Is the new Pizza Place equally quiet?" *(no)*
• To summarize, write on the board:
A is not as quiet as B. = A and B are <u>not</u> equally quiet.
• Write on the board:

BILL: *Did you hear that a new Pizza Place opened on Main Street last week?*

PAM: *Yes. But I prefer the one on Knight Street. It isn't as crowded.*

Have students study the conversation, and ask: "What is Pam comparing?" *(the new Pizza Place on Main Street with the one on Knight Street)* "Why doesn't Pam mention the Pizza Place on Main Street?" *(Because it isn't necessary. The context makes it clear that she is comparing the Pizza Place on Knight Street with the one on Main Street.)*
• Underline *It isn't as crowded* in the conversation. Call on a student to provide the full version of the comparison. *(It isn't as crowded as the new Pizza Place.)*

Note 2   *(Exercises 1, 3, 5)*
• Write the following example on the board:
<u>Comparatives with Than</u>
At the new Pizza Place the choices are more varied than at the other locations.
Have students study the example, and ask: "Are the choices varied at the new Pizza Place?" *(yes)* "Are the choices equally varied at the other locations?" *(no)*
• To summarize, write on the board:
A is more varied than B. = A and B are <u>not</u> equally varied.

Note 3   *(Exercises 1, 3, 5)*
• Write on the board more examples for each category, and clarify any confusion:
Short adjectives that use –er:
one-syllable adjectives: cheap—cheaper
two-syllable adjectives ending in -y: easy—easier
<u>*Spelling changes*</u>:
Adjectives ending in -e: only add -r (large—larger)
Adjectives ending in -y: change y to i (pretty—prettier)
Adjectives ending in consonant + vowel + consonant: double final consonant (thin—thinner)
<u>*Irregular comparative forms:*</u>
little—less
far—farther/further
<u>*Long adjectives that use less/more:*</u>
crowded—more/less crowded
varied—more/less varied
<u>*adjectives that can use either –er or more*</u>
lovely—lovelier, more lovely
cruel—crueler, more cruel
• Refer students to Appendix 23 on page A-11 for spelling rules for the comparative form of adjectives. Refer students to Appendix 10 on page A-6 for a list of irregular comparative adjectives.
• Refer students to Appendix 9 on page A-5 for a list of adjectives that use both forms of the comparative.

→ For additional practice, see the Supplementary Activities on page 152.

Note 4   *(Exercises 1, 3, 5)*
• Write on the board:

BILL: *Let's have the one with chicken. It's more interesting than the traditional pizza.*

PAM: *But it's also more expensive.*

Then ask: "What are Bill and Pam comparing?" *(a pizza with chicken with a traditional pizza)* "Why doesn't Pam mention the traditional pizza?" *(Because it is not* necessary. The context makes it clear that she is comparing the pizza with chicken with the traditional pizza.)

- Underline *It's also more expensive* in the conversation. Call on a student to provide the full version of the comparison. *(It's also more expensive than the traditional pizza.)*
- Have students work in pairs to create simple conversations comparing the new Pizza Place with the other Pizza Place restaurants. For example:

  A: *The new Pizza Place is more crowded than the other locations.*

  B: *Yes, but the pizza is better.*

Note 5 *(Exercises 1, 3, 5)*
- Write the following examples on the board:

  At Pizza Place the service is worse than at Crown Pizza. (not as . . . as)
  The pizzas at Crown Pizza are not as interesting as the ones at Pizza Place. (more)
  Crown Pizza is not as expensive as Pizza Place. (less)

  Working in pairs, have students restate the sentences on the board using the words in parentheses. Review as a class. *(At Pizza Place the service is not as good as at Crown Pizza. The pizzas at Pizza Place are more interesting than the ones at Crown Pizza. Crown Pizza is less expensive than Pizza Place.)*
- Write on the board:

  Pizza Place is <u>less quiet</u> than Crown Pizza.
  Pizza Place is <u>not as quiet as</u> Crown Pizza.

  Have students say which way of comparing is more common with short adjectives such as *quiet. (not as quiet as)*

Note 6 *(Exercises 1, 4, 5)*
- Write on the board:

  At Crown Pizza, the menu is getting more and more varied.
  Prices are getting lower and lower.
  The staff is becoming less and less professional.

  To check comprehension, ask: "Is variety increasing or decreasing at Crown Pizza?" *(increasing)* "Are prices increasing or decreasing?" *(decreasing)* "Is the quality of the service getting better or worse?" *(worse)*
- Write on the board:

  The pizza is worse each day.
  The waiters are more professional each day.
  The place is less crowded each day.

  To provide practice, have students work in pairs to restate each statement repeating a comparative adjective. Review as a class. *(The pizza is getting worse and worse. The waiters*

are becoming more and more professional. The place is getting less and less crowded.)

Note 7 *(Exercises 1, 4, 5)*
- Write the following examples on the board:
  The better the pizza, the higher the price.
  The fresher, the better.
  Point out that the nouns are given in the first example because the comparative adjectives *better* and *higher* give information about different things: the pizza and the prize. Point out that the nouns are left out in the second example because both adjectives give information about the same thing: the ingredients.
- Working in pairs, have students create their own statement using two comparative adjectives. Have volunteers share their statements with the class.

Focused Practice (pages 281–284)

Exercise 1
calorie: a unit measuring the amount of energy a particular food can produce

Exercise 2
serving: an amount of food that is enough for one person

Exercise 3
take-out menu: a list of the food that is available for you to buy at a restaurant and eat somewhere else

broccoli: a green vegetable with thick groups of small dark-green flower-like parts

beef: meat from a cow

sour: having an acid taste, like the taste of lemon

shrimp: a small curved sea animal that has ten legs and a soft shell, or the meat from this animal

pork: the meat from pigs

scallion: a young onion with a small round end and a long green stem

steamed: cooked using steam (the gas that water produces when it is boiled)

scallop: a small sea animal that has a hard flat shell, or the meat from this animal

hot: food that tastes hot or has a burning taste

spicy: food that is spicy contains a lot of spices (a powder or seed taken from plants that is put into food to give it a special taste)

Exercise 5
street vendor: someone who sells things in the street

muffin: a small, slightly sweet type of bread that often has fruit in it

Communication Practice (pages 284–288)

Exercise 6
- Books closed. Ask the class: "Do you comparison-shop for food? What do you compare?"
  Write students' ideas on the board.
  brands   *ingredients*
  prices   *number of servings*
  nutrition information   *expiration dates*
- After reviewing answers, ask students which brand of pizza the couple decided to buy. *(Angela's)*

Exercise 7
- Go over the adjectives in the box, and clarify the meaning of any of the words.
- Have students look at the pizza toppings. Encourage them to use the pictures to figure out the meaning of unknown words, and answer any questions students might have. Students might need help with the following words: *ground beef* (meat that has been cut into very small pieces), *jalapeño pepper* (a small very hot green pepper, used especially in Mexican food), *feta cheese* (a white cheese from Greece made from sheep's milk or goat's milk), *bean curd* (a soft white food, like cheese, that is made from soy beans)

Exercise 8
- To make sure students understand the types of food offered on a menu *(Soups and Appetizers/Starters, Entrees, Salads and Side Dishes, Desserts, Beverages)*, elicit from the class an example of each type.
- Brainstorm and write on the board a list of adjectives to discuss food. If necessary, have students look back at the unit and scan it for adjectives of this kind, for example:
  interesting   *fresh*   *hot*
  good   *flavorful*   *sweet*
  tasty   *salty*   *healthy*
  spicy   *nutritious* *expensive*
  cheap   *delicious*   *traditional*
  unusual   *filling*   *international*
- After working in groups, have students from different groups tell the class the name of their restaurant and what there is on the menu.
- Follow up by asking random students which restaurant they would like to go to and what they would like to eat there.

Exercise 9
- Go over the adjectives describing quality in the charts, and explain the meaning of any words. Students might need help with the

following words: *smooth* (a liquid mixture that is smooth is thick but has no big pieces in it), *chunky* (chunky food has large pieces in it), *flavorful* (having a strong pleasant taste), *fattening* (likely to make you fat), *nutritious* (food that is nutritious has a lot of substances that your body needs to stay healthy and grow).
- Before students work in pairs, have them say the adjectives from the list that can use *-er*. *(smooth, thick, chunky, sweet, salty, spicy)*
- Follow up by having a few volunteers tell the class which spaghetti sauce they would buy. Have students explain their choice.

Exercise 10
Questions to generate ideas and elicit vocabulary:
- What country would you like to compare your country's food with?
- What is food like in your country? What is food like in the other country? Which is more varied, spicier, healthier? Which is more flavorful?
- What's the name of a typical dish in your country? What does it consist of?
- What's the name of a typical dish in the other country? What does it consist of?
- Which food do you prefer—the one in your country or the one in the other country? Why?

Further Practice
Have students brainstorm different types of restaurants. For example: *fast food, sandwich or sub shops, fine dining, pizzerias, bars, ethnic restaurants.* Have pairs of students choose one type of restaurant to review. Have each partner choose a different restaurant within that category and review it according to the following criteria: value, quality of food, service, and location. Have partners compare their reviews and then report their findings to the class.

GRAMMAR OUT OF THE BOX . . . . . .

Food packaging. Bring in empty food containers such as boxes or cartons. Have students work in small groups. Give each group a few containers. If possible, give each group containers of the same food from different brands. Have students read the information on the container and compare the food(s) and the information on the container. If you don't have access to containers in English, print out information and/or nutrition facts from websites of companies that produce food. Follow up by having students report to the class on the food(s) they discussed.

UNIT 25 Adjectives: Superlatives

Unit Overview

Unit 25 focuses on the use of superlative adjectives to make comparisons.
• Superlative adjectives are used to compare one person, place, or thing with other people, places, or things in a group.
• Superlative adjectives are often used with words or expressions such as *in* and *of*, *one of* and *some of*, *second*, *third*, etc., and *ever* plus the present perfect (*the tallest tower in town, one of the tallest towers in the world, the second tallest tower in the world, the tallest tower I have ever visited*).

Grammar in Context (pages 289–290)

Background Note

The Toronto Transit Commission (TTC) operates the system of subways, buses, and streetcars that constitutes the second largest public transportation system in North America. (The largest is in New York.) In Toronto there are three subway lines, 161 bus routes, and eleven streetcar routes which operate in the downtown area. Many of the streetcar routes date from World War II.

Vocabulary

superlative: excellent

feature: an important, interesting, or typical part of something

Comprehension Questions

• Is Toronto the capital of Canada? *(No. It's the capital of the province of Ontario.)*
• Is Toronto larger than the capital of Canada? *(yes)*
• How do you know? *(because the brochure says Toronto is the largest city in Canada)*
• What proves that Toronto is a multicultural city? *(the fact that 100 languages are spoken there)*

• What makes it easy to get around in Toronto? *(its large public transportation system)*
• Is Toronto the safest city in the world? *(No. It's the safest on the continent/in America.)*
• What makes Toronto an exciting place to visit? *(its many unique features)*

Discussion Topics

• Have students tell their partners about a big city they have been to. Encourage students to describe the features that make the city an interesting place to visit.
• Have students discuss why they would/ wouldn't like to visit Toronto. Encourage students to share with their partners other information they might know about this city.

Grammar Presentation (pages 290–291)

Identify the Grammar

ADJECTIVES: SUPERLATIVES
Toronto is also the largest city in Canada.
Toronto is also one of the easiest towns to get around.
It has the second largest public transportation system in North America.
It is also the safest city on the continent . . .
All of these features, and many more, make Toronto one of the most exciting cities in the world.

Grammar Charts

• Write the following examples on the board:
Adjectives: Superlatives
In Toronto you can visit the tallest tower in the world.
Toronto is the biggest city in Canada.
Toronto is one of the easiest towns to get around.
—Ask students to name the superlative adjectives in the examples. *(the tallest, the biggest, the easiest)* Underline them as students say them.
—Then ask: "How do you form the superlative of short adjectives such as *tall*?" (the + *adjective* + -est) "What spelling change is there in *bigger*?" *(the final g is doubled to form the superlative)* "What spelling change is there in *easiest*?" *(the -y in easy changes to i)*
—Point out that spelling changes (as with forming the comparative) are sometimes necessary to form the superlative of short adjectives.

- Write new examples on the board:
  Toronto is one of the most exciting cities in the world.
  It is the least dangerous city on the continent.
  —Ask students to name the superlative adjectives in the examples. *(the most exciting, the least dangerous)* Underline them as students say them.
  —Then ask: "How do you form the superlative of long adjectives such as *exciting* or *dangerous*?" (the most OR the least + *adjective*)
- Write a new example on the board:
  Toronto has the second best public transportation system in North America.
  —Ask students to name the superlative adjective in the example *(best)* and underline it.
  —Then ask: "What is *best* the superlative of?" *(good)*
  —Point out that some adjectives such as *best* have irregular superlative forms. (These adjectives also have irregular comparative forms.)
- To summarize, write on the board:

Adjective	Comparative	Superlative
good	better	best
bad	worse	worst

Grammar Notes

Note 1 *(Exercises 1–5)*
- Write the following example on the board:
  <u>Adjectives: Superlatives</u>
  Toronto is the largest city in Canada.
  Have students study the example, and ask: "Is Toronto a large city?" *(yes)* "What is Toronto being compared with in the example?" *(other cities in Canada)* "Are other Canadian cities larger than Toronto?" *(No. Toronto is the largest of all.)*
- Point out that the superlative compares one person, place, or thing with other persons, places, or things in a group. In the example, the superlative compares Toronto with other cities in Canada.
- Emphasize that the superlative compares three or more things, and that it should not be used to compare only two things. Write two contrasting examples on the board:
  Toronto is <u>larger than</u> Montreal. (comparison of two cities)
  Toronto is <u>the largest</u> city in Canada. (comparison of more than two cities)

- Draw the following chart on the board:

My country
Largest city: _____
Tallest building: _____
Busiest area: _____
Most spectacular sight: _____

- Have students work in pairs to complete the chart with notes and use it as a guide to make sentences using the superlative. Follow up by calling on volunteers to read their sentences aloud.

Note 2 *(Exercises 1–5)*
- Write on the board more examples for each category, and clarify any confusion the students might have:
  <u>Short adjectives that use -*est*:</u>
  one-syllable adjectives: cheap—the cheapest
  two-syllable adjectives ending in -*y*: easy—the easiest
  <u>Spelling changes:</u>
  Adjectives ending in -*e*: only add -*r* (large—the largest)
  Adjectives ending in -*y*: change *y* to *i* (pretty—the prettiest)
  Adjectives ending in consonant + vowel + consonant: double final consonant (hot—the hottest)
  <u>Irregular superlative forms:</u>
  little—the least
  far—the farthest/furthest
  <u>Long adjectives that use *the most/the least*:</u>
  peaceful—the most/least peaceful
  multicultural—the most/the least multicultural

  <u>Adjectives that can use either -*est* or *the most*</u>
  lovely—the loveliest, the most lovely
  cruel—the cruelest, the most cruel
- Refer students to Appendices 9 and 10 on pages A-5–A-6, and have them choose six adjectives at random. Have them write down the adjectives on a slip of paper and then exchange lists with a partner. Students should write the superlative forms of the adjectives on the list. After discussing answers in pairs, students look back at the appendices to check their answers.

Note 3 *(Exercises 1, 3–5)*
- Write additional examples on the board:
  It's one of the safest cities.
  It's the safest city I've ever been to.
  It's the safest city in the country.
  It's the second safest city.

Working in pairs, have students find and underline in each example the words or expressions the superlative is used with. (*It's* <u>one of</u> *the safest cities. It's the safest city I've* <u>ever been</u> *to. It's the safest city* <u>in the country</u>*. It's the* <u>second</u> *safest city.*)

- Write the following incomplete sentences on the board:

  _____ is one of the smallest _____.
  _____ is the second largest _____.
  _____ is the _____ I've ever been to.
  _____ is the _____ in the world.

  Have students complete the sentences individually, and then share their sentences with a partner. Follow up by calling on volunteers to read a sentence aloud each.

→ For additional practice, see the Supplementary Activities on pages 152–153.

Focused Practice (pages 292–294)

Exercise 1
freestanding: standing alone without being fastened to a frame, wall, or other support

outing: a short enjoyable trip for a group of people

Exercise 2
average: calculated by adding several quantities and then dividing this by the total number of quantities

Exercise 3
recognize: to know someone or something because you have seen, heard, experienced, or learned about them before

reception: the quality of the sound of your radio or the picture of your television

staircase: a set of stairs inside a building, and the structure that supports it

Communication Practice (pages 295–296)

Exercise 6
- Before students listen, point out that the answers are not given in the order in which the items appear in the chart.
- To review answers have students say full sentences. (*Westin Harbour Castle has the best view of the three.*)
- After reviewing answers, ask students which hotel May and Dan decided to stay at. (*the Delta Chelsea*) Then have students explain why they decided to stay there.
- Follow up by asking students which of the three hotels they would like to stay at if they

had the chance to visit Toronto. Have students explain their choice.

Exercise 7
- Before students work in groups, as a class, brainstorm and write on the board aspects to discuss about a city, for example:

getting around	entertainment
safety	parks and gardens
restaurants	historic buildings
hotels	museums and galleries
shopping	the people
nightlife	other attractions (zoos, sports)

- Follow up by having volunteers report to the class on the cities they discussed.

Exercise 8
- As students discuss in groups, encourage them to ask follow-up questions to find out more.
- Follow up by calling on students to report to the class on one interesting experience someone in their group had.

Exercise 10
Questions to generate ideas and elicit vocabulary:
- What's the most famous tourist attraction?
- What are the best historic buildings and areas?
- Where can you eat the best food?
- What's the most convenient way to get around?
- Where can you eat the most relaxed meal?
- Where can you find the friendliest atmosphere?
- What's the most interesting tour?
- Where can you get the best views?
- What's the most beautiful park?
- What's the most convenient place to shop?
- Where can you get the best bargains?

Further Practice
In small groups, have students create a general-knowledge quiz of six to eight questions. Point out that students should use the superlative in all of their questions, and that they should know the answers to all of them. (*What's the fastest animal in the world? What's the longest river in the world? What's the oldest building in London?*) Have students submit their questions to you for correction. Then have groups exchange quizzes and answer the questions. Ask students how well they did. Follow up by having students report to the class on some of the questions they answered.

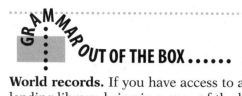

GRAMMAR OUT OF THE BOX ......

World records. If you have access to a lending library, bring in a copy of the book *Guinness World Records* or printouts from different sections of its website (http://www.guinnessworldrecords.com). Working in small groups, have students browse the book—or read the printouts—and write notes about world records using the superlative. (If students use the book, have each group choose a different topic to research—for example, travel and transportation, the natural world, or arts and media.) Then have a student from each group report to the class on their findings. [Example: *The East Japan Railway Company is the busiest railway in the world. It carries over 16 million passengers per day. On May 18, 1990, the French train TGV recorded the fastest speed on a railroad—515.3 km/h (320.2 mph).*]

Adverbs: *As . . . as,* Comparatives, Superlatives

UNIT 26

Unit Overview

Unit 26 focuses on the uses of adverbs to make comparisons with *as . . . as,* comparative adverbs with *than,* and superlative adverbs.

- *As* + adverb + *as* is used to compare actions and show how they are similar.
- *Not as* + adverb + *as* is used to compare actions and show how they are not the same or equal. Similarly, comparative adverbs + *than* show how the actions of two people or things are different.
- Superlative adverbs are used to compare one action with the actions of other people or things in a group.
- Comparative adverb + *and* + comparative adverb shows how something is increasing or decreasing.
- *The* + comparative adverb + *the* + comparative adverb shows cause and effect.

Grammar in Context (pages 297–298)

Background Note

The Los Angeles Sparks and the Detroit Shock are two women's professional basketball teams in the United States. Both teams are in the WNBA, a league of professional basketball. The Sparks wear purple and gold uniforms; the Shock wear black, teal, red, yellow, and metallic silver.

Vocabulary

halftime: a period of rest between two parts of a game such as football or basketball

aggressively: showing determination to succeed

battle: to compete with another team, often a very good team

cheer: to shout approval, encouragement, etc.

court: an area made for playing some type of sports such as tennis or basketball

score: (n.) the number of points that a person or team wins in a game, competition, or test; (v.) to win or earn points in a game, competition, or test

intensely: done in a way that shows strong feelings or opinions

consistently: always done, performed in the same way

defense: the act of preventing the other team from scoring points

block: to prevent the other person or team from scoring points

Comprehension Questions

- What two teams are playing? *(the Detroit Shock and the Los Angeles Sparks)*
- Who is winning? *(the Sparks)*
- Are the Shock playing badly? *(No. They scored almost as frequently as the Sparks in the first half.)*
- Which two players have scored the most of their teams? *(Ruth Riley from the Shock and Tamecka Dixon from the Sparks)*
- Why can't the sports commentators predict a winner? *(because both teams are playing well)*

Discussion Topics

- Have students discuss sports programs and sports commentators. Ask students to name their favorite sports programs and/or commentators and explain their choices.
- Basketball is one of the most popular sports in the United States. Have students share what they know about popular or top sports in other countries. Encourage students to account for the popularity of each sport.

Grammar Presentation (pages 298–300)

Grammar Charts

- Write the following example on the board:
  Adverbs: As . . . as
  The Shock scored as frequently as the Sparks.
  Have students study the example, and ask:
  "How can you make comparisons to show that
  two actions are the same?" *(as + adverb + as)*
- Write a new example on the board:
  *The Shock fans didn't cheer as loud as the
     Sparks fans.*
  Then ask: "How can you make comparisons
  to show that two actions are not the same?"
  (not + as + adverb + as) Be sure students
  understand that a negative verb is necessary.
  Give more examples: *Dixon isn't scoring as
  much as Riley. Dixon doesn't score as often as
  Riley.*
- Write the following examples on the board:
  Adverbs: Comparatives, Superlatives
  The Sparks played harder than the Shock.
  *The Sparks cheer the loudest of any fans in
     the game.*
  Ask students to name the comparative and
  superlative adverbs in the examples. *(harder,
  the loudest)* Underline them as students say
  them. Then ask: "How do you form the
  comparative of short adverbs such as *hard*?"
  (short adverb + -er) "What comes after
  harder?" *(than + the second part of the
  comparison)* "How do you form the
  superlative of short adverbs such as *loud*?"
  (the + adverb + -est)
- Note: You may want to point out that *loud* is
  the informal adverb, but in writing and more
  formal speech *loudly* should be used as the
  adverb.

- Write the following examples on the board:
  *The Sparks blocked Riley more effectively than
     any other team.*
  *Trigs got the ball less consistently than in other
     games.*
  *Riley scored the most consistently of anyone
     on the team.*
  *Trigs played the least intensely of anyone on
     the team.*
  Ask students to name the comparative and
  superlative adverbs in the examples. *(more
  effectively, less consistently, the most
  consistently, the least consistently)* Underline
  them as students say them. Then ask: "How
  do you form the comparative of long
  adverbs?" *(more OR less + adverb)* "How do
  you form the superlative of long adverbs?"
  (the most OR the least + adverb)
- Write the following examples on the board:
  *The first few minutes of the game the Sparks
     played better than the Shock.*
  Riley scored the most of her team.
  Ask students to name the comparative and
  superlative adverbs in the examples *(better,
  the most)* and underline them. Then ask:
  "What is *better* the comparative of?" *(well)*
  "What is *the most* the superlative of?" *(a lot)*
  Point out that some adverbs have irregular
  comparative and superlative forms.
  To summarize, write on the board:

Adverb	Comparative	Superlative
well	better	the best
a lot	more	the most
badly	worse	the worst

Grammar Notes

Note 1   *(Exercises 1–2, 3, 5)*
- Write the following example on the board:
  Adverbs: As . . . as
  The Shock played as well as the Sparks.
  Have students study the example, and ask:
  "Did the Shock play well?" *(yes)* "Did the
  Sparks play equally well?" *(yes)*
  Insert *just* between *played* and *as.* Then ask:
  "Is the comparison weaker or stronger now?"
  (stronger)
  To summarize, write on the board:
  *A played (just) as well as B. = A and B played
     equally well.*
- Write a new example on the board:
  Trigs didn't score as frequently as Jones.
  Then ask: "Did Jones score frequently?"
  (yes) "Did Trigs score with the same
  frequency?" *(no)*

To summarize, write on the board:
A did not score as frequently as B. = A and B didn't score the same.

→ For additional practice, see the Supplementary Activities on page 153.

Note 2 *(Exercises 1, 3–5)*
• Write the following example on the board:
<u>Comparative Adverbs + Than</u>
Jones ran faster than Trigs.
Have students study the example, and ask: "Did Jones run fast?" *(yes)* "Did Trigs run equally fast?" *(no)*
To summarize, write on the board:
A ran faster than B. = A and B did not run at the same speed.

→ For additional practice, see the Supplementary Activities on page 153.

Note 3 *(Exercises 1, 3–4)*
• Write on the board:
a. *Riley played intensely. Dixon played just as intensely.*
b. *Trigs played patiently. Jones played less patiently.*
To check comprehension, have students provide the full version of the comparisons. *(a. Dixon played just as intensely as Riley. b. Jones played less patiently than Trigs.)*

→ For additional practice, see the Supplementary Activities on page 153.

Note 4 *(Exercises 1, 3–5)*
• Write the following example on the board:
<u>Superlative Adverbs</u>
All the team played skillfully, buy Riley played the most skillfully.
Have students study the example, and ask: "Did Riley play skillfully?" *(yes)* "Who is Riley compared with in the example?" *(all the other players on the team)* "Did any of the other players play more skillfully than Riley?" *(no)*
Point out that the superlative compares one action with the action of other people in a group. In the example, the superlative compares the way Riley played with the way the other players on the team played. Emphasize that the superlative compares three or more things. It should not be used to compare only two things. Write two contrasting examples on the board:
Brad scored <u>more frequently than</u> Rost. *(comparison of two people)*
Brad scored <u>the most frequently</u> of anyone on the team. (comparison of more than two people)

• Write on the board additional examples of superlatives with expressions:
She runs the fastest of all the players.
She runs the fastest of anyone on the team.
She runs the fastest of all.
She runs the fastest of her team.

Note 5 *(Exercises 1, 3–5)*
• Draw the following chart on the board. (Note: Do not write the comparative and superlative forms.)

	Adverb	Comparative	Superlative
One-syllable adverbs	soon late loud	sooner later louder	the soonest the latest the loudest
Irregular adverbs	little a lot far	less more farther/ further	the least the most the farthest/ furthest
Long adverbs	cooperatively patiently	more/less cooperatively more/less patiently	the most/least cooperatively the most/least patiently

• As a class, elicit the comparative and superlative forms and fill in the chart.
• Working in pairs, have students use a few comparative and superlative adverbs from the chart in sentences. Follow up by having volunteers read their sentences aloud.
• Refer students to Appendix 10 on page A-6 for a list of irregular comparative and superlative adverbs.
• Refer students to Unit 23 for more information about adverbs.

Note 6 *(Exercises 1–5)*
• Write the following examples on the board:
The Sparks fans cheered louder than the Shock fans. (not as . . . as)
The Shock didn't play as fearlessly as the Sparks. (more)
The Sparks scored more consistently than the Shock. (less)
In pairs, have students restate the sentences on the board using the words in parentheses. Review as a class. *(The Shock fans didn't cheer as loud as the Sparks fans. The Sparks played more fearlessly than the Shock. The Shock scored less consistently than the Sparks.)*
• Write on the board:
The Tigers <u>cheered less loud than</u> the Vikings.
The Tigers <u>didn't cheer as loud as</u> the Vikings.
Have students say which way of comparing is more common with short adverbs such as *loud. (didn't cheer as loud as)*

Note 7 *(Exercises 1–2, 5)*
• Write the following sentences on the board:
  a. Jones played more skillfully than Whine.
  b. Jones blocked more skillfully his opponents than Whine.
  c. Jones blocked his opponents more skillfully than Whine.
  To check comprehension, have students in pairs decide which statements are correct. Review as a class. *(Correct statements: a and c)*

Note 8 *(Exercises 1, 3, 5)*
• Write on the board:
  Jones is training harder each day.
  The Whales are playing more accurately each day.
  The Tigers are playing less consistently each day.
  To provide practice, have students in pairs restate each statement repeating the comparative adverb. Review as a class. *(Jones is training harder and harder. The Whales are playing more and more accurately. The Tigers are playing less and less consistently.)*

Note 9 *(Exercises 1, 3, 5)*
• Write the following examples on the board:
  The better the pizza, the higher the price.
  The better he plays, the more he scores.
  To clarify the difference between the way comparative adjectives and comparative adverbs are used in this structure, point out that comparative adjectives are followed by nouns (*the pizza* and *the prize*), and comparative adverbs are followed by a subject and a verb (*he plays* and *he scores*).

Focused Practice (pages 301–303)

Exercise 1
delight: a feeling of great pleasure and satisfaction
handle: to control the movement of a vehicle, tool, or, in this case, ball

Exercise 2
support: to hold the weight of something, keep it in place, or prevent it from falling
fit: to be the right size and shape for someone or something
last: to continue to be effective, useful, or in good condition

Exercise 3
fearlessly: not being afraid of anything
cooperatively: made, done, or owned by people working together

shoot: to throw, hit, or kick a ball toward the place where you can make points

league: a group of sports teams or players who play games against each other to see who is best

Exercise 4
broad jump: a sport in which you jump as far as possible
pole vaulting: a sport in which you jump over a high bar using a special long pole (stick)
vault: to jump over something in one movement, using your hands or a pole to help you

Exercise 5
offensive: relating to trying to get points and win in sports games, or relating to the players who do this
coach: someone who trains a person or team in a sport

Communication Practice (pages 304–306)

Exercise 6
• Before listening to the tape, have students practice pronouncing the names of the horses so they can recognize the names while listening to the tape.
• You may want to point out that the horses are not mentioned in the order in which they finished the race.

Exercise 7
• As a class, have students choose a sport. Write the sport on the board.
• Brainstorm names of famous athletes for that sport. Write the names on the board.
• Go over the adjectives and adverbs in the box. Have students choose verbs that they would like to use to talk about the athletes. Have students match each verb they chose with an adverb from the box or an adverb of their choice. *(kick powerfully)*
• Go over the example. Point out students should use comparative and superlative adverbs.
  ⏱ After discussing as a class, have students write down three statements comparing the athletes.

Exercise 8
• Have students work individually to answer the questions and make up their own questions.
• After working in groups, students report their findings to the class.

Exercise 9

Questions to generate ideas and elicit vocabulary:

- Which two sports figures would you like to compare?
- What sport do they play?
- How well do they play it?
- What is one of the players better at?
- What is the other player better at?
- Who plays more intensely, aggressively, skillfully, or cooperatively?
- Who trains more seriously?
- Who scores more frequently or more consistently?

Further Practice

In small groups, have students choose a famous person they like—for example, a sportsperson, movie star, musician, singer, or dancer—and explain to their partners why they like them using comparative or superlative adverbs, for example: *My favorite ballet dancer is Julio Bocca from Argentina. I think he dances more gracefully than any other dancer I've seen.* Follow up by having volunteers tell the class about the people they like.

GRAMMAR OUT OF THE BOX ......

Sports news. Bring in the sports section of several newspapers. In small groups, have students browse the sports section in search of an article that reports on a game. Then have students find the answers to (some of) the following questions:

- Who played better?
- Who began more aggressively?
- Who played more skillfully by the end of the game?
- Who scored more in the first half/set/game?
- Who has been training more seriously?
- Which player on the team played the hardest?
- Which player on the team played the least consistently?

Follow up by having a member from each group report to the class on the article they read.

UNIT 27 Gerunds: Subject and Object

Unit Overview

Unit 27 focuses on the use of gerunds as subjects and objects of sentences.
- A gerund (base form + *-ing*) can be the subject of a sentence and is always singular.
- It can also be the object of certain verbs such as *admit, avoid, consider,* and *deny.*
- *Go* + gerund is often used to describe activities.

Grammar in Context (pages 316–317)

Background Note

An online bulletin board is a site on the Internet where users can post and read messages to one another. Users can also play games, download software or data, and read news. Online bulletin boards are usually free and open to the public.

Vocabulary

can't stand: to dislike something or someone very much

prohibit: to officially make an activity illegal

stink: to have a very strong bad smell

courtesy: polite and respectful behavior to other people

tolerance: willingness to allow people to do, say, or believe what they want

inhale: to breathe in air, smoke, or gas

second-hand smoke: smoke from someone else's cigarette that you breathe in

addicted: unable to stop taking drugs or something harmful

nicotine: a dangerous substance in tobacco

quit: to stop doing something that is bad

Comprehension Questions

- What can't Fumario stand? *(seeing all the new No Smoking signs)*
- Why does he think eating in a restaurant isn't fun any longer? *(because he can't smoke in restaurants)*
- Which does he think is worse—junk food or cigarettes? *(junk food)*
- Does Nuffsed agree with him? *(no)*
- What is she concerned about? *(the smell of second-hand smoke)*

- What does Swissfriend suggest? *(practicing courtesy and tolerance)*
- What does Cleanaire think about smoking? *(that it's an addiction)*

Discussion Topics

- Have students discuss who they agree with most. Have students support their views.
- Write the following questions on the board for students to share their personal experiences with their classmates:

Smokers	Non-smokers
When did you start smoking?	Did you ever try a cigarette?
Are you a heavy smoker?	If so, when was that?
Why do you smoke?	Why don't you smoke?
Have you ever tried to stop smoking?	If you used to be a smoker, was it easy to quit smoking?
Would you like to stop smoking?	What did you do?

Grammar Presentation (pages 317–318)

Identify the Grammar

GERUNDS: AS SUBJECTS

Eating in a restaurant or having an espresso in a café is no fun anymore!

. . . sitting in a room full of his cigarette smoke makes my hair and clothing stink.

GERUNDS: AS OBJECTS

I can't stand seeing all the new No Smoking signs.

I enjoy smoking, but I understand not wanting to inhale second-hand smoke.

Grammar Charts

- Write the following example on the board:
  Gerunds: As Subjects
  Smoking isn't allowed in restaurants.
  Have students study the example, and ask: "What's the subject of the sentence?" *(smoking)* "What's the verb phrase" *(isn't allowed)*
  Underline and indicate the subject and the verb phrase in the example on the board:
  Smoking isn't allowed in restaurants.
    subject   *verb*
  Then ask: "Is *smoking* a noun or a gerund?" *(a gerund)* "What's a gerund?" *(a base form of a verb + -ing)*

Point out that a gerund is a verb that is used like a <u>noun</u>, so it can be a <u>subject</u> of a sentence.

- Write the following example on the board:
  Gerunds: As Objects
  Fumario enjoys smoking.
  Have students study the example, and ask: "What's the subject of the sentence?" *(Fumario)* "What's the main verb?" *(enjoys)* "What's the object?" *(smoking)*
  Underline and indicate the subject, the verb, and the object in the example on the board:
  Fumario enjoys smoking.
    subject   *verb*   *object*
  Point out a gerund can also be the <u>object</u> of a sentence.

Grammar Notes

Note 1 *(Exercises 1–4)*
- Write the following sentences on the board:
  Gerunds: As Subjects and Objects
  Exercising is healthy.
  I don't like lying.
  She just started jogging.
  Have students say the gerunds in the examples. *(exercising, sleeping, jogging)*
- Write the following base forms and gerunds on the board:

exercise	exercising
jog	jogging
admit	admitting
lie	lying

- Working in pairs, have students study the spelling changes. You can refer students to Appendix 21 on page A-10 for spelling rules for verbs + -*ing*. To review as a class, have students explain the spelling rules.
- Write the following statements on the board:
  Smoking is difficult for Fumario.
  Getting enough sleep is unhealthy.
  I understand wanting to inhale second-hand smoke.
  To provide practice with forming the negative, have pairs insert *not* before the gerunds. Review as a class. *(Not smoking is difficult for Fumario. Not getting enough sleep is unhealthy. I understand not wanting to inhale second-hand smoke.)*

Note 2 *(Exercises 1–4)*
- Write the following examples on the board:
  Reading is fun.
  Smoking is an unhealthy habit.

Have students study the examples and name the subjects. (reading, smoking) Point out the singular verb. (is)
- Write new examples on the board:
  Reading travel magazines was my favorite pastime.
  Smoking in public places is not allowed.
  Point out that the subject can also be a gerund phrase. Have students name the subjects in the examples. (reading travel magazines, smoking in public places)
  Ask students if the verbs are singular or plural. (singular: was and is) Be sure students understand that the verb is always singular, even if the gerund is followed by plural nouns such as *magazines* or *places*.
- Write the following sentences on the board:
  a. I hate sitting in a room full of smoke.
  b. They are sitting at a table in a café.
  c. He is smoking a cigar.
  d. He started smoking when he was very young.
  To check comprehension, have students say which sentences have a gerund. (a and d)

Note 3 *(Exercises 1–4)*
- Write the following examples on the board:
  She quit smoking.
  I suggest going to a café.
  He enjoys swimming.
  Have students study the examples and name: the gerunds (smoking, going, swimming) and the verbs before the gerunds (quit, suggest, enjoys). Point out that certain verbs such as *quit, suggest,* and *enjoy* are often followed by gerunds.
- Point out that the objects can be either gerunds or gerund phrases. To check comprehension, have students look at the examples on the board again, and name the object that is a gerund phrase. (going to a café)
- Working in pairs, have students write three statements using verbs from Note 3 with gerunds. Have a few volunteers share their sentences with the class.
- Refer students to Appendix 13 on page A-7 for a more complete list of verbs that can be followed by gerunds.

→ For additional practice, see the Supplementary Activities on pages 153–154.

Note 4 *(Exercises 1, 3–4)*
To provide practice, address different students and ask questions using *go* + gerund. Encourage students to answer in complete sentences. You can ask: *Where do you usually* go shopping? Where did you use to go camping when you were a kid? Where do you like to go swimming? What's the best place to go skiing?

Focused Practice (pages 319–321)

Exercise 1
muscle: one of the pieces of flesh inside your body that join bones together and make your body move

low-impact: low-impact sports consist of mild exercise and do not cause injury to bones or muscles

high-impact: high-impact sports require effort and can cause injury to bones or muscles

recovery: the process of getting better after an illness, injury, etc.

consider: to think about something very carefully, especially before making a decision

Exercise 2
avoid: to prevent something bad from happening

Exercise 3
deny: to say that something is not true

admit: to accept or agree unwillingly that something is true or that someone else is right

mind: to feel annoyed, worried, or angry about something

Exercise 4
resist: to stop yourself from having something that you like or doing something that you want to do

Communication Practice (pages 321–323)

Exercise 5
- Before students listen, have them go over the list and predict what the doctor may say. If necessary, explain the meaning of *complex carbohydrates* (include fiber [found in fruits] and starches [such as rice], vegetables, whole grains, peas and beans).
- After reviewing answers, ask students whether they were right in their predictions. ⏱ Have students listen again and write down at the front of each item the verb the doctor uses before each gerund. Then have students make complete sentences using the verbs they wrote down and the items on the list. (*The doctor said the patient must stop smoking.*)

Exercise 6
Follow up with a class discussion. As the class discusses the survey results, have students determine whether smokers and non-smokers respond to questions differently. For example,

ask, "How many smokers agree with opinion 1? How many non-smokers?" You may also want to have a few students support their answers by saying why they agree or disagree with the statements.

Exercise 7
- After students have looked at the poster, point out that *CDC* stands for the Centers for Disease Control and Prevention of the U.S. Department of Health and Human Services.
- Before students discuss in groups, have them complete the sentences individually.
- Follow up with a discussion. To prompt discussion, say: "This poster was aimed at teenagers because most people become addicted to smoking in their teenage years. Do you think this poster reaches teenagers?" "What kind of poster do you think would reach teenagers?" "How can adults get teenagers to stop smoking?" "How can adults get teenagers to never start smoking?"

Exercise 8
- As students discuss in groups, have them take notes on the arguments for and against that are brought up in the discussion. Have students write the arguments in two lists under the headings *For* and *Against*.
- At the end of the discussion, encourage students to use their lists of arguments for and against to reach a conclusion.
- Follow up by asking students from different groups to share their conclusions with the class.

Exercise 10
Incomplete statements to generate ideas and elicit vocabulary:
- You should admit _____.
- You shouldn't deny _____.
- You must avoid _____.
- Why don't you consider _____.
- Remember that many people dislike _____.
- If you get through the first week you won't miss _____.
- I advise _____.
- Remember that if you stop smoking you will enjoy _____.

Further Practice
Have pairs of students choose a healthy habit to promote to the class. Give pairs of students five minutes to explain the habit, its benefits, and any special instructions. Possible topics are:
- Eating five to nine servings of fruit and vegetables a day

- Not eating snack food while watching TV
- Exercising every day
- Drinking eight glasses of water a day

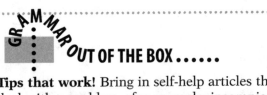

GRAMMAR OUT OF THE BOX . . . . . .

Tips that work! Bring in self-help articles that deal with a problem—for example, insomnia, stress, or depression. Hand out the material. Working in small groups, have students read the article and write a list of tips for dealing with that problem by completing (some of) the statements below. Then have groups report to the class on the problem they read about and the tips for dealing with it.

Tips for dealing with _____
- Avoid _____.
- Consider _____.
- Enjoy _____.
- Give up _____.
- Don't keep _____.
- Practice _____.
- When you feel like _____, you should _____.
- If you miss _____, you can _____.
- Experts recommend _____.
- They suggest _____.
- They also advise _____.

UNIT 28 Gerunds after Prepositions

Unit Overview

Unit 28 focuses on the use of gerunds after prepositions.
- Prepositions can be followed by nouns, pronouns, or gerunds.
- Many common expressions formed by verb + preposition or adjective + preposition can be followed by gerunds.
- Expressions with the preposition *to (look forward to, object to)* are followed by a gerund, not an infinitive.

Grammar in Context (pages 324–325)

Vocabulary

faculty: all the teachers in a school or college, or in a particular department of a school or college

get involved: to start taking part in an activity or event *make a difference:* to have a good effect on a situation or person

administration: the people who manage a company, institution, etc.

committee: a group of people chosen to do a particular job, make decisions, etc.

get active: get involved in an organization or activity by doing things for it

issue: a subject or problem that people discuss

be sick of: to be angry and bored with something that has been happening for a long time

link: a word or picture on a website or computer document that will take you to another page or document if you click on it

look forward to: to be excited and happy about something that is going to happen

Comprehension Questions

- What school is the student council from? *(Taylor College)*
- What is the student council concerned about? *(improving school life at Taylor College)*
- What does the student council want other students to do? *(to get involved/get active)*
- Where and when is the next meeting? *(in Buford Hall on October 23)*

Discussion Topics

- Have students discuss which links they would check out if this was the webpage of the Student Council in their school. Encourage students to explain why they would be interested in those links and to share ideas about improving those areas.
- Have students who are/have been members of a student government share their personal experience with the class. Ask students to say if they think student councils are an effective means of bringing about change in schools.

Grammar Presentation (pages 325–326)

Identify the Grammar

GERUNDS AFTER PREPOSITIONS
*Thank you <u>for visiting</u> the Student Council webpage.
Now is the time to think <u>about getting</u> involved and <u>making a difference</u>.
The Council is responsible <u>for developing</u> communication . . .
Because you are interested <u>in meeting</u> other students . . .
We <u>look forward to seeing</u> you there!*

Grammar Charts

- Write the following examples on the board:
*Gerunds after Prepositions
Now is the time to think about getting involved.
Are you interested in meeting other students?*
Have students study the examples and:
  —Name the gerunds in the examples. *(getting, meeting)*
  —Name the words that come before the gerunds. *(about, in)*
  —Say what kind of words *about* and *in* are. *(prepositions)*
- Underline and label the first example as indicated below:
Now is the time to think <u>about</u> <u>getting</u> involved.
                       prep. gerund
- Point out that only a gerund, not an infinitive, can follow a preposition.
- Circle *think* in the first example and ask: "What kind of word is *think*?" *(a verb)* "What preposition is it followed by?" *(about)*
- Point out that certain verbs like *think* are followed by a particular preposition. These verb + preposition combinations can be followed by a gerund.
- Write more examples on the board:
apologize for ⎤
insist on ⎦ + gerund
- Circle *interested* and ask: "What kind of word is *interested*?" *(an adjective)* "What preposition is it followed by?" *(in)*
- Point out that certain adjectives like *interested* are followed by a particular preposition. These adjective + preposition combinations can be followed by a gerund.
- Write more examples on the board:
excited about ⎤
responsible for ⎦ + gerund
- Have student use *apologize, insist, excited,* and *responsible* followed by the correct preposition and a gerund in sentences of their own.

Grammar Notes

Note 1 *(Exercises 1, 3, 5)*
- Write the following examples on the board:
*Gerunds after Prepositions
a. Think about the difference.
b. Think about it.
c. Think about making a difference.*
Have students say the preposition in the examples. *(about)* Ask students what kind of word the preposition *about* is followed by in each example. *(a. a noun b. a pronoun c. a gerund)*

Remind students that a gerund is a verb that is used like a noun, so it can follow prepositions just like nouns and pronouns can.

- Write on the board:
  He's responsible for _____. *(noun)*
  He's responsible for _____. *(pronoun)*
  He's responsible for _____. *(gerund)*
  To provide practice, have students complete the statements with their own ideas. Have students compare answers with a partner. To review, have a few volunteers read their sentences aloud.

Note 2 *(Exercises 1–2, 5)*
- Write on the board:
  She complained about having to study.
  She is good at solving problems.
  Have students study the examples, and ask: "What preposition is the verb *complained* followed by?" *(about)* "What preposition is the adjective *good* followed by?" *(at)*
- Point out that some verbs and adjectives are followed by a particular preposition.
  Write on the board:
  think _____
  responsible _____
  sick _____
  interested _____
  Working in pairs, have students write a preposition to follow each verb or adjective. To review answers, have students look back at the reading. *(think about, responsible for, sick of, interested in)*
- To provide practice, address different students and ask the following questions. Encourage them to answer using gerunds in complete sentences. "At school/work/home, what are you responsible for?" "What are you good at?" "What are you bored with?"

→ For additional practice, see the Supplementary Activities on page 154.

Note 3 *(Exercises 1–2, 4–5)*
- Make sure students understand that in expressions such as *look forward to, object to,* etc., *to* is a preposition, not part of the infinitive. Give more examples:
  He objects to doing that kind of work.
  I am opposed to working so late.
- To point out the difference between *be used to* and *get used to,* write on the board:
  I'm used to getting up early. = I always do it and it's not a problem.
  I've gotten used to getting up early. = I found it difficult at first, but now it's not a problem anymore.

- To point out the difference with *used to,* write on the board:
  I used to get up early. = I did it in the past, but I don't do it anymore.
  If necessary, refer students to Note 4 of Unit 5 on page 45 in the Student Book for more on the meanings of *used to, be used to,* and *get used to.*
- To provide practice, have students complete the following with true information about themselves. Write on the board:
  I'm looking forward to _____.
  I'm used to _____.
  I'm opposed to _____.
  Have volunteers share their sentences with the class.

Focused Practice (pages 327–330)

Exercise 1
concerned: worried about something important

Wi-Fi: wireless fidelity; a networking technology allowing connection to the Internet at high speeds

wireless: relating to a system of communication that does not use wires

count on: to depend on someone or something

hotspot: a place where the Internet can be accessed with a computer with Wi-Fi

undersigned: the person or people who have signed a piece of writing, used especially in formal letters

Exercise 2
banner: a long piece of cloth with writing on it; a belief or principle

Exercise 3
safety: the state of being free from danger or harm
run for: to be a candidate in an election

Communication Practice (pages 331–332)

Exercise 6
To help familiarize students with the vocabulary before they listen, write on the board:
class representative
activity fees
ethnic foods
campus safety
Elicit the meaning of the phrases from students, and clarify the meaning of unknown words.
⏱ After reviewing answers, write the following incomplete statements on the board.
I have been successful in _____.

I'm opposed to _____.
You can look forward to _____.
We are nervous about _____.
I will be aggressive about _____.

Point out that the statements on the board are fragments of the candidate's speech. Have students listen again to complete the statements with what the candidate says. Point out that students should use gerunds after the prepositions. Review as a class. *(I have been successful in bringing many new members into the Council. I'm opposed to raising student activity fees. You can look forward to eating better. We are nervous about walking back to our dorms at ten or eleven o'clock. I will be aggressive about talking to the school administration about student issues.)*

Exercise 7

Set a time limit of two minutes for each speech. After each speech, encourage the class to ask the speaker questions. Then conduct an election by secret ballot. Follow up with a discussion. Ask: "Would you like to have a student council?" "How can you set up a council?" "What kinds of issues would you like to address on the council?"

Exercise 8

After students have discussed in groups, have them report to the class. Ask: "In general, did you agree on your rankings?" "Which events were ranked as the most stressful?" "Why were they considered stressful?" "Which events were ranked as the least stressful?" "Why were they considered less stressful than the others?"

Exercise 9

• After students read, clarify the meaning of unknown words. Students may need help with the following: *academic adviser* (a professor at college who gives students advice on courses they should take, makes sure they are making good progress, and sometimes gives advice on personal problems); *transfer students* (a student who moves from one college or university to another).

• After reviewing the true/false statements, have students look back at the letter and underline the prepositions or expressions followed by gerunds.

• Write on the board a list of useful expressions students can use to write about the things they like and dislike.

Things I like
I'm happy about _____.
I'm excited about _____.

I feel confident about _____.
I approve of _____.
I'm satisfied with _____.
I'm content with _____.

Things I dislike
I'm concerned about _____.
I'm worried about _____.
I'm afraid of _____.
I object to _____.
I'm nervous about _____.
I'm tired of _____.

Further Practice

In groups of three, have students prepare 24 dominoes with a preposition on one half and a verb or adjective on the other. Tell students to use Appendices 17 and 18 on pages A-7 and A-8, for example:

of	good		at	happy		about	rely

Then have pairs use the dominoes they prepared to play dominoes.
How to play:
• Students place the dominoes facedown on the table.
• Each player takes six dominoes from the table. Then students make a pile with the others.
• Player A places a domino faceup on the table. *(at/happy)*
• Player B places another domino next to it. This domino should contain a verb or adjective that matches the preposition on the domino on the table *(good)* or a preposition that matches its verb or adjective *(about)*.
• If player B doesn't have a domino that can go with the one on the table, he/she picks a new domino from the pile, or passes if there are no more dominoes in the pile.
• The first player to get rid of all the dominoes—or the player who is left with fewer dominoes—wins the game.

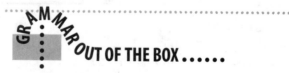

GRAMMAR OUT OF THE BOX . . . . . .

A great speech. Have students read or listen to an excerpt from Martin Luther King's speech, "I Have a Dream." (A good starting point is the paragraph starting "I say to you today, my friends . . . ", and a good finishing point is the paragraph ending "that we will be free one day.") Before students read/listen make sure they know who Martin Luther King was. Otherwise, give a brief introduction: Martin Luther King (1929–1968) was an African-American religious leader who became the most important leader of the Civil Rights Movement and worked hard to achieve social changes for African-Americans. Then have students write a short summary of the speech using some of the following opening lines, which you should write on the board:

- Martin Luther King dreams about _____
- He believes in _____
- He looks forward to _____
- He objects to _____
- He complains about _____
- He advises against _____
- He counts on _____
- He approves of _____
- He is angry at _____
- He is aware of _____
- He is concerned about _____
- He is opposed to _____
- He is worried about _____

Note: You may want to do a search on the Internet for **famous speeches** and select another speech. You can find famous speeches at http://www.historychannel.com/speeches/.

UNIT 29 Infinitives after Certain Verbs

Unit Overview

Unit 29 focuses on the use of infinitives after certain verbs.
- Some verbs can be followed directly by an infinitive.
- Some verbs need an object before the infinitive.
- Some verbs can be followed by either an infinitive or an object + infinitive.

Grammar in Context (pages 333–334)

Vocabulary

borrow: to use something that belongs to someone else and give it back to him/her later

overnight: here, suddenly

fail: to be unsuccessful in what you are trying to do

Comprehension Questions

- What does Lonely in Seattle want to find? *(new friends)*

- Why didn't her last relationship with a man work? *(because he asked to borrow money and wanted to correct her pronunciation)*
- Does Annie advise Lonely to find someone new to date? *(no)*
- What does she advise her to do? *(to relax, do the things she likes to do, and have fun)*

Discussion Topics

- Have students say whether they agree with Annie's advice. Encourage students to express their ideas about loneliness and making new friends. Ask questions to prompt discussion: "Why is it important to make friends when you move to a new place?" "What is the best way to make friends?" "Is it also important to fall in love?" Annie thinks that people shouldn't try to solve the problem of loneliness by falling in love. Ask students to say whether they agree with Annie and support their view.
- Lonely in Seattle resorted to a newspaper advice column for advice. Ask students to say what they would have done to seek advice if they had been in Lonely's situation.

Grammar Presentation (pages 334–335)

Identify the Grammar

INFINITIVES AFTER CERTAIN VERBS
. . . nothing *seems to work*.
. . . I *decided not to see* him again.
Now my roommate *would like* me *to go out* with her boyfriend's brother.
First, I'd just *like to find* some friends to hang out with.
I usually *advise* them *to make* friends first.

Grammar Charts

- Write the following examples on the board:
  Infinitives after Certain Verbs
  Nothing seems to work.
  I decided not to go.
  Have students study the examples, and ask: "What's the main verb in each sentence?" *(seems, decided)* "What words follow the main verbs?" *(to work, not to go)* "Are *to work* and *not to go* infinitives or gerunds?" *(infinitives)* Point out that some verbs such as *seem* and *decide* are followed by infinitives.
- Write the following examples on the board:
  I tell them to make friends first.
  I urge them not to focus on the problem.

If necessary, clarify the meaning of *urge (to strongly advise someone to do something)*. Ask students to name:
—the main verb in each sentence. *(tell, urge)*
—the infinitives. *(to make, not to focus)*
Then ask: "Do the infinitives directly follow the verbs?" *(no)* "What comes before the infinitives?" (them—*an object*) Point out that some verbs such as *tell* and *urge* need an object before the infinitive.
• Write on the board:
I'd just like to make friends.
She would like me to date her friend.
Have students study the examples, and ask: "Does the infinitive directly follow the verb in the first example?" *(yes)* "Does it directly follow the verb in the second example?" (*No. There's an object—me—between the verb and the infinitive.*) Point out that some verbs such as *would like* can be followed directly by an infinitive or by an object and an infinitive.

Grammar Notes

Notes 1–2 *(Exercises 1–2, 4)*
• Write on the board:
<u>Infinitives after Certain Verbs</u>
I decided to stay.
I told her to come.
• Ask students to: "Name the main verbs." *(decided, told)* "Name the infinitives that follow them." *(to stay, to come)* "Change *to stay* and *to come* into negative infinitives and say full sentences." (*I decided not to stay. I told her not to come.*)
• Erase *to stay* and *to come* in the examples and replace them with blanks.
• Have students use an affirmative and a negative infinitive to complete the blanks. Follow up by having volunteers read their sentences aloud with the class.

Note 3 *(Exercises 1–4)*
• Go over the verbs on the list, and clarify the meaning of any unknown words. Students might need help with *refuse (to say firmly that you will not do or accept something).*
• Write on the board:

	has failed	to develop friendships soon.
	refused	not to see that man again.
Lonely in Seattle	decided	to make new friends so far.
	hopes	to lend money to the man she was dating.

Have students match the main verbs with the infinitives to make true sentences about *Lonely in Seattle*.
• For further practice, have pairs use all the verbs on the list in simple sentences of their own. Have volunteers read their sentences aloud.
• Refer students to Appendix 14 on page A-7 for a list of verbs that are followed by the infinitive.

→ For additional practice, see the Supplementary Activities on page 154.

Note 4 *(Exercises 1–4)*
• Point out that the object can be a noun, a noun phrase, or a pronoun. To illustrate your point, write on the board:

| I invited | a few friends
Alice
her | to come with us. |

• Go over the verbs on the list, and clarify the meaning of any unknown words. Students might need help with *warn (to tell someone that something bad or dangerous might happen, so that she/he can avoid it or prevent it).*
• Write on the board:
Annie told Lonely _____.
She encouraged Lonely _____.
She warned Lonely _____.
To provide practice, have pairs use Annie's advice on the column to complete the sentences. Point out that more than one correct answer is possible. Review as a class. (Possible answers: *Annie told Lonely to relax a bit. She encouraged Lonely to join a sports club or learn to dance. She warned Lonely not to expect to develop friendships overnight.*)
• Refer students to Appendix 16 on page A-7 for a list of verbs that need an object before the infinitive.

→ For additional practice, see the Supplementary Activities on page 154.

Note 5 *(Exercises 1–4)*
• Point out that a verb followed by an infinitive may have a different meaning from a verb followed by an object and an infinitive. To illustrate your point, write on the board:
Sarah would like to write a letter to Annie. = Sarah is interested in writing to Annie.
Sarah would like her friend to write a letter to Annie. = Sarah is not interested in writing a letter herself. She thinks her friend should write to Annie.
• Write the following statements on the board, and have students say which are true.
a. Lonely wants to meet a man.

b. *Lonely's roommate wants her to meet a man.*

c. *Lonely's boyfriend wanted to improve his pronunciation.*

d. *Lonely's boyfriend wanted Lonely to improve her pronunciation.*

e. *Annie expects Lonely to make new friends soon.*

f. *Annie expects to make new friends soon.*

Review as a class. (*True statements: b, d, f*)

• To provide practice, have students write a sentence using a verb from the list followed by an infinitive and another sentence using the same verb followed by an object plus an infinitive.

• Refer students to Appendix 14 on page A-7 for a list of verbs that are followed by infinitives.

→ For additional practice, see the Supplementary Activities on page 154.

Focused Practice (pages 336–338)

Exercise 1

rafting: the sport of traveling down a fast-flowing river in a rubber raft

persuade: to make someone agree to do something by giving good reasons why she/he should

Exercise 2

mate: a husband, wife, or sexual partner

embarrassed: ashamed, anxious, or nervous, especially in front of other people

matchmaker: someone who tries to find suitable people for his/her friend to have romantic relationships with

Exercise 3

yawn: to open your mouth wide and breathe deeply, usually because you are tired or bored

ground: to stop a child from going out with his/her friends as a punishment for doing something wrong

Communication Practice (pages 338–340)

Exercise 5

• Before students listen, tell them they will listen to a couple talking about their blended family, and explain what a blended family is: "A blended family results when two adults with children from previous marriages get married. They blend their families. The new child is a stepdaughter or a stepson and the new parent is called a stepmother or stepfather."

• After reviewing answers, follow up with a brief discussion. Ask: "What kind of problem does this family have?" "What other problems might blended families have?" "Has this family managed to solve their problem?" "What would you advise them to do?"

Exercise 6

• After going over the questions, have students add their own questions individually.

• After working in pairs, students report to the class one or two interesting pieces of information about their partners' parents.

Exercise 7

• Before students discuss in groups brainstorm and write on the board useful verbs from this unit that students can use to talk about what parents and young people do. Write the verbs on the board for students to use as reference as they discuss. For example:

Parents		Young people	
allow	warn	want	persuade
forbid	expect	prefer	refuse
force	advise	ask	invite
prefer	encourage	try	choose

• After discussing in groups, students report their findings to the class.

Exercise 9

Questions to generate ideas and elicit vocabulary:

• What are you planning to do with your classmates?

• What do you want to do after that?

• Why would you like your friend to come?

• Who else did you invite to come with you?

• Where and when did you arrange to meet?

Further Practice

Have students work in pairs to classify some of the verbs in Appendices 14 and 16 on page A-7 into three semantic categories: "Speaking," "Making Decisions," and "Wanting or Expecting." Tell students that this will help them learn the verbs. (Speaking: *advise, encourage, convince, persuade, promise, remind, tell, urge, warn, ask, refuse, mean, offer, request.* Making Decisions: *agree, arrange, decide, plan, prepare.* Wanting or Expecting: *want, wish, would like, can't wait, hope, expect.*) Then have students write an example for each category. Each example should be suitable for three verbs from the same category, for example: *She advised/encouraged/persuaded me to join a club.*

We agreed/decided/are planning to go on vacation.
I want/would like/can't wait to make new friends.

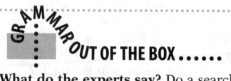 GRAMMAR OUT OF THE BOX ......

What do the experts say? Do a search on the Internet on **friendship and making friends,** and bring in several self-help articles about friendship written by psychologists or counselors. The articles should include tips for making new friends. Hand out the material and have students work in small groups and read the articles. Then have students report to the class on the tips for making friends suggested by the psychologist/counselor. Challenge students to only say sentences that contain the following verbs, which you should write on the board:

advise	*persuade*
encourage	*teach*
expect	*tell*
help	*urge*
remind	*warn*

 UNIT 30 **Infinitives of Purpose**

> ### Unit Overview
>
> Unit 30 focuses on the use of the infinitive to express the purpose of an action.
> - A purpose can be expressed with an infinitive (*to* + base form of verb) or *in order to* + base form of verb. *To* + base form of verb is more common in informal speech and writing.
> - A negative purpose can be expressed with *in order not to* + base form of verb. *Because* + a reason is more common in everyday spoken English.

Grammar in Context (pages 341–342)

Vocabulary

store: to keep facts or other information in a computer until you need them

journalist: someone who writes reports for newspapers, magazines, television, or radio

crew: a group of people with special skills who work together on something

meet a deadline: to finish something by a set time or date

surf: to look quickly at different places on the Internet for information that interests you

Comprehension Questions

- Why does Megan find her camera phone useful when she goes shopping? *(because she can ask friends for advice by sending them pictures of the items she wants to buy)*
- Why does Carlos find his camera phone useful at school? *(because he takes pictures of the teacher's notes on the board)*
- Why can a camera phone be particularly useful to a journalist? *(because it enables him/her to send stories with a photo or video instantly)*
- Can you also have fun with a camera phone? *(Yes. You can surf the Internet, e-mail friends, listen to music, watch videos, and play games.)*

Discussion Topics

- Have students discuss who—of all the people mentioned in the article—makes the best use of his/her camera phone. Encourage students to explain their choice.
- The article says that the camera phone has changed our lives. Have students discuss in what ways other technological items have brought about important changes in our lives.

Grammar Presentation (page 342)

> ### Identify the Grammar
>
> INFINITIVES OF PURPOSE
> *You can use it to send instant pictures home . . .*
> *Megan uses hers to get instant advice on shopping trips.*
> *I use the calendar to plan my week . . .*
> *I can instantly send my story with a photo or video in order to meet my deadline . . .*

Grammar Charts

- Write the following examples on the board:
  Infinitives of Purpose
  On shopping trips, Megan takes pictures to send them to her friends.
  She sends the pictures in order to get instant advice.
  Have students study the examples, and ask: "Why does Megan take pictures on shopping trips?" *(to send them to her friends)* "Why

does she send the pictures to her friends?" *(to get instant advice)*

Point out that the infinitive of purpose explains the <u>reason</u> to do something, for example, why Megan takes the pictures on shopping trips, or why she sends the pictures to her friends.

- Underline in the examples on the board *to send them to her friends* and *in order to get instant advice*.

Have students compare the way the infinitive is used to express purpose in each of the examples. Then ask: "How do you form the infinitive of purpose?" *(to + base form of verb* OR *in order to + base form of verb)*

- Then write on the board:

  Megan asks for advice in order not to make the wrong decision.

Have students study the example, and ask: "How do you express a negative purpose?" *(in order not to + base form of verb)*

Grammar Notes

Note 1 *(Exercises 1–4)*

- Write the following examples on the board:

  Infinitives of Purpose

  Gerry bought a camera phone to send pictures home to his family.

  Ask students: "Why did Gerry buy a camera phone?" *(to send pictures to his family)* Replace *send pictures home to his family* with a blank, and have students use their own ideas to complete the sentence. You may want to write some ideas on the board.

- To provide practice with *Why* questions and incomplete sentences as answers, ask random students: "Why do you come to English class?" "Why do you pay attention in class?" "Why do you take notes in class?" "Why do you ask questions in class?"

- Have students find in the opening reading a sentence that lists more than one purpose without repeating *to*. *(I use it to surf the Internet, e-mail friends, listen to music, watch videos, and play games.)* Then write this question on the board:

  What do you use your computer for?

  To provide practice with listing purposes in one sentence, have students individually write their answer to the question. Point out they should include several uses. Then call on volunteers to share their sentences with the class.

→ For additional practice, see the Supplementary Activities on pages 154–155.

Note 2 *(Exercises 1–4)*

- Emphasize that the longer form *in order to* is more formal. To provide practice, say several sentences using *to* + base form, and have students restate them using *in order to*. You can say: "Mee-Yon will hurry to meet his deadline." "He will send the story immediately to be the first to report it." "Carlos bought a camera phone to organize his life." "Yesterday he went to the mall to buy a new one."

- For further practice, write on the board.

  He went to the mall _____.

  He took a taxi _____.

  He bought a new printer _____.

  Have students complete the sentences with *in order to* and their own ideas. Then call on volunteers to share their sentences with the class.

→ For additional practice, see the Supplementary Activities on pages 154–155.

Note 3 *(Exercises 1, 3–4)*

- Write a new example on the board:

  He wrote it down in order not to forget about it.

  Point out that the infinitive shouldn't be split: *in order <u>not</u> to forget* NOT ~~in order to not forget~~

- Write the following questions on the board:

  Why did Harry get up early?

  Why did Brenda get the cheapest sweater?

  Why did Brian do all his homework yesterday?

  Why did Sue pretend to have a headache?

  To provide practice, have students make up answers to the questions using *in order not to*. Have students share their answers with the class. (Possible answers: *He got up early in order not to be late. She bought the cheapest sweater in order not to spend a lot of money. He did all his homework yesterday in order not to do it today. She pretended to have a headache in order not to go to the party.*)

- Remind students that in everyday speech we use *because*. You may want to have students restate their answers to the questions in the second step using *because*, for example: *He got up early because he didn't want to be late.*

→ For additional practice, see the Supplementary Activities on pages 154–155.

Focused Practice (pages 343–345)

Exercise 1

mean: unkind or nasty

digital: giving information in the form of numbers or changing electrical signals *shoplifting:* the crime of taking something from a store without paying for it

ban: an official order that does not allow something to be used or done

Exercise 2
tape: to record sounds or pictures onto a tape (videotape)

Exercise 3
exchange: to give something (such as American money) to someone who gives you something else (in this case, Canadian money)

Exercise 4
license plate: a sign with numbers and letters on it, usually at the front and back of your car

Communication Practice (pages 346–347)

Exercise 5
- Before students listen write on the board:
  touchtone telephone
  Explain what it is *(a telephone that produces different sounds when different numbers are pushed).*
- Have students go over the items and clarify the meaning of any words. Students might need help with the following words: *bill* (a list of things you have bought and the amount you have to pay for them), *merchandise* (things that are for sale in stores).
- To review answers, have students say complete sentences. *(To speak to a customer service representative, you should press 1.)*
- After students listen, ask: "What strategies do you use when you hear one of these long automated messages?" "Do you take notes?" "Do you hold on for an operator?" "Do you press the repeat button?"

Exercise 6
- Before students work in groups, elicit the names of the objects. Write them on the board.
  1. *shell*
  2. *cork*
  3. *jar*
  4. *binder clip*
  5. *notepad*
  6. *rubber band*
- Divide the class into groups. Tell students that they have a time limit of 10 minutes to try to imagine at least three different purposes for each object.
- Go over the example and point out the infinitives of purpose.
- Have students share their ideas with the class.

Exercise 7
- After students work in pairs, call on volunteers to say what they will/won't use their camera phone for. As you get feedback from students, list students' ideas in two columns on the board:
  I'll use it to . . .   I won't use it to . . .
- Working in pairs, have students take turns saying what electronic device they don't have and would like to have, and what they would use it for. Follow up by having a few volunteers share with the class interesting information they discussed.

Exercise 8
- Have students read the ad. Then ask: "What's the ad for?" *(a remote control)* "What's special about it?" *(It can operate several components.)* "Is it difficult to use?" *(no)*
- As students discuss, encourage them to be creative. You may want to have them list their ideas in note form.
- Have students share their ideas with the class.

Exercise 9
Questions to generate ideas and elicit vocabulary:
- What is the electronic gadget?
- What is it like? Is it high-tech? Is it revolutionary?
- What is it for?
- What special uses does it have?
- Why would someone want to buy it?
Note: You may want to ask students to draw a picture of the gadget next to the text.

Further Practice
Write the following pairs of low technology/ high technology items on the board:
paper dictionary vs. computer dictionary
paper mail vs. e-mail
bicycle vs. car
pen and paper vs. calculator
paper books vs. CD-ROM books
paper newspaper vs. Internet news
Have students discuss what they use each option for. Then have students discuss their responses as a class.

GRAMMAR OUT OF THE BOX . . . . . .

Antiques. Do a search on **antiques** and print out pictures of old objects whose uses students can guess at and discuss. They can be objects we no longer use, such as a warming pan (a copper pan that was used in the past to make your bed warm), or objects we still use but look different from the ones we use today. For example, at the BBC antiques website, you can find a flexible spice container with the shape of a fish. Divide the students into groups, hand out the pictures, and have students discuss what they think the objects were used for in the past. Encourage the use of the infinitive of purpose. Then have groups exchange pictures to discuss more objects. Follow up by having students share with the class what they think each object is and its possible uses. If students didn't guess correctly, provide the correct answer.

 Infinitives with *Too* and *Enough*

UNIT 31

Unit Overview

Unit 31 focuses on the use of the infinitive with *too* and *enough*.
- A reason can be expressed with *too* + adjective/adverb + infinitive or adjective/adverb + *enough* + infinitive.
- *For* + noun/pronoun can be placed before the infinitive to indicate what person, place, or thing the infinitive refers to.

Grammar in Context (pages 348–349)

Background Note

In the United States and Canada, people are considered adults for most purposes when they reach the age of 18. At that age, they can vote, sign contracts, get married, and serve in the armed forces without needing permission from their parents or guardians. Prior to 1971, Americans had to be 21 to vote. In the United States, young people cannot purchase alcohol until they are 21.

Vocabulary

vote: (n.) an act of making a choice or decision by voting (v.) to show which person you want to elect, which plan you want to support, etc., by doing something such as raising your hand, marking a paper using a pen or machine, clicking on a web page on the Internet, etc.

right: something that you are allowed to do or have according to the law or according to moral ideas

politician: someone who works in politics, especially an elected member of the government

argument: a set of explanations you use to try to prove that something is right or wrong, true or false, etc.

require: to demand officially that someone do something because of a law or rule

the law: the system of rules that people in a country, city, or state must obey

discriminate: to treat one person or group differently from another in an unfair way

curfew: time during which everyone must stay indoors

minorities: a group of people of a different race or religion than most people in a country, or someone in one of these groups

civil rights: the legal rights that every person in a particular country has. In the United States these include the right to have the same treatment whatever your race or religion is

Comprehension Questions

- Why does Kyle want the right to vote? *(to be taken seriously by politicians)*
- Why does Tina want the right to vote? *(to cause politicians to change the laws that discriminate against teenagers)*
- What would Micah like to decide for herself? *(how often she can see her father)*
- What contradiction does Kyle see in the law? *(According to the law, teenagers are responsible enough to work and pay taxes, but they are <u>not</u> responsible enough to stay out past 10:00.)*

Discussion Topics

- Have students discuss what they think about Kyle, Tina, and Micah's arguments. Who has the best argument? Encourage students to think of other arguments for and against lowering the voting age.
- Some people fight to get their rights. Other people don't exercise the rights they have: in countries where voting is not compulsory (where people have to vote), some people don't vote; in countries where voting is compulsory, some people cast blank votes. Why do you think this is so? What would you do if you had the right to vote?/Do you have the right to vote? What do you do?

Grammar Presentation (pages 349–350)

Identify the Grammar

INFINITIVES WITH *TOO* AND *ENOUGH*
. . . politicians won't take us <u>seriously enough</u>
  <u>to hear</u> our views.
. . . we're <u>old enough to vote</u>.
. . . the law says I'm <u>too young to decide</u> for
  myself.
I'm <u>responsible enough to work</u> . . .
. . . <u>too irresponsible to stay</u> out past 10:00.

Grammar Charts

• Write the following examples on the board:
Infinitives with Too and Enough
Kyle is too young to vote.
*He thinks the law is too unfair for teenagers to
  accept.*
Tina spoke too quietly to be heard.
—Have students study the examples, and ask:
  "Why can't Kyle vote?" *(because he's too
  young)* "Why can't teenagers accept the
  law?" *(because it's too unfair)* "Why couldn't
  Tina be heard?" *(because she spoke too
  quietly)*
—Point out that the infinitive with *too* gives a
  <u>reason</u> for something—for example, why
  Kyle can't vote, why teenagers can't accept
  the law, or why Tina couldn't be heard.
—Have students look at the examples again,
  and ask: "How can you give a reason with
  an infinitive with *too*?" (too + *adjective/
  adverb* + *infinitive* OR too + *adjective/adverb*
  + for + *noun* + *infinitive*)
• Write the following examples on the board:
Kyle thinks he's old enough to vote.
*The new law is fair enough for teenagers to
  accept.*
*Politicians don't take teenagers seriously
  enough to hear their views.*
—Have students study the examples, and ask:
  "Why does Kyle think he can vote?"
  (because he's old enough) "Why can
  teenagers accept the new law?" *(because it's
  fair enough)* "Why don't politicians hear the
  views of teenagers?" *(because they don't take
  them seriously enough)*
—Point out that the infinitive with *enough*
  also gives a <u>reason</u> for something—for
  example, why Kyle thinks he can vote, why
  teenagers can accept the new law, or why
  politicians don't hear the views of teenagers.

—Have students look at the examples again,
  and ask: "How can you give a reason with
  an infinitive with *enough*" (adjective/adverb
  + enough + *infinitive* OR *adjective/adverb* +
  enough + for + *noun* + *infinitive*)
• Be sure students are aware of the different
  ways in which *too* and *enough* are used: *too* is
  followed by an adjective or adverb and *enough*
  is preceded by an adjective or adverb. To
  summarize, you may want to write on the
  board:
  too + *adjective/adverb* + *(for* + *noun)* +
    infinitive
  adjective/adverb + <u>*enough*</u> + *(for* + *noun)* +
    infinitive

Grammar Notes

Note 1   *(Exercises 1–4)*
• Write the following examples on the board:
Infinitives with Too
Micah is too young to stay out past 10:00.
Then write on the board:
This sentence expresses the reason why

_____.

Have students complete the blank
individually. *(Micah can't stay out past 10:00)*
Review as a class and remind students that
infinitives with *too* give reasons.
• To provide practice with *too* + adjective +
  infinitive, ask the class the questions below
  one by one. Have students provide an answer
  with *because* and then restate the whole idea
  with an infinitive with *too,* for example:

TEACHER: Why can't you lift a car?

STUDENTS: Because it's too heavy.

TEACHER: Now restate the idea using *too.*

STUDENTS: A car is too heavy to lift.

The following are other questions you can
ask. (Possible answers are given in
parentheses.) "Why can't you learn Chinese in
a month?" *(Because it's too difficult. Chinese is
too difficult to learn in a month.)* "Why can't
you buy a Ferrari?" *(Because it's too
expensive. A Ferrari is too expensive to buy.)*
"Why can't you swim with sharks?" *(Because
they're too dangerous. Sharks are too
dangerous to swim with.)* "Why can't you live
on your own?" *(Because we're too young.
We're too young to live on our own.)*

→ For additional practice, see the Supplementary Activities on
  page 155.

Notes 2–3   *(Exercises 1–4)*

• Write the following example on the board:
Infinitives with Enough
Kyle is old enough to express his views on the
  radio.
Then write on the board:
This sentence expresses the reason why
  _____. Have students complete the blank
  individually. *(Kyle can express his views on*
  the radio) Review as a class and remind
  students that infinitives with *enough*—just
  as infinitives with *too*—give reasons.

• Write a contrasting example on the board:
Kyle isn't too young to express his views.
  Have students look at the examples and elicit
  the position of *too (before the adjective)* and
  the position of *enough (after the adjective).*
  Clarify any confusion the students may have.

• To provide practice with adjective + *enough* +
  infinitive, write on the board:
Chinese is too difficult to learn in a month.
  (easy)
A Ferrari is too expensive for everyone to buy.
  (cheap)
Sharks are too dangerous to swim with. (tame)
We're too young to live on our own. (old)
  Working in pairs, have students restate the
  statements using the adjectives in parentheses
  and *enough.* Review as a class. *(Chinese is not*
  easy enough to learn in a month. A Ferrari is
  not cheap enough for everyone to buy. Sharks
  are not tame enough to swim with. We're not
  old enough to live on our own.)

• To provide practice with adverb + *enough* +
  infinitive, write on the board:
He speaks French _____ enough _____.
She didn't work _____ enough _____.
They didn't play _____ enough _____.
  In pairs, students complete the sentences
  with an adverb and an infinitive. To review,
  have volunteers read their answers aloud.
  (Possible answers: He speaks French clearly
  enough for us to understand him. She didn't
  work quickly enough to finish on time. They
  didn't play well enough to win the game.)

→ For additional practice, see the Supplementary Activities on
   page 155.

Note 4   *(Exercises 1–4)*

• Write contrasting examples on the board:
It's too cold to go out. = General statement =
  No one should go out.
It's too cold for the children to go out. = The
  children can't go out.

Explain that the infinitive can be preceded by
a noun to make it clear who (or what) the
action expressed by the infinitive refers to.
Erase *the children* in the example and replace
it with *them.* Point out that a pronoun is also
possible.

• To check comprehension, have pairs study
  the difference in meaning between the
  following sentences: Write on the board:
a. *It's past 10:00. It's too late to go out.*
b. *It's past 10:00. It's too late for teenagers to*
   go out.
c. *This math exercise is too difficult to do.*
d. *This math exercise is too difficult for*
   Matthew to do.
  Review as a class. *(a. It's late. We shouldn't go*
  out. b. It's late. Teenagers can't go out. c. The
  exercise is very difficult. d. Matthew finds the
  math exercise hard to do. Other students might
  not find it hard.)

→ For additional practice, see the Supplementary Activities on
   page 155.

Note 5   *(Exercises 1–2)*

• To provide practice with *too* and *enough*
  without the infinitive, write these questions
  on the board:
a. *Why couldn't you hear him?*
b. *Why couldn't you understand her?*
c. *Why didn't you do your homework?*
d. *Why didn't you finish the task on time?*
e. *Why did you crash?*
  In pairs, students make up answers using *too*
  plus an adjective or adverb, or an adjective or
  adverb plus *enough.* To review, address
  individual students as you read each question
  aloud. Have students read their answers
  aloud. *(Possible answers: a. Because he spoke*
  too quietly./Because he didn't speak loudly
  enough. b. Because she didn't speak clearly
  enough./Because her English was too bad.
  c. Because it was too hard./Because it was too
  long. d. Because I didn't work quickly enough.
  e. Because I was driving too fast.)

Focused Practice   (pages 351–353)

Exercise 1

immature: behaving in a way that is not sensible for
your age

mature: behaving in a reasonable way, like an adult,
used especially about a child or young person

censorship: the practice or system of examining
books, movies, etc., in order to remove anything that
is offensive or politically dangerous

violent: violent actions are intended to hurt people

Exercise 2

steep: a road, hill, etc., that is steep goes down or up at a high angle

Exercise 3

access: the way you can enter a building to get to a place, or how easy this is

recreation center: a place or building where people can do activities for pleasure or fun

Exercise 4

weird: unusual and strange

Communication Practice (pages 354–355)

Exercise 5

• Before students listen, have students look at the pictures, spot the differences, and describe them.
• To review answers, have students explain their choice.

🕐 After reviewing answers, write the following cues on the board:

ramps / gradual / use without help
the automatic door opener / low / reach from a wheelchair
the water fountain / low / everyone / use
the new entrances / busy / teenagers / skate around

Have students use the cues to write sentences to describe picture 2. Point out they should use infinitives with *too* or *enough*.

Exercise 6

• As a class, brainstorm useful adjectives to describe the topics. List them on the board.

mature	*sensible*
immature	*careful*
responsible	*dangerous*
irresponsible	*safe*
concerned	*fair*
educated	*unfair*

• You may also want to brainstorm useful language to agree and disagree.

<u>Agreeing</u>	<u>Disagreeing</u>
I agree.	I disagree.
You're right.	I'm not so sure.
That's right.	I see your point, but . . .
I couldn't agree more.	You can't be serious!

• Pose one question at a time to the class. Write students' opinions on the board.
• After the discussion, have the class consider all the options on the board and try to identify two compelling (and opposing) opinions to vote on. Then conduct the vote by secret ballot.

Exercise 7

After students have discussed the meaning of the expressions in groups, have them report to the class. Elicit different occasions on which students would use the expressions.

Exercise 8

• Have students work individually to complete the sentences before they compare their ideas in groups.
• Have the groups report to the class any interesting ideas that arose in their discussions.

Exercise 9

Questions to generate ideas and elicit vocabulary:
• What topic have you chosen?
• Are you for or against it?
• What are some arguments in favor of [topic]?
• What are some arguments against [topic]?

Further Practice

Write the following on the board:
Make your argument for . . .
• *not wanting to have dinner at a particular restaurant this Sunday*
• *refusing to go shopping to a particular place*
• *not wanting to watch a particular movie*
Working in pairs, have students choose a real or fictional restaurant, mall, and movie. Then ask students to write as many reasons as they can think of to make a good argument for each of the topics on the board. Point out they should use *too* or *enough,* for example: *Reasons why we don't want to have dinner at Rosie's Cuisine on Sunday: It's too crowded on weekends. It's too expensive. The menu is not varied enough. The food is too spicy. The service is not fast enough.* Then have pairs share their arguments with the class. Who has the most convincing argument?

GRAMMAR OUT OF THE BOX . . . . . .

Let's be critical of the news. Bring in newspapers. Have students work in groups of four. Give each group two newspaper pages and have them read the news. All the students in the group should skim through both newspaper pages. (Pairs can share a newspaper page and then exchange it.) Have students discuss the news using infinitives with *too* and *enough,* for example: *I think this man is too old* *to rule his country. I don't think this project is sensible enough. These workers are demanding too much. This woman's ideals are too radical to be accepted in her country.* Follow up by having students share with the class their opinion of some of the news they discussed.

UNIT 32 Gerunds and Infinitives

Unit Overview

Unit 32 focuses on different uses of gerunds and infinitives. Some parts of this unit will be review for your students.
• Some verbs are followed by a gerund.
• Some verbs are followed by an infinitive.
• Some verbs can be followed by either a gerund or an infinitive, and the meaning is the same.
• Some verbs can be followed by either a gerund or an infinitive, but the meanings are different.
• To make general statements, you can use the gerund as subject or *it* + infinitive.

Grammar in Context (pages 356–357)

Vocabulary

put off: to delay something, or to delay doing something

unpleasant: not pleasant or enjoyable

time management: the process of controlling how your time is used

discouraging: making you lose the confidence you need to continue doing something

perfectionism: the attitude of not being satisfied with anything unless it is completely perfect

procrastinate: to delay doing something that you ought to do

Comprehension Questions

• What two examples of procrastination does the article give? *(a woman who puts off studying and a man who puts off making an appointment with the dentist)*
• Why do people tend to put off unpleasant tasks? *(because they are not fun to do. People prefer to do enjoyable things.)*
• Why do some people put off things they feel they won't be able to finish? *(because they get discouraged before starting)*
• Why do some people put off studying for tests? *(because tests make them feel nervous)*

• Why do perfectionists put off tasks? *(because the belief that they must do a perfect job prevents them from starting or finishing them)*

Discussion Topics

• Brainstorm with the class things people normally put off doing. Write students' ideas on the board. What types of things are they?
• Have students share with their partners methods/ideas they have tried to overcome procrastination. Were they effective? Encourage students to give concrete examples of their experiences.

Grammar Presentation (pages 357–358)

Identify the Grammar

GERUNDS AND INFINITIVES
. . . he decided to wait another week . . .
Procrastinating . . . is a universal problem.
Most people prefer to do enjoyable things.
Having too little time for a task is discouraging.
It's hard to get started on a project . . .
. . . you put off studying.

Grammar Charts

• Write the following examples on the board:
  Gerunds   *Infinitives*
  She put off studying.   *She decided not to study.*
  Have students study the examples, and ask:
  "What is *put off* followed by?" *(a gerund)*
  "What is *decided* followed by?" *(an infinitive)*
  Remind students that some verbs such as *put off* must be followed by gerunds, and other verbs such as *decide* must be followed by infinitives.
• Write below the examples on the board:
  They prefer going to   *They prefer to go to*
  the park.   *the park.*
  Then ask the class: "What is *prefer* followed by in the first example?" *(a gerund: going)*
  "What is *prefer* followed by in the second example?" *(an infinitive: to go)*
  Point out that a few verbs such as *prefer* can be followed by either a gerund or an infinitive with no change in meaning.
• Write below the examples on the board:
  Brad has stopped   *Tom was watching TV,*
  studying.   *but he has stopped*
                         to study.
  Then ask the class: "What is *stopped* followed by in the first example?" *(a gerund: studying)*

"What is *stopped* followed by in the second example?" (*an infinitive: to study*)
Point out that a few verbs such as *stop* can be followed by either a gerund or an infinitive, but the meaning is different. Brad stopped studying: he is not studying anymore. Tom stopped to study: he is now studying. (Tom stopped another activity—watching TV—in order to study.)
• Write below the examples on the board:
Getting started is not   It's not easy to get
* easy.   started.*
Have students name the gerund (*getting*) and the infinitive (*to get*) in the examples. Remind students that gerunds can be used as subjects. Point out that infinitives can be used after *it* + an adjective.
• Write below the examples of gerunds:
Tom is worried about not passing.
Remind students that prepositions such as *about* are followed by gerunds.

Grammar Notes

Notes 1–2   *(Exercises 1–4, 6)*
(Notes 1 and 2 are review for students.)
• Write the following examples on the board:
<u>*Gerunds and Infinitives*</u>
Todd avoids _____ an appointment with the dentist.
Todd plans _____ an appointment with the dentist.
Have students complete the sentences with a gerund or infinitive, as appropriate. *(making; to make)*
• Have students make up two sentences using a verb from each list and then share their sentences with the class.
• Refer students to Appendix 13 on page A-7 for a list of verbs followed by a gerund. Refer students to Appendix 14 on page A-7 for a list of verbs followed by an infinitive. Refer students to Unit 27 for more information on gerunds as objects. Refer students to Unit 29 for more information on infinitives after certain verbs.

→ For additional practice, see the Supplementary Activities on page 155.

Note 3   *(Exercises 1–2, 6)*
• Write on the board:
Eva hates to go to the library.
She prefers to go to the park.
Rod began writing his paper.
He likes writing papers.
Sheila loves reading.
Her teacher encouraged her to continue working hard.

Have students restate the statements on the board using gerunds or infinitives, as appropriate. Review as a class. (*Eva hates going to the library. She prefers going to the park. Rod began writing his paper. He loves to write papers. Sheila loves to read. Her teacher encouraged her to continue to work hard.*)
• For further practice, have students choose a verb from the list and write two sentences with the same meaning—one using a gerund, and the other using an infinitive. Have volunteers share their sentences with the class.
• Refer students to Appendix 15 on page A-7 for a list of verbs followed by a gerund or an infinitive.

Note 4   *(Exercises 1, 3–4, 6)*
• Write on the board:
a. Michael <u>stopped talking</u> on the phone.
b. Michael <u>stopped to talk</u> on the phone.
1. Michael was studying, but now he's talking on the phone.
2. Michael was talking on the phone, but now he's studying.
To check comprehension, have students match the examples a and b with the explanations 1 and 2. Review as a class. (*a—2; 1—b*)
• Continue in the same way with the following examples and explanations.
a. Liz <u>remembered going</u> to the library.
b. Liz <u>remembered to go</u> to the library.
1. Liz remembered the time when she used to go to the library.
2. Liz remembered that she had to go to the library, so she went.

a. John <u>forgot making</u> an appointment with the dentist.
b. John <u>forgot to make</u> an appointment with the dentist.
1. John made an appointment with the dentist, but then he forgot that he had made it.
2. John did not make an appointment with the dentist because he did not remember to do so.

Note 5   *(Exercises 1–3, 6)*
• This note is review for students. Ask students to say other expressions formed by adjective + preposition and verb + preposition that they remember. As you get feedback from students, write the expressions on the board. Then have volunteers use some of the expressions in sentences.
• Refer students to Unit 28 for more information on gerunds after prepositions.

Note 6   *(Exercise 1, 5–6)*
- Write a new example on the board:
  Having too little time for a task is discouraging.
  It is discouraging to have too little time for
  a task.
  Make sure students understand that both
  sentences have the same meaning.
- To provide practice, have students restate the
  following sentences using either gerunds as
  subjects or *it* + infinitive, as appropriate.
  Getting started is hard.
  It's fun to go to the park.
  Studying at the library is boring.
  It's interesting to learn a new language.

Focused Practice (pages 359–362)

Exercise 1

support group: a group of people who meet to help
each other with a particular problem

Exercise 2

postpone: to change an event to a later time or date

Exercise 3

reward: something that you get because you have
done something good or helpful or have worked hard

Exercise 5

reward: to give something to someone because
she/he has done something good or helpful or has
worked for it

Communication Practice (pages 362–366)

Exercise 7

After reviewing answers, have students share
their study habits with the class. Ask: "Which
things from the list don't you do?" "Why don't
you do them?" "Which things from the list do
you do?" "What else can you do to get better
results?"

Exercise 8

After working in groups, students share their
ideas with the class.
🕐 Have students write a short paragraph
about the kind of breaks they enjoy and the
new ideas they would like to try.

Exercise 9

- Write useful verbs on the board for students
  to use as reference:

avoid	keep
choose	prefer
decide	promise
delay	put off
end up	regret
fail	stop
forget	succeed

- Follow up by having students share with the
  class one of the things they do to stop putting
  things off.

Exercise 10

- Note: Students learned to use *advise* followed
  by an object and an infinitive. In the example,
  it is used followed by a gerund. If necessary,
  point out that *advise* is followed by an
  infinitive if it has an object. It is normally
  followed by a gerund if it has no object.
- After working in pairs, discuss the meaning
  of each quote as a class. Encourage students
  to say why they agree/disagree with them.
  You may want to take a poll to find out which
  quote is preferred by most students.

Exercise 11

Follow up with a brief discussion. Have
students discuss whether they would like to
join a support group. Ask: "Do you like sharing
your problems?" "Do you like sharing ideas
about how to solve problems?" "Do you think
that joining a support group can help you solve
problems?" "Why/Why not?"

Exercise 12

Questions to generate ideas and elicit
vocabulary:
- What's your goal?
- What's your deadline to achieve it?
- What will you stop doing to be able to
  accomplish it?
- What difficult things won't you put off/delay
  doing?
- What won't you fail to do?
- How long do you promise to spend on the
  task each day/week?
- What other things do you plan to do in order
  to achieve your goal?

Further Practice

In small groups, have students discuss these
questions:
- What do you expect to do this weekend?
- What do you look forward to doing?
- What do you need to do?
- What do you feel like doing?

 **OUT OF THE BOX** ......

Listening to the experts. Have students listen to a self-help audiocassette or compact disk about how to get organized or stop procrastinating, for example "Getting Organized," by Stephanie Winston, "Doing It Now—How to Cure Procrastination and Achieve Your Goals in 12 Easy Steps" by Edwin Bliss, or "Goals—Setting and Achieving Them on Schedule" by Zig Ziglar.

Have students listen to an excerpt and take notes about main ideas. To review the tips, read the items below one by one, and have different students say ideas about each. For example: *Stephanie Winston said you should remember to set priorities.*
• What you should remember to do
• What you should choose to do first
• What you should stop doing
• What you should try to do / not to do
• What you should plan to do
• What you shouldn't put off doing
• What you shouldn't forget to do
Note: If you don't have access to self-help audiocassettes or compact disks in English, do an Internet search on **tips to stop procrastinating.**

 UNIT 33

Preferences: *Prefer, Would prefer, Would rather*

Unit Overview

Unit 33 focuses on the uses of *prefer, would prefer,* and *would rather* to talk about things or activities that you like better than other things or activities.
• *Prefer* is often used to express a general preference.
• *Would prefer* and *would rather* are used to talk about a preference in a specific situation.
• A comparison with *to* can follow *prefer* or *would prefer* plus a noun or gerund.
• A comparison with *than* can follow *would rather* plus a base form.

Grammar in Context (pages 376–377)

Background Note

Market researchers conduct surveys about groups of people to find out about their lifestyles and buying habits, and they often show this information in bar graphs or pie charts. Companies use this information to market products and services more effectively.

Vocabulary

leisure time: time when you are not working and can do things you enjoy

thriller: a movie or book that tells an exciting story about murder, crime, etc.

portion: an amount of food for one person, especially when served in a restaurant

pastime: something enjoyable that you do when you are not working

Comprehension Questions

• What is the most popular pastime among adults? *(watching TV)*
• What is the least popular pastime among adults? *(doing exercise)*
• What are the most popular pastimes among teens? *(watching TV and listening to radio and recorded music)*
• What is the least popular pastime among teens? *(cooking)*
• What activities do adults prefer more than teenagers? *(cooking and shopping in stores)*
• What activities do teenagers prefer more than adults? *(listening to music, hobbies and exercise)*

Discussion Topics

• Have students discuss their preferences on the items in the survey. Encourage students to ask follow-up questions to find out more about their partners' favorite pastimes. Then take a poll to find out the most and least popular activities in the class.
• Watching TV seems to be the most popular pastime for both adults and teenagers. Ask students to provide possible reasons for the popularity of this pastime.

Grammar Presentation (pages 377–379)

Identify the Grammar

PREFERENCES: *PREFER*
I <u>prefer</u> big portions.
Which <u>do</u> you <u>prefer</u> . . . ?
I <u>prefer</u> e-mailing.

PREFERENCES: *WOULD PREFER*
Which <u>would</u> you <u>prefer</u> . . .?
I'd <u>prefer</u> to go to the game.

PREFERENCES: *WOULD RATHER*
. . . <u>would</u> you <u>rather see</u> a comedy or a
thriller?
I'd <u>rather try</u> interesting foods.

Grammar Charts

• Write the following examples on the board:

Preferences: Prefer	Preferences: Would prefer
I prefer e-mails.	I'd prefer a comedy.
He prefers e-mailing.	He'd prefer seeing a comedy.
They prefer (not) to e-mail.	They'd prefer (not) to see a comedy.

Have students study the examples on the left,
and ask: "Does *prefer* change when the
pronoun changes?" *(yes, because* prefer *is a
verb)* "What can *prefer* be followed by?" *(a
noun, a gerund, or an affirmative or negative
infinitive)* Have students study the examples
on the right, and ask: "What does *'d* in *I'd
prefer* or *He'd prefer* stand for?" *(would)* "Does
would change when the pronoun changes?"
(no, because would *is a modal)* "What can
would prefer be followed by?" *(a noun, a
gerund, or an affirmative or negative infinitive)*
Point out that both *prefer* and *would prefer*
are used to express preferences (things that
we like better than other things).
—Point to the first example under
"*Preferences: prefer,*" and provide the *yes/no*
question. (*Do you prefer e-mails?*) Write the
question on the board. Call on a student to
provide the two possible short answers. *(Yes,
I do. No, I don't.)*
Follow the same procedure for the second
and third question under "*Preferences:
prefer.*"
—Point to the first example under
"*Preferences: would rather,*" and provide
the *yes/no* question. (*Would you prefer a
comedy?*) Write the question on the board.

Call on a student to provide the two possible
short answers. *(Yes, I would. No, I wouldn't.)*
Follow the same procedure for the second
and third question under "*Preferences:
would prefer.*"
• Write the following examples on the board:
Preferences: Would rather
I'd rather watch a thriller.
He'd rather not watch a comedy.
Have students study the examples, and ask:
"What does *'d* in *I'd rather* and *He'd rather*
stand for?" *(would)* "Does *would* change
when the pronoun changes?" *(no)* "What can
would rather be followed by?" *(the base form
of the verb)*
—Point out that *would rather*—such as *prefer*
and *would prefer*—is also used to express
preferences.
—Point to the first example under
"*Preferences: would rather,*" and provide the
yes/no question. (*Would you rather watch a
thriller?*) Write the question on the board.
—Call on a student to provide the two possible
short answers. *(Yes, I would. No, I wouldn't.)*
—Point out that another possible negative
short answer is *No, I'd rather not.* You may
want to write on the board:
No, I wouldn't. = No, I'd rather not.

Grammar Notes

Note 1 *(Exercises 1–3, 5)*
• To help clarify how to express general
preferences and preferences in a specific
situation, write the following examples on the
board:

TONY: *I usually prefer thrillers, but tonight I'd
prefer a comedy.*

SALLY: *I usually prefer pizza, but right now I'd
rather eat a hamburger.*

Ask the class: "What does Tony usually prefer
to watch?" *(thrillers)* "Does he want to watch
a thriller tonight?" *(no)* "What would he
prefer to watch?" *(a comedy)* "What does
Sally usually prefer to eat?" *(pizza)* "Does she
want to eat pizza right now?" *(no)* "What
would she rather eat?" *(a hamburger)*
Then ask: "What do we use to express general
preferences?" *(prefer)* "What do we use to
express preferences in a specific situation?"
(would prefer or *would rather)*
• To provide practice, erase *thrillers, a comedy,
pizza,* and *a hamburger,* and replace them
with blanks. Have students copy the
sentences and complete the blanks with their
own ideas.

Follow up by calling on volunteers to share their sentences with the class.

→ For additional practice, see the Supplementary Activities on page 156.

Note 2 *(Exercises 1, 3, 5)*
• To provide practice, write on the board:

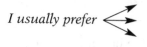

I usually prefer

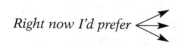

Right now I'd prefer

• Complete the diagrams with your own reading preferences using nouns, gerunds, and infinitives to express the same idea.

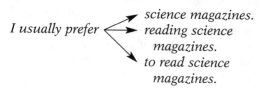

I usually prefer — science magazines.
reading science magazines.
to read science magazines.

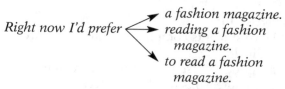

Right now I'd prefer — a fashion magazine.
reading a fashion magazine.
to read a fashion magazine.

• Erase the information about yourself. Have students copy the diagrams and complete them with their own reading preferences. Point out that for each opening line they should express the same idea in three different ways.

→ For additional practice, see the Supplementary Activities on page 156.

Note 3 *(Exercises 1–3, 5)*
• To provide practice, write the following conversation on the board:

A: *What would you like to have? <u>The grilled salmon</u> sounds delicious.*

B: *I'd rather not eat <u>fish</u> today. I think I'd rather have <u>the grilled chicken</u>.*

Tell students that the conversation takes place in a restaurant. Have students work in pairs and practice the conversation replacing the underlined fragments with their own ideas. Make sure both students play both roles.
• For further practice, write on the board:

A: *[make a suggestion]*

B: *[refuse the suggestion] [provide an explanation] [express your preference]*

Have students work in pairs and use the instructions on the board to create guided conversations. You may want to provide an example:

A: *Why don't we go jogging?*

B: *I'd rather not. It's cold outside. I think I'd rather stay home today.*

Make sure both students play both roles.

→ For additional practice, see the Supplementary Activities on page 156.

Note 4 *(Exercises 1, 4–5)*
• To help clarify, write new examples on the board:

I prefer	football swimming	*to*	tennis. skiing.
I'd prefer	a thriller renting a DVD	*to*	a horror movie. going to the movies.

Point out the patterns <u>noun + *to* + noun</u> and <u>gerund + *to* + gerund</u> to make comparisons with *prefer* or *would prefer.*
• To provide practice with *prefer* for general preferences, write the following cues on the board:
books—magazines
cookies—potato chips
brisk walking—cycling
eating out—cooking at home
In pairs, have students take turns using the cues to express their preferences. (*I prefer books to magazines. I prefer brisk walking to cycling.*) Follow up by having volunteers share some of their preferences with the class.
• To provide practice with *would prefer* for preferences in a specific situation, write the following cues on the board:
a cup of coffee—a soda
a sandwich—a piece of cake
doing a written exercise—talking with a partner
going on working—taking a break
In pairs, have students take turns using the cues to express what they would prefer to do at the moment. (*I'd prefer a cup of coffee to a soda. I'd prefer talking with a partner to doing a written exercise.*) Follow up by having volunteers share some of their preferences with the class.

Note 5 *(Exercises 1, 4–5)*
• Write a new example on the board:
I'd rather rent a DVD <u>than</u> go to the movies.
Point out the pattern <u>base form + *than* + base form</u> to make a comparison with *would rather.*

- Have students restate the preferences they previously expressed with *would prefer* using *would rather*. (*I'd rather drink a cup of coffee than a soda. I'd rather talk with a partner than do a written exercise.*)

Focused Practice (pages 380–383)

Exercise 2

anchovy: a very small ocean fish that tastes very salty

be in the mood: to want to do something, here, to want to eat something

pepperoni: a spicy dry Italian sausage

heartburn: a slightly painful burning feeling in your stomach or chest caused by indigestion

give someone the creeps: to make someone feel nervous and frightened

Exercise 3

aisle: a long passage between rows of seats in a theater, airplane, church, etc.

World Series: the last series of baseball games that is played each year in order to decide the best professional team in the United States and Canada

Exercise 4

shoot hoops: informal, play basketball

cricket: a game in which two teams try to get points by hitting a ball and running between two sets of sticks

whopping: very large

figure skating: a type of skating in which you move in patterns on the ice

wrestling: a sport in which you try to throw your opponent to the ground and hold him/her there

Communication Practice (pages 384–387)

Exercise 6

- Before students listen, go over the menu as a class. Clarify the meaning of any unknown words.
- To review answers, have students say full sentences using *She'd prefer* or *She'd rather.* (*She'd rather have the onion soup.*) Students in pairs take turns saying what they would prefer to order.

Exercise 7

- Go over the example. Point out that students should make suggestions, accept or refuse suggestions, and express their preferences.
- Give students a time limit of five minutes to agree on a program.

- Have students share their decisions with the class. Ask, "What did you learn about your classmates?" "Do you have similar tastes?"

Exercise 8

After students work in pairs, have them share their preferences with the class. Encourage them to support their views.

Exercise 9

- Have students look at the bar graphs and clarify any confusion the students may have.
- Go over the examples. Point out the use of *or* (NOT ~~and~~) in *Fifteen percent prefer cheese to chips or popcorn.* You may want to point out the same applies to questions:
  What percentage of people would rather eat chips to cheese or popcorn?
- Follow up by having volunteers compare their own preferences with what most people prefer. (*Most people prefer chips to cheese or popcorn. I prefer cheese. It's tastier and healthier!*)

Exercise 10

- Have students complete the questionnaire individually.
- As students discuss, encourage them to express reasons for their preferences.
- Follow up by having volunteers share their preferences with the class.

Exercise 11

Questions to generate ideas and elicit vocabulary:
- Which two choices will you write about?
- Which of the two choices do you prefer?
- What are the main advantages of the choice you selected?
- Are there any disadvantages?
- What are the main disadvantages of the choice you didn't select?
- Are there any advantages to the choice you didn't select?

Further Practice

Have students choose a topic to survey each other about their preferences. Ask them to create a questionnaire for that topic similar to the one on page 376. (Note: Point out the use of *which* (NOT ~~what~~) for questions that provide two choices.) Have students submit the questionnaires to you for correction. Then have students circulate around the room conducting the survey. Have students report to the class on their findings or write up a report on them and then submit it to you.

Let your imagination flow! Bring in magazine or newspaper advertisements for expensive cars, luxury cruises, exotic adventure vacations, five-star vacation resorts, etc. Have students work in small groups. Give each group a wide array of advertisements. Tell students to imagine they won $75,000 to spend on the items advertised in the ads. Have students discuss the choices, express their preferences, and decide what they'd rather spend the money on. Follow up by having students share their decisions with the class.

UNIT 34 — Necessity: *Have (got) to, Must, Don't have to, Must not, Can't*

Unit Overview

Unit 34 focuses on the uses of *have (got) to, must, don't have to, must not,* and *can't* to express different degrees of necessity.

- The affirmative forms *have, have got to,* and *must* express necessity.
- The negative form *don't have to* expresses lack of necessity.
- The negative forms *must not* and *can't* express prohibition.

Grammar in Context (pages 388–389)

Vocabulary

inspect: to examine something carefully

expire: if a document expires, you cannot legally continue to use it beyond a particular date

valid: a valid ticket, document, or agreement can be used legally or is officially acceptable

renew: to arrange for something such as a contract to continue

customs: the place where your bags are checked for illegal goods when you go into a country

permit: an official written statement giving you the right to do something

rent: to pay money for the use of something for a short period of time

regulation: an official rule or order

differ: to be different

hassle: something that is annoying because it causes problems, or is difficult to do

Comprehension Questions

Why does the columnist recommend . . .

- carrying your passport for all international travel? *(because it's the best form of identification)*
- renewing you passport if it will expire in three months? *(because for many countries your passport must be valid for at least six months after you enter the country)*
- not bringing fresh food into foreign countries? *(because many countries have strict rules about bringing in food)*
- getting an IDP for an around-the-world tour? *(because it is required in many countries)*
- moving around and drinking plenty of water on long flights? *(because otherwise, you won't stay healthy)*

Discussion Topics

- To draw on prior knowledge, have students share other rules an international traveler should know. Encourage students to explain why it is important to know them.
- To draw on students' prior experience, ask students to say whether they often/sometimes travel abroad. Encourage students to talk about their personal experience.

Grammar Presentation (pages 389–391)

Identify the Grammar

NECESSITY: *HAVE (GOT) TO, MUST*
. . . your passport <u>must be</u> valid . . .
. . . you'll <u>have to check</u> the rules . . .
<u>Do I have to get</u> an International Driver's Permit (IDP)?
. . . you'<u>ve got to get up</u> . . .

NECESSITY: *DON'T HAVE TO*
. . . you <u>don't have to put</u> them through the X-ray equipment.
. . . in Canada you <u>don't have to have</u> one . . .

NECESSITY: *MUST NOT, CAN'T*
You <u>can't bring</u> most types of cheese . . .
In Germany you <u>must not drive</u> without one . . .

Grammar Charts

- Write the following examples on the board:

Necessity: Have to	Necessity: Have got to
He has to renew his passport.	She has got to get an IDP.
They have to board from Gate 10.	We have got to check the rules.
Do they have to carry their passport?	They've got to move around.
Does she have to make connecting flights?	He's got to drink plenty of water.
What time do they have to be at the airport?	

Have students study the examples of *have to,* and ask: "Does *have to* change when the pronoun changes?" *(yes)* "How do you express necessity with *have to*?" *(form of* have to + *base form of verb)* "Do *have to* and *has to* have short forms?" *(no)* "How do you form *yes/no* questions with *have to*?" *(do/does + subject + * have to + *base form)* "How do you form *wh-* questions?" *(wh- word + do/does + subject +* have to + *base form)*

- Call on a student to provide the two possible short answers for each *yes/no* question on the board. *(Yes, they do. No, they don't. Yes, she does. No, she doesn't.)*

- Have students study the examples of *have got to,* and ask: "Does *have got to* change when the pronoun changes?" *(yes)* "How do you express necessity with *have got to*?" *(form of* have + got to + *base form of verb)* "Do *have got to* and *has got to* have short forms?" *(yes)* "What do *'ve* in *They've* and *'s* in *He's* stand for?" (have *and* has)

- Do not erase the examples already on the board, and write:

Necessity: Must
He must renew his passport.
They must board from Gate 10.
She must get an IDP.
We must check the rules.

Have students study the examples, and ask: "Do the examples with *must* have the same meaning as the ones with *have to* and *have got to*?" *(yes)* "Does *must* change when the pronoun changes?" *(no)* "How do you express necessity with *must*?" (must + *base form of verb)*

- Write the following contrasting examples on the board:

Necessity: Don't have to	Necessity: Must not
You don't have to have an IDP in Canada.	You must not drive without an IDP in Germany.
He doesn't have to get an IDP.	He must not forget his IDP.

Have students study the examples, and ask: "What are the negative forms of *have to* and *has to*?" *(don't have to* and *doesn't have to)* "What does *don't have to* express?" *(that something is not necessary)* "What is the negative form of *must*?" *(must not)* "What does *must not* express—that something is not necessary or that something is not permitted?" *(that something is not permitted)*

- Write the following examples on the board:

Necessity: Can't	Necessity: Must not
He can't park here.	He must not park here.

Have students study the examples, and ask: "Do both examples mean the same?" *(yes)* Emphasize that both *must not* and *can't* express prohibition.

- To summarize, you may want to draw the following diagrams on the board:

have to
have got to ⎤— necessity
must

don't have to ⎤— lack of necessity

must not
can't ⎤— prohibition

Grammar Notes

Note 1 *(Exercises 1–4, 6)*

- To check comprehension, write on the board:
  1. *Which is more common in everyday speaking?*
     You must get an IDP.
     You have to get an IDP.
  2. *Which is used in writing?*
     You have to go through customs.
     You must go through customs.
  3. *Which expresses stronger feelings?*
     You have to renew your passport.
     You've got to renew your passport.
  4. *Which expresses a stronger obligation?*
     You must go to bed.
     You have to go to bed.

Working in pairs, have students close their books and answer the questions. Then ask them to open their books to confirm their answers. Review as a class. *(1. You have to get an IDP. 2. You must go through customs. 3. You've got to renew your passport. 4. You must go to bed.)*

• Point out that in informal speech *have to* is often pronounced "hafta" and *got to* is often pronounced "gotta." Have students practice these reductions in pronunciation by repeating the following sentences after you:
"You <u>have to</u> (hafta) get an IDP."
"They <u>have to</u> (hafta) carry their passport."
"You've <u>got to</u> (gotta) get an IDP."
"They've <u>got to</u> (gotta) carry their passport."

→ For additional practice, see the Supplementary Activities on page 156.

Note 2 *(Exercises 1, 3, 6)*

• To help clarify, write on the board:
<u>Simple Present</u>: *She has to check in now.*
<u>Future</u>: *They will have to declare the new camera.*
<u>Simple Past</u>: *He had to be at the airport at 4:00.*
<u>Present Perfect</u>: *She has had to travel ever since she got that job.*
Point out that *have to* can be used in all tenses. Have students look at the examples and name the simple present, future, simple past, and present perfect forms of *have to.* *(has to, will have to, had to, has had to)*

• To provide practice, erase the examples and replace them with blanks. In pairs, have students write their own examples. Then call on volunteers to share their sentences with the class.

• To check comprehension of present and future meaning, write on the board:
You've got to be there at 10:00.
You've got to sign here.
Have students look at the examples and ask: "Which example refers to the present?" *(You've got to sign here.)* "What does the first example refer to?" *(the future)* "How do you know?" *(because it says at 10:00)*

Note 3 *(Exercises 1, 3, 6)*

• Emphasize that *must* and *have got to* are not normally used in questions.

• To provide practice, rewrite the examples in Note 2 on the board:
She has to check in now.
They will have to declare the new camera.
He had to be at the airport at 4:00.
She has had to travel ever since she got that job.
Working in pairs, have students write a *yes/no* question and a *wh-* question for each item. Review as a class. *(Does she have to check in now? When does she have to check in? Will*

they have to declare the new camera? What will they have to declare? Did he have to be at the airport at 4:00? What time did he have to be at the airport? Has she had to travel since she got that job? How long has she had to travel?)

Note 4 *(Exercises 1–6)*

• To check comprehension, write new examples on the board:
a. You must not check in yet.
b. You don't have to check in yet.
Have students explain the difference in meaning between the two sentences. *(a. It is not allowed to check in yet, so the person can't check in. b. It is not necessary to check in right now, but the person can do so if he/she wants to.)*

• To provide practice with *can't*, write on the board:
You don't have to renew your passport.
Passengers must not check in before 6:00.
He doesn't have to get an IDP.
You must not bring fresh food into the country.
Working in pairs, have students restate the sentences with *can't* <u>whenever possible</u>. Review as a class. *(Passengers can't check in before 6:00. You can't bring fresh food into the country.)*

→ For additional practice, see the Supplementary Activities on page 156.

Focused Practice (pages 392–395)

Exercise 1

consulate: the official building where a consul lives and works (a consul is an official who lives in a foreign city and whose job is to help citizens of his/her own country who also live or work there, or citizens from the country where he/she is living who need information about his/her country)

visa: an official mark that is put on your passport that allows you to enter or leave another country

insurance: an arrangement with a company in which you pay it money regularly and the company pays the costs if anything bad happens to you or your property, such as an illness or an accident

certificate: an official document that states the facts about something or someone

rental: an arrangement by which you rent something

set: a set time, amount, price, etc., is fixed and is never changed

Exercise 3

security: the area that people must pass through where guards who protect a business's buildings, equipment, and workers check people and their belongings for anything dangerous

endless: continuing for a very long time, especially in a way that is annoying

Exercise 4
carry-on: a carry-on bag is one that you can take on a plane with you

overhead compartment: a small enclosed space above the seats of an airplane

label: a piece of paper or other material that is attached to something and has information about that thing printed on it

Communication Practice (pages 396–397)

Exercise 7
• Before students listen, have them look at the signs.
• After reviewing answers, ask students to explain what the signs mean using *have to, must,* or *can't.* (*a. You have to/must stop. b. You can't stop. c. You can't drive more slowly than 30 miles per hour. d. You can't pass another car. e. You can't drive faster than 80 miles per hour. f. You have to/must turn left. You can't turn right.*)

Exercise 8
• Give the class a time limit of 10 minutes to discuss the signs.
• After working in pairs, students share their ideas with the class.
⏱ Have students choose a sign and write a short paragraph about it. Point out that students should use the questions that prompted discussion as a guide.

Exercise 9
• Bring in colored pens and pencils and different-colored and textured paper to class.
• Encourage students to be creative. Point out that they can make signs for their cars, their homes, for the classroom, for their bedroom door, or for anywhere else.
• Give students a time limit of 10 minutes to draw the sign and write a few sentences about its meaning. Circulate and provide help as needed.
• After showing their sign to a classmate, students share their signs with the class. Invite students to come to the front and show the sign for the whole class to discuss its meaning.

Exercise 10
• Have students write their list individually. Emphasize that students should include things that they have already done this week and things that they haven't done yet.
• After working in pairs, students report to the class on what their classmates have to do and don't have to do this week.

Exercise 11
Questions to generate ideas and elicit vocabulary:
• What application procedure will you write about?
• Have you ever applied for that? If so, when? Why?
• What must you do? (Think about what is mandatory or essential.)
• What do you have to do? (Think about what is important to do.)
• What don't you have to do? (Think about what is not really necessary to do.)
• What is a "must not"? (Think about what is not permitted or what you strongly recommend not to do.)

Further Practice
Working in small groups, have students choose a place—for example, a zoo, a museum, or a train station—and write a list of 10 useful rules for that place. Point out that each rule should use one of the modals that students learned in this unit. After writing the rules, students read the rules aloud to the class, withholding the name of the place. The class guesses the place.

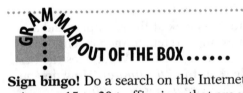

Sign bingo! Do a search on the Internet and print out 15 to 20 traffic signs that are used in the United States. (Print out several copies of the signs or make several copies of the signs you selected.) Cut out a colored card for each pair or group of three. Paste nine signs in a 3 × 3 grid on each colored card. Each colored card should have at least one sign which is from the ones on the other cards. The following are three examples of cards:

Give pairs or groups of three a card each, and play bingo: say the rules one by one as students check if they have the corresponding sign on their card. Whenever possible, use the ways to express necessity that students learned in this unit to describe the signs, for example: *This sign indicates that you can't park in this place.*

UNIT 35 Expectations: *Be supposed to*

Unit Overview

Unit 35 focuses on the use of *be supposed to* to express expectations.
- *Be supposed to* is used to express expectations that have their origin in rules, customs, predictions, hearsay, and plans or arrangements.
- It is used in the simple present to express present or future expectations, and in the simple past to express past expectations

Grammar in Context (pages 398–399)

Background Note

There are several popular books on etiquette. A traditional favorite was written by Emily Post. Judith Foster, known as Miss Manners, has written several more recent ones. She also writes a newspaper column, answering questions about etiquette (or manners). Ms. Etiquette is a fictional character.

Vocabulary

bride: a woman at the time she gets married, or just after she is married

maid of honor: the main bridesmaid (a woman who helps the bride and stands beside her in a wedding)

ceremony: a formal or traditional set of actions used at an important social or religious event

wedding: a marriage ceremony, especially one with a religious service

groom: a man at the time he gets married, or just after he is married

best man: the man at a wedding who stands beside and helps the man who is getting married (groom)

value: to think that something is important and worth having

marriage certificate: an official document that proves that two people are married

Comprehension Questions

- What has the reader been invited to do? *(to be the maid of honor at her best friend's wedding)*
- Why does the columnist think the reader should feel proud? *(because her friend's invitation means that she values their friendship)*
- Who was the maid of honor in the past? *(the bride's sister)*
- What is the maid of honor supposed to do? *(help the bride choose the bridesmaids' dresses, help the bride send the invitations, hold the bride's flowers during the ceremony, and sign the marriage certificate)*
- What is the best man supposed to do? *(drive the groom to the ceremony and sign the marriage certificate)*

Discussion Topics

- Have students compare the wedding customs in the United States with the ones in their own country. Encourage them to also share what they might know about wedding customs in other countries.
- Ask students to discuss their views on customs and traditions. To prompt discussion, you may want to write the following questions on the board:
Why do different countries usually have different customs and traditions?
Are customs and traditions important?
Is it important to respect traditions?
Is it important to keep them alive?
Encourage students to explain their views.

Grammar Presentation (pages 399–400)

Identify the Grammar

EXPECTATIONS: *BE SUPPOSED TO*

What is the maid of honor <u>supposed to do</u> in a wedding ceremony?

. . . the bride <u>is supposed to select</u> my dress.

. . . the bride's sister <u>was supposed to serve</u> as her maid of honor . . .

. . . the groom's brother <u>was supposed to be</u> his best man.

. . . these two <u>are supposed to help</u> the couple prepare for the ceremony.

. . . the best man <u>is supposed to drive</u> the groom to the ceremony.

. . . the maid of honor and the best man <u>are both supposed to sign</u> the marriage certificate . . .

Grammar Charts

- Write the following examples on the board:
  Expectations: *Be supposed to*
  The bride is supposed to be on her way.
  We are supposed to sign the marriage certificate after the wedding.
  Have students study the examples, and ask: "Does the first example express an expectation about the present or the future?" *(the present)* "Does the second example express an expectation about the present or the future?" *(the future)* "How do you express present or future expectations?" *(present form of* be (am, is, are) + supposed to + *base form of verb)*
- Write new examples on the board:
  In the past the groom's brother was supposed to be the best man.
  The bride was supposed to be there at 6:00.
  Have students study the examples, and ask: "Do these examples express expectations about the present, the past, or the future?" *(the past)* "How do you express past expectations?" *(past form of* be (was, were) + supposed to + *base form of verb)*
- Write the following questions on the board:
  Is she supposed to sign the marriage certificate?
  Was he supposed to drive the groom to the ceremony?
  Were the bridesmaids supposed to arrive at 5:00?
  Have students study the examples, and ask: "How do you form questions with *be supposed to*?" *(present or past form of* be + *subject* + supposed to + *base form)*
  Call on different students to provide the two possible short answers for each question.

Have them come to the front and write the answers on the board. *(Yes, she is. / No she isn't. Yes, he was. / No, he wasn't. Yes, they were. / No they weren't.)*
- Have students turn the *yes/no* questions on the board into *wh-* questions starting with *what, where,* and *what time,* respectively. *(What was she supposed to sign? Where was he supposed to drive the groom? What time were the bridesmaids supposed to arrive?)*

Grammar Notes

Note 1 *(Exercises 1–2, 4)*
- If necessary, point out that *be supposed to* is an idiomatic phrase and is distinct from the regular verb *to suppose,* which means *to consider as probable* or *to believe.* (*I suppose I should go home. It's late.*)
- Write on the board:

a. *It's supposed to be sunny tomorrow.*	hearsay
b. *We're supposed to leave at 8:00.*	rule
c. *The maid of honor is supposed to help the bride.*	prediction
d. *You're not supposed to drive without a license.*	custom
e. *The Argentineans are supposed to be friendly to foreigners.*	plan or arrangement

  To check comprehension have students match the examples with the different kinds of expectations. Review as a class. *(a. prediction b. plan or arrangement c. custom d. rule e. hearsay)*
- To provide practice, have students work in pairs and write their own example for each kind of expectation. Follow up by having volunteers share their sentences with the class.

→ For additional practice, see the Supplementary Activities on pages 156–157.

Note 2 *(Exercises 1–4)*
- Point out that when we use *be supposed to* for present or future expectations, what we expect may or may not happen.
- To provide practice, have students take turns sharing their expectations for the weekend. You may want to write an example on the board:

  I'm going to the movies with Jane on Saturday. We are supposed to meet at the movie theater at 6:00. We might meet later, though, because Jane is never on time. After the movie, we are supposed to go out for dinner. It all depends on how tired we are!

- Give additional examples of how *supposed to* in the past describes something that was expected to happen but didn't. Write on the board:

  We were supposed to get married this June, but we changed the date to August.

  He was supposed to pick the bride up at her house, but he went directly to the church instead!

- To provide practice with *was/were going to*, have students restate the sentences above using *was/were going to*. (*We were going to get married . . . He was going to pick the bride up . . .*)

- To provide practice with *was/were supposed to*, write the following incomplete sentences on the board:

  _____, but it rained.
  _____, but we just didn't meet.
  _____, but he forgot.
  _____, but they put it off.

  In pairs, have students complete the sentences with their own ideas using *was/were supposed to*. To review, have students share their sentences with the class.

→ For additional practice, see the Supplementary Activities on pages 156–157.

Focused Practice (pages 401–404)

Exercise 1

elope: to go away secretly with someone to get married

site: a place where something important or interesting happened

mayor: someone who is elected to lead the government or a town or city

setting: the place where something happens, and all the things that surround it

burst into: to suddenly start to do something

bouquet: a group of flowers given to someone as a present or carried at a formal occasion

cyclist: someone who rides a bicycle

weather forecaster: someone who reports on the television or radio what the weather will be like

Exercise 2

handkerchief: a piece or cloth that you use for drying your nose or eyes

rehearsal: a period of time or a particular occasion when all the people in a play, concert, ceremony, etc., practice it before giving a public performance

Exercise 3

bridal shower: a party for a woman who is going to be married, given by her friends and family

Exercise 4

fiancée: the woman whom a man is going to marry

hire: to employ someone to work for you; here, to pay money for the use of something for a short time

limousine: a big expensive car, driven by someone who is paid to drive

reception: a large formal party to celebrate something

newlyweds: a man and a woman who have recently gotten married

Communication Practice (pages 404–405)

Exercise 5

- Before students listen, have them go over the sentences.
- After reviewing answers, ask students to say the customs that spring from the conversations. List them on the board.

  The bride's family is supposed to sit on the left during the ceremony.

  The maid of honor isn't supposed to walk behind the bride.

  Guests are supposed to tell the bride that she looks beautiful.

  They are supposed to say "Congratulations" to the groom.

  Guests are supposed to throw rice at the bride and the groom, but they don't do it anymore because it can hurt birds.

  Then ask students which of these customs are true in other cultures.

Exercise 6

- Point out that students can discuss plans about studies, jobs, vacations, moving to a different town or country, getting married, or their own ideas.
- Go over the example and point out the use of *be supposed to* and *be going to*. Point out that students should ask follow-up questions.
- After working in pairs, students report on how their partner's plans changed to the class.

Exercise 7

- Have students look at the picture and describe it. Then go over the example.
- Encourage students to write notes about customs for each event on the list.
- To review, call on a group to report on the first item on the list. Have the other groups listen carefully and provide additional information. Continue in the same way for the other events on the list.

Exercise 8

Questions to generate ideas and elicit vocabulary:

- What are the people supposed to wear?
- What are they supposed to do?
- What are they supposed to say?
- What kind of gifts are they supposed to give?
- Is there any special food that is prepared/ served?
- If there is a ceremony, where is it supposed to take place?
- Are the people supposed to do anything in particular after the event?

Further Practice

Have students think about things that they were supposed to do last week but they didn't do in the end, or things that they expected to happen but did not happen in the end. In pairs, have students take turns sharing their expectations and the things that actually happened.

GRAMMAR OUT OF THE BOX ......

Table manners. Bring in questions posted to an Internet column about table manners. Have students work in small groups. Give each group at least one question. Have students write an answer to the question as if they were the columnist. Point out that some of their sentences should use *be supposed to*. After students have finished writing, hand out the columnist's replies to the questions for students to compare with their own answer. Then have groups report to the class on the question, their own reply, and the columnist's reply.

UNIT 36 Future Possibility: *May, Might, Could*

Unit Overview

Unit 36 focuses on the uses of *may, might,* and *could* to express expectations.

- The affirmative forms *may, might,* and *could* express the possibility that something will happen.
- The negative forms *may not* and *might not* express the possibility that something will not happen. *Couldn't,* however, expresses that something is impossible.
- *May, might,* and *could* are not often used in questions about possibility. The future (*will, be going to,* the present progressive) is used instead. Phrases such as *Do you think . . . ?* or *Is it possible that . . . ?* are also used. Answers to these questions often use *may, might,* or *could.*

Grammar in Context (pages 406–407)

Background Note

This unit talks about temperature in both Celsius and Fahrenheit measurements. Here is a conversion table:

Celsius degrees	Fahrenheit degrees
0	32
10	50
20	68
30	86
40	104

Vocabulary

high: the highest temperature recorded in a particular time or period

low: the lowest temperature recorded in a particular time or period

flurries: a small amount of snow that falls

bundle up: to dress in a lot of warm clothes because it is cold

Comprehension Questions

- Will it definitely snow in London tomorrow? *(No, it might snow.)*
- How strong are the winds going to be? *(They could reach 40 mph.)*
- Will it be stormy in France tomorrow? *(Yes, stormy conditions may move into France.)*
- Will it definitely snow in Paris tomorrow? *(No, rain could turn to snow in the evening.)*
- Will Rome be warm tomorrow? *(Yes, it may be warm in Rome.)*
- Will the temperature reach the twenties? *(It could reach the twenties.)*

Discussion Topics

- Have students discuss the importance of weather forecasts. To prompt discussion, write the following questions on the board: *Why are weather forecasts useful? Do you sometimes check the weather forecast? When? What for?*

Where do you usually get information about the weather—in the newspaper, on the Internet, on the radio, on TV? Why?

- Have students talk about their favorite season and the type of weather they prefer. Follow up by asking students, "Which country or region has the 'ideal' climate for you? Why?"

Grammar Presentation (pages 407–408)

Identify the Grammar

FUTURE POSSIBILITY: *MAY, MIGHT, COULD*
Temperatures <u>may drop</u> . . .
We <u>might</u> even <u>see</u> some snow flurries . . .
. . . winds <u>could reach</u> 40 miles per hour.
. . . you <u>may not need</u> your coat at all . . .
I <u>might!</u>

Grammar Charts

- Write affirmative sentences on the board:
<u>Future possibility: May, Might, Could</u>
Temperatures may drop.
We might see some snow.
Winds could reach 40 miles per hour.
Have students study the examples, and ask: "Do the examples express a possibility or a fact?" *(a possibility)* "Do they refer to the future or the past?" *(the future)* "How do you express future possibility?" (may/might/could + *base form of verb*)
- Write negative sentences on the board:
Temperatures may not drop.
We might not see snow.
Winds may not reach 40 miles per hour.
Winds might not stop until Sunday.
Have students study the examples, and ask: "Do these sentences express a possibility that something will happen or a possibility that something will not happen?" *(a possibility that something will not happen)* "How can you express a possibility that something will not happen?" (may/might + not + *base form of verb*) Point out that *could not* is not used to express a possibility that something will not happen. *Could not* has a different meaning: impossibility.
- Write the following questions on the board:
Will it snow in Paris?
Is it going to rain in London?
Are you taking the 5:00 P.M. flight?
Have students study the examples, and ask: "Do we use *may, might,* or *could* to ask about future possibility?" *(no)* "What do we use

instead?" *(a way to express the future:* will, be going to, *or the present progressive)*
Add possible short answers next to each question, for example:
Will it snow in Paris? It may./It might./It could.
Is it going to rain in London? It may not./It might not.
Will it be hot tomorrow? It may be./It might be./It could be.
Point to the first question and its answers and say, "*May, might,* and *could* are used for affirmative short answers." Point to the second question and its answers and say, "*May* and *might* (NOT ~~could~~) are used for negative short answers." Point to the third question and its answers and say, "*May, might,* and *could* are often followed by *be* if the question uses *be* as a main verb."

Grammar Notes

Note 1   *(Exercises 1–3, 5)*
- Write two contrasting examples on the board:
It <u>may</u> be sunny tomorrow.
<u>Maybe</u> it will be sunny tomorrow.
Direct students' attention to the first example. Point out that *may* is a modal that expresses future possibility. Ask students what other modals could replace *may* in the first example. *(might, could)*
- Direct student's attention to the second example. Point out that *maybe* is not a modal but an adverb that expresses possibility. It comes at the beginning of the sentence. Point out the use of *will* to express the same meaning as the first sentence (future possibility).
- Write the following sentences on the board:
It might snow.
Maybe it will be windy.
She may go skiing.
Maybe she will need her new jacket.
To provide practice, have students restate the sentences using modals or *maybe,* as appropriate. *(Maybe it will snow. It may/might/could be windy. Maybe she will go skiing. She may/might/could need her new jacket.)*

Note 2   *(Exercises 1–2, 5)*
- Write on the board:
a. *I may not travel with my aunt. She's too bossy!*
b. *I might not travel with my aunt. She's too bossy!*

c. *I couldn't travel with my aunt. She's too bossy!*

To check comprehension ask students "Which sentences express a possibility that the person will not travel with his/her aunt?" *(a and b)* "What does the last sentence express?" *(That the person doesn't even consider traveling with his/her aunt because she is so bossy. That's impossible.)*

- Write on the board:
  Someone you may travel with one day: _____
  Someone you might never travel with: _____
  Someone you couldn't travel with: _____
  Have students complete the item with notes, and then write a sentence for each item using *may, might not,* and *couldn't.* Have students share sentences with a partner and explain their choices. Follow up by having a few volunteers share their sentences with the class.

Note 3   *(Exercises 1, 4–5)*

- Emphasize that *may, might,* and *could* are not normally used in questions about possibility. However, *may, might,* and *could* are normally used in answers.
- To exemplify further, write on the board:
  Will it rain tomorrow?
  Is it going to rain tomorrow?
  Do you think it will rain tomorrow?

  | *Well, the forecast says it* | *may* *might* *could* | *rain in the evening.* |

- To provide practice, have pairs use the questions on the board as a guide to create three new questions using *will, be going to,* and *Do you think . . . ?* Have them also provide a full sentence as an answer.
- To provide practice with short answers, write on the board:
  a. *Will you come?*
  b. *Are you going to stay?*
  c. *Is he still in the office?*
  d. *Do you think it will get hot?*
  e. *Will she be late?*
  Working in pairs, have students create a short answer for each question. Remind students that questions that use *be* as the main verb usually use *be* in the answer. Review as a class. (Possible answers: *a. I might. b. I could. c. He may be. d. It might. e. She might be.*)

→ For additional practice, see the Supplementary Activities on page 157.

Focused Practice (pages 409–411)

Exercise 1
cut class: to deliberately not go to class or school

shovel: to dig or move earth, stones, snow, etc., with a shovel (a tool with a long handle)

takeout: a meal you buy from a restaurant that you eat somewhere else

Exercise 2
notice: a written or printed statement that gives information or a warning to people

day-care center: a place where young children are taken care of while their parents are at work

master's degree: a university degree that you get by studying for one or two years after your first degree

Exercise 5
El Niño: the condition when the surface of the Pacific Ocean becomes warmer near the west coast of South America, affecting the weather around the ocean

crop: a plant such as corn, wheat, rice, etc., that is grown by a farmer and is used as food

pollution: the process of polluting (making air, water, soil, etc., dangerously dirty) a place

Communication Practice (pages 412–413)

Exercise 6
- Before students listen, have them look at the charts. Point out that all the weather conditions in the charts are mentioned in the forecast. Students should listen carefully to find out if they are <u>certain</u> or <u>possible</u>. Also point out that temperatures are given in the Fahrenheit scale.
- To review answers, have students say complete sentences using future tenses or modals of possibility, as appropriate. *(It might be sunny on Friday. It will be sunny on Saturday.)*
  Ask the class, "What will the weather be like tomorrow?" Write students' predictions on the board using future tenses and modals of possibility, depending on the certainty.

Exercise 7
- Have students read the profiles and the future possibilities in the box. Clarify any confusion they might have.
- Go over the example and point out the modals.
- After working in groups, students share their ideas with the class.

- Individually, have students write about their own possibilities using the listed categories of occupations, hobbies, and achievements.
- Have students share their writing in groups and then submit it to you for correction.

Exercise 8

Questions to generate ideas and elicit vocabulary:
- What are you going to do <u>next year</u>?
- What may/might/could you do?
- What may/might you not do?
- What do you think you will do <u>in the next ten years</u>?
- What may/might/could you do?
- What may/might you not do?

Topics to generate ideas and elicit vocabulary:
- Studies
- Work
- Vacations
- Hobbies
- Achievements
- Living at home or abroad
- Getting married
- Having children

Further Practice

Working in small groups, have students write a list of ten goals that people may be interested in achieving. *(break a record, become a millionaire, travel around the world, etc.)* Then have students interview another group by asking "Do you think you will . . . ?" *(Do you think you will ever break a record?)* Ask students to answer the questions about their future using modals expressing future possibility. Point out that they can give serious or amusing answers. Follow up by having students report to the class on their partners' answers.

GRAMMAR OUT OF THE BOX . . . . . .

What's behind the headlines? Bring in magazine or newspaper articles about the environment, global warming, and how the weather is changing. Bring material from both serious and sensational newspapers. Have students compare how bad news seems more certain in sensational news stories than in serious ones. You may want to write two headlines as examples on the board:

ICE CAP TO MELT SOON
SCIENTISTS STUDY POSSIBLE EFFECTS OF GLOBAL WARMING

Point out how the first headline states a fact: that the ice cap will definitely melt soon. The second headline, however, states that scientists still don't know what might happen. After discussing in groups, have students share the topics they discussed, and describe the future of the environment using future tenses and modals of possibility, depending on the certainty.

UNIT 37 — Conclusions: *Must, Have (got) to, May, Might, Could, Can't*

Unit Overview

Unit 37 focuses on the uses of *must, have (got) to, may, might, could,* and *can't* to express conclusions.

- The affirmative forms *must, have to,* and *have got to* express that we are almost 100 percent certain that something is possible. *May, might,* and *could* express that something is possible, but we are less certain about it.
- The negative forms *can't* and *couldn't* express that we are almost 100 percent certain that something is impossible. The negative form *must not* expresses that we are slightly less certain, and *may not* and *might not* express that we are even less certain.
- Only *can* and *could* are used in questions about guesses.

Grammar in Context (pages 414–415)

Background Note

Sir Arthur Conan Doyle wrote the Sherlock Holmes stories at the end of the 19th century. Holmes, a fictional character, was one of the first detectives. He used his powers of observation to make deductions that helped him solve crimes. He was often accompanied by his friend, Dr. Watson, who was not as brilliant as Holmes. Usually Holmes had to explain his conclusions to Dr. Watson in great detail.

Vocabulary

cuff: the end part of a sleeve (the arm of a shirt, dress, etc.)

worn: a worn object is old and slightly damaged because it has been used a lot

Comprehension Questions

- Why is Wilson visiting Holmes? *(because he wants Holmes to solve a case)*
- What does Wilson look like? *(He is fat and has red hair.)*
- How does Watson know that Wilson writes a lot? *(because his right shirt cuff is worn and he has a hole in the sleeve of his jacket)*
- Where did Wilson work for two months? *(at the Red-Headed League)*
- What's the Red-Headed League? *(an organization to help red-headed men)*
- How did Wilson learn about the job? *(his clerk, Vincent, showed him an advertisement for an open position)*
- What did Wilson do at the League? *(copied the encyclopedia by hand)*

Discussion Topics

- Have students share their views on the story so far. Ask questions to prompt discussion: "Does the Red-Headed League sound like a serious organization to you? Does Wilson's work at the League seem like useful work? Do you think Wilson was cheated?" Have students also say what they think might happen next.
- Have students tell their partners about the best mystery novel or suspense movie they have read or watched. Encourage students to explain why they liked it.

Grammar Presentation (pages 415–418)

Identify the Grammar

CONCLUSIONS: *MUST, HAVE (GOT) TO, MAY, MIGHT, COULD, CAN'T*
Mr. Wilson *must write* a lot . . .
You *could be* right.
Your methods *may be* useful after all.
They *couldn't pay* someone just for having red hair . . .
It *might not be* . . .

Grammar Charts

- Write affirmative sentences on the board:
Conclusions: *Must, May, Might, Could*
Wilson *must write* a lot.
He *may be* in danger.
He *might be* in trouble.
He *could be* a liar.

Have students study the examples, and ask: "What do all the examples express?" *(conclusions)* "How do you express affirmative conclusions?" (must/may/might/could + *base form of verb*)

- Write negative sentences on the board:
Conclusions: *Must, May, Might, Could, Can*
Wilson *must not be* very smart.
He *may not have* a shop.
He *might not know* his clerk very well.
They *couldn't pay* him for copying an encyclopedia.
Vincent *can't be* an honest man.

Have students study the examples, and ask: "Do these examples also express conclusions?" *(yes)* "How do you express negative conclusions?" (must/may/might/could/can + not + *base form of verb*) "Which modals can be contracted in sentences expressing conclusions?" *(couldn't, can't)* "Which modals are <u>not</u> often contracted in sentences expressing conclusions?" (*must not, may not,* and *might not*)

- Write new examples on the board:
Conclusions: *Have (got) to*
Wilson *has (got) to be* worried.
Watson and Holmes *have (got) to suspect* Vincent.

Have students study the examples, and ask: "Do these examples also express conclusions?" *(yes)* "How do you express conclusions with *have (got) to?*" (*form of* have to/have got to + *base form of verb*) "Are *have to* and *have got to* used in affirmative or negative conclusions?" *(affirmative conclusions)*

- Write the following questions on the board:
Could they pay Wilson for having red hair?
Can Wilson be a liar?
Have students study the examples, and ask: "What modals do you use for questions about guesses?" *(can* and *could)*
Write possible short answers next to each question:
Could they pay Wilson for having red hair?
They could./They couldn't./They may not.
Can Wilson be a liar? He might be./He has got to be./He can't be.
Point out that in short answers all the modals can be negative, except for *have (got) to.* Also point out that modals are often followed by *be* if the question uses *be* as a main verb.

- Erase *Could, Can,* and *be* from the questions and replace the modals with *Do* and *Is:*
Do they pay Wilson for having red hair? They could./They couldn't./They may not.
Is Wilson a liar? He might be./He has got to be./He can't be.

Point out that questions that don't use modals can also be answered with modals to express that we are unsure of the answer.

Grammar Notes

Note 1   (Exercises 1–4, 7)

- Direct students' attention to the continuum that illustrates the degree of certainty expressed by each modal. You may want to explain that in sentences expressing conclusions some modals are only used in the affirmative and others are only used in the negative. (*Have to/have got to* is only used in the affirmative and both *can* and *couldn't* are only used in the negative.) You can also explain that the affirmative and negative form of the same modal might not express the same degree of certainty. (The affirmative form *must* and the negative form *must not* do not express the same degree of certainty.)
- To check comprehension, write on the board: *Which speaker is more certain?*
  A: He has got to be a good detective. OR B: He must be a good detective.
  A: He can't be a criminal. OR B: He must not be a criminal.
  A: He may not be honest. OR B: He might not be honest.
  A: He could be a millionaire. OR B: He has to be a millionaire.
  Working in pairs, have students close their books and decide which speaker is more certain in each case. Then ask them to open their books to confirm their answers. Review as a class. (*He must be a good detective. He can't be a criminal. He may not be honest. He has to be a millionaire.*)

Note 2   (Exercises 1–4, 7)

- To provide practice, write the following facts on the board:
  Holmes solves many mysteries.
  Holmes and Watson have worked together for years.
  Holmes is not married and he has no friends.
  Holmes plays the violin.
  Read the first fact aloud and draw a conclusion: *He must be very intelligent.* As a class, have students draw other conclusions for the same fact. (*He must be famous. He has to have a lot of experience. He's got to like riddles. He must be a brave man.*)
- In pairs, have students draw one or two conclusions for the other facts on the board. To review as a class, have volunteers say some of the conclusions they have drawn.

- For further practice, bring a brown paper bag to class. Put an object in the bag without students seeing it. Allow students to touch, lift, press, and shake the bag. Elicit statements with *must, have to,* or *has got to* and explanations. For example:
  A: It must be a book because it's rectangular and hard.
  B: It has to be our workbook because it's thinner than our grammar book.
  TEACHER: Right. It's our workbook.
  Once students have guessed the object, replace it with another.
- Remind students that in informal speech *have to* is often pronounced "hafta" and *got to* is often pronounced "gotta."

→ For additional practice, see the Supplementary Activities on page 157.

Note 3   (Exercises 1–2, 6–7)

- To provide practice, rewrite the facts from Note 1 on the board:
  Holmes solves many mysteries.
  Holmes and Watson have worked together for years.
  Holmes is not married and he has no friends.
  Holmes plays the violin.
  Read the first fact aloud and draw a conclusion about which you are not too certain: *He might ask the police for help.* Point out how this conclusion does not necessarily spring from the fact. You're less certain about it, so you use *might.* As a class, have students draw other less certain conclusions for the same fact. (*He may be a busy man. He might have a lot of enemies. He could work for the police.*)
- In pairs, have students draw a new conclusion for the other facts on the board. Point out that this time they shouldn't be so certain about the conclusions they draw. To review as a class, have volunteers say some of the conclusions they have drawn.
- For further practice, as in the Note 2 paper bag activity, put an object in the bag without students seeing it, but do not allow students to touch the bag. You may shake the bag or otherwise demonstrate some small clue of what is inside, but do not give the class solid evidence. Elicit statements with *may, might,* and *could.* Once students have guessed the object, replace it with another.

→ For additional practice, see the Supplementary Activities on page 157.

Note 4 *(Exercises 1–4, 6–7)*

- Write additional examples on the board:

  Copying an encyclopedia is not a serious job. You can't be paid for that.

  Wilson sounded honest when he talked to Holmes. He couldn't be a liar.

  Point out that we use *can't* and *couldn't* for negative conclusions when we are almost 100 percent certain.

- To provide practice with *can't* and *couldn't*, write on the board:

  This book _____. It can't be a best seller.

  Sam phoned from home a moment ago. That man _____.

  That printer _____. It couldn't be so expensive.

  Tom has never sent me flowers before. These flowers _____.

  In pairs, have students use their own ideas to complete the supporting statements and conclusions. Review as a class. (Possible answers: *This book is terrible. That man can't be him. That printer is an old model. These flowers couldn't be from him.*)

- To provide practice with *must not, may not,* and *might not*, write on the board:

  a. Alexandra never cooks.

  b. John won't go on vacation.

  c. Sandra never watches TV.

  In pairs, have students draw one or two negative conclusions for each item. Review as a class. (Possible answers: *a. She must not like cooking. She may not have time. b. He may not have enough money. He might not like traveling. c. She might not like it. She may not have a TV.*)

→ For additional practice, see the Supplementary Activities on page 157.

Note 5 *(Exercises 1, 6–7)*

To provide practice, as in the Notes 2 and 3 paper bag activities, put an object in the bag without students seeing it. Do not allow students to touch the bag. You may shake the bag or otherwise demonstrate some small clue of what is inside, but do not give the class solid evidence. Elicit student questions with *can* or *could*, for example:

A: Could it be a book?

TEACHER: Yes.

B: Can it be a heavy book?

TEACHER: Yes.

C: Could it be a dictionary?

TEACHER: Right! It's a dictionary!

Once students have guessed the object replace it with another.

Note 6 *(Exercises 1, 5–7)*

To provide practice, ask these questions, and have volunteers answer them with short answers. "Could Wilson be a liar?" "Is Vincent a criminal?" "Is the Red-Headed League a serious organization?" "Does Wilson have more money than he said he has?" "Do you think Holmes is a good detective?" "Is Watson as smart as Holmes?"

Focused Practice (pages 418–423)

Exercise 1

fault: a part of someone's character that is not perfect

scar: a permanent mark on your skin from a cut or wound

tunnel: a passage that has been dug under the ground

hollow: having an empty space inside

Exercise 3

trust: to believe that someone is honest and will not hurt you, cheat you, disobey you, etc.

clever: able to use your intelligence to do something, especially in a slightly dishonest way

Exercise 5

throat: the passage from the back of your mouth down the side of your neck

cough: the action of coughing (if you cough, air suddenly comes out of your throat with a short loud sound, especially because you're sick)

syrup: thick liquid made from sugar

Exercise 6

rattle: if something rattles, it shakes and makes a short repeated knocking sound

Communication Practice (pages 423–425)

Exercise 8

- Before students listen, have them read the statements.
- Point out that the conversation provides the conclusion to the mystery "The Red-Headed League."
- After reviewing answers, call on a volunteer to summarize the end of the story.

Exercise 9

- As a class, have students describe the pictures.
- Have students work individually to interpret the pictures.
- Before students discuss the pictures in pairs, point out that if they feel the evidence is solid, they should use *must* or *have (got) to*.

If the evidence is not so sound, they should use *may, might,* or *could.*

- Follow up by having students share their ideas with the class.

Exercise 10

- Go over the example and point out the modals.
- Encourage students to be creative.
- Have each pair come to a conclusion about each situation and then share their ideas with the class.

Exercise 11

Questions to generate ideas and elicit vocabulary:

- Is the murder suspect a man or a woman?
- Why does he/she talk to the exercise instructor?
- Who is Dr. Lorenzo? Is he a friend?
- Do you think the suspect is ill? Or does he/she want to find out information about a drug?
- Is the hairdresser a friend?
- What does the suspect pick up at the pharmacy? What is it for?
- Why does the suspect need $10,000?
- The suspect has quite a lot of money in the bank. Is he/she a robber?
- Who is Mr. Jordan? What is his relationship with the suspect?
- Why does the suspect call the travel agency? Is he/she planning a trip?
- Why does the suspect ask for a vegetarian meal?

Further Practice

Individually, have students write three true statements about themselves. In pairs, have students take turns sharing information about themselves with a partner and making relevant guesses. Write two examples on the board:

A: I never go cycling.

B: You might not have a bicycle then.

A: Well, I have one, but I never use it!

B: I'm planning a vacation to Italy.

A: You must like historical places.

B: I do!

OUT OF THE BOX ......

Solving a mystery. Play the first scenes of a movie about a mystery or bring in the beginning of a mystery story. Have students watch the scenes or read the first part of the story. In small groups, have students draw conclusions about the characters or what might happen next. Follow up by having students share their conclusions with the class. (Note 1: If some of the students have already watched the movie you selected, have them get together and write questions to ask to their classmates.) (Note 2: If appropriate, have students watch the rest of the movie, or read the rest of the story to confirm their guesses.)

Supplementary Activities

Unit 1   Note 1

- Ask students to describe an imaginary week, using the present progressive. Have them describe some of the things they use every day—for example, their washing machine, microwave oven, toaster, coffee maker, car—that have broken down.
- Ask students to make a list of four or five machines or appliances and tell their classmates what they are temporarily doing while their things are being serviced. *(This week I'm having breakfast in the café around the corner, I'm getting takeout for dinner, and I'm taking my clothes to a laundromat. I'm not driving to work these days—I'm taking the train.)*
- Follow up by having a few volunteers describe their imaginary week to the class.

Unit 2   Note 1

- Have students practice using the imperative for orders and warnings. Give students three minutes to write down a list of orders and warnings they were given by their parents when they were young children. Ask students to write as many orders/warnings as they can. Students should use both affirmative and negative imperatives. *(Go to bed. Go and take a bath. Wash your hands. Brush your teeth. Don't speak to strangers. Don't shout. Don't talk back. Clean up your room. Sit up straight. Don't chew with your mouth open. Clean up that mess. Hurry up! Don't touch that.)*
- After three minutes, ask students how many warnings/orders they were able to write. Call on individual students to read a sentence aloud, and write the sentences on the board, making any necessary corrections.

Unit 3   Note 2

- *Group work.* Have students play a game using simple past statements with time expressions and follow-up questions. (Note: Each group will need a small ball.) Have students sit in a circle.
- Explain the game. Student A says a simple past statement with a time expression and throws the ball to Student B. Student B catches the ball and quickly asks a follow-up question. As soon as Student A answers the question, Student B says a new statement and throws the ball to Student C. Point out that the game should be fast and agile.

  A: I moved here two years ago.

  B: Where did you live before?

  A: In Mexico.

  B: I saw a good film yesterday.

  C: What did you see?

- Circulate as students play the game, listening to make sure students form correct simple past questions.

Unit 4   Notes 2–4

- Have students practice the past progressive and simple past by describing scenes from a movie. In groups of three, have students choose a movie that all the group members have seen and write six sentences describing different scenes from the movie. Give an example: *She was walking out of the building when she met him.* Point out that each sentence should contain either *when* or *while,* and that students should use pronouns instead of the characters' names.
- After students have finished writing their sentences, have students submit them to you for correction.
- Have each group read their sentences aloud to the class, who should try and guess the movie after listening to the six sentences.

Unit 5   Note 4

- Have students practice comparing the past and the present with *used to.* Draw the following chart on the board:

	THEN: About _____ years ago	NOW
Family life		
Cost of living		
Standard of living		
Communications		
Transportation		
Health issues		

- Have students work in small groups to choose a time in the past to compare with the present, and fill in the blank in the chart with the corresponding number of years. Then have students complete the chart with notes for each of the topics.
- After students have completed the chart, have each group report to the class. *(People used to grow their own fruits and vegetables. Now people buy food in supermarkets.)* After each group has finished reporting, have students ask a few questions to the class. *(What did people use to eat?)*

Unit 6   Note 3

- Have students create conversations, practicing different ways to express the future. Write the following conversation on the board, underlining as shown:

A: What are you doing <u>tonight</u>?

B: I'm going to <u>go to the movies</u>.

A: And on <u>Saturday</u>? What are you going to do?

B: I don't really know. I think I'll <u>go shopping</u>.

- In small groups, have students write down the conversation replacing the underlined parts with their own ideas. Then have students practice the conversation without reading it.
- Have volunteers role-play the conversation for the class.

Unit 7   Note 2

- Have students practice using future time clauses by talking about goals. Draw the following event chain on the board, or enlarge and photocopy.

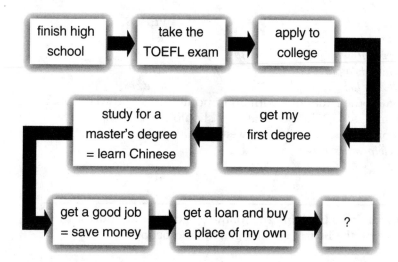

- Explain that the event chain on the board is about Brenda's goals in life. Point out that the two events joined by an equals sign (=) will happen at the same time.
- Ask students to work in pairs to write their own idea in the last box. Then have pairs write down Brenda's story using time clauses. Give examples. You can say, "Brenda will take the TOEFL exam as soon as she finishes high school. She will learn Chinese while she studies for a master's degree. She's not going to get a loan until she gets a good job."
- Have volunteers read their stories aloud to the class.

Unit 8   Note 4

- Have students practice using *wh-* questions by putting together jumbled cards. First, have students draw the following cards, or enlarge these and photocopy.

- Have students cut out the cards.
- Ask students to combine all or some of the cards to make up as many questions as they can think of. Students should write every question they make up on a sheet of paper. Set a time limit of three minutes.
- When time is up, review the questions as a class. Write them on the board.
  Who saw you?
  Who did you see?
  What did you see?
  Which defendant did you see?
  Which defendant saw you?
  Where did you see the defendant?

Unit 9   Note 2

• Have students practice using imperative sentences with reflexive pronouns by doing the following matching activity. First write the following situations and verbs on the board.

SITUATIONS	VERBS
An elementary teacher talking to her students	*help*
A father talking to his teenage son, who will go on a trip	*enjoy*
A man talking to a friend who has a party	*behave*
A woman offering sandwiches to her guests	*take care of*

• In pairs, have students match the situations with appropriate verbs and write what they think the people actually said. Point out that they should use the imperative and appropriate reflexive pronouns. (Possible answers: *Behave yourselves. Take care of yourself. Enjoy yourself. Help yourselves.*)

Unit 10   Notes 3–4

• Have students review phrasal verbs by doing the following activity. First draw the following graphic organizer on the board, or enlarge and photocopy:

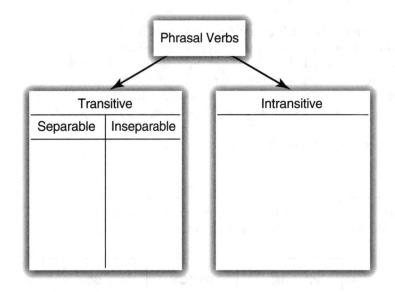

• List on the board the phrasal verbs students have seen so far.

pick up	look up	get by	grow up	figure out	pick out
take off	start over	help out	bring up	wake up	drop off
put on	get back	point out	go on	set up	

• Books closed. In pairs, have students classify the phrasal verbs. Encourage students to use them in sentences to confirm their classification.
• To review, refer students to Appendices 4 and 5 on pages A-3–A-4.

Unit 11   Notes 2–3, 5–6

• Have students describe the development (different stages) of an ability they have, practicing *can, could,* and *be able to.* Ask them to think about something they wanted to be able to do in the past, they can do now, and they think they will be able to do better in the future. Write an example on the board:
When I was a child I could draw pretty well, but I wanted to be able to draw like an artist. I took lessons, and I was soon able to draw nice pictures of animals. Now I can paint beautiful landscapes. I'm still taking lessons because I want to be able to paint portraits.

- Have students write a paragraph about their ability. Circulate as students write, providing help as needed.
- Call on volunteers to read their paragraphs out loud to the class.

Unit 12   Notes 1, 3

- Have students practice asking for permission and making requests by creating a new conversation.
- Write the following conversation on the board, underlining as shown:

A: <u>My computer is broken</u>. Can I <u>use yours for a few hours</u>?

B: I'm sorry. <u>I need it right now</u>.

A: Could I <u>use it this evening</u>?

B: Sure. <u>I will be finished by then</u>.

- *Pairs*. Have pairs write down the conversation replacing the underlined parts with their own ideas. Then have students practice the conversation without reading it.
- Have volunteers role-play their conversation for the class.

Unit 13   Notes 1–4

- Have students practice making and responding to requests by doing a matching activity. Write the information below on the board, or make photocopies for each student, enlarging the text.
- Have students match the sentence parts in column A with the sentence parts in column B to form a question. Then have them choose an appropriate reply for each request from column C. Point out there is only one possible combination. Ask students to write the requests and the replies, and then add a new possible reply to each request.
- Review as a class.

A	B	C
Could you please	mail this letter for me, please?	Sure I will.
Would you mind	drive me to the stores?	Not at all.
Would you	calling me back later?	Of course I can.

Unit 14   Note 1

- Have students practice giving advice about the Internet using *should* and *should not*. Write the following topics on the board, or make photocopies for each group, enlarging the text.
  Forwarding other people's messages
  Posting a private e-mail to a bulletin board
  Reading other people's e-mail
  Sending e-mail advertising messages to a lot of people
  Using offensive language
  Copying people on your messages
  Pointing out other people's spelling or grammar mistakes
  Posting incorrect information
  Posting messages that are not clear
  Sharing your knowledge with a discussion group
  Forgiving other people's mistakes
  Lurking before participating

- Have students work in small groups to choose eight topics from the board and write eight statements giving advice about what you should do and should not do on the Internet. *(You shouldn't forward a message if you don't have the author's permission.)* Encourage students to use the different ways to give advice they learned.
- Have students share their ideas with the class.

  ⏱ As a class, students prepare a poster of the rules of netiquette. Pass the poster around and have each group contribute a sentence.

Unit 15   Notes 1–4

- Have students practice making suggestions by doing a scrambled word activity. Have students draw the following cards, or make photocopies for each pair, enlarging the text.

LET'S	WHY	HOW
NOT	MAYBE	ABOUT
WE	DON'T	COULD
GET	GETTING	TAKEOUT

- Have students cut out the cards.
- Ask students to combine all or some of the cards to make up as many suggestions as they can think of. Students should write down on a sheet of paper every suggestion they make up. Set a time limit of three minutes.
- When time is up, review the suggestions as a class. Write them on the board. *(Let's get takeout. Let's not get takeout. Maybe we could get takeout. Why don't we get takeout? How about getting takeout? How about takeout? Why not get takeout?)*

Unit 16   Notes 1–4

- Have students practice making sentences with *for* and *since*. First, draw the following diagram on the board.

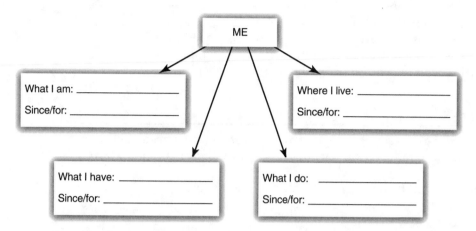

- Have students complete the diagram with information about themselves. Any kind of information that will answer the questions is valid. Write two examples on the board:

What I am: *a student*	What I am: *a basketball fan*
~~Since~~/for: *9 years*	Since/~~for~~: *I turned six*

- Ask students to use the diagram as a guide to tell the class about themselves. Remind students they should use the present perfect with *since* or *for*.

Unit 17   Notes 1–5

- Have students practice the present perfect with *already* and *yet* by talking about what they've done today. First have students imagine that yesterday they wrote their To Do list for today. Ask them to write this list. Point out that on their list they should mix things they've already done today and things they haven't done yet, for example:
reply to Sarah's e-mail
get takeout on the way home
pick up jacket from dry cleaner's
walk the dog
pay telephone bill
- Ask students to use their list as a guide to talk to their partners about the things they have already done today and the things they haven't done yet. (*I've already replied to Sarah's e-mail, but I haven't paid the telephone bill yet.*)

Unit 18   Notes 1–2, 4

- Have students practice describing someone using the present perfect. Write the following information on the board, or enlarge and photocopy.

My _____
    A place she/he has been to: _____
    A place she/he has never been to: _____

Something she/he has always done: _____

Something she/he has done many times: _____

Something she/he has always liked: _____

Something she/he hasn't done lately: _____

Something she/he has done recently: _____

- Have students choose a close relative or friend and complete the information about him/her. Then ask students to use the information as a guide to write sentences about their friend or relative using the present perfect.

Unit 19   Note 3

- Have students practice the present perfect with an unfinished time period. Tell students they are going to conduct a survey about the things their classmates have done so far today.
- Draw the following chart on the board, or enlarge and photocopy.

	cups of coffee have you had e-mails have you replied to buses have you taken people have you greeted _____ _____ _____ _____	
How many		today?

- Have students use their own ideas to write four more questions.
- Have students interview three classmates and take notes about their answers.
- Follow up by having students share the results of their survey with the class.

Unit 20   Notes 1–2

- Have students practice the present perfect and the present perfect progressive by creating new conversations. Write the following conversation on the board, underlining as shown:

A: <u>Kate</u>, you look tired.

B: I know. I've been <u>cleaning</u> <u>for three hours</u>.

A: What have you been <u>cleaning</u>?

B: <u>The kitchen</u>. I've <u>cleaned two cupboards</u>, but I haven't <u>cleaned the floor</u> yet.

- Have students study the conversation. Point out the use of the present perfect progressive for something the person has been doing for some time and has not finished doing (*I've been cleaning for three hours*) and the present perfect for something the person has done/not done. (*I've cleaned two cupboards. I haven't cleaned the floor yet.*)
- Have pairs write down the conversation replacing the underlined parts with their own ideas. You may want to brainstorm some ideas for the reasons why someone might look tired, and write possible replacements for *cleaning* on the board: *working / writing / typing / painting / reading / doing a search on the Internet*
- Then have students practice the conversation without reading it.
- Have volunteers role-play their conversation for the class.

Unit 21   Notes 1–2

- Have students practice using proper and common nouns by playing a game.
- Enlarge and photocopy the following charts:

Proper nouns				
People	Places	Months	Nationalities	Seasons

Common nouns		
People	Places	Things

- Place students in small groups. Give each student a photocopy of the charts, and have students put it facedown on their desk as you explain the game. Students will be given two minutes to complete the charts. The student with the most correct answers will be the winner. When time is up, have students correct each other's charts. Circulate to answer any questions and provide help as needed.

Unit 22   Notes 2–5

- Have students practice using indefinite and definite articles, and *some* by completing a story. Enlarge and photocopy the following incomplete text of the story "The Town Mouse and The Country Mouse."

_____ town mouse went to visit his cousin in _____ country. _____ country cousin was poor, but he gladly served his town cousin _____ only food he had—_____ beans and _____ bread. _____ town mouse ate _____ bread and laughed. He said, "What poor food you country mice eat! Come home with me. I will show you how to live." _____ moon was shining brightly that night, so _____ mice left immediately.

   As soon as they arrived at _____ town mouse's house, they went into _____ dining room. There they found _____ leftovers of _____ wonderful dinner, and soon _____ mice were eating jelly and cake and many nice things. Suddenly, _____ door flew open, and _____ enormous dog ran in. _____ mice ran away quickly. "Good-bye, Cousin," said _____ country mouse. "Are you leaving so soon?" asked _____ town mouse. "Yes," his honest cousin replied. "This has been _____ great adventure, but I'd rather eat bread in peace than cake in fear."

- Have students complete the story individually with *a, an, the,* or *some.*

- Have students compare answers with a partner. Encourage students to explain their choices.
- Have students use the reading on page 250 to check their answers. Clarify any confusion.

Unit 23   Note 7

- Have students practice using participial adjectives. In pairs, have students go over the list of participial adjectives (Appendix 11 on page A-6), and ask them to choose three adjectives to look up in a dictionary. Have students copy on a sheet of paper an example of each of the participial adjectives they chose.
- Have students write down examples of their own using the same adjectives. Point out that students can base their own examples on the ones they copied from the dictionary. Circulate as students write to provide help as needed.
- Follow up by having a few volunteers share their examples with the class.

Unit 24   Note 3

- Have students practice classifying the comparatives of adjectives by completing a chart. Draw the following box and chart on the board:

good	quiet	professional	long
bad	fresh	interesting	happy

a. short adj. + -er	
b. *more/less* + long adj.	
c. irregular comparative forms	
d. adjs. that can use either -er or *more*	

- In pairs, have students use the chart to classify the adjectives in the box. Point out that students can refer to Appendix 23 on page A-11 for spelling rules for the comparative form of adjectives, Appendix 10 on page A-6 for a list of irregular comparative adjectives, and Appendix 9 on page A-5 for a list of adjectives that use both forms of the comparative. Review as a class. *(a. long, fresh; b. professional, interesting; c. good, bad; d. quiet, happy)*

Unit 25   Note 3

- Have students practice using the superlative + *ever* + the present perfect by finding out about a classmate's experiences. Tell students they are going to conduct an interview about their classmates' experiences.
- Write the following questions on the board:

_____ *the funniest story* _____ ?

_____ *the most exciting sport* _____ ?

_____ *the most difficult thing* _____ ?

_____ *the most enjoyable experience* _____ ?

_____ *the most delicious meal* _____ ?

_____ *the worst mistake* _____ ?

_____ *the most expensive thing* _____ ?

_____ ?

- Have students use their own ideas to complete questions. Point out that they should use the last line to make up their own question.
- Have students interview a classmate and take notes about his/her answers.
- Follow up by having students share the results of their interview with the class.

Unit 26   Notes 1–3

- Have students practice describing people using comparative adverbs and *as . . . as*. Draw on the board the following box and Venn diagram, or provide handouts.

study hard	speak loud	dance gracefully
work fast	drive carefully	pass exams easily
cook well	speak English fluently	arrive at school/work early

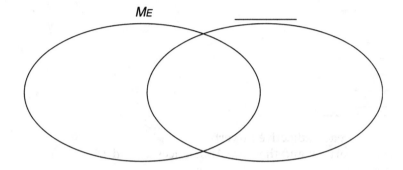

- Ask students to choose a friend or family member to compare themselves with, and write his/her name on the line above the second circle.
- Then have students use the Venn diagram to classify six actions from the box. Give some examples:

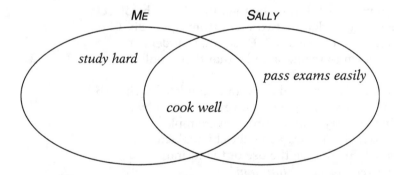

- Have students use the diagram as a guide to write statements using *as . . . as* and comparative adverbs. *(I study harder than my friend Sally. Sally passes exams more easily. I cook just as well as Sally.)*

Unit 27   Note 3

- Have students practice using verbs followed by gerunds. Have pairs choose and underline four verbs from Appendix 13 on page A-7. Encourage students to choose verbs whose meaning is unknown to them, or verbs that they would like to see used in examples.
- Have students look up the verbs in a dictionary, and copy an example of each verb. Point out that if the dictionary provides an example of the verb followed by a gerund, they should copy that example.

- Have students use their own ideas to replace segments of the examples they copied and make up new sentences. Encourage the use of the gerund.
  Example from the dictionary: *How can you justify spending so much money on a coat?*
  Example by students: *How can you justify wasting so much time?*
  Example from the dictionary: *Simmons denied murdering his wife.*
  Example by students: *Simmons denied witnessing the accident.*
- Have students share their examples with the class.

Unit 28   Note 2

- Have students practice using common adjective/verb + prepositions. Write the following adjectives and verbs on the board, or provide handouts:

afraid _____	interested _____
apologize _____	look forward _____
concerned _____	sick _____
believe _____	object _____
famous _____	tired _____
complain _____	rely _____
glad _____	worried _____
count _____	succeed _____

- Have students write a preposition next to each adjective or verb.
- Ask students to compare answers with a partner, and then use Appendices 17 and 18 on pages A-7–A-8 to confirm their answers.
- Have students use four words from the box in sentences of their own.
- Follow up by having volunteers share some of their sentences with the class.

Unit 29   Notes 3–5

- Have students practice using common verbs followed by the infinitive or by objects and the infinitive. Have pairs choose and underline two verbs from Appendix 14 on page A-7 and two verbs from Appendix 16 on page A-7. Encourage students to choose verbs whose meaning is unknown to them, or verbs that they would like to see used in examples.
- Have students look up the verbs in a dictionary, and copy an example of each verb. Point out that if the dictionary provides an example of the verb followed by an infinitive or an object plus an infinitive, they should copy that example.
- Have students use their own ideas to make up new sentences by replacing segments of the examples they copied. Encourage the use of the infinitive.
  Example from the dictionary: *Bob never intended to hurt him.*
  Example by students: *Bob never intended to offend you.*
  Example from the dictionary: *Cooder's father encouraged him to play the guitar.*
  Example by students: *Cooder's father encouraged him to save part of his salary.*
- Have students share their examples with the class.

Unit 30   Notes 1–3

- Have students practice expressing reasons using *to* + infinitive, *in order to* + infinitive, and *in order not to* + infinitive.
- Write the following questions on the board:
  —What do you eat a lot of? Why?
  —What don't you eat much of? Why?
  —What did you buy? When? Why?

—What don't you buy? Why?
—Where did you go? When? Why?
—Where did you travel? When? Why?
—What public transportation do you sometimes take? Why?
—What are you studying? Why?
—What did you borrow? When? Why?
—What don't you do? When? Why?

- Have students answer each set of questions in one sentence using the infinitive of purpose. Encourage the use of all the forms students have seen: *to* + infinitive, *in order to* + infinitive, *in order not to* + infinitive. You may want to give a few examples:
  I eat a lot of fruit to stay healthy.
  I don't eat much chocolate in order not to gain weight.
  Last month I went to my hometown to visit my grandmother.
  I sometimes take the subway to get to work earlier.
  I don't go jogging in winter in order not to catch a cold.
- Follow up by having volunteers share some of their sentences with the class.

Unit 31   Notes 1–4

- Have students practice giving reasons with infinitives and *too* or *enough*. First, write the following sentences in two columns on the board:

A	B
He arrived late.	She won't be a good assistant.
The bridge was narrow.	The audience couldn't understand him.
She didn't work hard.	He couldn't get tickets for the concert.
That house is expensive.	She didn't get a passing grade.
She isn't reliable.	The truck couldn't go through.
He didn't speak clearly.	She can't possibly buy it.

- Have students match the sentences in column A with the ones in column B. Then have them combine the ideas using the infinitive with *too* or *enough*. Point out that students should make any necessary changes and that some sentences require *for* plus a noun or pronoun.
- Have students compare answers with a partner. Follow up by having volunteers read their sentences aloud. (Possible answers: *He arrived too late to get tickets for the concert. The bridge was too narrow for the truck to go through. She didn't work hard enough to get a passing grade. The house is too expensive for her to buy. She isn't reliable enough to be a good assistant. He didn't speak clearly enough for the audience to understand him.*)

Unit 32   Notes 1–2

- Have students practice using verbs followed by gerunds or infinitives by writing a paragraph. Write the following cues on the board:
  Procrastinators / keep / put off / things they need to do
  They / want / avoid / bad feelings / and / do / enjoyable things instead
  They / expect / be able to / do things better another day
  They / end up / do / things the last minute / and / feel / worse
- Have students use the cues to make sentences using verbs followed by gerunds and infinitives. Review as a class. (*Procrastinators keep putting off the things they need to do. They want to avoid bad feelings and do enjoyable things instead. They expect to be able to do things better another day. They end up doing things the last minute and feeling worse.*)

Unit 33   Notes 1–3

- Have students practice expressing preferences using *would prefer* and *would rather*. To remind students of the different ways to express general preferences and preferences in a specific situation, provide handouts of the chart below. Have students study the chart and clarify any confusion they might have.

		General Preferences	Preferences in a Specific Situation

1	Nouns	I prefer [something].
		I prefer [something] to
		    [something else].
			I'd prefer [something].
			I'd prefer [something] to
			    [something else].

2	Gerunds	I prefer [doing something].
		I prefer [doing something] to
		    [doing something else].
			I'd prefer [doing something].
			I'd prefer [doing something] to
			    [doing something else].

3	Infinitives	I prefer [(not) to do something].	I'd prefer [(not) to do something].
4	Base forms	—	I'd rather [(not) do something]. I'd rather [do something] than [do something else].

- Ask students to write their own examples replacing the items in brackets. Point out they should use the following topics for each row in the chart: Row 1: Movies; Row 2: Food; Row 3: Reading Materials; Row 4: Sports.

Unit 34   Notes 1, 4

- Have students practice talking about necessity using *have to, don't have to, must, must not,* and *can't*. Write a list of verb phrases on the board. For each item, have students write two sentences, using different modals of necessity in each, for example: *Drivers must respect traffic lights and speed limits. Ambulance drivers don't have to respect traffic lights or speed limits, but they have to be careful.*
  —respect traffic lights and speed limits
  —feed the animals in a zoo
  —carry their passports
  —support their family
  —wear their seatbelts
  —go through customs
- Have students compare their sentences with those of a partner, and then share some of them with the class.

Unit 35   Notes 1–2

- Have students practice using *supposed to* by talking about expectations. Write the following "formulas" and examples on the board, and have students provide their own example for each item. (You can also provide handouts.)

[present expectation about a person] + [what the person is actually like]
Teachers are supposed to be patient, but our math teacher doesn't have much patience when we don't understand.

[past expectation about an outing] + [what actually happened]
We were supposed to go out for dinner, but we had to put it off because I had to work late.

[present expectation about a rule] + [what some people actually do]
Drivers are supposed to wear their seat belts, but some drivers just don't wear them.

[present expectation about a custom] + *[what someone did]*
Brides are supposed to wear white, but my friend Susan got married in pink.

[past expectation about a vacation] + *[what you actually did]*
I was supposed to go to Africa last summer, but it was so expensive that I went to Mexico instead.

- Have students compare their sentences with those of a partner, and then share some of them with the class.

Unit 36   Note 3

- Have students practice talking about future possibility using *may, might,* and *could.* Write the following questions on the board. Have students write an appropriate response for each using either full answers or short answers.
Do you think it will rain tomorrow?
Are you going to go out with your friends on Friday?
Will you work/study late tomorrow?
Do you think you will pass all your exams this term?
Are you going to buy yourself anything this week?
- After students have written their responses, have them ask the questions to a partner. Follow up by addressing different students as you ask each of the questions. You may want to ask each question more than once to different students.

Unit 37   Notes 2–4

- Have students practice talking about conclusions with *must, have to, may, might, could,* or *can't.*
- Write the following conversation on the board:

A: *What's the noise in the kitchen?*

B: *It may be the cat.*

A: *It can't be the cat. The cat's over there, under that chair.*

- Point out the affirmative conclusion *(It may be the cat.),* the negative conclusion *(It can't be the cat.),* and the reason *(The cat's over there, under that chair.).*
- Then write on the board:
Who's that man at the door?
Someone left this gift for you.
What's that box on the floor?
- Have students work in pairs to write three conversations starting with the items on the board. Point out the conversations should include an affirmative conclusion, a negative conclusion, and a reason. Have students submit the conversations to you for correction, and then practice them without reading.

Scoring Rubric for Speaking

Tips for using the speaking rubric

- Give a copy of the rubric to the class before you use it.
- Tell students that you will evaluate their speaking using the rubric.
- The speaking rubric can also be found in a printable format on the Power Point® presentations CD-ROM found in the back of this Teacher's Manual.
- Give feedback for the different areas identified in the rubric: vocabulary, grammar, pronunciation, fluidity, topic organization, and communication.
- Point out some strong points and weak points. Use language that a student can understand and give examples of what the student did or didn't say when possible. Example comments: *You used a lot of vocabulary and expressions from the unit.* OR *You need to work on verb forms. Review the verb forms needed for the future conditional.* OR *Your sentences were usually complete and clear, but sometimes you hesitated a lot.*
- It's recommended that you discuss the assigned rating and your feedback with each student in order to be most effective and helpful.

SPEAKING RUBRIC

Rating	Vocabulary	Grammar	Pronunciation	Fluidity	Topic	Communication
4	Uses variety, with few errors	Uses a variety of structures, with few errors	Almost always clear and accurate	Speaks smoothly, little hesitation	Successfully organizes and develops topic	Communicates information and opinions effectively
3	Uses variety, makes some errors in word choice	Uses a variety of structures, makes some errors	Usually clear and accurate, some problem areas	Speaks with some hesitation, does not usually interfere with communication	Topic is organized, needs more development	Most information and opinions are communicated clearly
2	Uses limited vocabulary and expressions, some errors	Uses basic structures, makes frequent errors	Errors sometimes make it difficult to understand student	Speaks with hesitation, frequently interferes with communication	Topic not organized, needs development	Information and opinions are not clear
1	Uses basic vocabulary and expressions, makes many errors	Uses basic structures, makes many errors	Very weak; student cannot be understood	Hesitates frequently when speaking, interferes with communication	Does not stay on the topic	Is not able to communicate information and opinions

Scoring Rubric for Writing

Tips for using the writing rubric

- Give a copy of the rubric to the class before you use it.
- Tell students that you will evaluate their writing using the rubric.
- The writing rubric can also be found in a printable format on the Power Point® presentations CD-ROM found in the back of this Teacher's Manual.
- Give feedback by writing comments for the different areas identified in the rubric: topic, sentence structure, vocabulary, grammar.
- Use language that a student can understand and, when possible, give examples of what the student did or didn't do. Example comments: *You addressed the topic and gave very clear examples to support your ideas.* OR *You tried to use a lot of vocabulary and expressions from the unit, but review the meanings of the items I marked in red.* OR *You need to work on verb forms. Review regular and irregular verb forms in the simple past.*
- It's recommended that you discuss the assigned rating and your feedback with each student in a timely manner in order to be most effective and helpful.

Rating	WRITING RUBRIC
5	• Topic is addressed and well organized; includes clear explanations or details • Includes mostly complex sentence types, with few errors • Uses a variety of vocabulary and idiomatic expressions; makes few errors in word choice • Uses complex grammar structures, with few errors
4	• Topic is addressed and generally well organized; includes some explanations or details • Includes some variety of sentence types, but with occasional errors • Varies vocabulary and expressions, but makes occasional errors in word choice • Uses some complex grammar structures, but with errors
3	• Topic is not addressed completely, but writing is organized; explanations or details need more development • Uses little variety in sentence type, but does not have many errors • Attempts to vary vocabulary and expressions, but makes some errors in word choice • Does not use complex grammar structures, but does not make many grammar errors
2	• Topic is somewhat addressed, but writing is not organized and lacks explanations or details • Uses only basic sentence types and makes frequent errors • Uses limited vocabulary and with frequent errors • Uses simple grammar structures, but with some errors
1	• Topic is not addressed; there are no explanations or details • Most sentences have errors • Has many errors in vocabulary usage, even at the basic level • Uses only simple grammar structures, and makes many errors

Audioscript

Unit 1

Exercise 8 (page 11)

INTERVIEWER: Today's the end of your first week of classes here. How do you feel?

MARIA: Pretty good. Things are going well. Everyone's friendly, and I'm learning a lot.

INTERVIEWER: You're living in a new country, a new culture. What's the most difficult part?

MARIA: Well, there are many changes. The language is the biggest. Right now I'm speaking English, of course. At home I speak Spanish all the time.

INTERVIEWER: Where in Mexico do you come from?

MARIA: A very small town in Durango.

INTERVIEWER: And now you're living in a big city.

MARIA: That's right. It's very different. The pace of life, especially.

INTERVIEWER: The pace of life. What do you mean?

MARIA: When I'm in Mexico, I walk slowly. Everyone does. People never seem in a hurry. But here, everyone moves very quickly.

INTERVIEWER: And what about you?

MARIA: I find myself moving quickly too. And I'm wearing a watch!

INTERVIEWER: You don't usually wear a watch?

MARIA: No. But people here expect you to arrive exactly on time, so I don't want to be late. Oops, speaking of late, I'd better go. My next class starts in exactly five minutes.

INTERVIEWER: What are you studying?

MARIA: Computer science. This is something new for me too. Back in Mexico, I study history.

INTERVIEWER: Well, thank you very much for your time. And good luck!

MARIA: Thank you.

Unit 2

Exercise 5 (page 18)

Good morning, and welcome to "Cooking Light and Easy"—where we cook healthy food that tastes delicious. I'm Danny Morgen, and today I'm going to show you an easy and healthy breakfast that everyone loves—pancakes.

- To start with, beat two egg whites in a large bowl . . . Don't overbeat. You just need to beat them a little bit . . . like this.
- Now, measure one and a quarter cups of flour— you can use white flour, but I prefer to use whole wheat flour.
- Add the flour to the beaten egg whites, like this . . . OK.
- Now, we're going to add a cup of milk. Again, you can use regular milk, or you can use low-fat milk. I'm adding milk with 2% fat . . .
- Mix thoroughly . . . Again, don't overmix . . . That looks right . . .
- At this point, we can add some fruit. Any kind of fruit works well. Today, I have some nice fresh blueberries, so I'm going to blend those in like this . . .
- Now, we're ready to heat a frying pan and melt a small piece of butter in it. You could use margarine, but I prefer the taste of real butter, and you really only need to use a little bit . . . like that. OK.
- The butter is melted and the pan is nice and hot, so I'm going to gently pour some of the pancake mixture into the frying pan . . . just like this. In about two to three minutes, you'll see little bubbles forming on the outside edge of the pancakes. That means it's time to flip the pancakes over . . . like this. Good. That's nice and brown . . .
- Now, wait a few minutes to allow the other side to brown too, and then remove it from the pan . . . These look beautiful. Top them with more fruit or yogurt, and you and your family are in for a real treat!

If you want a copy of this recipe, send a self-addressed stamped envelope to WCTV or get a free copy at our website at www.litecooking.com. See you tomorrow with some more recipes that are "light and easy"!

Unit 3

Exercise 8 (page 31)

JANA: Good morning. You're listening to "Literary Notes." With us in the studio today is prize-winning poet Murat Veli. Welcome.

MURAT: Thank you, Jana. It's a pleasure to be here.

JANA: Murat, in your poetry, you often write about your memories of Turkey. Were you born there?

MURAT: Yes, I was. But I came to the United States in 1980, when I was ten. My parents came here in

1975—five years before me. They found jobs and bought a house. Then I joined them.

JANA: Who did you live with between 1975 and 1980?

MURAT: With my grandparents. Our family farm is in Sivas, in central Turkey. I missed my parents, of course, but my life with my grandparents was wonderful. My grandmother told stories, and she knew hundreds of riddles. Very entertaining for a little boy.

JANA: So then, in 1980, you left Turkey and joined your parents in the U.S.

MURAT: That's right. We lived in Baltimore. You know, Jana, I hated the city at first. I had no freedom. I rode a school bus instead of my grandfather's horses. I had no friends. So . . . I read. I escaped into books.

JANA: When did you start to write poetry?

MURAT: Well, first, you know, I wrote stories in Turkish all the time, from when I was only six or seven. But I wrote my first poem when I was twelve. I wrote poetry in English.

JANA: Did you study poetry in school?

MURAT: No, I didn't. In college I majored in farming—agriculture. But I wrote every day.

JANA: You won an award for your poetry at a very young age. When was that?

MURAT: That was in 1992. A year after I graduated from college.

JANA: And what do you do when you *aren't* writing poetry?

MURAT: I teach it! I became a teacher in 1994, and I've been teaching since then. When I'm not farming, that is.

JANA: We have to pause for a break. When we return. Murat Veli will read one of his poems.

Unit 4

Exercise 2 (page 38)

REPORTER: What was the cause of the accident, Officer?

OFFICER: Well, it looks like there were many causes. First of all, when the accident happened, the driver was driving much too fast. The driver is a suspect in a burglary, and she was leaving town. While she was driving, she was speaking to someone on her cell phone. When she saw the pedestrian, she immediately stepped on the brakes, but it was too late. The victim wasn't paying attention, either. He was crossing the street against a red light when the car hit him. He didn't see the approaching car because he was talking to his friend. The friend wasn't paying attention, either. He was listening to music with his headphones. When he noticed the car, he tried to push his friend out of the way, but it was too late.

REPORTER: How is the victim doing?

OFFICER: Well, when the ambulance arrived, he was bleeding from a head wound, but the doctors stopped the bleeding and they think he'll be OK.

Exercise 6 (page 41)

OFFICER: Did you see the accident, miss?

WITNESS: Yes, I did, officer.

OFFICER: Can you tell me what happened?

WITNESS: I'll try, but it all happened so quickly . . .

OFFICER: That's OK, just tell me what you saw.

WITNESS: Well, I was walking down the street when I heard this car honking. The driver was driving much too fast. In fact, I'm sure he was speeding. The two men were just starting to cross the street. They were talking to each other and not paying attention to traffic. When they finally saw the car, they started to move out of the way, but it was too late. The car was moving too fast and was too close to the men to stop. They were both hit by the car.

Unit 5

Exercise 5 (page 49)

SANDRA: Do you ever think back, say, to ten years ago? We were so different then.

ROSA: Ten years?

SANDRA: Yeah, I don't know about you, but when I was a kid my life was really different. You know what I mean? I always used to get up really early and I never used an alarm clock. Today, without an alarm clock, forget it. I'd never wake up.

ROSA: You're telling me? I can hardly get up *with* the alarm clock.

SANDRA: No kidding! And I remember, as soon as I woke up, I used to have a huge breakfast; I mean huge—cereal, eggs, toast, the works.

ROSA: Me too. These days we're lucky if we have time for a quick cup of coffee and a brief look at the newspaper.

SANDRA: Really! And when we were kids, we had endless energy. I used to run from morning to night. Now I'm exhausted after 15 minutes of aerobics.

ROSA: Those were fun days. We used to hang out with our friends every weekend and take trips in Linda's car, remember?

SANDRA: I sure do. Well, now we're too busy to hang out. You know, we only see each other once a year at the school reunion. I can't remember the last car trip I took.

Rosa: We'd better stop talking like this. Imagine in another ten years . . . Then, what will we say we used to do?

Unit 6

Exercise 6 (page 62)

Jason: I just heard the weather report. It's going to rain tomorrow.

Ariel: Oh, no. I hate driving in the rain. And it's a long drive to the conference.

Jason: Wait! I have an idea. We'll take the train instead!

Ariel: Good idea! Do you have a train schedule?

Jason: Yes. Here's one. There's a train that leaves at 7:00 A.M.

Ariel: What about lunch? Oh, I know, I'll make some sandwiches for us.

Jason: OK. You know, it's a long trip. What are we going to do all those hours?

Ariel: Don't worry. We'll think of something.

Jason: You know, we have to get up really early. I think I'll go home now.

Ariel: OK. I'll see you tomorrow. Good night.

Exercise 8 (page 63)

1. **A:** I'm glad it's Friday. Let's go home.

   B: What are you doing tonight?

   A: The usual. I'm just staying home and watching TV.

2. **A:** Hi, Pete. What are you watching?

   B: Oh. It's a program about space travel. It's pretty interesting. Want to watch with me?

3. **A:** There's a phone call for Professor Starr.

   B: Oh. He's working on his speech for the space conference next week. Can you take a message?

4. **A:** There's a lecture at the Community Center tonight.

   B: Really? What's it on?

   A: Some professor's talking about space travel. Do you want to go?

5. **A:** I wish I could go to the lecture, but my parents are flying in from Florida.

   B: Oh. Are you going to meet them at the airport?

   A: No. They're going to take a taxi to my place.

6. **A:** Excuse me. What time does the train to Boston leave?

   B: The train to Boston? It leaves at 2:05. You'd better hurry, it's 2:00.

   A: Oh. Thanks.

Unit 7

Exercise 5 (page 71)

Man: Hello, Jobs Are Us. How can I help you?

Woman: Hi. Do you have any jobs for people with desktop publishing skills?

Man: Yes. Have you had any work experience?

Woman: No, not really. I just graduated from college. But I did some desktop publishing while I was in school.

Man: OK. Do you have a résumé?

Woman: Yes, I do.

Man: Fine, why don't you e-mail or fax us your résumé. As soon as we receive it, we'll set up an interview for you in our office.

Woman: OK. And what happens after that?

Man: Well, after we interview you, you'll take a little skills test. Then as soon as we see your test results, you'll meet with one of our job counselors. Together we'll find the best job for you.

Woman: Sounds great. Will you send me on interviews at different companies?

Man: Yes. But before we send you to any companies, you'll probably receive more job training.

Woman: I see. Do you have any written information about your agency that you could send to me?

Man: Sure. I'll send you one of our brochures as soon as I get off the phone.

Woman: Thank you. And I'll send you my résumé.

Unit 8

Exercise 5 (page 78)

1. I saw . . . at the restaurant.
2. The . . . car hit the truck.
3. It happened at . . .
4. . . . mother called me.
5. I reported it to . . .
6. There were . . . shouts.
7. . . . saw the man.
8. I have to hang up now because . . .

Unit 9

Exercise 2 (page 97)

1. **A:** Listen guys! The food and drinks are over here. Please come and help yourselves.

   B: Thanks. We will.

2. **A:** Isn't that the new head of the accounting department over there?

   B: I think so. Let's go over and introduce ourselves.

3. **A:** I'm really nervous about my date with Nicole after the party. I cut myself twice while shaving, and then I lost my car keys.

   B: Come on. This is a party. Just relax and be yourself. You'll do fine.

4. **A:** What are you giving your boss for the holidays this year?

   B: We always give each other the same holiday gifts. Every year I give him a book, and he gives me a box of candy.

5. **A:** What do you think of the new computer program?

   B: I'm not sure. In our department, we're still teaching ourselves how to use it.

6. **A:** Jessica looks upset. Didn't she get a promotion?

   B: No, and she keeps blaming herself. I'll lend her that article about self-talk.

7. **A:** The Aguayos are going to Japan on vacation this year.

   B: Are they going by themselves or with a tour group?

8. **A:** This was a great party.

   B: Yeah. We really enjoyed ourselves.

Exercise 6 (page 101)

1. **A:** The guys in Mark's department did a great job this year.

   B: I know. They should be really proud of each other.

2. **A:** What's wrong? You look upset.

   B: I just heard Ed and Jeff talking. You know Ed blames himself for everything.

3. **A:** I hear you're going to Japan on vacation this year. Are you going by yourself or with a tour?

   B: Oh, with a tour.

4. **A:** Jennifer looks happy tonight. Did Megan give her the promotion?

   B: No, not yet. Megan keeps asking herself if she can do the job.

5. **A:** How do you like the new computer system?

   B: I'm not sure. In our department, we're still teaching ourselves how to use it.

6. **A:** So long, now. Thanks for coming. It was good to see you.

   B: Oh, it was a great party.

   A: I'm glad you enjoyed yourselves.

Unit 10

Exercise 7 (page 112)

1. **A:** What's Terry doing?

   B: She's handing out some lab reports.

2. **A:** Are you done with your report, Rea?

   B: Almost. I just have to look up some information.

3. **A:** Hey, guys. That music is disturbing us.

   B: Sorry. We'll turn it off.

4. **A:** Jason is discouraged.

   B: I know. He says he can't keep up with the class.

5. **A:** Did you hear about Lila?

   B: Yes. We were all surprised when she dropped in yesterday.

6. **A:** OK, class. It's time to take off your lab coats.

   B: Oh, could we have a few more minutes? We're almost done.

7. **A:** Hi. Can I help you?

   B: Yes, thanks. I need to pick out a book for my biology report.

8. **A:** Did you see Professor Diaz in lab today?

   B: Yes. He brought back those plants from the field trip. Very interesting.

Unit 11

Exercise 6 (page 132)

ANNE: Our office is very busy, Karl. We get a lot of phone calls.

KARL: Oh, that's no problem. I can handle phones.

ANNE: Good. Can you speak any other languages? Many of our students are foreign.

KARL: Well, I used to be able to speak Spanish, but I'm out of practice now.

ANNE: That's OK. Maybe with a little practice, you'll be able to get along. Now, what about computer skills? Can you use the computer?

KARL: Yes, I can do word processing and spreadsheets.

ANNE: How fast can you type?

KARL: 50 words per minute.

ANNE: That's good. Can you do any desktop publishing? We're thinking of designing a monthly newsletter.

KARL: Well, I can't right now. But I *am* taking a course in desktop publishing, so I imagine I'll be able to do it pretty soon.

ANNE: You also have to schedule appointments. Many of our students take private dance lessons.

KARL: I can do that.

ANNE: Let's see. What else? Oh, can you drive?

KARL: Sure.

ANNE: That's good. I might need you to do some errands from time to time.

KARL: No problem.

[swing music]

ANNE: Oh! As you can hear, one of our classes is beginning right now. Can you dance, Karl?

KARL: No, but I hope I'll be able to take some classes here if I get the job.

Unit 12

Exercise 5 (page 141)

1. A: May I see your driver's license please?
   B: Certainly. Here it is.

2. A: Hey, can I borrow a pen? All mine have disappeared.
   B: No problem. Keep it if you want. I've got plenty.

3. A: Mom, can I leave the table now? I'm finished eating, and I want to watch TV.
   B: No, you can't. Not yet. I want you to wait until we're all finished.

4. A: I feel awful. I've got a headache, and I'm sick to my stomach. Do you mind if I leave work now?
   B: Not at all. Go home and get some rest.

5. A: Could I take a make-up exam, Professor O'Dell? I didn't feel well during the test.
   B: Sorry, but that won't be possible this time.

6. A: Hi, Mrs. Carter. This is Jeff. May I speak to Linda?
   B: Hi, Jeff. I'm sorry, Linda's sleeping. Could I take a message?

7. A: This is Globe Travel, Mr. Sanchez. Have you decided what day you want to leave for Chicago?
   B: No, I haven't. Could I tell you tomorrow? I need to talk to my wife first.
   A: I'm sorry, but I'm afraid I have to know today. This is the last day I can book your flight.

Unit 13

Exercise 5 (page 152)

1. DARA: Hey Mom, can you drive me to the library on Saturday morning? I have a report to do for school.
   MARCIA: Sorry, I can't. I'm taking Ethan to the dentist on Saturday morning.
   DARA: Will you take me in the afternoon?
   MARCIA: Sure. We can all go to the library in the afternoon.

2. KELLY: Hello, Marcia? This is Kelly. I have to ask you a big favor. We're going to a party on Saturday night. Could you babysit for us?
   MARCIA: I'd like to, but I can't. We're going to the movies Saturday night. Why don't you try Ann? She babysits for us sometimes.

3. MOM: Hi, Marcia. This is Mom. Listen, we're going away for the day on Sunday. Could you come and walk the dog on Sunday morning?
   MARCIA: Sure. I'd be glad to. What time should I come?
   MOM: Come at about 8:00. Thanks a lot.

4. JADE: Hi, Marcia, this is Jade. Are you going to the gym on Sunday afternoon?
   MARCIA: Yes, I am.
   JADE: Would you mind giving me a ride? My car broke down this week.
   MARCIA: Not at all. I'd be glad to.

Unit 14

Exercise 6 (page 162)

TIM: Good morning! And welcome to the Tim Tommando Show! I'm your host, Tim Tommando. Today we're talking about buying a new computer. Got a question? Give me a call at 1-800-555-ENTER. I'm here to help you. OK, we've got Amy on the line from Miami. Go ahead, Amy.

AMY: Hi Tim. I'm a first-time caller.

TIM: Welcome, Amy! How can I help you?

AMY: My computer is seven years old. It's still working, but it's beginning to do some strange things. I don't know what to do. Should I get it repaired or should I buy a new one?

TIM: Don't even think of getting it repaired, Amy! Seven years is *very* old for a computer. You really should get a new one.

AMY: OK. But, I know there have been a lot of changes in the last seven years. How do I get information about all the features in new computers?

TIM: Good question, Amy. There are a lot of excellent websites with computer reviews. You should read them and see what the issues are. You'll learn what's available and what you want. And, a word of advice to *all* my listeners. You shouldn't throw away your old computer if it's still working. Keep it in case you have trouble with your new one. You won't regret it!

AMY: Thanks, Tim.

TIM: You're welcome. We've got Jason from Toronto. Jason, you're on the air.

JASON: Good morning Tim. Thank you for taking my call. I'm ready to buy a new computer. Here's my question: Should I buy it from one of those big companies online, or should I get it at a local computer store?

TIM: Good question, Jason. A computer from a big online company is cheaper, but if you want to be satisfied, you'd better not decide on price alone. Service is *very, very* important. For the best service, you should shop at a local computer store. And you really ought to consider paying a little extra for a service contract. That way if there's a problem, they'll repair it for you—fast and at no cost. We've got Marta on the line from Texas . . .

MARTA: Hi, Tim. I'm getting a new computer. What's the most important thing to look for?

TIM: RAM. That's computer memory. You should always get as much memory as you can afford. Well, we've run out of time for today. Tune in next Friday for more computer tips on the Tim Tommando show. I'm Tim Tommando. Good-bye, and happy computing!

Unit 15

Exercise 5 (page 172)

EMILY: Lantau looks beautiful. Why don't we stay overnight? I think there's a hostel on the island.

MEGAN: You're right. According to this map, the S. G. Davis Hostel is right over there. And there are quite a few interesting things we could do right around the hostel.

EMILY: Hmmm. How about going to see the Tian Tan Buddha? They say it's the largest seated outdoor Buddha statue in the world.

MEGAN: Oh wow, that sounds good. And it's just a few minutes' walk from here. Oh, look at that. There's a riding school right near the hostel. Maybe we could go horseback riding later on.

EMILY: Oh—I don't like horseback riding. Sorry.

MEGAN: No problem. There's plenty of other things we could do.

EMILY: Oh, let's have lunch at the Tea Gardens Restaurant.

MEGAN: I have another idea. Why don't we spend some time at the Po Lin Monastery? It's supposed to be very beautiful, and we could have lunch there. They serve vegetarian meals all day.

EMILY: Hey, that's a good idea! Any ideas for later on?

MEGAN: How about hiking the Lantau Trail?

EMILY: Why don't we do that tomorrow? If we stay at the hostel, we can get up in time to hike the trail and then watch the sunrise at Lantau Peak. It's supposed to be spectacular!

MEGAN: Great idea! Hey, let's get started! We've got a lot to do!

Unit 16

Exercise 7 (page 191)

INTERVIEWER: So, tell me, Antonio, how long have you been a sports announcer?

ANTONIO: For 20 years. My first job was with Channel 8 News. I covered tennis and baseball for them. I left in 1990 when the station was sold.

INTERVIEWER: I see. And how many jobs have you had since then?

ANTONIO: Since 1990? Just two. I was a tennis coach for two years, and then I announced sports on radio WQRT until last year. That's when I moved here to Los Angeles.

INTERVIEWER: So you've been here for a year. How do you like it?

ANTONIO: Very much.

INTERVIEWER: Have you worked at all since you moved here?

ANTONIO: No, not since last year. I decided to go back to school. I've been enrolled in the business program at UCLA since September, but I really miss sports announcing. That's why I'd like this job.

Unit 17

Exercise 5 (page 198)

MAN: Have we found a place yet for the party next week? We've already invited everyone!

WOMAN 1: Jason said we can have it at his place.

MAN: Really? Is it big enough? There are going to be more than 20 people.

WOMAN 1: He says it's no problem. And he's already borrowed extra chairs from his parents.

MAN: That's great. What are we going do about food?

WOMAN 2: Well, we haven't figured that one out yet. We might just have things like chips and soda.

MAN: That's OK. Everyone likes that. Has anyone bought the soda yet?

WOMAN 2: Not yet. But we've got time for that.

MAN: I can do that on Friday. Now, what about music?

WOMAN 1: Ella has already taken care of that. Relax! It's going to be a great party.

Unit 18

Exercise 2 (page 205)

TT: As a travel writer, you've visited many places. Any favorites?

RG: Thailand. It's a beautiful, amazing country. I have been there five times, and I can't wait to go back.

TT: What's been your most unusual travel experience?

RG: My *most* unusual? I've had so many! I've swum near sharks (in a cage, of course!), I've eaten dinner next to an active volcano, I've slept in an ice hotel in Finland . . .

TT: The world has become a lot smaller. There are fewer and fewer "undiscovered" places. Have you ever found a really great place and decided not to tell your readers about it?

RG: No. I've thought about doing that a few times, but I've never kept a place secret. I've always written about it.

TT: Where have you just come back from?

RG: I've just returned from a hot-air ballooning trip in Australia. It was really fantastic.

TT: Where are you going next?

RG: On an African safari! I've never gone on one, and I'm really excited.

TT: Good luck! I look forward to your African safari article.

Exercise 4 (page 207)

EVAN: Hot-air ballooning! What's it like? I've never done this before!

ANDY: You'll love it. I've gone up a few times, but I haven't done it lately.

EVAN: Have you traveled a lot?

ANDY: Yes, I have. I'm a travel writer, so it's part of my job.

EVAN: That's great! Have you ever been on a safari?

ANDY: No, I haven't, but I've always wanted to go.

EVAN: Me too. I've been to Africa several times. In fact, I've just gotten back from a trip there. But I've never been on a safari.

ANDY: Look. They've just finished getting the balloon ready. It's time to go up!

Exercise 7 (page 210)

AGENT: So, what type of vacation are you interested in?

OLIVIA: Well, I've done a lot of adventure traveling, and I've enjoyed things like white water rafting. But this time I'm looking for something *really* unusual. Something exciting and challenging. Something I've never done before.

AGENT: Well, you've come to the right place. Here at Adventure Travel, we have lots of exciting possibilities. Take a look at this . . . Have you ever gone hang gliding? We've got a great trip in Australia that includes hang gliding.

OLIVIA: Hang gliding's great, but I've done it. Quite a few times, actually.

AGENT: OK. What about sky diving? I bet you haven't tried that!

OLIVIA: No, I haven't. But I think that's a little *too* adventurous for me. I don't want this to be my *last* vacation, after all!

AGENT: I understand. How about *shark* diving then? Have you ever been shark diving?

OLIVIA: Shark diving? You're kidding, right?

AGENT: No. It's probably a lot safer than sky diving. You get really up close and personal with the sharks, but you're in this cage. See?

OLIVIA: I don't think so . . . Maybe I should stay on land.

AGENT: OK. How about snow mobiling in Canada?

OLIVIA: Been there, done that. But, you know, all this talk about adventure has made me think. Maybe what I *really* need is a nice, quiet vacation.

AGENT: Well, then this may be the perfect vacation for you! Here, take a look at this brochure.

Unit 19

Exercise 3 (page 216)

MARIA: Hello?

JOE: Hi, hon! How was your day? I bet you're glad it's over.

MARIA: I'm OK—a little tired. I only slept a few hours last night. I'm writing this big report, and I haven't stopped worrying about it all week.

JOE: You've been tired for weeks. You need to relax a little. Listen—why don't I come see you this weekend? We've seen each other only twice this month.

MARIA: Sounds great, but remember the last time you came? I didn't do any work, and I still haven't caught up.

JOE: I understand. Now, why don't you have a cup of coffee and relax?

MARIA: Coffee! You're kidding! I've already had five cups today. And yesterday I drank at least six. I can't drink another drop.

JOE: You've had a rough week. Try to get some sleep.

MARIA: I can't go to sleep yet. I haven't finished my report, and it's due tomorrow.

JOE: Well, I hope it goes fast. Good night, hon. I'll call you tomorrow.

MARIA: Bye, honey. Speak to you tomorrow.

JOE: Bye, bye.

Exercise 7 (page 219)

INTERVIEWER: As you know, we've been interviewing married faculty members. How long have the two of you been married?

MAN: For ten years.

WOMAN: Yeah, but we lived in different cities for most of that time.

MAN: That's right. It was very hard, I should say impossible, to get a job in the same city.

WOMAN: Yeah, in fact, this is the first time we've been at the same university since we were graduate students back in Boston.

INTERVIEWER: How long did you live in Boston?

MAN AND WOMAN: Six years.

INTERVIEWER: And how long have you been in Austin?

WOMAN: Oh let's see, how long has it been? A year now?

MAN: That's right. We've been here for almost a year. July will be exactly a year.

WOMAN: Yes. We *finally* managed to find jobs in the same city *and* at the same university. It's been great!

MAN: Yeah, and now that we don't have to pay rent for two apartments, we've been able to buy a house.

WOMAN: We've only had it for a month, and we love it.

MAN: It sure beats driving six hours every weekend to see each other!

WOMAN: Yeah.

Unit 20

Exercise 7 (page 229)

1. **A:** Isn't it awful?
   B: What's awful?
   A: Haven't you seen it? They've cut down that tree.

2. **A:** You must be so excited about your safari trip.
   B: Well, we've planned the first few weeks, and we've packed all our stuff.

3. **A:** We haven't spoken in a while, Jane. How is that elephant family doing?
   B: Much better. It's rained since we spoke, and there's plenty of water and food now.

4. **A:** Will she ever stop?
   B: I don't know. She's been eating leaves all morning.

5. **A:** What's Professor Owen doing these days?
   B: She's been writing a book about elephants.

Unit 21

Exercise 2 (page 245)

JASON: There's still a lot of work to do this evening. We have to plan the food for the trip.

MEGAN: I've been reading this book about camping. There's some good advice about food in it.

JASON: What does it say?

MEGAN: We should bring a lot of beans and rice.

JASON: Potatoes are good on camping trips too.

MEGAN: Fresh vegetables are too heavy to carry. Maybe we can get some when we pass through a town.

JASON: Is the equipment ready? We should go over the checklist.

MEGAN: I did that. We need some batteries for the radio.

JASON: Why do we need a radio? I thought we were running away from civilization.

MEGAN: But the news never stops. I still want to know what's happening.

JASON: That's OK with me. By the way, do we have enough warm clothing? It gets chilly in the mountains.

MEGAN: That's true. And the cold really bothers me at night.

JASON: But we have warm sleeping bags.

Unit 21

Exercise 5 (page 247)

JASON: That book you found has a good recipe for cookie bars.

MEGAN: Let's make some and bring them along. What are the ingredients?

JASON: It says two cups of butter.

MEGAN: Hmmm. We don't have that much butter left. We'd better get some more.

JASON: How about brown sugar? We need three cups of that.

MEGAN: We still have a lot of brown sugar. What's next?

JASON: Oatmeal.

MEGAN: We only have a little oatmeal. What else? Is there any flour in this recipe?

JASON: Four cups.

MEGAN: Then there isn't enough flour either.

JASON: We'll also need a cup of cornflakes and some eggs.

MEGAN: OK. We have a lot of cornflakes. How many eggs do we need?

JASON: Eight.

MEGAN: Eight? What are we making, an omelet?

JASON: I'm just reading the recipe. It says eight eggs.

MEGAN: We don't have that many. We only have four.

JASON: The last things are raisins and chocolate chips. I know we have a lot of *those*.

MEGAN: We ate the chocolate chips last night, remember?

JASON: Oh, yeah.

MEGAN: But you're right. We still have a lot of raisins.

JASON: Why don't you make the list, and I'll go shopping.

Unit 22

Exercise 7 (page 258)

1. AMY: What's that?

   BEN: Oh. It's the new video game. Do you want to try it?

2. AMY: I'm reading the story you recommended now. Who's Angelica? I can't figure it out.

   BEN: She's the princess with magic powers.

3. AMY: What about Aesop? Have you read the fable?

   BEN: No. I'm going to tonight.

4. AMY: You know, I'd like to buy a book of fables for Ava.

   BEN: Good idea. She loves fables.

5. AMY: Let's go to the bookstore this weekend.

   BEN: OK. We can go on Sunday after lunch.

6. AMY: Speaking of lunch, I'm hungry.

   BEN: Here. Why don't you have a sandwich?

Unit 23

Exercise 4 (page 273)

MAGGIE: What's the matter with Alice?

LUIS: Who knows? She's always annoyed about something.

MAGGIE: I know, but this time I'm really confused.

LUIS: Why? What's so confusing this time?

MAGGIE: Oh, I thought she was happy. She met an interesting man last week.

LUIS: Great. Was she interested in him?

MAGGIE: I thought so. She said they saw a fascinating movie together. So I thought . . .

LUIS: Maybe she was fascinated by the movie, but she was disappointed with the guy.

MAGGIE: Maybe. It's hard to tell with Alice. Her moods are often very surprising.

Exercise 6 (page 274)

MAN: I found four apartments in today's paper that I think we should take a look at.

WOMAN: Good! Tell me about them.

MAN: Well, they're all two bedrooms, and they all cost between 450 and 600 a month.

WOMAN: Sounds good so far.

MAN: Let's see. The first one is described as a large, two bedroom in a new building. It's also near public transportation. It doesn't say anything else about it.

WOMAN: Right. So let's forget about that one.

MAN: Now, the second one has more information. It sounds like it's sunny. It says it's just been painted and is in excellent condition. It's also near stores and schools.

WOMAN: That sounds better. What about the other two?

MAN: OK. The third one is described as "cute and cozy."

WOMAN: Uh-oh. You know what that usually means!

MAN: Yeah, it's probably very small.

WOMAN: What else does it say?

MAN: It says it's in a quiet area.

WOMAN: Hmmm. That could mean there are no stores or anything around.

MAN: Right. *[sound of dog barking]* And we couldn't bring Loki. . . . Listen to this one. It says the apartment's in a completely renovated building with a modern kitchen and bathroom.

WOMAN: What's wrong with that?

MAN: Nothing. And it's available right away.

Unit 24

Exercise 6 (page 284)

WOMAN: How about pizza for dinner?

MAN: Sounds good. Any special brand?

WOMAN: Well, here's the frozen food section. Let's see what they have.

MAN: OK . . . there's Di Roma's and there's Angela's. Ever hear of those?

WOMAN: No. How do they compare in price?

MAN: Let's see. Angela's is $5.38, and Di Roma's is $4.41.

WOMAN: Di Roma's is cheaper, but the pizza isn't as big as Angela's.

MAN: Right. Angela's is bigger. You get five and a quarter slices from a Di Roma's pizza, but you get six slices from an Angela's.

WOMAN: Hmmm.

MAN: What are you looking at?

WOMAN: The nutrition information. Listen to this. Angela's uses low-fat cheese, so there are fewer grams of fat.

MAN: Sounds like Angela's is the healthier choice. What else does the label say? What ingredients do they list for the sauce?

WOMAN: Well, in addition to tomatoes and water, Angela's sauce just has basil and black pepper. Di Roma's has basil, oregano, garlic, onions, salt, and pepper.

MAN: Di Roma's sounds a lot tastier.

WOMAN: It's hard to choose. Let's see if there's an expiration date.

MAN: Di Roma's says sell by February 15 of this year.

WOMAN: That's in two weeks! The Angela's says sell by April 15 of next year.

MAN: Then, let's get the Angela's. It's fresher, and we can always add our own spices.

Unit 25

Exercise 6 (page 295)

MAY: If we're going to go to Toronto next summer, we'd better make reservations soon.

DAN: It's only January!

MAY: But the guidebooks all say hotels fill up fast, so let's not wait.

DAN: OK, this won't be too hard. We've already gotten our choices down to three hotels—the Westin Harbour Castle, the Hôtel Le Germain, and the Delta Chelsea.

MAY: Westin Harbour Castle has the best view of all three. It's right on the lake, and a lot of the rooms have good views. Oh, and they have a restaurant with views of both the lake and the city.

DAN: Sounds beautiful, but we're going to see a lot of shows, so we want to be close to the Entertainment District. Unfortunately, the Westin Harbour Castle is the least convenient for that. Also, it's really big, and we both like small hotels.

MAY: OK, let's see . . . The Hôtel Le Germain is very close to the Entertainment District. From there we could walk to the theater, to the sports arena, and to the CN Tower. *And* it has only 122 rooms. Here, look at these pictures.

DAN: Wow, it looks comfortable. It says "we give our guests every comfort, including in-room stereos, high-quality bath products, and a library with a fireplace and coffee bar."

MAY: Sounds great. It's the smallest, the most comfortable, *and* the most convenient of all. How much are the rooms?

DAN: They start at $240.

MAY: Ouch. So it's also the most expensive. And the Westin Harbour Castle is only a little cheaper.

DAN: OK, maybe we don't need absolutely the *best* view or the *most* convenient location.

MAY: Right. Then I think the Delta Chelsea is probably our best choice. It's the least expensive of the three, and the guidebook says it's the best value in Toronto.

DAN: It has 1,600 rooms! Is that OK with you? It's the biggest hotel in the city.

MAY: Sure. We can afford it, and it's not too far from the Entertainment District.

DAN: Great! I'll get online and make the reservation, OK? This is going to be the best vacation we've ever had!

Unit 26

Exercise 3 (page 302)

LOBO: Why do people still take female basketball players less seriously than male players? Do women really play less aggressively than men?

BARD: Absolutely not! We play just as aggressively. And when we fall, we hit the floor just as hard as the guys do.

LOBO: You could sure see that in tonight's game. Jackson played the most fearlessly of any player I've seen, male or female.

BARD: Yes. And the more often women athletes compete, the sooner audiences are going to see that.

LOBO: Some people say women play more cooperatively than men.

BARD: I agree. I think we have better teamwork—we play better on a team. We also play more patiently. Women players will wait longer for a good chance to shoot.

LOBO: Tickets for women's basketball games cost less than tickets for men's games. Does that bother you?

BARD: Sure, but the faster women players attract fans, the faster the women's leagues will make money.

LOBO: So as time goes on you'll be paid better and better.

BARD: We certainly hope so.

Exercise 6 (page 304)

And what a race that was, ladies and gentlemen. Up until the last minute, those horses sure had us guessing. Nobody fell asleep during this race, I can tell you that.

Of course, you know that Get Packin' was the winner. He did come in first, but for a long time it looked like Inspired Winner was going to win. He was running as fast as Wild Whirl, and then suddenly he started to run slower and slower. The next thing we knew he was in last place, and he stayed last the rest of the race. Yes, Inspired Winner came in last, while Wild Whirl finished a close second to Get Packin'.

Now Señor Speedy and Exuberant King started running as slowly as two turtles in a sandbox. Then, after the second turn, Señor Speedy took off like lightning. That's all Exuberant King needed to see, and he was off, too. It was amazing. They were moving as fast as any horse can move, but it was too

late to catch up. As fast as they were running, they still couldn't catch up with Get Packin' or Wild Whirl. They ran side by side most of the way, but at the end Exuberant King ran a little slower, and Señor Speedy came in third place.

Unit 27

Exercise 5 (page 321)

PATIENT: So, doctor, what do you think?

DOCTOR: Well, first of all, you must stop smoking. You should also quit drinking coffee.

PATIENT: What about my weight?

DOCTOR: Avoid losing any more weight. Stay at 160 pounds. That's the perfect weight for you. As for your diet, you eat enough protein, but I suggest eating more complex carbohydrates.

PATIENT: And what about exercise?

DOCTOR: Well, exercise is very important, but avoid running every day. It's too stressful.

PATIENT: But I want to do some form of exercise every day.

DOCTOR: Have you considered riding a bike? Cycling is something you can do every day without harm.

PATIENT: OK. Any other advice?

DOCTOR: Yes. Keep working eight hours a day. Being active mentally and physically is the best thing for you.

Unit 28

Exercise 6 (page 331)

Good evening, everyone, and thanks for coming tonight. My name is Latoya Williams, and I want to be your next Student Council president.

I believe that I am the best person for this position because of my experience in working for student government. For two years I have been a class representative to the Student Council. As a representative, I have been successful in bringing many new members into the Council. Elect me president, and I can do much more for you.

First of all, I am opposed to raising student activity fees. We pay the highest student activity fees of any college in this area, and the college plans on raising these fees again this year. I will insist on discussing this issue with the administration.

Second, when I am president you can look forward to eating better. Right now you have to choose between eating school cafeteria food or buying fast foods on campus. We need some more choices—how about some ethnic foods and health foods on campus?

The third and most important issue is campus safety. Many of us want to use the computer labs and libraries at night. However, we are nervous about walking back to our dorms at ten or eleven o'clock. I will ask the school administration for more campus security guards on campus at night.

I am experienced, and I will be aggressive about talking to the school administration about student issues. I believe that these three issues—lower fees, better food, and most importantly, greater safety—are going to make a big difference. Vote for me next week and get the campus you deserve.

Unit 29

Exercise 5 (page 338)

1. **WOMAN:** I've been married once before. I have a teenage daughter from my first marriage. She and my new husband always used to argue. I really wanted them to discuss their problems, but that was impossible at first.

2. **MAN:** I guess I'm a slow learner, but I finally learned not to argue with my stepdaughter.

3. **WOMAN:** Blended families always have a lot to learn. I expected to have problems with my daughter.

4. **MAN:** But it was much, much worse than we thought. For a while, my stepdaughter refused to talk to me at all. To be honest, sometimes I just wanted her to leave the house for a few hours.

5. **WOMAN:** I know what you mean. But we always tried to understand her feelings. After all, she didn't choose to live with us. I made that choice for her.

6. **MAN:** I almost gave up. Then one day, she asked me to go on a family vacation—the three of us went to California.

7. **WOMAN:** I was amazed. I didn't expect to have a good time, but it was wonderful.

8. **MAN:** We're still having problems, but we can talk about them now. In fact, sometimes, I'd like her to stop talking for a few minutes.

    WOMAN: Oh, come on . . .

Unit 30

Exercise 5 (page 346)

Hello, you have reached Lacy's Department Store.
- If you are calling from a touchtone telephone, please press 0 now.
- To speak to a customer service representative, please press 1 now.
- To report a lost or stolen credit card, please press 2 now.

- To place an order through our teleservice, please press 3 now.
- To ask about billing accounts or merchandise delivery, please press 4 now.
- To get information about our locations and hours, please press 5 now.
- To listen to this recording again, please press 6 now, and thank you for calling Lacy's.

Unit 31

Exercise 5 (page 354)

We're excited to report that our new recreation center is open to the public. The outside areas are all completely accessible by wheelchair, and soon the indoor pool and other indoor areas will be too.

You'll notice that there are now ramps for all the steps going into the new building. These ramps are gradual enough to use without help. Each door also has an automatic door opener, and it's placed low enough so that you can reach it from a wheelchair.

The old water fountains were too high to reach from a wheelchair. We've put in new ones that everybody can use—we know you get thirsty out there on the basketball courts.

Unfortunately, we haven't been able to change the outdoor telephones yet. They are still too high to reach from a wheelchair. However, indoor public telephones are already wheelchair accessible.

Oh—and some important news for you skateboarding dudes! These new entrances are too busy for you to skate around. Check out our new skate park instead. You'll find plenty of challenge there.

Unit 32

Exercise 7 (page 362)

INTERVIEWER: You recently joined a support group for procrastinators. Tell me about it.

EVA: Yes. I decided to join after trying to solve the problem on my own and failing. The support group has taught me a lot of useful tips to deal with my problem.

INTERVIEWER: What have you learned?

EVA: Well, for one thing, I now always clean my work area before I start working. I know this sounds simple, but in the past, I didn't do it. I thought it was a waste of time. But it's distracting sitting at a messy desk, and I wasted a lot of time *that* way.

INTERVIEWER: OK. Let's say you have an important test. When do you start studying for it?

EVA: Well, in the past, I put off studying until the night before the test. Not anymore. I start preparing a week before the test—at least. As a result, I feel much less nervous, and I do better on the test. I also choose to study the hardest thing first.

INTERVIEWER: Why is that?

EVA: It makes the whole thing easier, and that way I'm sure I can study everything.

INTERVIEWER: What else do you do?

EVA: I've learned to write down all my tasks on a To Do list—along with their deadlines. I tape it on my computer monitor and look at it frequently. That way I don't forget to do anything.

INTERVIEWER: Do you take breaks?

EVA: I used to take breaks—long breaks. It was a way of avoiding work. I stopped doing that. I still take breaks now, but I limit them to just ten minutes. During my breaks I like to do relaxation exercises. This helps me work better when I start again.

INTERVIEWER: Do you give yourself a reward when you finish a project?

EVA: No. Finishing the project, getting good grades, and feeling less nervous is more than enough reward for me!

Unit 33

Exercise 6 (page 384)

WAITER: Have you decided what you'd like?

EMMA: What are your specials tonight?

WAITER: We have a fish dinner and a steak dinner.

EMMA: I think I'll have the fish dinner. What does that come with?

WAITER: Well, you have a choice of soup or a salad.

EMMA: Hmmm. I think I'd prefer soup to a salad. What kind of soup do you have today?

WAITER: We have onion and tomato. The tomato soup is very good.

EMMA: I think I'd rather have onion soup.

WAITER: OK, onion soup. And would you prefer rice or potatoes with your fish?

EMMA: Could I have a vegetable instead?

WAITER: Sure. We have fresh broccoli today.

EMMA: I'd rather not have broccoli. I guess I'll have the rice after all.

WAITER: And to drink?

EMMA: A small soda. I prefer diet soda, if you have it.

WAITER: Yes, we do. And you have a choice of apple pie or ice cream for dessert.

EMMA: Do you have strawberry ice cream?

WAITER: No, vanilla or chocolate.

EMMA: Then I'd prefer the pie.

Unit 34

Exercise 7 (page 396)

1. **A:** Should I go left or right at the corner?

   B: You have to turn left. You can't make a right turn here.

2. **A:** Why are you driving so slowly?

   B: Because the speed limit is 30 kilometers an hour.

   A: No, it isn't. The blue sign means you have to drive at least 30 kilometers an hour. You can't drive more slowly than that.

3. **A:** This scenery is beautiful. Let's stop and take some pictures.

   B: You can't stop here.

   A: Not even for a few minutes?

   B: Nope. That big red X means "no stopping."

4. **A:** Slow down a little. It's starting to rain.

   B: I can't. Look at the sign.

   A: I know. But that's the *maximum* speed. You don't *have to* drive 80 kilometers an hour!

5. **A:** You have to stop here.

   B: Why? There's no traffic.

   A: You've got to come to a complete stop when you see this sign.

6. **A:** That car is going awfully slow.

   B: Why don't you pass?

   A: I have to wait. I can't pass here. It's not allowed.

Unit 35

Exercise 5 (page 404)

1. **A:** Where's Netta? It's 2:00 already.

   B: Relax. She isn't supposed to be here until 2:30.

   A: Oh, OK. I guess I am a little nervous.

2. **A:** Do you know how she's getting here?

   B: Well, she wasn't going to walk!

3. **A:** What's the photographer doing up there? He isn't supposed to take pictures during the ceremony.

   B: It's OK. He's just checking the light.

4. **A:** Let's go sit down. The ceremony's going to start soon.

   B: Where do we sit?

   A: We're with the bride's family, so we're supposed to sit on the left.

5. **A:** Here come the bridesmaids now. Ooh, don't they look beautiful!

   B: Yes! But I'm a bit surprised. I thought they were going to wear pink.

   A: They were, but Netta changed her mind.

6. **A:** Where is Sophie?

   B: She'll come in later. She's the maid of honor, so she's supposed to walk behind the bride.

7. **A:** I've never been to an American wedding. What are we supposed to say to the bride and groom?

   B: Tell the bride she looks beautiful. Say "congratulations" to the groom.

   A: OK.

8. **A:** Hey, I thought that we were supposed to throw rice at the bride and groom on their way out of the church.

   B: No, not anymore. People say it can hurt the birds.

   A: Really?

Unit 36

Exercise 6 (page 412)

And now for the weekend forecast.

A lot of you are still shoveling snow from Wednesday's storm, but take heart. Warm, dry air is moving in from the south. We might see sunny skies and temperatures in the low 50s by Friday.

Plan to get out on Saturday—it's going to be a beautiful day. It will be bright and sunny, and temperatures may reach 60 by Saturday afternoon. There will be some wind, though, with gusts reaching 20 miles per hour, so bring a jacket.

Unfortunately, this beautiful weather won't stay with us for the whole weekend. A new storm front is right behind this good weather. Cold, windy weather could be here again by Sunday afternoon, and there might even be some flurries Sunday evening.

Don't put away the snow shovel yet. Winter is still with us.

Unit 37

Exercise 6 (page 422)

MRS. WILSON: Shh! I hear someone at the door. It's 9:30. Who could it be?

MR. WILSON: It could be a late customer.

MRS. WILSON: No, it couldn't be. It's much too late. Maybe it's the cat.

MR. WILSON: It can't be. I put the cat out before we went to bed.

MRS. WILSON: Could it be Vincent? He's always down in the basement with his camera.

MR. WILSON: No, Vincent went out an hour ago. He can't be back this early. Wait a minute. It could be Holmes and Dr. Watson. They said they wanted to talk to me.

MRS. WILSON: Could they really be here so late?

MR. WILSON: No. You're right. It can't be them.

MRS. WILSON: What could it be then?

MR. WILSON: That door rattles whenever the wind blows. It could be the wind.

MRS. WILSON: That must be it. Let's go to sleep.

Exercise 8 (page 423)

HOLMES: Dr. Watson, this is Captain Rogers from the Police Department.

CAPTAIN: How do you do, Dr. Watson? Well, we're all here now. It must be 10:00. Let's go down to the basement.

HOLMES: You lead, captain. We'll follow you.

CAPTAIN: The storeroom is in here. Please close the door.

HOLMES: Let's get comfortable. We may have a long wait.

WATSON: I'm going to sit on one of these boxes. Uh . . . what's in all these boxes, captain?

CAPTAIN: Gold. Two months ago, the bank borrowed a large amount of gold from France. There may be 2,000 gold coins in that box, Dr. Watson.

HOLMES: John Clay must know about this gold. That's why he took the job at Wilson's.

WATSON: And he invented the Red-Headed League to keep Wilson away from the shop. While Wilson was working at the League, John Clay was digging a tunnel to the bank.

HOLMES: But Clay just ended the Red-Headed League. So his tunnel has to be finished.

CAPTAIN: You're right, Mr. Holmes! This floor is hollow. The tunnel has got to be right here, under this floor!

HOLMES: Did you bring your gun, Watson? John Clay could be dangerous.

WATSON: Yes, I did. But what is he waiting for? It's after 10:00.

HOLMES: He may want Wilson to be asleep before he comes.

CAPTAIN: Shhh! I heard a noise in the tunnel!

HOLMES: It might be him! Get ready!

CLAY: Police?!

HOLMES: How do you do? You must be Mr. John Clay!

CAPTAIN: You're under arrest, Mr. Clay.

Student Book Answer Key

NOTE: In this answer key, where the contracted form is given, the full form is also correct, and where the full form is given, the contracted form is also correct.

UNIT 1 Present Progressive and Simple Present (pages 2–13)

After You Read
1. Tomás
2. Claude
3. Nicole
4. Sheila
5–6. *Answers will vary.*

1

JUNE 28: I'm sitting in a seat 30,000 feet above the earth en route to Argentina! I usually have dinner at this time, but right now I have an awful headache from all the excitement. My seatmate is eating my food. I guess it's good. She looks happy.

JUNE 30: It's 7:30 P.M. My host parents are still working. Carlos, my father, works at home. My little brother, Ricardo, is cute. He looks (and acts) a lot like Bobby. Right now, he's looking over my shoulder and trying to read my journal.

JULY 4: The weather is cold here. I usually spend the first weekend of July at the beach. Today I'm walking around in a heavy sweater.

AUGUST 6: I usually feel great in the evening because we take long naps in the afternoon, but tonight I feel really tired.

AUGUST 25: I'm feeling very comfortable here now—but it's almost time to go home! My host parents usually cook a light dinner, but tonight they're cooking a special dinner for me. I miss them already!

2

2. attends class, is going on a field trip to the museum
3. eats lunch
4. is eating lunch
5. takes a nap, is working on the family web page
6. works in the cafeteria
7. isn't doing homework, is calling home
8. isn't playing tennis, is watching a video with Eva
9. is having dinner
10. has dinner
11. writes letters, is taking a walk with the family
12. isn't taking a shower, is doing homework

3

A.
2. 'm waiting
3. seem
4. 'm working
5. 's talking
6. 's not looking
7. seems
8. doesn't mean

B.
1. 's talking
2. 're taking
3. 're standing
4. Do you think
5. 're dating
6. don't think
7. means
8. come
9. usually stand

4

A.
2. starts
3. has
4. walks
5. appear

B.
1. are . . . shaking
2. know
3. shake
4. meet
5. Do . . . shake

5

2. cause
3. Are . . . living
4. traveling
5. do . . . feel OR are . . . feeling
6. go

6

2. treat
3. annoy
4. 'm living, don't think
5. want
6. improve

7. 'm making OR am making
8. don't understand, feel OR 'm feeling

7

I'm sitting
It's 12:30 and ~~I sit~~ in the library right now. My classmates are eating lunch together, but I'm

never eat
not hungry yet. At home, we ~~eat never~~ this early. Today our journal topic is culture shock. It's a good topic for me right now because I'm ~~being~~ pretty homesick. I miss my old routine.

eat
At home we always ~~are eating~~ a big meal at 2:00 in the afternoon. Then we rest. But here

I have
in Toronto ~~I'm having~~ a 3:00 conversation class. Every day I almost fall asleep in class, and my

asks
teacher ~~ask~~ me, "Are you bored?" Of course I'm not bored. I just need my afternoon nap! This

is always   *we're working*
class ~~always is~~ fun. This semester, ~~we work~~ on a project with video cameras. My team is filming groups of people from different

analyzing
cultures. We are ~~analyze~~ "social distance." That means how close to each other these people stand. According to my new watch, it's 12:55,

I'm leaving
so ~~I leave~~ now for my 1:00 class. Teachers here

don't like
really ~~aren't liking~~ tardiness!

8

Usually: 2, 3, 5
Now or These Days: 1, 4, 6, 7

9–13

Answers will vary.

UNIT 2 Imperative   (pages 9–21)

After You Read
Jab: 2, 3
Power Kick: 4, 5, 6
Both: 1

1

2. e   **4.** b   **6.** d   **8.** h
3. c   **5.** g   **7.** a   **9.** f

2

2. Wash six strawberries.
3. Cut the strawberries in half.
4. Pour orange juice into the blender.
5. Add the fruit to the orange juice.
6. Blend the ingredients until smooth.

3

2. Learn
3. Decrease
4. Increase
5. Become
6. Don't miss

7. Take
8. Choose
9. Don't wait
10. Register

4

For the Black Belt essay, Master Gibbons gave

Write
us this assignment: ~~You write~~ about something important to you. My topic was "The Right Way," the rules of life for the martial arts. Three of these rules are very important to me.

respect
• First, ~~respects~~ other people—treat them the way you want them to treat you.

help
• Second, ~~helped~~ people in need. In other

don't
words, use your strength for others, ~~not~~ use it just for your own good.

don't
• Third, ~~no~~ lie or steal. You can't defend others when you feel guilty.
There are many other rules, but these are the most important ones to me.

5

____6____ Heat a frying pan and melt a small piece of butter in it.
____1____ Beat two egg whites in a large bowl.
____2____ Add one and a quarter cups of whole wheat flour to the egg whites.
____8____ Flip the pancakes over.
____5____ Blend in some fruit.
____4____ Mix thoroughly.
____9____ Top them with fruit or yogurt.
____7____ Pour some of the pancake mixture into the frying pan.
____3____ Add a cup of low-fat milk.

Answers will vary.

UNIT 3 Simple Past (pages 22–33)

After You Read
True: 1, 4
False: 2, 3

1

As the son of a samurai, Basho <u>grew up</u> in the household of Todo Yoshitada, a young lord. After his father's death in 1656, Basho <u>stayed</u> in the Yoshitada household. He and Todo <u>wrote</u> poetry together, and in 1664 they <u>published</u> some poems. Two years later, Todo <u>died</u> suddenly. Basho <u>left</u> the area.

Basho <u>moved</u> around for several years. In the 1670s, he <u>went</u> to Edo and <u>stayed</u> there. He <u>found</u> friendship and success once again. Basho <u>judged</u> poetry contests, <u>published</u> his own poetry, and <u>taught</u> students. His students <u>built</u> him a home outside the city in 1681. They <u>planted</u> a banana tree (*basho* in Japanese) in front and <u>called</u> his home "Basho Hut." That is how the poet <u>got</u> his name: Basho.

In spite of this success, Basho <u>became</u> unhappy. He often <u>wrote</u> about loneliness. His mother <u>died</u> in 1683, and he <u>began</u> his travels a year later. His trip to the northern part of Honshu in 1689 <u>was</u> difficult, but his travel diary about this journey, *Narrow Road to the Deep North*, <u>became</u> one of Japan's greatest works of literature.

As a famous poet, Basho <u>had</u> many visitors—too many, in fact. In 1693 he <u>locked</u> his gate for a month, <u>stayed</u> alone, and <u>wrote</u>. The following year he <u>took</u> his final journey, to Osaka. He <u>died</u> there among his friends.

1664	Basho (and Todo) published poems.
1666	Todo died.
	Basho left the area.
1681	Students built the Basho Hut.
1683	Basho's mother died.
1684	Basho began his travels.
1689	Basho traveled to northern Honshu
1693	Basho locked his gate to visitors.
1694	Basho took his final journey.
	Basho died.

2

2. wrote
3. were
4. led
5. became
6. left
7. didn't have
8. wore

3

2. studied
3. became
4. read
5. used
6. didn't write
7. wrote
8. didn't address
9. did
10. appeared
11. was

4

2. saw
3. bit
4. ate
5. drank
6. hopped

5

3. **A:** Did Dickinson become famous during her lifetime?
   B: No, she didn't.
4. **A:** Did Dickinson receive many visitors?
   B: No, she didn't.
5. **A:** Did Dickinson travel a lot?
   B: No, she didn't.
6. **A:** How many poems did Dickinson write?
   B: She wrote 1,700 poems.
7. **A:** What did Dickinson write about?
   B: She wrote about love, nature, and time.
8. **A:** When did Dickinson die?
   B: She died in 1886.

6

Answers may vary slightly.

2. That's wrong. She didn't live in Chicago until 1977. She lived there until 1985.
3. That's wrong. He wasn't very shy. He was outgoing.
4. That's right.
5. That's right.
6. That's wrong. She didn't teach Spanish. She taught English and Mexican history.
7. That's wrong. She didn't go to France for her Ph.D. She went to Germany.

7

Today in class we read a poem by American poet Robert Frost. I really ~~enjoy~~ *enjoyed* it. It was about a person who ~~choosed~~ *chose* between two roads in a forest. Many people believed the person ~~were~~ *was* Frost. He ~~thinked~~ *thought* about his choice for a long time. The two roads didn't ~~looked~~ *look* very different. Finally, he didn't ~~took~~ *take* the road most people take. He took the one less traveled on. At that time, he didn't ~~thought~~ *think* it was an important decision, but his choice ~~change~~ *changed* his life.

Sometimes I feel a little like Frost. Two years ago I ~~decide~~ *decided* to move to a new country. Did I ~~made~~ *make* the right choice?

8

1975	parents left Turkey
1980	moved to the U.S.
1982	began to write poetry
1991	graduated from college
1992	won a poetry award
1994	became a teacher

9

Vladimir Liapunov was born on May 6, 1981, in Kiev. His mother was a dressmaker, and his father made shoes. At home they spoke Russian. In 1999 Vlad and his family moved to Boston. At first Vlad felt lonely. Then he got a part-time job as a cook. He worked in a Russian restaurant. He met Elena at work, and they got married in 2001. They had a baby in 2002. A month ago, Vlad enrolled at the local community college. His goal is to own his own restaurant someday.

10–13

Answers will vary.

UNIT 4 Past Progressive and Simple Past
(pages 34–42)

After You Read

Checked: 1, 4

1

2. b **4.** a
3. b **5.** b

2

3. was leaving
4. was driving
5. was speaking
6. saw
7. stepped
8. was crossing
9. hit
10. didn't see
11. was talking
12. wasn't paying
13. was listening
14. noticed
15. tried
16. arrived
17. was bleeding
18. stopped

3

2. Who exactly were you visiting?
3. Was she working at 7:00?
4. Was anyone else working with her?
5. What were you doing while she was working?
6. What did you do when the lights went out?
7. What was she doing when you found her?
8. Then what did you do?
9. Why were you running when the police saw you?

4

2. When the wind began to blow, the electricity went out.
3. While he was driving home, he was listening to his car radio.
4. He pulled over to the side of the road when he couldn't see anything.
5. While he was listening to the news, he heard about the burglary.
6. When it stopped snowing, Mr. Ligo went to the police station.

5

What ~~was happening~~ *happened* to me this morning was so unbelievable! I ~~walked~~ *was walking* down the street ~~while~~ *when* a woman stopped in front of me and asked me for directions to the nearest bank. At that moment, I ~~was seeing~~ *saw* my friend Bill across the street. I called out to him and asked him to wait for me. Luckily for me, he did. Bill saw everything: While I ‸*was* talking to the woman, a pickpocket ~~was~~ put his hand into my backpack. Bill started to walk away. I thought he didn't want to wait for me, but I was wrong. When Bill saw the pickpocket he went to call the

police. They ~~were arriving~~ ^{arrived} immediately. The police arrested the woman and the pickpocket. What an experience!

6

Set 2

7–10

Answers will vary.

UNIT 5 *Used to* (pages 43–51)

After You Read
True: 3, 4, 5
False: 1, 2, 6, 7

1

Underlined verb forms: used to play, used to listen, never used to bother, used to be, did . . . use to do

2

1. **b.** used to have
2. **a.** used to stop
3. **a.** Did . . . use to play
   b. used to practice
   c. used to come
4. **a.** didn't use to like
5. **a.** used to sit
   b. didn't use to wear
   c. used to be

3

2. used to wear
3. used to drive
4. used to be
5. used to play
6. used to visit
7. used to love

4

The high school reunion was great! I talked to Eileen Edwards. Well, she's the famous Shania Twain now. In high school, she ~~was~~ used to be just one of us, and tonight we all called her Eileen. She graduated in 1983, a year before me. Today she lives in a chateau in Switzerland

and models for Revlon, but her life didn't ~~used~~ ^{use}
to be like that at all! She ~~uses~~ ^{used} to be very poor, and her grandma used to ~~made~~ ^{make} all her clothes because her family couldn't afford to buy them. She was always a good musician, though. In fact, she used to earn money for her family that way. She performed with a local rock band, and my friends and I ~~use~~ ^{used} to go hear her. She could really sing! Her new name, Shania, means "on my way" in Ojibwa (her stepfather's Native American language). After she left Timmins, I ~~got~~ used to think that Timmins wasn't important to her anymore—but I was wrong. She is always doing good things for our community. And tonight she was just the way she used ^{to} be in high school—simple and friendly!

5

Past: 1, 3, 6, 9
Now: 2, 4, 5, 7, 8

6–9

Answers will vary.

UNIT 6 Future (pages 52–64)

After You Read
Collins: 1. T, **2.** F, **3.** F, **4.** T, **5.** T, **6.** T, **7.** F, **8.** T
You: *Answers will vary.*

1

Underlined Verb Forms:
2. is going to talk
3. is coming
4. is going to be
5. 'll tell
6. will . . . be able to afford
7. will be
8. 'll cost
9. is . . . going to create
10. will improve
11. will have
12. will want
13. won't stop
14. won't take
15. will have
16. is speaking
17. is moving
18. begins

2

2. He isn't going to drive. OR He's not going to drive.
3. It's going to rain.

4. He isn't going to get very wet. OR He's not going to get very wet.

5. He's going to give a speech.

6. He's going to answer the phone.

7. He's going to have dinner.

8. He isn't going to watch TV. OR He's not going to watch TV.

9. He isn't going to go to sleep. OR He's not going to go to sleep.

10. He's going to get out of bed.

3

2. he's taking the train to Tokyo.

3. he's meeting friends from England for dinner.

4. he's doing an interview for *The Space Show.*

5. he's answering questions from the online chat.

6. he's working on the Space Future website.

7. he's going to an exercise class.

8. he's flying to New York for the Space Transportation Conference.

9. he's answering e-mails from the Space Future website.

10. he's writing a speech for the next space travel conference.

4

3. 'll feel	**11.** won't look
4. 'll become	**12.** will get
5. Will . . . feel	**13.** won't recognize
6. won't last	**14.** Will . . . float
7. will . . . be able	**15.** 'll bump
8. 'll need	**16.** Will . . . be able
9. 'll get	**17.** 'll have
10. Will . . . look	**18.** 'll use

5

2. A: How many shuttle flights leave this year?
B: Six shuttle flights leave this year.

3. A: How often does the shuttle depart for the Moon each month?
B: The shuttle departs for the Moon twice each month.

4. A: When does the earliest morning flight leave Earth?
B: The October 15th flight leaves at 4 A.M.

5. A: At what time does the latest shuttle leave Earth?
B: The November 19th flight leaves Earth at 6 P.M.

6

2. We'll take	**6.** We'll think
3. leaves	**7.** I'll go
4. I'll make	**8.** I'll see you
5. are we going to do	

7

Both astronauts and space tourists will ~~traveling~~ *travel* in space, but tourists *are* going to have a much different experience. Space tourists ~~is~~ *are* going to travel for fun, not for work. So, they ~~willn't~~ *won't* have to worry about many of the technical problems that astronauts worry about. For example, space tourists ~~will need not~~ *won't need* to figure out how to use a screwdriver without gravity. And they ~~isn't~~ *aren't* going to try new experiments outside the space shuttle. For the most part, space tourists will just ~~going~~ *go* to see the sights and have a good time.

Still, there will be similarities. Regular activities *will* be the same for astronauts and space tourists. For example, eating, washing, and sleeping will ~~turned~~ *turn* into exciting challenges for everyone in space. Everyone is going to ~~doing~~ *do* exercises to stay fit in zero gravity. And both astronauts and space tourists will ~~going to~~ have many new adventures!

8

Now: 2, 3,

Future: 4, 5, 6

9–12

Answers will vary.

UNIT 7 Future Time Clauses   (pages 65–72)

After You Read

1. a

2. a

3. b

1

2. a	**7.** b
3. b	**8.** b
4. a	**9.** b
5. b	**10.** b
6. b	

2

2. graduate
3. get
4. 'll have / 'm going to have
5. save
6. 'll buy / 'm going to buy
7. 'll feel / 'm going to feel
8. am
9. 'll learn / 'm going to learn
10. work
11. get up
12. 'll buy / 'm going to buy
13. talk
14. 'll ask / 'm going to ask
15. 'll look / 'm going to look
16. go
17. go
18. 'll improve / 'm going to improve
19. do
20. 'll write / 'm going to write
21. contact
22. 'll work / 'm going to work

3

2. They are going to move to a larger apartment as soon as Jeff gets a raise.
3. After they move to a larger apartment, they're going to have a baby.
4. Sandy will get a part-time job after they have their first child.
5. When their child is two, Sandy will go back to work full-time.
6. Sandy will work full-time while Jeff goes to school.
7. Jeff will find another job when he graduates.

4

Graduation is next month! I need to make
                              start
some plans now because when exams ~~will start~~,
won't OR *'m not going to*
I ~~don't~~ have any free time. What am I going to
do when I ~~will~~ finish school? My roommate is

                                    looks
going to take a vacation before she ~~will look~~
for a job. I can't do that because I need to
earn some money soon. I think that after I
                    ,
~~will~~ graduate ^I am going to take a word

processing class. As soon as I learn word
        , I'll look OR *I'm going to look*
processing ^~~I look~~ for a job as a bilingual

office assistant. It's hard to find full-time
jobs, though. Part-time jobs are easier to find.
                              before
Maybe I'll take a part-time job ~~after~~ I find a
good full-time one. Or maybe I'll take a
workshop in making decisions~~x~~ before I do
anything!

5

a. 4	**c.** 1	**e.** 6
b. 2	**d.** 5	**f.** 3

6–9

Answers will vary.

UNIT 8 *Wh-* Questions: Subject and Object (pages 73–81)

After You Read
True: 1, 3, 4
False: 2

1

2. a	**4.** b	**6.** c
3. d	**5.** e	

2

2. How did you get home?
3. Who gave you a ride?
4. What happened next?
5. Who (OR Whom) did you see?
6. Who is Deborah Collins?
7. What did you do?
8. When did the police arrive?
9. What did they ask you?
10. How many police officers came?

3

2. What happened?
3. How many witnesses testified?

4. Who (OR Whom) did the witness recognize?
5. Who recognized Harry Adams?
6. Who (OR Whom) did the district attorney question?
7. Who spoke to the jury?
8. What was the verdict?
9. Why did the jury find Adams guilty?
10. How long did the trial last?
11. How much did Adams pay his lawyer?

4

did Jones go
Where ~~Jones went~~ on January 15?
Who went with him?
did
What time ^ he return home?
did he call
Who ~~he called~~?
did he have
How much money ~~he had~~ with him?
Who
~~Whom~~ saw him at the station the next day?
How did he look?
How many suitcases did he have?
did
When ^ the witness call the police?
happened
What ~~did happen~~ next?
was his alibi
What ~~his alibi was~~?

5

2. b	6. b
3. a	7. a
4. b	8. a
5. a	

6

Answers will vary.

7

Suspect	Time	Location	Other Witnesses
Rick Simon	8:00 P.M.	*Al's Grill*	the waiter
Alice May	7:30 P.M.	*Fifth Avenue*	*Bob May*
Jake Bordon	6:30 P.M.	the office	*the janitor*
Lilly Green	7:15 P.M.	in the park	*some children*
John Daniels	*7:00 P.M.*	Tony's Pizza	two customers

8–10

Answers will vary.

PART I From Grammar to Writing (pages 82–84)

1

I always exchange holiday presents with my girlfriend, Shao Fen. Last year, while I was shopping for her, I saw an umbrella in her favorite color. As soon as I saw it, I thought of her. I bought the umbrella and a scarf in the same color. When Shao Fen opened the present, she looked really upset. She didn't say anything, and she didn't look at me. I felt hurt and confused by her reaction. Later she explained that in Chinese the word for *umbrella* sounds like the word for *separation*. When she saw the umbrella she misunderstood. She thought I wanted to end the relationship. After I heard that, I was very upset! I decided that next year, before I buy something, I'm going to check with her sister!

2

Answers may vary.

As soon as I got home, I noticed that my wallet was missing.

While I was thinking about the situation, my brother came home.

When I called the police, they weren't very encouraging.

Tomorrow, when I go to the movies, I'll keep my wallet in my front pocket.

3–6

Answers will vary.

UNIT 9 Reflexive and Reciprocal Pronouns (pages 94–104)

After You Read

Tom: 2, 4

Sara: 1, 3

Tom and Sara: 5

1

Positive self-talk can make the difference between winning and losing. Top athletes not only compete against <u>one another</u>, they also compete against <u>themselves</u> when they try to improve their performances. Many athletes use self-talk to help <u>themselves</u> reach new goals. For example, golf pro Jack Nicklaus used to imagine <u>himself</u> making a winning shot just before he played. Olympic swimmer Summer Sanders prepares <u>herself</u> for a race by smiling.

One sports psychologist believes that Olympic athletes are not very different from <u>one another</u>—they are all the best in their sports. When two top athletes compete against <u>each other</u>, the winner is the one with the most powerful positive "mental movies."

Psychologists say that ordinary people <u>themselves</u> can use these techniques as well. We can create "mental movies" to help <u>ourselves</u> succeed in difficult situations.

2

2. ourselves
3. myself, yourself
4. each other
5. ourselves
6. herself
7. themselves
8. ourselves

3

2. myself
3. one another
  OR each other
4. yourselves
5. one another's
  OR each other's
6. itself
7. themselves
8. himself
9. myself
10. myself

4

2. Tom cut himself.
3. Sara smiled at herself.
4. Tom talked to himself.
5. Tom and Sara talked to each other (OR one another) on the phone.
6. Sara drove herself.
7. Tom and Sara greeted each other (OR one another).
8. They introduced themselves.

5

Jan's birthday was Wednesday, and I forgot to call him. I reminded ~~me~~ *myself* all day, and then I forgot anyway! I felt terrible. My sister Anna said, "Don't be so hard on ~~yourselves~~ *yourself*," but I didn't believe her. She prides herself on remembering everything. Then I remembered the article on self-talk. It said that people can change the way they explain problems to ~~theirselves~~ *themselves*. Well, I listened to the way I talked to ~~me~~ *myself*, and it sounded really insulting—like the way our high school math teacher used to talk to us. I thought, Jan and I are good friends, and we treat each ~~others~~ *other* well. In fact, he forgave ~~myself~~ *me* for my mistake right away. And I forgave him for forgetting our dinner date two weeks ago. Friends can forgive ~~themselves~~ *each other*, so I guess I can forgive myself.

6

2. himself
3. yourself
4. herself
5. ourselves
6. yourselves

7–12

Answers will vary.

UNIT 10 Phrasal Verbs (pages 105–114)

After You Read

1. grew up
2. went on
3. get by
4. brought up
5. pick out
6. takes off
7. turned into
8. puts on

In Eloy Rodriguez's elementary school in Edinburg, Texas, teachers passed [Chicano] [students] over for special honors classes. They also punished them for speaking Spanish. When Rodriguez became the first U.S.-born Chicano biology instructor at his university, he worked 18 hours a day and slept in his lab. "I was very aware that I was the first this, and the first that, and I knew that some people were waiting for me to slip up." Rodriguez didn't slip up. However, he knows that when students feel teachers don't treat them fairly, it turns [them] off education. Many of them just give up.

Today, Dr. Rodriguez is passing [his own] [success] on. When he became a professor at Cornell University, he set out to find Latino graduate students. He takes these students with him on many of his trips and works hard to turn [them] into top scientists. In 1990 he set up [KIDS] (Kids Investigating and Discovering Science)—a science program for minority elementary school children. They put on [white lab coats] and investigate science with university teachers who treat them like research scientists. They observe nature and figure out [problems]. In interviews, Rodriguez always brings up [role models]. "I saw my first snowflake before I saw my first Chicano scientist," he says. Because of Rodriguez's efforts, many students will not face the same problem.

2. T	**5.** T	**7.** T
3. T	**6.** F	**8.** F
4. F		

2. setting up	**8.** get up
3. Pick up	**9.** keep on
4. fill . . . out	**10.** talk . . . over
5. Hand . . . in	**11.** try out
6. find out	**12.** pass up
7. work . . . out	

2. up	**6.** over
3. up	**7.** out
4. out	**8.** out
5. up	

2. take them off	**5.** call it off
3. turn it on	**6.** wake him up
4. cover it up	

2. Set up the experiment. OR Set the experiment up.
3. Carry it out.
4. Sit down when you're done.
5. Go on to page 26.
6. Write up your reports. OR Write your reports up.
7. Hand them in.
8. Take off your lab coats. OR Take your lab coats off.
9. Put them away.
10. Clean up the lab. OR Clean the lab up.

I just got ^back^ from Venezuela ~~back~~! I spent two weeks in the Amazon rain forest with Dr. Rodriguez's research group. We carried out research there on plants that the Piaroa people use as medicine. We made ~~down~~ ^up^ a list of these plants, and we're going to analyze them when we get back to school next week.

We set ~~down~~ ^up^ camp near the Orinoco River, hundreds of miles from any major city. Life there is hard. You get ^up^ very early ~~up~~ every morning. You must always watch ~~up~~ ^out^ and never touch a new insect or plant. If you pick ~~up it~~ ^it up^, you can get a bad skin rash. But plants can also cure. One day, I felt sick. One of the Piaroa gave me the stem of a certain plant to chew. It worked! Later I found ~~at~~ ^out^ that the same plant helps cure insect bites. And believe me, insects are a big problem in the rain forest. I used up many bottles of repellent. But even when I put ~~on it~~ *it on*, it didn't totally keep the insects away.

This trip changed my life! I'm now thinking about changing my major to pharmacology. I want to find ~~over~~ *out* more about how people can use the same plants that animals use as medicine.

7

2. look up   6. take off
3. turn it off   7. pick out
4. keep up   8. brought back
5. dropped in

10. T   14. F
11. F   15. T
12. T   16. T
13. T

8–11

Answers will vary.

PART II From Grammar to Writing

(pages 115–117)

1

Dear Felicia,

Thanks for staying in my apartment this weekend and taking care of the dog. Help *(Felicia)* yourself to the food in the fridge—*(Felicia)* you can use *(food)* it all up if *(Felicia)* you want. *(Ted)* I rented some videos for *(Felicia)* you. *(videos)* They're on top of the TV. *(Ted)* I picked out some action movies. *(Ted)* I hope you like *(action movies)* them. The VCR is easy to use, but remember to turn *(VCR)* it down at 11:00 P.M. My upstairs neighbor is very touchy about noise. There are just a few other things to remember. Red's friendly, but please keep *(Red)* her away from my neighbor's poodle. *(Red + poodle)* They don't like *(Red + poodle)* each other. Her bowl is on the kitchen counter. Fill *(bowl)* it up once a day with dry food. Please walk *(Red)* her twice a day. *(Felicia)* When you go out, remember to turn on the answering machine. *(answering machine)* It's in the living room. The Sunday newspaper arrives at about 8:00 A.M. Pick *(newspaper)* it up early—sometimes *(newspaper)* it disappears! *(Felicia)* When you leave for work Monday, just leave the keys with Mrs. Delgado next door. *(Ted)* I'll get *(keys)* them from *(Mrs. D.)* her when *(Ted)* I get back.

Thanks again!

Ted

2

Dear Dara,

Welcome! I hope you enjoy staying here this week. Here are a few things to keep in mind:

• The mail is delivered every day around noon. You'll find ~~the mail~~ *it* in the mailbox in front of the building. Please pick ~~up the mail~~ *it up* and put ~~the mail~~ *it* on the dining room table.

• Feel free to use the air conditioner, but please turn ~~off the air conditioner~~ *it off* when you leave the house.

• There's plenty of food in the refrigerator! Please feel free to use ~~up the food~~ *it up*.

• I'm expecting a few phone calls. If you're home, could you please take a message? Just write ~~down the message~~ *it down* on the yellow pad in the top left desk drawer.

I think you'll find that the apartment is pretty comfortable. I hope you enjoy staying in ~~the apartment~~ *it*. Make yourself at home!

See you in a week
Rachel

Answers will vary.

UNIT 11 Ability: *Can, Could, Be able to* (pages 124–134)

After You Read

True: 1, 3, 5

False: 4

Don't Know: 2

1

2. F	**7.** T
3. F	**8.** T
4. ?	**9.** ?
5. T	**10.** F
6. ?	

2

1. b. can't
   c. can
   d. can
2. a. couldn't
   b. can

3. a. couldn't
   b. can OR could
   c. can
4. a. couldn't
   b. can
   c. can
   d. can't

3

1. b. isn't able OR 's not able to do
2. a. be able to dance
3. a. Were . . . able to find
   b. 'll be able to compete
   c. being able to do
4. a. Were . . . able to speak
   b. was able to speak
   c. Are . . . able to speak
5. a. wasn't able to practice
   b. Will . . . be able to practice

4

1. b. can see
   c. can't see
   d. 'll be able to see
2. a. can dance
   b. could get
   c. couldn't get
   d. can pronounce

3. a. can't get
   b. can lend
   c. 'll be able to pay
4. a. Can . . . do
   b. 'll be able to do

5

The Dance Desk

How ~~They Can~~ *Can They* Do That?

Last night was the first time I saw the group Pilobolus perform. And what a performance it was! I would like to ~~can~~ *be able to* tell you that I fully understood the performance, but I can't. I *can* ~~to~~ say, however, that the experience was completely wonderful.

Pilobolus is a very unusual group. The performers have no background in dance. When they began, they thought, "Maybe we can't ~~dancing~~ *dance*, so why try?" So they just made interesting shapes with their bodies. Well, this group certainly ~~cans~~ *can* dance, and they are able to do much more. The six dancers in the group are athletic, artistic, and very talented. They are able ⌄*to* do amazing things with their bodies.

In many dances, they move together as a single unit.

My theater companion and I had great seats. We could ~~saw~~ *see* the entire stage (not always true in some theaters). The sound system, though, had a few problems, and we ~~didn't~~ *weren't* able to hear the music clearly all the time.

Some people in the audience asked: "Is it dance or is it gymnastics?" You can decide for yourself. Many people weren't able to ~~got~~ *get* tickets for the first two performances of this series, but you can still buy tickets for next week. This is the type of dance performance everyone can ~~enjoys~~ *enjoy*.

6

Items Checked: 1, 3, 4, 6, 7

7

Dances	March	April	May
Argentine tango			✓
Cha-cha	✓		
Fox-trot		✓	
Hip-hop		✓	
Hustle			✓
Mambo		✓	
Merengue	✓		
Salsa			✓
Swing	✓		
Tango		✓	
Waltz	✓		

8–10

Answers will vary.

UNIT 12 Permission: *Can, Could, May, Do you mind if* (pages 135–143)

After You Read
True: 1, 3, 4
False: 2

1

Underlined Phrases:
2. c. Do you mind if I have
3. c. Can I wash
4. b. Sure.
5. a. May I please borrow
6. a. Could we have

2

2. **a.** can play
   b. Can . . . borrow
3. **a.** May . . . ride
   b. Sure. OR Certainly.
4. **a.** Could . . . bring
   b. No, you can't.
5. **a.** May . . . use
   b. No, you may not.

3

2. —Can I borrow your black sweater?
   —Sorry.
3. —Do you mind if my sister stays in our room?
   —No, not at all. OR No, I don't.
4. —May we please have the party in the dormitory lounge?
   —Sure.
5. —May we please hang decorations from the ceiling of the lounge?
   —No, you may not.
6. —Could we please party until midnight?
   —Sorry. You can't.
7. —Could we play some of your CDs at the party?
   —Sure. OR Certainly.
8. —Can I study here (OR in the lounge)?
   —I'm sorry, you can't.

4

1. **A:** May we board the train yet?
   B: No, you ~~mayn't~~ board until 12:30. *(can't OR may not)*
2. **A:** Can he ~~comes~~ on the train with me? *(come)*
   B: Sorry. Only passengers can board.
3. **A:** Do you mind if ~~I'm sitting~~ here? *(I sit)*
   B: ~~No, I don't.~~ My friend is sitting here. *(Yes, I do.)*
4. **A:** Could I ~~looked~~ at your newspaper? *(look)*
   B: Yes, of course you ~~could~~. *(can)*
5. **A:** Do you mind if my son ~~play~~ his computer game? *(plays)*
   B: No, not at all. It won't disturb me.
   A: Thanks.

5

a. 2 (given)
b. 3 (refused)
c. 7 (refused)
d. 1 (given)
e. 6 (refused)
f. 4 (given)
g. 5 (refused)

6–9

Answers will vary.

UNIT 13 Requests: *Can, Could, Will, Would, Would you mind*   (pages 144–153)

After You Read
True: 1, 3
False: 2, 4

Underlined Phrases:
2. would you help
3. Would you like, Can you get, Will you answer
4. would you mind making
5. Could you tell
6. Could you take, would you mind offering
7. Could you give

2

2. a	**5.** a
3. a	**6.** b
4. b	

3

First Part:

2. e	**6.** i
3. g	**7.** b
4. f	**8.** c
5. h	**9.** a

Second Part:
Position of please *can vary.*
2. Would you please shut the door?
3. Will you please buy some cereal
4. Can you close the window, please?
5. Would you mind waiting for a few minutes, please?
6. Would you mind washing your cups and dishes?
7. Could you please call back later?
8. Can you get that book, please?
9. Could you please repair the photocopier?

4

The meetings are going well but they have been

extended a day. Could you ~~call please~~ *please call* Doug
Rogers to try to reschedule our sales meeting?
Sure OR *Certainly* OR *Of course*
~~Not at all~~. **I'll do it right away.**

We'll need three extra copies of the monthly
sales report. Would you ask Ann to take care
of that?
Sure OR *Certainly* OR *Of course*
~~Yes, I would~~. **(Ann—could you do this?)**

I won't have time to return Emma Lopes' call
this week. Would you mind ~~to call~~ *calling* her and
telling her I'll call her back next week?
**No problem. Could you e-mail me her
phone number?**

I hate to ask, but would you mind ~~to work~~ *working* on
Saturday? We'll need the extra time to go over
the new information I've gotten.
**Sorry, but I ~~couldn't~~ *can't*. My in-laws are coming
for a visit. But Rob Lin says he can come
into the office to help out.**

One last thing. I was going to pick up those
new business cards, but I won't be back in
time. Would you mind doing that for me?
~~Yes, I would~~ *Not at all*. **I'll stop at the printer's during
my lunch break.**

5

Items Checked: 2, 5, 6, 8

6–8

Answers will vary.

UNIT 14 Advice: *Should, Ought to, Had better*   (pages 154–164)

After You Read
OK: 1, 4, 6, 9
Not OK: 2, 3, 5, 7, 8

1

Underlined Phrases:
'd better not forget, shouldn't . . . be
should stop, ought to ask
'd better not do
should get
shouldn't fight

2

2. 'd better not rent
3. 'd better keep
4. ought to see
5. should get
6. shouldn't use

7. should listen
8. ought to read
9. ought to watch
10. 'd better not give

3

2. Should I ask them to stop
   Yes, you should.
3. Should I try to repair it
   No, you shouldn't
4. Should I forward the e-mail
   No, you shouldn't
5. Should I buy one online
   Yes, you should
6. Should I check the spelling
   Yes, you should

4

2. You'd better not give out any personal information.
3. You shouldn't give it to anyone.
4. You ought to get virus protection and use it.
5. You should keep your virus protection up-to-date.
6. You'd better not believe any "get rich quick" offers.
7. You shouldn't open any e-mail attachments from strangers.
8. You should be careful

5

JUSTME: My friend asked me to dinner and she told me I should ~~to~~ bring some food! What kind of an invitation is that?

should I
What ~~I should~~ bring to this strange dinner party?

SASHA: LOL! Your friend is having a potluck—a dinner party where everybody brings something. It's
to
really a lot of fun. You ought ^ bring a dish from your country. People will enjoy that.

TOBY: HELP! My first day of class, and I
should
lost my wallet! What ~~ought~~ I do first? My student ID, credit card, and cash are all gone.

R2D2:
better not
First of all, you'd ~~not better~~ panic because you need to be calm so you can speak clearly. You should ~~to~~ call your credit card company right away. Did you lose your wallet at school?

go
Then you ought to ~~going~~ to the Lost and Found Department at your school.

SMILEY: What should an international student
do
~~does~~ to make friends? At my college, people always smile and say, "Hi, how are you?" but they don't wait for an answer!

4GUD:
join
New students should ~~joining~~ some clubs and international student organizations. They also ought to find a student in each class to study with and ask about homework assignments.

NEWGUY: Hi. I'm new to this board. I'm from Vietnam, and I'm going to school in Canada next year. How should I ~~will~~ get ready?

SMILEY: Welcome Newguy! I'm at school in Montreal, and my best advice is—
you'd
~~you're~~ better bring a lot of warm clothes. You won't believe how cold it gets here.

to
SASHA: You ought ^ check the school's website.

They might have a Vietnam Students' Association. If they do, you should e-mail the Association with your questions. Good luck!

6

Items Checked: 6, 7, 8

7–11

Answers will vary.

UNIT 15 Suggestions: *Let's, Could, Why don't, Why not, How about*
(pages 165–173)

After You Read
Items Checked: 3, 5

EMILY: Why don't we go to the races? I hear they're really exciting.

MEGAN: I'd like to, but I need to go shopping.

EMILY: Then let's go to the Temple Street Market tonight. We might even see some Chinese opera in the street while we're there.

MEGAN: That sounds like fun. If we do that, why not go to the races this afternoon?

EMILY: OK, but let's get something to eat first in one of those floating restaurants.

MEGAN: I don't think we'll have time. Maybe we could do that tomorrow. Right now, how about getting *dim sum* at the Kau Kee Restaurant next door? Then we could take the Star Ferry to Hong Kong Island and the racecourse.

EMILY: Sounds good. Here's an idea for tomorrow. Why not take one of those small boats—*kaido*—to Lantau Island? When we come back, we could have dinner at the Jumbo Palace.

MEGAN: Let's do that. It's a little expensive, but it sounds like fun.

Items checked in guidebook:

Temple Street Night Market

Happy Valley Racecourse

The Star Ferry

Kaido

Jumbo Palace

Kau Kee Restaurant

2. How about

3. Why don't we

4. Maybe we could

5. Let's not

2. going to the beach?

3. buy another one.

4. we could take a trip together.

5. she come with us?

6. try that new seafood place.

The rooms here are very nice, but why don't you ~~having~~ *have* better lamps so we can read at night?
Petra De Graff, Netherlands

How about ~~have~~ *having* a list of inexpensive restaurants in the area?
Jessica Edwards, Canada

The breakfast is delicious, but why not ~~has~~ *have* music in the breakfast room? Everyone likes music.
Liv Lindberg, Sweden

The countryside around here is very beautiful. Maybe you could ~~having~~ *have* some bikes for us to use so we could explore a little.?
Yan Ying Tan, Taiwan

I like staying in old, historic hostels, but I miss some of the modern conveniences. How about having Internet access? It would be nice to send and get e-mail! And why not ~~accepting~~ *accept* credit cards?
Carlos Ezcurra, Argentina

You provide sheets, so why ~~you don't~~ *don't you* provide towels too? They're just as important as sheets!
Ian Harlow, Scotland

Here's a suggestion for all of us hostel guests. Let's ~~don't~~ *not* be so messy! It will be more pleasant for everyone if we clean up our own stuff.
Anonymous

Items checked on map:

The S. G. Davis Hostel

Tian Tan Buddha

Po Lin Monastery

Lantau Trail

Lantau Peak

Answers will vary.

PART III From Grammar to Writing
(pages 174–175)

1

Answers may vary.
Chen,—Here is our project summary. <u>Read it.</u>
I really think it's much too long. What <u>do you
think? Tell me whether to shorten it. We will
meet tomorrow to discuss it. My advice is that
we finish the draft by Friday.</u> By the way,
Nadia is in town. <u>I want to invite her to our
meeting.</u>—Ed

2

Possible answers.
Chen,—Here is our project summary.
<u>Would you mind</u> reading it? I really think it's
(make a request)

much too long. What do you think? <u>Should</u> I
(ask advice)

shorten it? <u>Let's</u> meet tomorrow to discuss it.
(make a suggestion)

We <u>should</u> finish the final draft by Friday. By
(give advice)

the way, Nadia is in town. <u>Could</u> I invite her to
(ask permission)

our meeting?—Ed

3

Possible answers.
Ed—Sorry, I was very busy this morning, so I
wasn't able to finish reading the summary until
now. I think you should shorten it. Maybe we
could meet tomorrow morning instead. Could
you please reserve the conference room for the
meeting? Of course Nadia can come to the
meeting. Why don't we have lunch together
after the meeting? See you tomorrow morning.
—Chen

4–5

Answers will vary.

UNIT 16 Present Perfect: *Since* and *For*
(pages 182–192)

After You Read
True: 1, 4
False: 2, 3

1

2. b   **3.** a   **4.** b   **5.** b   **6.** a

2

2. for   **6.** for
3. Since   **7.** since
4. for   **8.** for, since
5. since

3

2. hasn't stopped   **7.** have gone
3. has been   **8.** has skated
4. have lived   **9.** has won
5. have had   **10.** has wanted
6. haven't taken   **11.** has come

4

3. have been   **10.** have opened
4. since   **11.** Since
5. have changed   **12.** have gone
6. since   **13.** Since
7. Since   **14.** has become
8. have taken   **15.** hasn't competed
9. Since   **16.** for

5

2. —How long have you had your M.A. degree?
   —I've had my M.A. degree since 1995 OR for
   9 years.
3. —Have you had any more training since you
   got your M.A.?
   —Yes, I have.
4. —How long have you been a physical
   education teacher?
   —I've been a physical education teacher
   since 1997. OR for 9 years.
5. —How long have you worked as a sports
   trainer?
   —I've been a sports trainer since 1995 OR
   for 11 years.
6. —How long have you had a black belt in tae
   kwon do?
   —I've had a black belt for two months.
7. —Have you won any awards since then?
   —Yes, I have.

8. —How long have you been a member of
NEA?
—I've been a member of NEA since 1998 OR
for 8 years.

I've had
~~I have~~ my skateboard for two years. For me, it's
much more than just a sport. It's a form of
transportation. It's much faster than walking!
Jennifer, USA

for
I've been a skater ~~since~~ five years. Since
I've won
December ~~I won~~ two contests. I'd love to go
pro one day.
Paulo, Brazil

since
Help! I've broken three boards ~~for~~ January!!! Is
have you
this normal? How long ~~you have~~ had your
board?
Sang-Ook, Korea

broken
Broken boards?! That's nothing! I've ~~break~~ my
wrist twice since I started skating!
Marta, Mexico

Last year, my board hit a rock while I was
skating in the street. I fell and hit my head and
have
had to go to the emergency room. I ˄ always
worn a helmet since then!
Megan, Australia

have lived
I ~~live~~ in California since 2001. My first love is
surfing, but when there aren't any waves, I
jump on my skateboard and take to the streets!
Ming, USA

Wow! Yesterday, my friend gave me a copy of
watched
the video "OP King of Skate." I've ~~watch~~ it
three times since then. The Burnquist part is
awesome!
Todd, Canada

At last! A skate park opened near my home last
have
week. Since then I ˄ gone every day. It's a lot
more fun than skating in the streets!
Sylvie, France

2. since 1990
3. for a year
4. since he moved here OR since last year
5. since September

Answers will vary.

UNIT 17 Present Perfect:
Already and *Yet*   (pages 193–201)

After You Read
Items Checked: 1, 3, 4, 5

2. T **5.** T
3. F **6.** F
4. T

2. 've already met
3. 've already had
4. Has . . . left already
No . . . hasn't
5. Have . . . seen . . . yet
Yes . . . have
haven't seen . . . yet
6. have already planned

3. He's already found a location.
4. He's already written a guest list.
5. He's already bought invitations.
6. He hasn't sent invitations yet.
7. He hasn't asked friends to help yet.
8. He hasn't planned the menu yet.
9. He's already picked out music.
10. He hasn't shopped for food yet.
11. He hasn't cleaned the house yet.
12. He's already borrowed some chairs.

Doug asked: Help! My party is next week and
yet   *already*
I haven't figured out the food ~~already~~! I've ~~yet~~
wasted three days worrying, and I still don't
have any ideas. What should I do?

The Party Planner's Advice is: Don't panic!

Your guests ~~have~~ *haven't* started arriving yet, so there's still time. Ask everyone to bring something!

(You've already ~~invite~~ *invited* people, right?) Or order pizza. I haven't met anyone ~~already~~ *yet* who doesn't like pizza.

Rosa asked: I'd like to find a "theme" for my next birthday party. I've already ~~have~~ *had* a pasta party (10 kinds of pasta!), and I've already ~~gave~~ *given* a movie party (everyone dressed up as a movie character). Any ideas?

The Party Planner's Advice is: Sure. ~~Has~~ *Have* you tried this one yet? ~~No~~ *Not* yet? Ask each guest to bring a baby photo of him- or herself. Collect the photos. People try to match the photos with the guests! Your guests will love it!

5

Items Checked: 2, 3, 6

6

To Do—Helmut
~~buy film~~
~~bake the cake~~
put the turkey in the oven
~~mop the floor~~
wash the dishes
~~cut up the vegetables~~

To Do—Gisela
vacuum the carpet
~~buy flowers~~
~~wash the windows~~
set the table
~~hang the balloons~~
wrap the gift

7–9

Answers will vary.

UNIT 18 Present Perfect: Indefinite Past

After You Read

Items Checked: 4, 5

1

---
2. F   5. F
3. T   6. T
4. F

2

2. 've been
3. has been (OR 's been)
4. 've had
5. 've swum
6. 've eaten
7. 've slept
8. has become (OR 's become)
9. Have . . . found
10. 've thought
11. 've . . . kept
12. 've . . . written
13. have . . . come
14. 've . . . returned
15. 've . . . gone

3

3. He hasn't ridden a camel. OR He's never ridden a camel.
4. He's jumped out of an airplane with a parachute.
5. He's gone up in a hot-air balloon.
6. He hasn't spent time on a desert island. OR He's never spent time on a desert island.
7. He's eaten some really unusual food.
8. He hasn't taken photos of wild animals up close. OR He's never taken photos of wild animals up close.
9. He hasn't crossed the Andes on horseback. OR He's never crossed the Andes on horseback.
10. He's sailed a boat on the Nile River.
11. He's swum with dolphins in the ocean.
12. He hasn't been on a safari. OR He's never been on a safari.
13. He hasn't flown around the world. OR He's never flown around the world.
14. He hasn't gone on an organized trip. OR He's never gone on an organized trip.

4

2. I've gone up
3. I haven't done it lately
4. Have you traveled a lot
5. I have
6. Have you ever been
7. I haven't

Student Book Answer Key | **193**

8. I've always wanted to go
9. I've been to Africa several times
10. I've just gotten
11. I've never been
12. They've just finished

5

Answers will vary.
2. She's ridden (on) a camel.
3. She's traveled (a lot). OR She's seen a lot of countries.
4. She's stayed at the Hotel Roma.
5. She's written *Traveling Solo*.
6. She's seen *Cats* three times.

6

We ~~has~~ received many comments from our
have
clients. We'd like to share some with you.

Comments

I have always ~~be~~ afraid of heights. But after I
been
saw the beautiful photos on your website, I

knew I had to go hot-air ballooning! This ~~have~~
has
been one of the best experiences of my life.
Thank you!
Britta Kessler, Germany

We've ~~returned just~~ from the best vacation
just returned
we've ever ~~have~~. I've told all my friends about
had
your company.
James Hudson, Canada

I've always wanted to go up in a hot-air balloon.
I was not disappointed!
Antonio Vega, Mexico

I ~~just gotten~~ my photos back! Fantastic!
've just gotten OR *just got*
Bill Hampton, USA

I've never ~~went~~ hot-air ballooning, but after
gone
visiting your wonderful website I've decided to
sign up!
Amalia Lopes, Brazil

We gave our parents a balloon trip as an
anniversary gift. They've just ~~wrote~~ to say it
written

was fantastic. They've ~~ever~~ been very
never
adventurous, but now they want to go rafting!
Pat Calahan, Ireland

~~You have~~ ever seen the face of a kid on a
Have you
hot-air balloon ride? The cost of the ride: a lot.
That look on her face: priceless!
Lydia Hassan, New Zealand

I broke my leg last month, so I haven't ~~lately~~
lately
been able to do sports ︿—boring! Your mountain

balloon trip has just ~~gave~~ me a lift—in more
given
than one way!
May Roa, Philippines

7

Items Checked: 1, 3, 5
Item Circled: 4

8–10

Answers will vary.

UNIT 19 Present Perfect and Simple Past (pages 212–221)

After You Read
True: 1, 3, 4, 5
False: 2

1

2. a	6. b
3. b	7. a
4. a	8. a
5. b	9. b

2

2. began	6. didn't get
3. 've written	7. saw
4. has been	8. 've lived
5. 've worked	

3

2. slept	8. haven't caught up
3. haven't stopped	9. 've already had
4. 've been	10. drank
5. 've seen	11. 've had
6. came	12. haven't finished
7. didn't do	

4

2. In the 1990s Joe was clean shaven. Since then, he has grown a beard.
3. In the 1990s Joe was heavy. Since then, he has lost weight.
4. In the 1990s Joe was a student. Since then, he has become a professor.
5. In the 1990s Joe lived in a dormitory. Since then, he has bought a house.
6. In the 1990s Joe was single. Since then, he has gotten married.

5

2. How long did you live in Detroit?
3. When did you get a job offer?
4. When did your company move?
5. How long have you lived apart?
6. How often did you see each other last month?
7. How often have you seen each other this month?
8. When did you start to communicate by e-mail?

6

I've just finished reading a fascinating article

                              've read

about Felicia Mabuza-Suttle. Actually, I ~~read~~
several articles about her this year. She's a very
famous international businesswoman and
talk-show host in South Africa. Guess what!
We have something in common! She and her

                 have had

husband ~~had~~ a "commuter marriage" for more
than 15 years, and they are still happily
married! She lives in Johannesburg, South
Africa; he lives in Atlanta, Georgia. That's a

                     met

whole ocean apart! They ~~have met~~ in the
1970s. In the first 10 years of their marriage

          lived

they ~~have lived~~ in more than 10 cities. Then, in

                 returned

the early 1990s she ~~has returned~~ to South

                 hasn't been

Africa to help her country. It ~~wasn't~~ an easy life,
but they both feel it's been very worthwhile.

Their situation makes our problems seem
not that bad. Joe and I are only 3,000 miles
apart, and we have managed to see each other
a lot since we left Detroit. But, to be honest,

          was   *lived*

I ~~have been~~ happier when we ~~have lived~~
together in Detroit. I hope we can live together
again someday soon.

7

Items Checked: 1, 3, 5, 6

8–12

Answers will vary.

UNIT 20 Present Perfect Progressive and Present Perfect   (pages 222–231)

After You Read

True: 1, 3

False: 2, 4

1

2. T	5. T	7. F
3. T	6. T	8. T
4. F		

2

2. has published
3. have already died
4. has given
5. has spoken
6. has created
7. have been studying
8. have been waiting
9. has lived OR has been living
10. has worked OR has been working

3

2. hasn't been following
3. 's been writing
4. hasn't been reading
5. 's been drinking
6. hasn't been drinking
7. hasn't been eating
8. hasn't been watching
9. she's been working
10. 's been raining

2. 've . . . seen
3. has lived OR has been living
4. has experienced
5. has survived
6. have tested
7. have hunted
8. have saved
9. has been moving
10. has been eating
11. (has been) resting
12. has rained OR has been raining
13. have been finding
14. has been

5

2. —How much vegetation has he eaten?
   —He's eaten about 1,000 pounds of vegetation.
3. —How often has he stopped OR been stopping for water?
   —He's stopped for water four times.
4. —How much water has he drunk?
   —He's drunk about 160 gallons of water.
5. —How long has he been walking today?
   —He's been walking for nine hours.
6. —How far has he traveled today?
   —He's traveled 45 miles.

6

This year in class we've been ~~studied~~ *studying*

endangered species. We've already ~~been studying~~ *studied* the panda and the tiger. Now we're learning

about the African elephant. Elephants ~~has~~ *have* been roaming the Earth for millions of years! I have to write a research paper on the topic. I've

~~researched~~ *been researching* it on the Web since Monday. It's now Friday, and I haven't finished yet. There's

so much information! I've already ~~been reading~~ *read* more than ten articles, and I've even ~~been~~ ordered a book about endangered species. I really find this topic interesting, and I've been learning a lot! The paper has to be ten pages

long. So far, ~~I've been writing~~ *I've written* about five pages. I've been thinking about a title for my paper,

but I haven't ~~been deciding~~ *decided* on one yet.

7

2. a   4. a
3. b   5. a

8–10

Answers will vary.

PART IV From Grammar to Writing   (pages 232–233)

1

My restaurant experience has prepared me for a position with your company. While I was in high school, I worked as a server at Darby's during the summer and on weekends. ~~Summers here are very hot and humid~~. I worked with many different kinds of customers, and I learned to be polite even with difficult people. ~~They serve excellent food at Darby's~~. I received a promotion after one year. Since high school, I have been working for Steak Hut as the night manager. I have developed management skills because I supervise six employees. ~~One of them is a good friend of mine~~. I have also learned to order supplies and to plan menus. ~~Sometimes I am very tired after a night's work~~.

2

Possible answers. (See diagram on next page.)

3–4

Answers will vary.

UNIT 21 Nouns and Quantifiers   (pages 240–248)

After You Read
True: 2, 4
False: 1, 3, 5

1

Proper Nouns: Katya, New York, May, Panama, Typhoon, Thanksgiving

Count Nouns: journey, world, boat, birthday, years, miles, things, stars, ports, markets, pot, cat, family, trip, sight, harbor

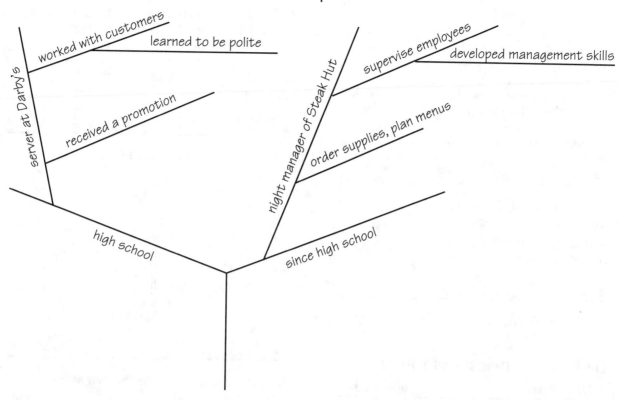

Non-Count Nouns: courage, equipment, money, technology, food, cooking, water, time, news, music, reading, loneliness

2

3. 's	**12.** equipment
4. advice	**13.** batteries
5. beans	**14.** news
6. rice	**15.** stops
7. Potatoes	**16.** clothing
8. are	**17.** cold
9. vegetables	**18.** bothers
10. are	**19.** bags
11. Is	

3

1. b. A few	**4. a.** any
c. A little	**b.** How many
2. a. a great deal of	**c.** How many
b. many	**d.** How much
c. a great deal of	**e.** enough
3. a. a	**5. a.** little
b. much	**b.** a few
c. some	**c.** a little
d. many	**d.** few

4

October 27. I've been on the ~~canary~~ *Canary* Islands for three days now. I'll start home when the ~~weathers~~ *weather* ~~are~~ *is* better. I was so surprised when I picked up my ~~mails~~ *mail* today. My family sent some birthday presents to me. My ~~Birthday~~ *birthday* is the 31st.

~~october~~ *October* 29. I think the weather is getting worse. I heard ~~thunders~~ *thunder* today, but there wasn't ~~many~~ *much* rain. Typhoon and I stayed in bed. I started reading ~~brave~~ *Brave* New World.

October 30. I left the Canary Islands today— just like ~~columbus~~ *Columbus*. There's a strong wind and plenty of sunshine now. I went 250 miles.

October 31. I'm 21 today. To celebrate, I drank ~~little~~ *a little* coffee for breakfast and I opened my presents. I got some perfume and some

pretty silver ~~jewelries~~. *jewelry*

November 1. The ~~electricities~~ ~~are~~ low. I'd *electricity is*

better save ~~them~~ until I get near land. I'll *it*
need the radio then. It rained today, so I

collected ~~a few waters~~ for cooking. *a little water*

5

Ingredients they have enough of: brown
sugar, cornflakes, raisins

Shopping List: butter, oatmeal, flour, eggs,
chocolate chips

6–8

Answers will vary.

UNIT 22 Articles: Indefinite and Definite

(pages 249–261)

After You Read

The Ant and the Dove: 5, 3, 2, 1, 4

The Town Mouse and the Country Mouse: 3,
4, 2, 5, 1

1

2. a   **3.** b   **4.** b   **5.** b   **6.** a

2

2. the	**9.** a	**16.** the
3. the	**10.** the	**17.** the
4. a	**11.** the	**18.** the
5. an	**12.** Ø	**19.** The
6. the	**13.** the	**20.** a
7. a	**14.** Ø	**21.** the
8. Ø	**15.** the	**22.** the

3

2. a	**5.** the	**8.** the, a
3. the	**6.** a, a	**9.** a, the, the
4. a	**7.** the, an	**10.** an, the

4

2. (blank)	**8.** (blank)	**14.** the
3. (blank)	**9.** (blank)	**15.** the
4. the	**10.** the	**16.** the
5. the	**11.** the	**17.** (blank)
6. (blank)	**12.** (blank)	**18.** (blank)
7. the	**13.** the	**19.** the

5

1. b. a	**4. a.** (blank)
c. the	**b.** The
d. a	**c.** (blank)
2. a. the	**d.** (blank)
b. An	**e.** the
c. (blank)	**5. a.** an
3. a. the	**b.** the
b. (blank)	**c.** the
c. (blank)	**6. a.** the
	b. (blank)
	c. (blank)

6

Once there was a plumber named Mario.
~~Plumber~~ had ^ beautiful girlfriend. One day, ~~a~~ *The plumber a ... an*
ape fell in love with the girlfriend and
kidnapped her. The plumber chased ^ ape to *the*
rescue his girlfriend. This simple tale became
Donkey Kong, ~~a~~ first video game with a story. *the*
It was invented by Sigeru Matsimoto, ~~a~~ artist *an*
with Nintendo, Inc. Matsimoto loved ~~the~~ video
games, but he wanted to make them more
interesting. He liked fairy tales, so he invented ^ *a*
story similar to a famous fairy tale. ~~Story~~ was *The story*
an immediate success, and Nintendo followed
it with *The Mario Brothers* and then with *Super
Mario.* The third game became popular all over
~~a~~ world, and it is still ^ most famous game in *the ... the*
video history. Nintendo has continued to add
~~the~~ new characters to the story, but success
does not change Mario. He is always ^ brave *the*
little plumber in a red hat and work clothes.

Part 1:
2. the   5. the
3. the   6. a
4. a

Part 2:
2. a   5. a
3. a   6. b
4. b

The Big Dipper · crescent moon · tower · castle · superhero · sword · cape · magic wand · laser gun · magician · warrior · flask · gold · coffer · princess · silver coins · medicine

9–12

Answers will vary.

PART V From Grammar to Writing
(pages 262–263)

1

2. We also decorate the altar with candy skulls.
3. For my sister, we offer toys.
4. My family always hires a mariachi band.

2

1. *Los Días de los Muertos*, November 1 and 2
2. To remember our relatives who have died
3. **a.** food, loaves of bread called "souls," candy skulls
   b. special gifts for the dead, a new hat for my grandfather, toys for my sister
   c. music, we hire a mariachi band, we all sing

3–6

Answers will vary.

UNIT 23 Adjectives and Adverbs
(pages 268–276)

After You Read
True: 2, 4, 5, 6
False: 1, 3

1

Are you looking for a place to live? This <u>lovely</u> apartment is in a <u>new</u> building and has two <u>large</u> bedrooms and a <u>sunny</u> kitchen. The building is [very] <u>quiet</u>—[absolutely] <u>perfect</u> for two <u>serious</u> students. You'll be <u>close</u> to campus. The bus stop is a <u>short</u> walk, and the <u>express</u> bus goes [directly] into town. You can <u>run</u> or <u>ride</u> your bike [safely] in <u>nearby</u> parks. The rent is [very] <u>affordable</u>. <u>Small</u> <u>pets</u> are <u>welcome</u>. <u>Interested</u> students should call Megan at 555-5050. Don't wait! This apartment will <u>rent</u> [fast]. Nonsmokers, please.

2

2. really
3. new
4. beautiful
5. hard
6. happily
7. gorgeous
8. great
9. nice
10. shy
11. good
12. quickly
13. usually
14. exciting
15. terribly

3

2. terribly disappointed
3. surprisingly easy
4. extremely expensive
5. amazingly cheap
6. incredibly fast
7. very clearly
8. awfully loud
9. very accurately
10. exceptionally friendly
11. absolutely perfect
12. really upset

4

2. confused
3. confusing
4. interesting
5. interested
6. fascinating
7. fascinated
8. disappointed
9. surprising

1

2. T	6. T
3. T	7. T
4. F	8. F
5. T	9. T

5

Mr. Delgado is an ~~exceptionally~~ *exceptional* teacher. He prepared ~~careful~~ *carefully* for classes, and his lessons were almost always ~~interested~~ *interesting*. He explained ~~clearly the material~~ *the material clearly*, and he ~~returned always~~ *always returned* our tests on time. This was not an easy class, but the time always passed ~~fastly~~ *fast* because the students were ~~exciting~~ *excited* by the material. I studied ~~hardly~~ *hard* for this class—more than two hours a night—because Mr. Delgado gave hard tests. His tests were very ~~fairly~~ *fair* though. We were never ~~surprising~~ *surprised* by test questions because they were all from class work or the textbook. I did ~~good~~ *well* in this class, and I'm sure other students will too. I recommend ~~highly his class~~ *his class highly*.

2

2. is not as expensive as
3. tastes as good as
4. doesn't taste as good as
5. doesn't smell as nice as
6. smells as nice as

3

2. hotter than
3. less expensive than
4. spicier than
5. less salty than
6. milder than
7. healthier than
8. cheaper than
9. oilier than
10. sweeter than
11. shorter than
12. shorter than
13. less expensive
14. sweeter than

6

1. Smithfield
2. Foster
3. Cumberland
4. Lincoln

4

2. better and better, the better . . . the higher
3. less and less crowded; heavier and heavier
4. more and more popular; The harder . . . the more popular
5. worse and worse; the spicier . . . the better
6. faster and faster; The faster . . . the shorter

7–11

Answers will vary.

UNIT 24 Adjectives: Comparisons with *As . . . as* and *Than* (pages 277–288)

After You Read

True: 2, 3, 6
False: 1, 4, 5

5

When I was a teenager in the Philippines, I was an expert on snacks and fast foods. I was growing fast, so the more I ate, the ~~hungry~~ *hungrier* I felt. The street vendors in our town had ~~the~~ better snacks than anyone else. In the morning, I used to buy rice muffins on the way to school. They are much sweeter ~~that~~ *than* American muffins. After school, I ate fish balls on a stick or *adidas* (chicken feet). Snacks on a stick are ~~small~~ *smaller* than American hot dogs and burgers, but they are much *more* varied. My friend thought *banana-cue* (banana on a stick) was really great. However, they weren't as sweet ~~from~~ *as* *kamote-cue* (fried sweet potatoes and brown sugar), my favorite snack.

When I came to the United States, I didn't

less

like American fast food at first. To me, it was ^

tasty

interesting than my native food and less ~~tastier~~
too. Now I'm getting used to it, and it seems

more and more delicious

~~deliciouser and deliciouser~~. Does anyone want
to go out for a pizza?

6

Di Roma's: 1, 4
Angela's: 2, 3, 5

7–8

Answers will vary.

9

Spaghetti Sauce:

● ◒ ○

more   equal   less

Quality	Frank's	Classic's
smooth	●	○
thick	◒	◒
chunky	○	●
flavorful	○	●
sweet	●	○
salty	●	○
spicy	○	●
garlicky	●	○
fresh-tasting	◒	◒
fattening	○	●
nutritious	○	●
expensive	●	○

10–11

Answers will vary.

UNIT 25 Adjectives: Superlatives
(pages 289–296)

After You Read
True: 3, 4, 5
False: 1, 2

1

• **Go to the CN Tower.** It's the tallest
free-standing structure in the world—even
taller than the Petronas Towers in Malaysia.
From there you can get the best view of the
city and countryside.
• **Drive along Yonge Street.** At 1,200 miles
(1,800 km) it's the longest street in the world.
For one weekend in July it's one of the liveliest
too. Come and join 1 million others for the
exciting Yonge Street Festival.
• **Visit PATH,** the world's largest underground
shopping complex.
• **Explore the Old Town of York.** It has the
most historic buildings in the whole city.
• **Take the Yuk Yuk Comedy Tour** of the
Entertainment District—you'll have a good
time on the funniest bus ride in town.
• **Visit the Toronto Zoo.** There's always
something new and fascinating going on.
Local people call it the best family outing in
Toronto.

2

1. the biggest
2. the biggest
3. the smallest
4. the coldest
5. the coolest
6. the coolest, the warmest,
   the most comfortable
7. The driest, the hottest
8. the rainiest
9. the cheapest
10. The most expensive

3

2. the most famous   5. the clearest
3. the heaviest   6. the fastest
4. the most popular   7. the longest

4

Answers will vary.
2. X is the most comfortable place I've ever
   stayed.
   Y is the least comfortable place I've ever
   stayed.
3. X are the friendliest (OR the most friendly)
   people I've ever met.
   Y are the least friendly people I've ever met.
4. X is the most expensive trip I've ever taken.
   Y is the least expensive trip I've ever taken.

5

Greetings from Toronto—the ~~beautifulest~~ *most beautiful* city
I've ever visited. Yesterday we went to the CN

Tower—the ~~more~~ *most* recognizable structure in all
of Canada. From there you get the best view of

the city. The restaurant was the most ~~expensivest~~ *expensive*
I've ever seen, so we just enjoyed the view and
then went to Kensington Market to eat. This

place has the ~~baddest~~ *worst* crowds but the cheapest

and the ~~goodest~~ *best* food we've had so far. We're

staying in East Toronto. It's not the ~~closer~~ *closest* place

to downtown, but it has some of ^*the* most historic

buildings. In fact, our bed-and-breakfast is called
1871 Historic House. John Lennon slept here!
Love, Marissa

6

the most convenient: Hôtel Le Germain

the least convenient: Westin Harbour Castle

the most comfortable: Hôtel Le Germain

the most expensive: Hôtel Le Germain

the least expensive: Delta Chelsea

the biggest: Delta Chelsea

the smallest: Hôtel Le Germain

7–10

Answers will vary.

UNIT 26 Adverbs: *As . . . as,*
Comparatives,
Superlatives   (pages 297–306)

After You Read

True: 1, 2

False: 3, 4, 5, 6

1

In the first basketball game of the season, the
Comets beat the Lions, 90 to 83. The Lions
played a truly fantastic game, but their defense
is still weak. The Comets defended the ball
much <u>more aggressively than</u> the Lions did.

Of course, Ace Hernandez certainly helped
win the game for the Comets. The Comets' star
player was back on the court today to the
delight of his many fans. He was hurt badly at
the end of last season, but he has recovered
quickly. Although he <u>didn't play as well as</u>
people expected, he still handled the ball like
the old Ace. He certainly handled it <u>the most
skillfully</u> of anyone on the team. He controlled
the ball <u>the best</u>, shot the ball <u>the most
accurately</u>, and scored <u>the most consistently</u> of
any of the players on either team. He played
hard and helped the Comets look good. In fact,
<u>the harder</u> he played, <u>the better</u> the Comets
performed. Watch Ace this season.

And watch the Lions. They have a new coach,
and they're training <u>more seriously</u> this year. I
think we'll see them play <u>better and better</u> as the
season progresses.

2

2. doesn't fit as comfortably as

3. supports the ankle as well as

4. don't support the ankle as well as

5. doesn't protect the feet as effectively as

6. protects the feet as effectively as

7. lasts as long as

8. doesn't last as long as

3

2. less aggressively than

3. as aggressively

4. as hard as

5. the most fearlessly

6. the more often

7. the sooner

8. more cooperatively than

9. better

10. more patiently

11. longer

12. less than

13. the faster

14. the faster

15. better . . . better

4

3. the slowest OR the most slowly

4. slower than OR more slowly than

5. the farthest

6. faster than

7. higher than

8. the best

9. the worst

Last night was the last game of the season, and

the Lions played the ~~goodest~~ *best* they've played for months. Both the Cubs and Lions play a great offensive game, but this time the Lions really

played defense much more effectively ~~as~~ *than* the Cubs. Hernandez, the Cubs' star player, has

been shooting more ~~aggressively and~~ *and more* aggressively all season. But in last night's

game, the more ~~aggressive~~ *aggressively* he played, the ~~most~~ *more* closely the Lions guarded him. Then, in the last two minutes, "Tiny Tim" O'Connell made the winning shot for the Lions. "He's less than six

feet tall, but he runs ~~more fastly~~ *faster* than anyone else on the court," the Cubs' coach said.

"O'Connell doesn't shoot as often ˄ *as* other players,

but he's a lot more ~~accurately~~ *accurate* than the bigger guys." The Cubs played a great game last

night too, but they just didn't play as ~~good~~ *well* as the Lions.

_4_	Exuberant King	_3_	Señor Speedy
_1_	Get Packin'	_2_	Wild Whirl
_5_	Inspired Winner		

Answers will vary.

1. b **2.** a **3.** b **4.** c

(Yelena Isinbayeva didn't compete in the women's high jump—she is a pole vaulter.)

PART VI From Grammar to Writing
(pages 307–308)

I live in a ⬭small ⬭comfortable ⬭one-bedroom apartment that is ⬭close to school. The living room is my ⬭favorite room. It's ⬭sunny, ⬭warm, and ⬭cheerful. There's an ⬭old ⬭brick fireplace, which I use on ⬭cold ⬭winter nights. In the corner there's a ⬭large ⬭soft ⬭green couch. I like to sit there and read. Next to it is a ⬭small ⬭wood table with a ⬭beautiful ⬭antique lamp from my favorite aunt. It's a ⬭cozy living room, and I enjoy spending time there.

See figure below.

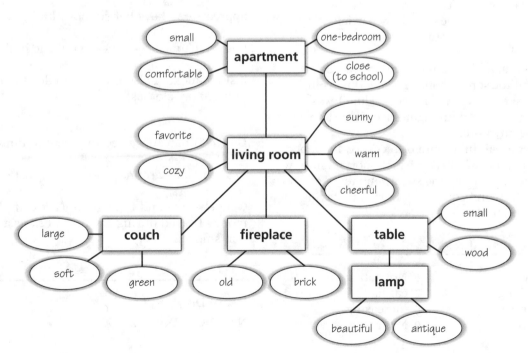

Words in parentheses fit into more than one category.

a. things that are big: large, enormous, huge

b. things that are small: little, tiny, (cozy), (cute)

c. things that look good: attractive, (cute), gorgeous, lovely, (cozy)

d. things that look bad: run-down, hideous, ugly

e. things that feel good: soft, comfortable, (cozy)

f. things that feel bad: hard, coarse, rough

4–6

Answers will vary.

UNIT 27 Gerunds: Subject and Object

(pages 316–323)

After You Read

Grofumeur: 1, 3

Nuffsed: 4

Swissfriend: 1, 5

Cleanaire: 2

1

SWIMMING is a great exercise. It's healthy, fun, and relaxing. Because swimming is a low-impact sport, people can enjoy participating in this activity without fear of injury to bones or muscles.

Jogging, a high-impact activity, can be harmful for some people. I know this from personal experience. Last year while I was jogging, I injured my right knee. I don't go jogging anymore.

After a painful month of recovery, I stopped running and switched to water sports. I'm now considering joining the swimming team at my health club and competing in races. Staying fit should be fun!

2

2. Staying
3. smoking
4. Exercising
5. starting
6. Not eating
7. eating
8. increasing
9. Not going

3

2. enjoy running
3. quit smoking
4. go swimming
5. admitted (OR admits) being
6. avoids eating
7. mind exercising
8. are considering taking

4

Day 1 I quit ~~to smoke~~ smoking! This was the first day of the rest of my life as a non-smoker. ~~Get~~ Getting through the day wasn't too difficult. I quit drinking coffee today too, and I think that helped. I used to enjoy ~~had~~ having a cigarette with a cup of coffee in the morning.

Day 3 Today was harder. I called Dinah and admitted ~~wanted~~ wanting to smoke. She advised ~~takeing~~ taking deep breaths and staying busy. That worked. I have to resist ~~eat~~ eating too much. Gaining five pounds ~~aren't~~ isn't a big deal, but I don't want to gain more than that.

Day 5 I got through the workweek smoke free. My boss keeps ~~tells~~ telling me, "You can do it." I really appreciate ~~to have~~ having her support. I miss smoking, but I don't miss ~~to standing~~ standing outside in the cold just to smoke. I also don't mind ~~don't~~ not burning holes in my clothes!

Day 7 Dinah suggested ~~to go~~ going out to dinner, but I can't risk ~~be~~ being around smokers . . . Instead, we went ~~shoping~~ shopping and I bought a shirt with the money I saved during my first week as a non-smoker.

5

OK to Do: 4, 6, 7

Not OK to Do: 1, 2, 3, 5

Answers will vary.

UNIT 28 Gerunds after Prepositions (pages 324–332)

After You Read
Items Checked: 1, 2, 4, 6, 7

1

To President Hacking:
We are concerned <u>about improving</u> Internet access at Taylor College. Times are changing. With Wi-Fi (for Wireless Fidelity, or a wireless Internet connection), students can get on the Internet anywhere on campus. Many schools have succeeded <u>in making</u> their campuses completely wireless. Taylor College has been slow <u>at developing</u> this technology, but it is becoming more necessary. Taylor College instructors are putting more and more course material online. With only a few Wi-Fi areas, busy students cannot count <u>on finding</u> a place to connect when they have the time to work on course material. <u>By having</u> more Wi-Fi areas, the college will make education more efficient. We are asking the administration to consider increasing the number of "hotspots" for wireless connections. We look forward <u>to having</u> a completely wireless campus in the next few years.

2

2. about getting
3. about going
4. about driving
5. to staying
6. (to) relaxing
7. for having
8. about not doing
9. on coming
10. (on) going

3

2. We can make changes by telling the administration about our concerns.
3. The administration can help by listening to our concerns.
4. In some cases, students just complain instead of making suggestions for improvements.
5. Students get annoyed with some teachers for not coming to class on time.
6. You can improve your grades by studying regularly.

7. We're proud of our school for having the latest computer technology.
8. Students should learn about issues before voting for the next Student Council president.
9. You have great ideas for solving some problems on campus.
10. Our school has been slow at improving food services.
11. Latoya is happy about running for Student Council.

4

2. have
3. have
4. being
5. going, studying
6. doing
7. earn, spend, spending
8. living

5

I'm a new student and I'm not used to ~~live~~ *living* on a college campus. Before ~~to come~~ *coming* here, I lived at home and had a lot of friends. I'm very happy about being here, but I'm getting sick of ~~spend~~ *spending* all my time alone in the library. I'm really interested in ~~meet~~ *meeting* more people. Would it be possible to have more social events on campus—especially for new students? I'm planning ~~at~~ *on* joining some clubs too. Is there a list? I'm looking forward to ~~hear~~ *hearing* your response. Thank you for ~~to give~~ *giving* us the opportunity to make suggestions online!

6

2. F
3. T
4. F
5. F
6. T

7–8

Answers will vary.

9

2. F
3. F
4. F
5. T
6. T
7. T

Answers will vary.

UNIT 29 Infinitives after Certain Verbs (pages 333–340)

After You Read
True: 2, 3, 5
False: 1, 4

1

Underlined Phrases:

advised me to join, decided to join,
want to go, decided to go, didn't want to sign up,
urged me not to miss, asked me to go out,
hoped to make, expect everyone to be,
persuaded me not to give up

2

2. attempt to find
3. warns single people not to leave
4. urges them to use
5. fail to plan
6. plan to fail
7. wish to meet
8. Ask two friends to read
9. Tell them not to worry
10. Choose to participate
11. advises people not to feel
12. wants to be

3

2. reminded Lily to get stamps.
3. invited Mary to go out for coffee.
4. agreed to come home by 10:30.
5. forgot to go to the staff meeting.
6. encouraged Lisa (OR her) to try once more.
7. needs to use the car.

4

     make
You'd like to ~~making~~ some new friends. Maybe
you're at a new school or job, or, possibly, you

           to
have changed and the "new you" wants ⌃meet

          you
new people. First, I strongly advise ⌃to turn off

the TV. Those people on *Friends* are not YOUR
       to
friends. You need⌃go out with real people.

          not to
Decide right now ~~to don't~~ refuse invitations.
When a classmate or co-worker invites you for
coffee, just say "Yes." Join a club and volunteer
    do
to ~~doing~~ something. That responsibility will
force you to attend the meetings. By doing
             to meet
these things, you will manage ~~meeting~~ a lot of
new people. But don't rush to become close
friends with someone right away. Learn to
          talk
listen. Encourage the person to ~~talks~~ by asking
         to develop
questions. Allow relationships ~~develops~~
naturally, and soon you'll have a group of
people you're really comfortable with.

5

2. b   6. b
3. a   7. a
4. b   8. b
5. a

6–9

Answers will vary.

UNIT 30 Infinitives of Purpose (pages 341–347)

After You Read
Items Checked: 2, 5, 6

1

New technology is great, but it often brings
new problems. Most people use camera phones
for good things, for example, to take pictures
of their family and friends. But some people
use them to play mean jokes on other people
or even to steal. When camera phones first
came out, some places had to prohibit their
use. People were using them to take secret
pictures in health clubs and other private
places! Not very nice! And what about "digital
shoplifting"? Here is an example: My friend
Ned (not his real name) often goes to
bookstores to look at magazines. Sometimes
he sees an interesting article, but he doesn't
want to buy the magazine. In order not to pay

for the article, he secretly photographs it with his camera phone. Then he goes home <u>to read</u> it! Did Ned steal the article? Should stores ban camera phones <u>in order to prevent</u> digital shoplifting?

2. d
3. a
4. e
5. f
6. c

2. He took the bus in order not to be late.
3. We turned our phone off in order not to get calls.
4. She taped her favorite TV show in order not to miss it.
5. He enrolled in French 101 (in order) to learn the language.
6. She went to the electronics store (in order) to buy a new camera phone.

2. (in order) to drive to Montreal
3. (in order) to pass it
4. (in order) to get more gas
5. (in order) to exchange money
6. (in order) to buy fruit and vegetables
7. (in order) to have coffee
8. (in order) to communicate with her

Click <u>here</u> ~~for telling~~ *to tell* us how you've used your camera phone.

I was riding my bike when I saw an accident. A car hit a truck, but it didn't stop. I used my camera phone ⌃*to* take a picture of the car and the license plate number. Then I used it to call the police.
Jason Harvey, England

I was at a great concert in Mexico City. I wanted to share the experience with my best friend back home. I picked up my camera phone and used it to take a photo, record a little bit of a song, and ~~writing~~ *write* a short message. Instantly my friend was "there" with me. Awesome!
Emilia Leale, Italy

My brother needed a new part for his refrigerator. He called the supply store on his camera phone and tried to describe the broken part. They told him to use his phone to ~~takes~~ *take* a picture. He did it, and the supply store was able to send him the correct part right away.
Min-Soo Kim, Korea

I sell houses. I always use my camera phone in order ~~no~~ *not to* waste my customers' time. When I see an interesting house, I immediately send a photo. Then, if they are interested, I make an appointment for them.
Andrea Cook, USA

While I was traveling, I got a terrible skin rash. I used my camera phone ~~for calling~~ *to call* my doctor and send her a photo of it. She was thousands of miles away, but she used the photo to give me instant advice!
Ana Diaz, Spain

One of my classmates was sick and had to miss class. I used my camera phone to call him and ~~taking~~ *take* a picture of the teacher's notes on the board. He heard the class fine, but had trouble reading the teacher's handwriting. But that's not the fault of the camera phone!
James Gordon, Australia

5

1. 3   **4.** 4   **6.** 1
2. 5   **5.** 4   **7.** 6
3. 2

Answers will vary.

UNIT 31 Infinitives with *Too* and *Enough* (pages 348–355)

After You Read
Items Checked: 2, 3

2. b   **5.** a   **8.** a
3. a   **6.** b   **9.** a
4. a   **7.** b   **10.** b

2

2. c	**5.** a	**8.** f
3. i	**6.** g	**9.** h
4. b	**7.** d	

3

2. cheap enough for us to afford
3. too good for you to miss
4. too late to stop
5. old enough to stay
6. early enough to come
7. too slow to beat

4

The Hologram concert was awesome! Now I'm
too excited ~~for sleeping~~ *to sleep*. That Eve Durkin can
really sing. My voice isn't ~~enough good~~ *good enough* to sing
in the shower! After the concert we were really
hungry, but it was ~~to~~ *too* late to go for pizza. I
HATE this stupid curfew! It's too weird ^*to*
understand. My friend Todd works and has
to pay taxes, but the law says he's too young
~~for staying~~ *to stay* out past 10:00 P.M.! That's really
crazy! Well, I'd better try to get some sleep or
I'll be too tired ~~too~~ *to* get up in the morning.

5

Picture 2

6–10

Answers will vary.

UNIT 32 Gerunds and Infinitives
(pages 356–366)

After You Read
Items Checked: 2, 3, 4

1

Like many students, Eva is a procrastinator.
She keeps putting off her school work. When
she studies, she often stops to go for a walk in
the park. She wants to improve her study
habits, but she isn't sure how. Eva decided to
make a list of things she needs to do every day.
She always remembers to make her list, but
she often forgets to read it. It's very frustrating.
Last night Eva remembered reading an article
in the school newspaper about a support group
for procrastinators. She thinks being in a
group is a good idea. She likes sharing ideas
with other students.

2. F	**6.** T
3. T	**7.** T
4. T	**8.** T
5. F	

2

2. starting	**9.** to work
3. to study OR studying	**10.** to do
4. finishing	**11.** making
5. making	**12.** being
6. doing	**13.** to do
7. working	**14.** to improve
8. to do OR doing	**15.** putting

3

2. doing	**8.** to take
3. starting	**9.** to give
4. to do	**10.** finishing
5. to spend	**11.** doing
6. doing	**12.** joining
7. working	

4

2. meeting Todd.
3. taking too many breaks.
4. listening to music.
5. to go home.
6. to give Eva a ride home.
to stay a little longer.
7. to drive carefully.

5

3. Working on a long project is difficult.
4. It feels great to complete a job on time.
5. It's a good idea to reward yourself for finishing a project.
6. It's very helpful to be in a support group.
7. Meeting people with the same problem is good.

6

For months I was thinking about ~~to go~~ *going* to a support group for procrastinators, but I kept putting it off! Last night I finally decided ~~going~~ *to go*, and I'm glad I did. I'm not alone! There were a lot of people there with the same problem as me. I expected ~~being~~ *to be* bored, but it was really quite interesting—and helpful. I even knew some of the other students there. I remembered ~~to meet~~ *meeting* a few of them at a school party last year. I really enjoyed ~~to talk~~ *talking* to Todd, and before I left I promised ~~coming~~ *to come* again.

I have a math test tomorrow, so I really should stop ~~to write~~ *writing* now and start studying.

See, I've already learned something from ~~to be~~ *being* in this group! I have to stop making excuses and start my work! Now!

7

Things Eva Does: 3, 4, 6
Things Eva Doesn't Do: 2, 5, 7

8–10

Answers will vary.

11

EVA:	I remember meeting you.
TODD:	I hope to see you here again.

PAT:	I quit making excuses.
LEE:	I decided to join the group.

UTA:	I keep trying to change.
KAY:	I can't afford to fail.

LEV:	I finished writing my paper!
JEFF:	I learned to start projects early.

12–13

Answers will vary.

PART VII From Grammar to Writing

1

2. but	**7.** and
3. and	**8.** or
4. but	**9.** and
5. but	**10.** so
6. and	

2

2. or
3. but
4. so

3–6

Answers will vary.

UNIT 33 Preferences: *Prefer, Would prefer, Would rather*

After You Read
True: 1, 2, 3
False: 4, 5, 6

1

Underlined Clauses and Sentences:

I think I'd rather get the things for my project first.

I really prefer them for science projects.

I'd prefer looking for DVDs at Goodly's.

I'd rather do that too.

. . . I'd rather not.

I always prefer romantic comedies to action movies.

I'd rather just get a taco.

Items Checked:

Goodly's Music
Breakfast in Bogotá
Taco Bill's

2

2. I'd rather not cook
3. I'd rather not
4. I'd rather have

Student Book Answer Key **209**

5. I'd rather not
6. I'd rather see

2. Does . . . prefer
3. Would . . . prefer
4. Do . . . prefer
5. Would . . . rather
6. Would . . . prefer

4

2. soccer to basketball
3. shooting hoops to making goals
4. play basketball than soccer
5. watching to playing
6. soccer to other TV sports
7. it to basketball or soccer
8. watch a pro than participate

5

For my study, I interviewed 50 men and women. There was no real difference in men's and women's preferences for television. I found that everyone prefers watching television ~~than~~ *to* going to the movies.

Men and women both enjoy news programs and entertainment specials. However, men would rather ~~watching~~ *watch* adventure programs and science fiction, while women prefer soap operas. Men also like to watch all kinds of sports, but women would rather see game shows ~~to~~ *than* sports events.

I found a big difference in reading preferences. Men prefer to ~~reading~~ *read* newspapers while women would much rather read magazines and books. When men read books, they prefer ^*to* read nonfiction and adventure stories. Women ~~will~~ prefer novels.

6

Items Circled:
Fish Dinner, soup, onion; rice; soda, diet; apple pie

7–8

Answers will vary.

9

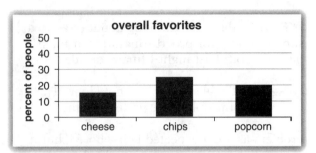

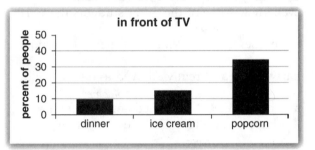

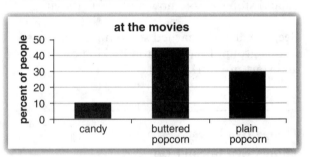

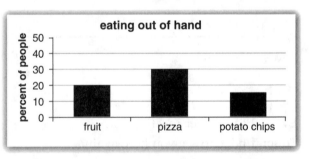

10–12

Answers will vary.

UNIT 34 Necessity:
Have (got) to, Must, Don't have to, Must not, Can't (pages 388–397)

After You Read
True: 2, 3
False: 1, 4

1

BEN: Hello. I'm Australian, and I'm planning to spend several weeks in Europe with my family. I have some questions. First, <u>do we have to get</u> visas to visit Italy?

CLERK: Not for a short visit. But you <u>can't stay</u> for longer than 90 days without a visa. Australians also need a Permit to Stay for visits in Italy longer than eight days. You <u>must apply</u> for the permit at a local police station within eight days of your arrival.

BEN: Can my wife and I use our Australian driver's licenses in Italy?

CLERK: You <u>have to carry</u> your Australian license, but you <u>must</u> also <u>have</u> an International Driver's Permit. And you've <u>got to be</u> at least 18 years old.

BEN: When <u>do we have to get</u> the IDPs? Is it possible to apply for them when we get to Europe?

CLERK: No, you <u>must apply</u> before you leave. The Australian Automobile Association can help you. You'll also <u>have to get</u> an International Insurance Certificate to show you have insurance. But you'll be able to get that at the car rental agency.

BEN: We'll be in Italy in January. We don't have a set schedule, so we haven't made any reservations.

CLERK: Oh, you've <u>got to have</u> reservations, even in January—especially in major cities like Rome, Florence, or Venice.

BEN: OK. Thanks a lot. You've been very helpful.

Necessary: 2, 7

Not Necessary: 1, 4

Prohibited: 3, 5, 6

Answers may vary.

Ann has to buy phone cards online, and she has to buy batteries for the digital camera.

She doesn't have to call Pet Care or stop the mail for two weeks.

Sean and Maya don't have to pack clothes.

They have to choose DVDs and CDs for the trip, and they have to say good-bye to friends.

1. b. can't start
  c. have to (OR have got to) check in
  d. Do . . . have to get
  e. we do
  f. has to (OR has got to) park
2. a. can't weigh
  b. 'll (OR will) have to pay
  c. Do . . . have to bring
  d. I do
  e. 've got to (OR have to) have
  f. 've got to (OR have to) go
3. a. 've (OR have) had to wait
  b. won't have to wait
4. a. 've got to (OR have to) call
  b. can't use
5. a. 've got to (OR have to) walk
  b. do . . have to get
  c. can't sit
6. a. won't have to be

2. must	**7.** must not
3. must not	**8.** must
4. must	**9.** must
5. must not	**10.** must not
6. must	**11.** must not

2. don't have to bring	**5.** don't have to go
3. must not play	**6.** don't have to leave
4. must not dive	**7.** must not stay

We're on our way back to Australia. We ~~have~~ *had* to leave the hotel at 5:30 this morning, and then we had ~~got~~ to wait in line at the airport for hours. This flight is great. There are computers and TVs at every seat and hundreds of movies to watch. But we can't sit for more than three hours at a time because it's unhealthy, and we must ~~to~~ drink water every hour when we're not sleeping. This flight is 14 hours long, so we have to ~~taking~~ *take* care of ourselves. Thanks for the camping knife. I used it a lot in Italy, but before we left, I ~~has~~ *had* to put it in my suitcase. You ~~don't have to~~ *can't OR must not* bring knives '*ve* OR *have*

in carry-on bags. Well, I got to get up and walk
around again. E-mail me. We'll be on this plane
for 10 more hours!

7

a. 5		**d.** 6
b. 3		**e.** 4
c. 2		**f.** 1

8–12

Answers will vary.

UNIT 35 Expectations: *Be supposed to*

(pages 398–405)

After You Read

Items Checked: 2, 5, 6

1

PROVIDENCE, July 19—The Stricklands wanted a
small, quiet wedding—that's why they eloped
to Block Island, off the Atlantic Coast of the
United States.

The ferry they took to their wedding site
doesn't carry cars, so the Stricklands packed
their bikes for the trip.

The couple found a lonely hill overlooking
the ocean. The weather <u>was supposed to be</u>
beautiful, so they asked the town mayor to
marry them on the hill the next afternoon.
They <u>were going to have</u> a small, private
ceremony in this romantic setting.

"When we got there, we found a crowd of
cyclists admiring the view," laughed Beth
Strickland.

When Bill kissed his bride, the audience
burst into loud applause and rang their bicycle
bells. "We <u>weren't supposed to have</u> 50 wedding
guests, but we love biking, and we're not sorry,"
Bill said.

When they packed to leave the island the
next day, Beth left her wedding bouquet at the
hotel. She remembered it minutes before the
ferry <u>was going to leave</u>. Bill jumped on his
bike, recovered the flowers, and made it back
to the ferry before it departed.

"Cyclists <u>are supposed to stay</u> fast and fit,"
he said. "Now I know why."

True: 3, 4, 6
False: 1, 2, 5

2

2. a. Were . . . supposed to do
   b. were supposed to deliver
3. a. is supposed to start
   b. are . . . supposed to stand
4. a. 're not (OR aren't) supposed to be
   b. isn't supposed to see
5. a. 'm supposed to wear
   b. 's supposed to rain
6. a. 's supposed to be
7. a. were supposed to stay

3

Answers may vary.
2. Netta's parents were going to mail 180
invitations, but they mailed 210 invitations.
3. Netta was going to order a vanilla cake, but
she ordered a chocolate cake.
4. Gary's parents were going to hire a rock
band, but they ordered a jazz band.
5. Sophie was going to give the bridal shower
on May 10, but she gave it on May 20.
6. Gary was going to plan the rehearsal
dinner, but Gary's parents planned it.
7. Netta was going to find a photographer, but
Jack found a photographer.
8. Jack was going to rent a limo, but he rented
a red sports car.
9. Sophie was going to order flowers by April
1, but she ordered by OR on April 15.
10. Netta's parents were going to buy candles as
bridesmaid's gifts, but they bought clocks.
11. Gary was going to send the wedding
announcement to the newspaper, but Jack
sent it.

4

Remember my old college roommate Gary?
He's getting married tomorrow, and I'm the

were

best man! He and his fiancée supposed to have
a small wedding, but they ended up inviting
more than 200 people! As best man, I have
some important responsibilities. For one thing,

supposed

I'm ~~supposing~~ to make sure Gary gets to the
wedding ceremony on time—not an easy job for

were

me. At first we ~~was~~ going to hire a limousine
and driver, but I decided to drive him there
myself in a rented red sports car. I'm also
supposed to hold the wedding rings during the
ceremony. Then, at the end of the reception

party, I'm supposed to ~~helping~~ *help* the newlyweds leave quickly for their honeymoon. They're going straight to the airport (I'm also ~~suppose~~ *supposed* to hold the plane tickets for them). They ~~are~~ *were* going to go to Hawaii, but they changed their minds and are going to Aruba instead. Oh! I just looked at the clock. I'd better sign off now, or I'll be late for the rehearsal dinner. I *was* going to leave five minutes ago! By the way, Sophie, the maid of honor, will be there too. I've never met her, but she ~~supposes~~ *'s (OR is) supposed* to be very nice. I'll let you know how it goes!

5

2. wasn't	**6.** is
3. isn't	**7.** are
4. aren't	**8.** aren't
5. were	

6–9

Answers will vary.

UNIT 36 Future Possibility: *May, Might, Could*   (pages 406–413)

After You Read

True: 2, 4

False: 1, 3, 5

1

Underlined Phrases:

might, may snow, might take, Maybe I'll take, couldn't do, might not catch, maybe I'll rent, might be

Cody's Schedule:

Certain: 3, 5, 7

Possible: 1, 2, 6, 8

Impossible: 4

Anna's Schedule:

Certain: 2, 3, 6, 7, 8

Possible: 1, 5

Impossible: 4

2

2. could	**5.** 'm going to
3. might	**6.** may
4. may not	**7.** might

3

2. She may (OR might) buy some notebooks before class.

3. She's going to go to a meeting with Mrs. Humphrey at 11:00.

4. She may (OR might) have coffee with Sue after class.

5. She's going to go to work at 1:00.

6. She may (OR might) go shopping after work.

7. She may (OR might) take the 7:00 train.

4

2. They couldn't	**5.** It could be
3. It could be	**6.** It could be
4. It could	

5

Every few years, the ocean near Peru becomes warmer. This change is called El Niño. An El Niño ~~maybe~~ *may* cause big weather changes all over the world. The west coasts of North and South America might have very heavy rains. On the other side of the Pacific, New Guinea might ~~becomes~~ *become* very dry. Northern areas could have warmer, wetter winters, and southern areas ~~maybe~~ *may* become much colder. These weather changes affect plants and animals. Some fish ~~mayn't~~ *may not* survive in warmer waters. They may die or swim to colder places. In addition, dry conditions could ~~causing~~ *cause* crops to die. When that happens, food may get very expensive. El Niño does not happen regularly. It may happen every two years, or it ~~could~~ *may OR might* not come for seven years. Will El Niños get worse in the future? They could ~~be~~. Pollution might increase the effects of El Niño, but no one is sure yet.

6

Friday
      Possible: Sunny, Low 50s
Saturday
      Certain: Sunny, Windy
      Possible: 60°
Sunday
      Possible: Cold, Windy, Snow Flurries

7–9

Answers will vary.

UNIT 37 Conclusions:
Must, Have (got) to, May, Might, Could, Can't (pages 414–425)

After You Read
True: 1, 4
False: 2, 3, 5

1

Underlined Phrases:

could be serious, couldn't be dishonest, might be the key, has to have a very special reason, may want to be alone, must spend his time, must not be here

Statements:
Possible: 2, 4,
Almost Certain: 3, 5, 6

2

2. might   **5.** could
3. might   **6.** might not
4. could   **7.** may

3

2. Vincent must not be the clerk's real name.
3. He must not know about the poster.
4. He must be very clever.
5. Number 27 Carlisle Street must be City Bank.
6. Vincent's tunnel must not lead to those shops.
7. Vincent's tunnel must lead to the bank.
8. The tunnel must be almost finished.

4

2. That's got to be wrong.
3. It's got to cost less than $50.
4. It can't be after 11:00.
5. It's got to be nearby.
6. You can't be sick.

5

2. might be   **5.** must be
3. might   **6.** might not
4. might   **7.** must

6

2. could be   **7.** could be
3. couldn't be   **8.** Could . . . be
4. can't be   **9.** can't be
5. Could . . . be   **10.** could . . . be
6. can't be   **11.** could be

7

The main character, Molly Smith, is a college ESL teacher. She is trying to find her dead grandparents' first home in the United States. It may ~~being~~ *be* in a nearby town. The townspeople there seem scared. They could ~~be~~ have a secret, or they ~~must~~ *might* just hate strangers. Molly has some old letters that might lead her to the place. They are in Armenian, but one of her students ~~mights~~ *might* translate them for her. They ~~hafta~~ *have to* be important because the author mentions them right away. The letters must contain family secrets. I'm sure of it. Who is the bad guy? It couldn't be the student because he wants to help. It might ~~to~~ be the newspaper editor in the town.

8

Possible: 2, 6, 7, 8
Almost Certain: 3, 4, 5, 9

9–12

Answers will vary.

PART VIII From Grammar to Writing

(pages 426–427)

1

I am writing this letter of complaint although / [because] one of your cashiers treated me rudely. Because / [Even though] I was sure I paid her with a $20 bill, I only received change for $10. I told her that there was a mistake. She said, "You're wrong." Later the manager called. He said the cashier was right although / [because] the money in the cash drawer was correct.

Because / [Even though] the mistake was mine, I believe the cashier behaved extremely rudely.

[Although] / Because I like Hardly's, I also value polite service. I hope I won't have to change restaurants although / [because] I can't get it there.

2

2. contrasting idea
3. comma
4. must also
5. doesn't have to
6. sender's
7. before
8. colon

3–6

Answers will vary.

License Agreement

READ THIS LICENSE CAREFULLY BEFORE OPENING THIS PACKAGE. BY OPENING THIS PACKAGE, YOU ARE AGREEING TO THE TERMS AND CONDITIONS OF THIS LICENSE. IF YOU DO NOT AGREE, DO NOT OPEN THE PACKAGE. PROMPTLY RETURN THE UNOPENED PACKAGE AND ALL ACCOMPANYING ITEMS TO THE PLACE YOU OBTAINED THEM. *THESE TERMS APPLY TO ALL LICENSED SOFTWARE ON THE DISK EXCEPT THAT THE TERMS FOR USE OF ANY SHAREWARE OR FREEWARE ON THE DISKETTES ARE AS SET FORTH IN THE ELECTRONIC LICENSE LOCATED ON THE DISK:*

1. **GRANT OF LICENSE and OWNERSHIP:** The enclosed data disk ("Software") is licensed, not sold, to you by Pearson Education, Inc. Publishing as Pearson Longman ("We" or the "Company") for academic purposes and in consideration of your purchase or adoption of the accompanying Company textbooks and/or other materials, and your agreement to these terms. This license allows instructors teaching the course using the Company textbook that accompanies this Software (the "Focus on Grammar") to use, and display the data on a single computer (i.e., with a single CPU) at a single location for <u>academic</u> use only, so long as you comply with the terms of this Agreement.

   We reserve any rights not granted to you. You own only the disk(s) but we and our licensors own the Software itself.

2. **RESTRICTIONS ON USE AND TRANSFER:** You may <u>not</u> transfer, distribute or make available the Software or the Documentation, except to instructors and students in your school in connection with the Course. You may <u>not</u> reverse engineer, disassemble, decompile, modify, adapt, translate or create derivative works based on the Software or the Documentation. You may be held legally responsible for any copying or copyright infringement that is caused by your failure to abide by the terms of these restrictions.

3. **TERMINATION:** This license is effective until terminated. This license will terminate automatically without notice from the Company if you fail to comply with any provisions or limitations of this license. Upon termination, you shall destroy the Documentation and all copies of the Software. All provisions of this Agreement as to limitation and disclaimer of warranties, limitation of liability, remedies or damages, and our ownership rights shall survive termination.

4. **DISCLAIMER OF WARRANTY: THE COMPANY AND ITS LICENSORS MAKE NO WARRANTIES ABOUT THE SOFTWARE, WHICH IS PROVIDED "AS-IS." IF THE DISK IS DEFECTIVE IN MATERIALS OR WORKMANSHIP, YOUR ONLY REMEDY IS TO RETURN IT TO THE COMPANY WITHIN 30 DAYS FOR REPLACEMENT UNLESS THE COMPANY DETERMINES IN GOOD FAITH THAT THE DISK HAS BEEN MISUSED OR IMPROPERLY INSTALLED, REPAIRED, ALTERED OR DAMAGED. THE COMPANY DISCLAIMS ALL WARRANTIES, EXPRESS OR IMPLIED, INCLUDING WITHOUT LIMITATION, THE IMPLIED WARRANTIES OF MERCHANTABILITY AND FITNESS FOR A PARTICULAR PURPOSE. THE COMPANY DOES NOT WARRANT, GUARANTEE OR MAKE ANY REPRESENTATION REGARDING THE ACCURACY, RELIABILITY, CURRENTNESS, USE, OR RESULTS OF USE, OF THE SOFTWARE.**

5. **LIMITATION OF REMEDIES AND DAMAGES: IN NO EVENT, SHALL THE COMPANY OR ITS EMPLOYEES, AGENTS, LICENSORS OR CONTRACTORS BE LIABLE FOR ANY INCIDENTAL, INDIRECT, SPECIAL OR CONSEQUENTIAL DAMAGES ARISING OUT OF OR IN CONNECTION WITH THIS LICENSE OR THE SOFTWARE, INCLUDING, WITHOUT LIMITATION, LOSS OF USE, LOSS OF DATA, LOSS OF INCOME OR PROFIT, OR OTHER LOSSES SUSTAINED AS A RESULT OF INJURY TO ANY PERSON, OR LOSS OF OR DAMAGE TO PROPERTY, OR CLAIMS OF THIRD PARTIES, EVEN IF THE COMPANY OR AN AUTHORIZED REPRESENTATIVE OF THE COMPANY HAS BEEN ADVISED OF THE POSSIBILITY OF SUCH DAMAGES.** SOME JURISDICTIONS DO NOT ALLOW THE LIMITATION OF DAMAGES IN CERTAIN CIRCUMSTANCES, SO THE ABOVE LIMITATIONS MAY NOT ALWAYS APPLY.

6. **GENERAL:** THIS AGREEMENT SHALL BE CONSTRUED IN ACCORDANCE WITH THE LAWS OF THE UNITED STATES OF AMERICA AND THE STATE OF NEW YORK, APPLICABLE TO CONTRACTS MADE IN NEW YORK, EXCLUDING THE STATE'S LAWS AND POLICIES ON CONFLICTS OF LAW, AND SHALL BENEFIT THE COMPANY, ITS AFFILIATES AND ASSIGNEES. This Agreement is the complete and exclusive statement of the agreement between you and the Company and supersedes all proposals, prior agreements, oral or written, and any other communications between you and the Company or any of its representatives relating to the subject matter. If you are a U.S. Government user, this Software is licensed with "restricted rights" as set forth in subparagraphs (a)-(d) of the Commercial Computer-Restricted Rights clause at FAR 52.227-19 or in subparagraphs (c)(1)(ii) of the Rights in Technical Data and Computer Software clause at DFARS 252.227-7013, and similar clauses, as applicable.